I0189337

WEYMOUTH AND MELCOMBE REGIS MINUTE BOOK
1617–1660

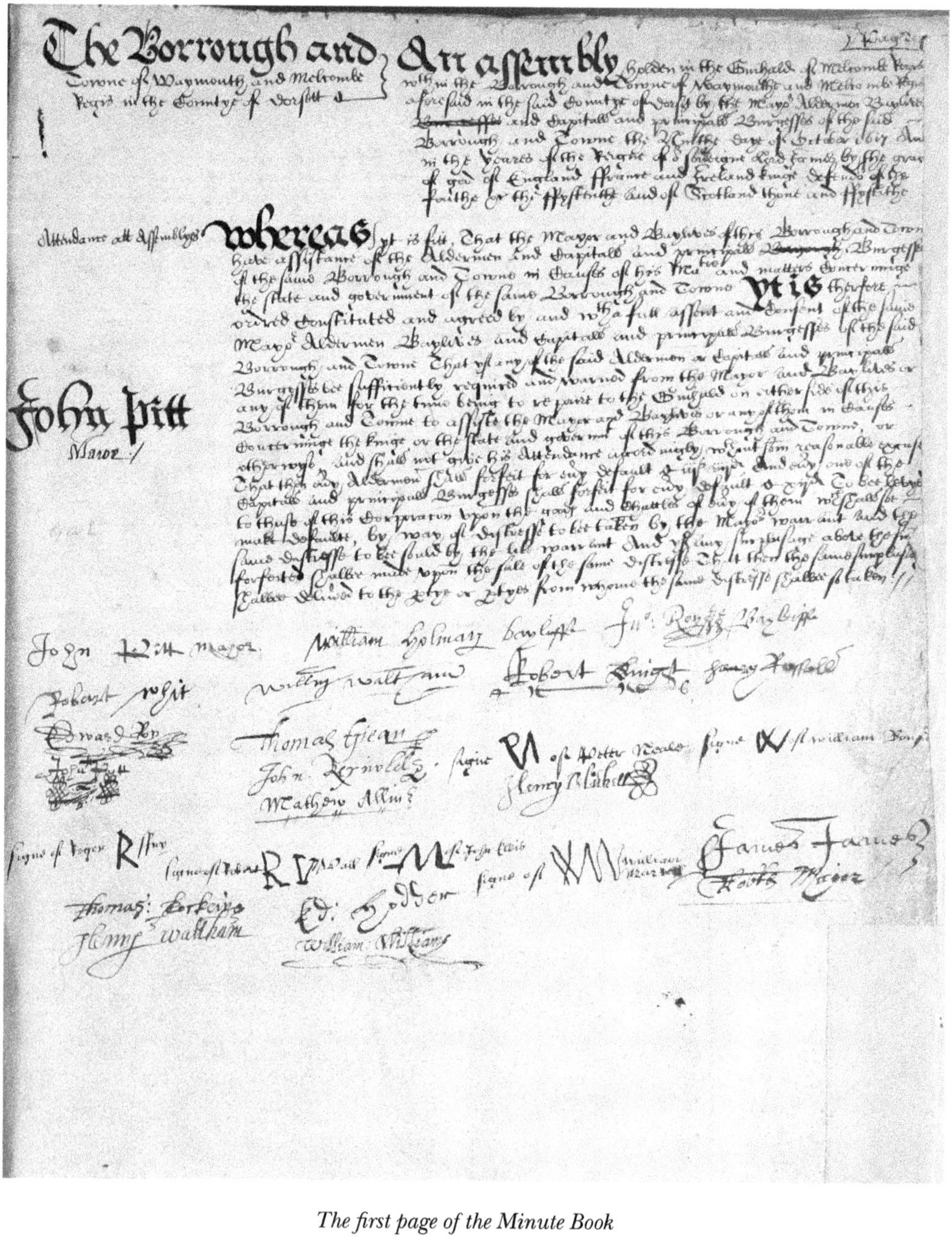
The Borrough and Towne of Waymouth and Melcombe Regis in the Countye of Dorsett — An assembly holden in the Guildhall of Melcombe Regis within the Borrough and Towne of Waymouth and Melcombe Regis aforesaid in the said Countye of Dorset by the Mayor Aldermen Bayliffs and Capitall and principall Burgesses of the said Borrough and Towne the [illegible] day of October 1617 Anno in the yeare of the Reigne of our soveraigne Lord James by the grace of God of England ffrance and Ireland kinge defender of the faithe &c the ffifteenth and of Scotland the one and ffiftithe

Attendance att Assemblyes

Whereas yt is fitt, That the Mayor and Bayliffs of this Borrough and Towne have assistance of the Aldermen and Capitall and principall Burgesses of the same Borrough and Towne in Causes of his Matie and matters concerninge the state and government of the same Borrough and Towne Yt is therefore ordered constituted and agreed by and with a full assent and consent of the said Mayor Aldermen Bayliffs and Capitall and principall Burgesses of the said Borrough and Towne That yf any of the said Aldermen or Capitall and principall Burgesses bee sufficiently required and warned from the Mayor and Bayliffs or any of them for the time being to repaire to the Guildhall on either side of this Borrough and Towne to assiste the Mayor and Bayliffs or any of them in Causes concerninge the Kinge or the State and government of this Borrough and Towne, or otherwyse, and shall not give his attendence accordingly without some reasonable cause That then every Alderman shall forfeit for every default [illegible] and every one of the Capitall and principall Burgesses shall forfeit for every default [illegible] To bee levyed to thuse of this Corporacon upon the goods and Chattells of every of them which shall soe make default, by way of distresse to bee taken by the Mayors warrant and the same distresse to bee sould by the like warrant And yf any surplusage above the forfeiture shall be made upon the sale of the same distresse That then the same surplusage shall be delivered to the partye or partyes from whome the same distresse shall be taken

John Pitt Mayor

John Pitt Mayor — William Holman bayliffe — [illegible] Bayliffe

[illegible signatures]

Thomas [illegible] — John Reynolds — Mathew Allin — Henry [illegible]

[illegible signatures]

William Williams

The first page of the Minute Book

WEYMOUTH AND MELCOMBE REGIS MINUTE BOOK

1617–1660

Edited by

KAY KEARSEY AND MAUREEN WEINSTOCK

DORSET RECORD SOCIETY

VOLUME 20

© Dorset Record Society 1960, 2020

First published 1960
Second edition published 2020 by Dorset Record Society
Dorset History Centre, Bridport Road, Dorchester, Dorset DT1 1XA

General Editor: Dr Mark Forrest

All rights reserved. No part of this publication may be reproduced, in any form or by any means, without permission from the publishers.

Typeset in ITC New Baskerville by John Chandler,

British Library Cataloguing in Publication Data:
A catalogue record for this book is available from the British Library.

ISBN 978-0-900339-23-3

CONTENTS

Maureen Weinstock MA FRHist Soc (1905-1996) was a keen local historian and principal of Weymouth Teacher Training College. She published numerous articles in *Somerset and Dorset Notes and Queries* and the *Proceedings of the DNHAS* as well as a volume of Hearth Tax returns for the Oxfordshire Record Society. Her volumes of collected essays *Studies in Dorset History* and *More Dorset Studies* form the basis of the introduction to the present volume. Her obituary appears in the *Proceedings of the DNHAS*, v.114, pp.288-9.

Kay Kearsey developed an interest in local history growing up in Dorset. She is co-author of *The Book of Stinsford: Thomas Hardy's Melstock*. She has spent many years cataloguing and calendaring Tudor and Stuart documents as a volunteer at the Dorset History Centre including the deeds of the Crichel, Ilchester and Floyer Acland estates.

PREFACE TO THE FIRST EDITION

Dorset Record Society

To preserve for posterity what might so easily perish and to enable the many to read that which before was solely possible for the few, may be said to be the main function of a Record Society. It must surely, therefore, be a matter of pleasure and encouragement to all those who take an interest, or even a pride, in the history of their own neighbourhood to possess this first volume of the newly founded Dorset Record Society. When we read printed records of the kind admirably transcribed by Miss Weinstock we can feel that we are actually in contact with the real stuff of History and are making acquaintance with the past at first hand. The professional scholar will find one use for such material, the local patriot another but all have their sheaves to gather.

In these days of high costs it is a courageous venture to embark on a new county record society and if the format be unfamiliar and the absence of the usual printed page be a surprise we must remember that it is the high cost of printing that has led to the extinction of record societies in many another county. The Dorset Record Society by pursuing this new method of publication should be able to issue volumes year by year without due financial anxiety for the future.

Miss Weinstock's edition of The Minute Book of the Borough of Weymouth and Melcombe Regis is therefore warmly to be welcomed, not only on account of its own interest but as the prelude of things to come.

Aelred Watkin
General Editor, 1960

PREFACE TO THE SECOND EDITION

It is sixty years since the launch of the Dorset Record Society with the publication of Maureen Weinstock's edition of the Minute Book of Weymouth and Melcombe Regis. It was a good choice of text for the first volume of the Society as its popularity with both academic and local historians remains undiminished.

In the mid-twentieth century Record Societies published faithful transcripts of texts with almost no introduction. Maureen Weinstock was not unusual in writing a single page to introduce her text and followed the conventions of her age in reproducing the language, grammar and punctuation of the original text in her transcription.

Times have changed. It is now possible to replicate sections of the text as photographs to provide a sample of the style and language. Scholars who wish to make detailed analysis of capitalisation or punctuation can easily obtain copies. For the great majority of readers producing a faithful reproduction by leaving dates in Latin or retaining archaic spellings and abbreviations makes the text less accessible and adds little to their appreciation of the content. This is the approach taken to the revision of Maureen Weinstock's text and by Kay Kearsey in her transcript of the earlier part of the Minute Book,

Sadly Aelred Watkin's optimism concerning the Society was misplaced. It was impossible to meet the production costs, produce a volume each year to maintain a subscription base. Dorset Record Society ceased to be a subscription society in 1975 when it was adopted as a committee of the Dorset Natural History and Archaeological Society. Following a restructure of committees in 2015 the Dorset Record Society became an independent charity and continues to publish texts reflecting aspects of the history of the county.

This second edition was prepared during the 'lockdown' Spring and Summer of 2020. Kay and I are most grateful to Antony Wilsdon for assisting with the Latin section pp.160-161 and John Chandler for his support with typesetting and editorial decisions in these most unusual circumstances.

Mark Forrest
General Editor, 2020

INTRODUCTION

For a number of years at the end of the sixteenth century bitter rivalry existed between the boroughs of Weymouth and Melcombe Regis. Melcombe Regis had been the principal customs port for Dorset in the thirteenth and fourteenth centuries, but it had been burned by French forces in the Hundred Years War and it was eclipsed by the more secure habour at Poole. Disputes had arisen between Melcombe Regis and Weymouth in the later fourteenth century over rights within the channel that separated the two towns. But in spite of these difficulties the strategic and commercial advantages of the secure deep water harbour enabled them to retain some trade and Parliamentary support through tax concessions. In the sixteenth century new contacts across the Atlantic increased the towns' economic potential and the war with Spain highlighted the necessity for a secure harbour west of Poole.

The merchants of Melcombe Regis and Weymouth were slow to put aside their differences. When negotiations could not persuade them to establish cordial relations a charter was granted in 1571; uniting the two towns on either side of the harbour. This increased rather than diminished the ill feeling and it was not until 1597 that any real union was effected.

A further charter granted in 1616 decreed that the government of the united town should consist of a mayor, two bailiffs, six principal burgesses to be aldermen and twenty-four capital burgesses "of good, faithful and honest demeanour" to form a council. Their appointments, duties, decisions and ordinances were recorded in a Minute Book the first 269 pages of which, covering the period 1617-1660, are printed in this edition. The book is part of the Weymouth and Melcombe Regis Borough Collection at the Dorset History Centre, reference DC-WYM/AD/1/2.

Besides those appointments specified in the town's charter other officers were appointed by this council. The town clerk was a permanent appointment and critical to the effective administration of the town. Financial affairs were managed by a treasurer, receiver and auditors selected from the burgesses; the treasurer was usually a burgess who had previously served as mayor. Public order was maintained by two constables for Melcombe Regis and two for Weymouth, two sergeants at mace, a beadle "appointed for the punishing of rogues, vagabonds and wandering idle persons" and several watchmen drawn from among the residents of the borough who were to serve in turns (see entry for 22 April 1625) and assisted by rounders (16 April 1629). The Minute Book sets out their duties and salaries, but their daily actions were recorded elsewhere in the records of the borough courts which survive in an incomplete series in the Weymouth and Melcombe Regis Borough collection at the Dorset History Centre (series DC-WYM/CO). Additional to the officers who maintained public order were the two scavengers who cleaned the streets, six pilots to guide boats into the harbour and several porters who made sure that the quays were kept safe and assisted with the loading and unloading of freight. Perhaps surprisingly the scavenger, usually responsible for cleaning the streets, was to be paid 12d to administer corporal punishment (entry for 25 February 1658). Officers and employees might be called upon to carry out a range of duties, while they primarily transported goods and cargoes the porters were also required to round up any stray pigs belonging to the inhabitants (27 October 1620).

Weymouth and Melcombe Regis was an Incorporated Borough, so the meetings of the mayor, aldermen, bailiffs and burgesses are generally called assemblies of the Corporation or Incorporation. These were meetings held in the Melcombe Regis Guildhall, and sometimes referred to as a "hall", but more usually as an "assembly". Here the attendees enjoyed a meal (27 October 1620) after discussing the business which makes up the majority of the entries in this volume. The meetings were frequent, but not regular; there were six in 1625 and 15 in 1633, at some times meeting on several occasions in a month at others leaving several months between assemblies. While only one meeting is recorded in each of the years 1642 and 1643 and two in 1644 when the Civil War brought conflict directly to the heart of the town, the aftermath was recorded in some detail with 22 meetings in 1645 and 28 in 1649.

Besides appointing officers the Corporation took action when immediate problems presented themselves or collective action was required: by putting a ship carrying the plague in quarantine (26 July 1625), repairing public assets such as the town pump (23 February 1649), or sending representatives to Parliament (4 August 1625). Sometimes a dispute might arise between the town and an individual merchant like Denis Bond of Dorchester who refused to pay the petty customs (30 October 1623) or with another town, such as the protracted dispute about requirements of merchants from the City of Exeter to pay customs duties (18 October 1630).

Appointments of pilots and porters were part of the general concern that the harbour was properly managed. The level of trade passing through the quays at Weymouth and Melcombe Regis determined the prosperity of the town and its inhabitants and many of the mayors and burgesses recorded in the Minute Book are also found as ship owners in State Papers and merchants whose cargoes are detailed in the Port Books which record the amount of customs duties payable on them.[1] In this Minute Book a long list of the petty customs provides the rates for different goods that were brought into Weymouth and Melcombe Regis. Regulated pilots and porters were supplied and licenced by the town to ensure that the harbour was properly managed. Maintenance of the quays was expensive: stone was purchased (19 April 1619), £50 was set aside for repairs on 1 February 1622, up to a further £40 was made available 14 March 1623, a further £50 in March the following year, by 12 October 1638 it was necessary to conduct extensive renovations and general surveys were undertaken in October 1639 and August 1641. In July 1647 the harbour was regarded as so important to the nation that a grant of £500 was made for repairs by the committee

1 *Calendar of State Papers Domestic: Charles I, 1625-49 Addenda*, ed. William Douglas Hamilton and Sophie Crawford Lomas (London, 1897), *British History Online* http://www.british-history.ac.uk/cal-state-papers/domestic/chas1/addenda/1625-49. The Port Books for Dorset harbours are held at The National Archives class E190

for the navy and further work was undertaken in May 1648, but the quays were still reported to be in a state of decay 12 May 1651. This is despite certain duties imposed on the use of the town bridge and ballast being used exclusively for the repairs (27 August 1647). Like the quays the town bridge and streets needed regular repairs: in February 1622 the town's contingency fund known as the 'town stock' provided £20 for piles, planks and works to repair the bridge and similar payments were granted in the following years, particularly to repair the substantial damage incurred during the hostilities of 1645. The town lighter: a vessel maintained at public expense to assist in the management of the harbour and conveyance of goods. A new lighter was commissioned from the shipwright John Damon according to a detailed specification at a cost of £45 (4 December 1633). For loading and unloading goods a new crane was constructed at the expense of the Corporation (23 December 1631). The town beam and weights were brought out to weigh the sugar belonging to Henry Russell, John Blachford and John Gardner (22 December 1623). The Corporation had responsibility for ensuring that goods were sold according to standard measures and those who did not do so were prosecuted in the town's courts. Weights and measures were provided and replaced at the expense of the town: sea coal, which had previously been sold by the heap or bucket, was ordered to be sold by a newly commissioned bushel, a half Bushell or peck, subject to a 10s fine (26 July 1646).

Merchants were charged to use the quays and various facilities provided by the Corporation including the crane. Imported goods were subject to a range of customs duties which were listed in 1618 and provide an indication of the range of goods imported. Charges depended upon whether the merchants were freemen of the town and the Minute Books frequently uses of the term "foreign bought and foreign sold" to describe goods in transactions between traders who were not freemen of the borough. Sometimes the minutes reveal aspects of the town's trading network: 22 April 1625 two hogsheads of Gascoigne wine were sold by the merchant Thomas Combes of Southampton to the vintner Thomas Meryfield of Bridport. At other times inhabitants of the town became involved in deception: in 1646 George Churchey, a freeman, was fined £8 for claiming that the goods of his his brother James, who was not a freeman, were his own.

There are pages used to record the enrolment of apprentices, the period 1618-1641 is covered in a haphazard way on pages 26-37; another list of enrolments after 1641 appears on page 211. Apprentices were important to the prosperity of the town. The tailors Thomas Baldwin and John Reynolds were licenced to work on the condition that they took on Weymouth born apprentices. In February 1621 the Mayor paid 20s from the poor stock to John Pope for taking Launcelot Growte to be apprentice for eight years. Apprenticeship was an important route to qualification as a freeman of the town and they usually paid the nominal fee of 3s 4d for admittance at the end of their terms. The sons of freemen might be admitted by patrimony also for a fine of 3s 4d. "*ex gratia*" freemen were admitted for no fine as an honour for providing some service to the town such as the members of parliament Gerard Napper and Sir Walter Erle or Colonel James Hearne the governor of the garrison. The largest group of freemen were those who paid fines from £1 to £30 for their admittance and the associated right to trade within the town. The variation in the entry fine depended upon the applicant's pre-existing association with the town, with the son-in-laws of freemen achieving the largest reductions. Freemen might be elected capital burgesses which qualified them to serve as members of the assembly. Like the lists of apprentices the lists of freemen and capital burgesses are interspersed among the council minutes. There seems to be no particular order and the fact that some of the pages are left blank indicates that it was intended to use the book for various other records which were never completed or inserted.

The assembly was full of merchants and tradesmen who were not above doing a deal or bending the rules when it suited them. John Frye, a glazier, was given permission to open a shop in Melcombe Regis, although he was a foreigner, on the condition that he repaired the church windows (6 June 1634).

In addition to collecting customs and charges for the import and export of goods the town raised revenues in a number of ways. The rentals of Weymouth and Melcombe Regis detail the sums that came to the Corporation through residential and commercial properties. The town also owned areas of waste and common land which were let out on short leases. Also leased were the markets, town bridge and rights to collect duties which might be quite profitable: in October 1621 John Reade paid £5 10s to manage the market and to take any profits from leasing stalls and fines for minor offences, at the same time John Pope paid £15 10s to manage the town bridge and to take any charges from those who used it, Henry Russell paid £5 15s for the right to manage the quays and harbours taking any payments for the disposal of ballast, use of the crane and the charges to be moored at the quayside. In October 1621 it was also agreed that the right to collect the petty customs should be leased. Following a competitive tender and with the provision of securities they were granted to John Pitt the elder for £121.

Poor relief was a significant aspect of the business of the Corporation which overlapped with the roles of churchwardens. It is likely that the Corporation took a more active role in an area where parochial authority was weaker than in other towns: as Weymouth was a dependent chapelry of Wyke Regis and Melcome Regis a dependent chapelry of Radipole. Poor relief might take many forms: Joan Gold left £20 in her will to be used by the mayor for the relief of the poor (30 March 1632), when new porters were appointed they were required to pay 6d from their wages to an old and infirm porter (8 October 1641) and the Corporation acted as a credit union loaning money to young merchants and craftsmen who paid the interest to the churchwardens (16 March 1649). In February 1622 money was provided to Matthew Allin and Richard Harrisson to buy flax "to set the poor to work" in Weymouth and Melcombe Regis, in this and other matters of relief the sum was specifically allotted to ensure that each town received an equal sum. The Corporation also took measures to ensure that it did not adopt people who might become dependent upon the community: Roger Devenisshe was allowed to work as a glazier, but not to bring his wife and children into the town (3 October 1629); John Wall was ordered to remove the foreigner Henry Tizer and his wife and children from his house because they were likely to become chargeable upon the town (10 November 1648).

The unusual parochial status of both Weymouth and Melcombe Regis meant that the Corporation has a considerable interest in the appointments of preachers and activities in a blurring of roles between the secular and ecclesiastical. When William Reape was appointed parish clerk he was to teach poor children to read and write with no further reward beyond his salary (7 January 1648); several burgesses were ordered to review what repairs to Melcombe church were necessary and to audit the churchwarden's accounts (12 October 1650), Weymouth Chapel and Melcombe Regis church were each given £20 from the town stock towards the fabric of their buildings (20 July 1621). The Corporation paid for a replacement clock for Melcombe Church (5 November 1619), no doubt necessary to ensure that the bell was rung at the required times of four in the morning and eight in the evening.

Teachers like William Reape were drawn from the clergy, but the Corporation also appointed a schoolmaster for whom a stipend of £4 towards accommodation was allowed (29 January 1647) and the old medieval Friary site was set aside for a school (8 August and 30 October 1651).

Weymouth and Melcombe Regis formed a significant urban centre, but they were close to the countryside, retained their own rural hinterlands. Rights to the commons were reasserted in November 1649 when the sergeants, constables and scholars of the town sowed wheat to the Melcombe Regis town boundary following a period of disputed lease. Mr Waltham made a trip to London to establish the town's rights in August 1651, but by 1656 the farmer of Radipole contested them once more and this friction remained for several years.

The Corporation was responsible for various aspects of coastal defence. Weymouth and Melcombe Regis had been burnt several times by French and Spanish raiders in the late fourteenth and early fifteenth centuries which had resulted in Melcombe Regis losing its status as the principal customs port to the more secure town of Poole in 1433. The subsequent decline in the town's fortunes had only begun to be reversed in the sixteenth century and the events of Elizabeth's reign had highlighted the potential risks faced by southern harbours. Some provision was made for immediate defence by maintaining canons and a blockhouse (6 October 1625) and as part of a wider network the town beacon might attract assistance from the Dorset militia and warn the rest of the country of an impending attack (7 May 1622). When residents were obliged to provide lodgings for troops billeted in the town they were paid 3s 6d per week for each soldier (10 October 1626).

The Minute Book covers the period of the Civil War, in which Weymouth and Melcombe Regis characteristically took opposing sides; disappointingly the it does not make explicit reference to the conflict as it occurred. On 25 September 1640 the town's revenues were used to provide a soldier to fight in the wars against the Scots. In January 1645, just before the conflict came to the town itself, the clerk gives the regnal year as well as the year of grace at the start of his entry, perhaps suggesting some Royalist sympathy, there are no entries for February 1645, and when order was restored in March it was necessary to appoint several new constables. On 21 March 1645 Fabian Hodder, a leader of the local Royalists had his status of burgess removed for non-attendance at the assembly. Hodder's status was restored at the Restoration, as were those fifteen burgesses who resigned their status in 1649. Meanwhile, in November 1645 Colonel Sydenham, the Parliamentary commander, was selected as the town's representative in Parliament. Clearly deep divisions remained throughout the Commonwealth, for which the text of the Minute Book returns to a more detailed account of the decisions made within the town.

Details of the reconstruction provide evidence of some of the damage that occurred in the conflict and how long it took to make matters right. On 21 April 1651 two Parliamentary officers allocated thirty trees to be brought from Hampshire for repairs to the town bridge which had incurred serious damage six years previously. In August 1651 it was noted that the town had suffered greatly from the loss of trade and that considerable damage had occurred to Weymouth Marsh where much of the fighting had taken place, £70 was borrowed from the Melcombe Regis parish funds to make repairs. By October 1653 the Minute Book records the sale of stones from the various forts to raise funds for the town.

In the seventeenth century commercial contacts with the world were expanding and Weymouth and Melcombe Regis were perfectly placed to take advantage of the increase in long range maritime contacts. In January 1618 the plantation of Newfoundland was discussed at the assembly and it was considered again in 1620. In 1621 the mayor of Exeter was contacted regarding his interests in the plantation and fishing in New England. Transatlantic travel was dangerous, but waters closer to home could present problems too: payments were authorised to repatriate men enslaved by the Turks (3 September 1623) and for redeeming captives from Algiers (15 January 1647).

From the Minute Book it is possible to reconstruct a partial geography of the seventeenth century town. Among the surveys included at the beginning of the volume is one of the rents in Weymouth and a more detailed survey of the houses and premises in Melcombe Regis. From this second survey Maureen Weinstock produced three maps to indicate the sites of the plots and the development of the town, Originally published in her collection of *More Dorset Studies* (1960), they are reproduced here to illustrate the residential and commercial development of Melcombe Regis by the early seventeenth century.[2] The goods were stored in cellars beneath the merchant's houses. The survey of Melcombe Regis compiled in August 1617 takes care to list them and from this it is possible to reconstruct something of the commercial geography of the town. Trades men and artisans were concentrated to the north and east of the town, with the merchants congregated along the harbour facing Weymouth or along the backwater with their cellars beneath their houses. St Nicholas and St Edmund Streets, a short distance from the quay, were home to most of the warehouses. The bailiffs and aldermen were called upon to regulate construction. They ensured that the buildings did not encroach upon public areas and reviewed substantial construction projects like the new windmill (3 November 1619).

Although Dorset's main county gaol was in Dorchester the larger towns found it necessary to have small prisons in Melcombe Regis, in a converted shop beneath a building adjacent to the town hall (18 October 1622), and another in Weymouth (26 October 1621) both of which were maintained at the expense of the Corporation.

2 Maureen Weinstock produced two collections of essays *Studies in Dorset History* (Dorchester, 1953) and *More Dorset Studies* (Dorchester, 1960), which each contain several essays on Weymouth and Melcombe Regis in the seventeenth century, both long out of print they are available in local libraries.

This was a short term lock-up or bridewell where offenders might be held pending their appearance at the Quarter Sessions (26 June 1646) and was probably used as a short term lock-up for drunks and brawlers. Some minor crimes were judged and punished locally in the town courts and a new pillory and ducking stool was provided at the expense of the Corporation (9 October 1634).

While the Minute Book reveals a the infrastructure of the town in some detail it is through the interactions of the inhabitants that the environment is brought to life. Members of the Allin, Maunsell, Gyer and Leddoze families had, with others, represented inhabitants of Melcombe Regis and Weymouth when the towns were brought together in 1585 and continued to figure prominently throughout the period covered by the Minute Book. Sir Samuel Mico, whose bequest to the Weymouth Town Charities is still administered in the twenty first century, appears as both a merchant and a Parliamentary candidate. Mico was not the only former resident to remember the town with a bequest. The London merchant Robert Middleton's will, made in 1618, included the sum of £25 for the benefit of the poor was still being lent at interest by the Corporation in 1651. Fabian Hodder can be seen carrying out the administrative duties of a member of the town's ruling group before the Civil War. The unfortunate suicide John Dry whose goods were listed in March 1618, the widow Margaret Payge who cooked the junor's dinner, and the poor man Robert Welman, who was allowed to live rent free, represent the less fortunate and poorer residents upon who the Corporation might look kindly: 3 January 1651 Gregory Babbidge came to the assembly and paid £7 17s 3d which the Corporation had allowed his grandmother 'old Mrs Babbidge' to accrue in arrears, £5 was used to pave the street outside her house and the remaining £2 17s 3d was returned to him.

Compilation of the volume

The book is a large folio volume in a good state of preservation. It was compiled by several scribes who appear to have written up the notes of meetings at a later date and copied in certain other significant documents to maintain a permanent record. It begins with an alphabetical index to the whole volume which has not been reproduced in the present edition. Each clerk then added their minutes and other records sequentially. At certain points the scribes left space for further information or returned to previous sections, such as the lists of apprentices and freemen, where the contents were updated.

The first minutes of the town council are dated 9 October 1617, and the last recorded in the book is for 10 April 1695. This Dorset Record Society edition covers the period 1617-1660.

Editorial Conventions.

The text presented in this edition is the core text of the volume as it was compiled. Marginalia has not been included unless it is important to clarify a specific point within the main body of the text. The additions to lists of freemen and apprentices have been transcribed as they are of general interest and the original clerks left space intending that they should form part of the on going compilation of the volume.

All abbreviations have been expanded, spellings have been modernised and capitals used sparingly as seventeenth century scribes used capitals more frequently than a modern reader expects.

Some punctuation has been added by the editors to long or difficult sections to provide clarification. Certain archaic forms such as *bounden, appeareth, paieth* and *saieth* have been replaced by 'bound', 'appears', 'pays' and 'says'. Where a word has obviously been omitted by accident it has been inserted in square brackets. Where an obscure word might be of particular interest, as a technical term of unusual spelling, it has been included in italics or followed by the modern form in round brackets. As far as possible a faithful transcript has been made except that all marginalia have been omitted. These merely give the heading and gist of the minute or resolution.

All Latin sections have been translated and are preceded by [Latin] in the text with [English] where the language reverts to the vernacular. Occasional Latin words such as *inprimis* (firstly) have been silently translated, except where they convey a particular technical meaning such as *ex gratia* for those burgesses who were granted their status without payment of the usual fines.

Forenames have been modernised, but surnames appear in their manuscript forms and the reader should note that any individual may have several spellings of their surname. Place names have also been left as they appear in the manuscript, most notably Waymouth being the usual form, with a clarification in square brackets where the location is not obvious.

All Roman numerals have been reproduced as Arabic and dates have been standardised to the modern calendar with the year beginning 1 January rather than 25 March. Dates in headings have been standardised to the form 1 January 2021, but dates within the text have been left in their original formats with the year of grace added in square brackets where only the regnal year is provided.

LIST OF MAPS AND IMAGES

Photographs reproduced with permission of the Dorset History Centre, references [D-DPA/1/WY/208, 222 and 273, and D-HBT/5726a]

Front Cover image, sailing ships at the quay, late nineteenth century [DPA/1/WY/160]

Back cover image, Melcombe Regis Guildhall, engraving by John Upham, 1825 [D-DPA/1/WY/316]

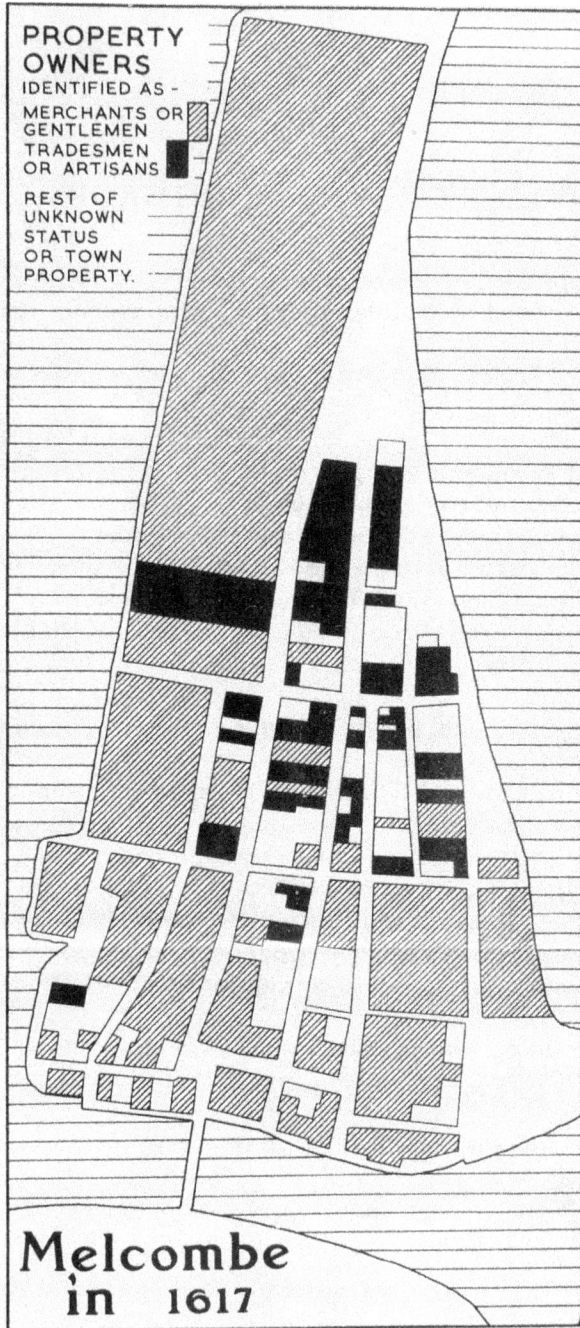

1 *Map of Melcombe Regis by Maureen Weinstock to accompany 1617 survey showing locations of properties*

MELCOMBE
REGIS
in 1617

PROPERTY BOUNDARIES AND
OTHER DETAILS RECONSTR-
UCTED FROM THE TOWN
RENTAL, LEASES, AND
LATER CADASTRAL MAPS.
● HOUSE
Ⓑ BUTCHERY
Ⓢ STABLE
Ⓢⓗ SHOP
Ⓦ WAREHOUSE OR STORE

NORTHWARD CONTINUATION:
ONE-THIRD SCALE

SCALE OF FEET

Site of
MOUNTJOY FORT

The Bay

The Backwater

The Haven

BLOCKHOUSE

ST. THOMAS STREET
ST. MARY STREET
ST. NICHOLAS STREET
MAIDEN STREET
NEW STREET
EAST STREET
WEST STREET
PETTICOAT LANE
CONEYGAR
DITCH   Site of Maypole
ST. EDMUND STREET
FRIARY BUILDINGS
FRIARY LAND
FRIARY LANE
CHURCH YARD
CHURCH
TOWN HALL
TOWN LAND
HELL LANE
QUAY
BRIDGE
Town Crane
Parsonage

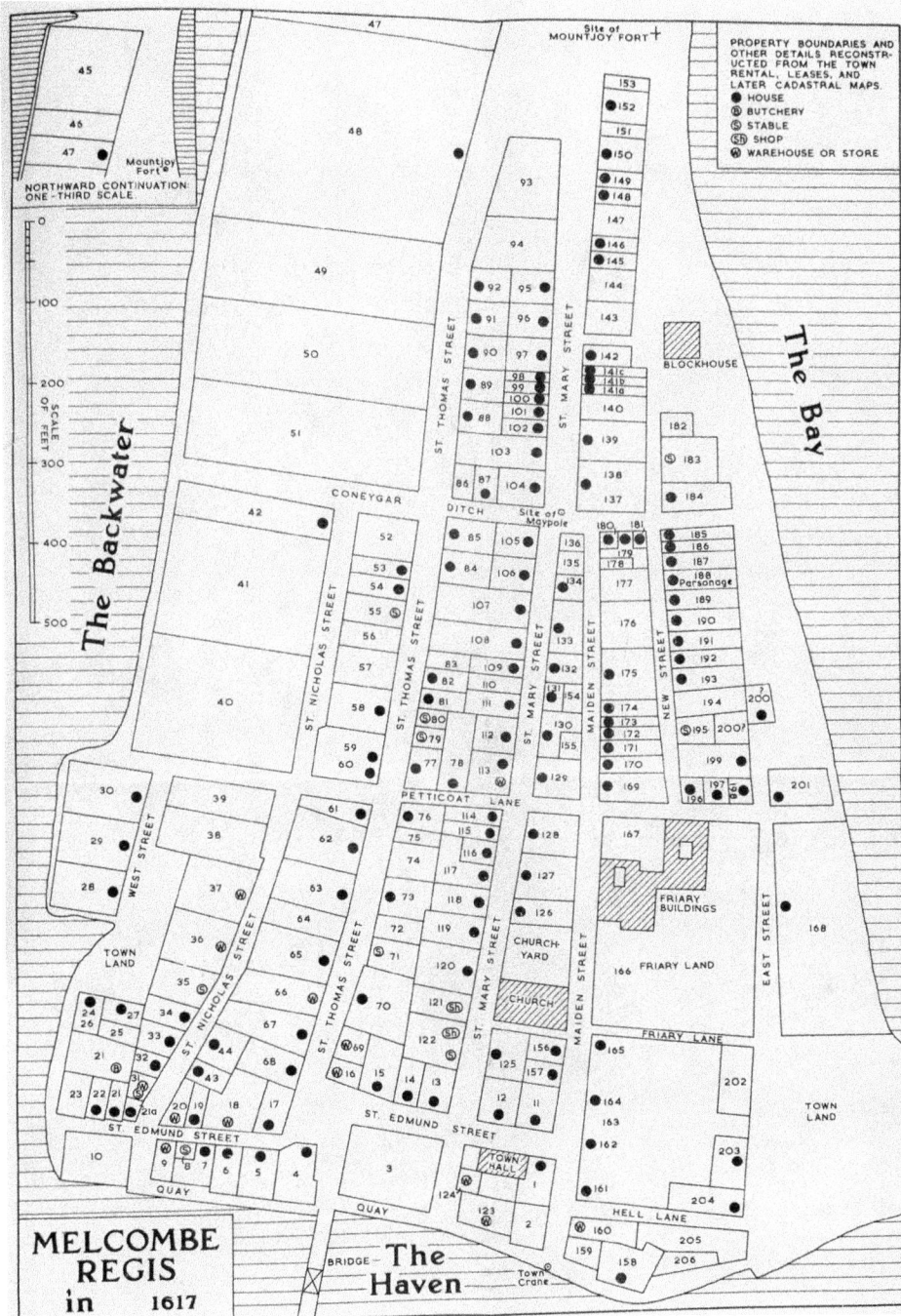

2 Map of Melcombe Regis by Maureen Weinstock showing classes of property holders circa 1617

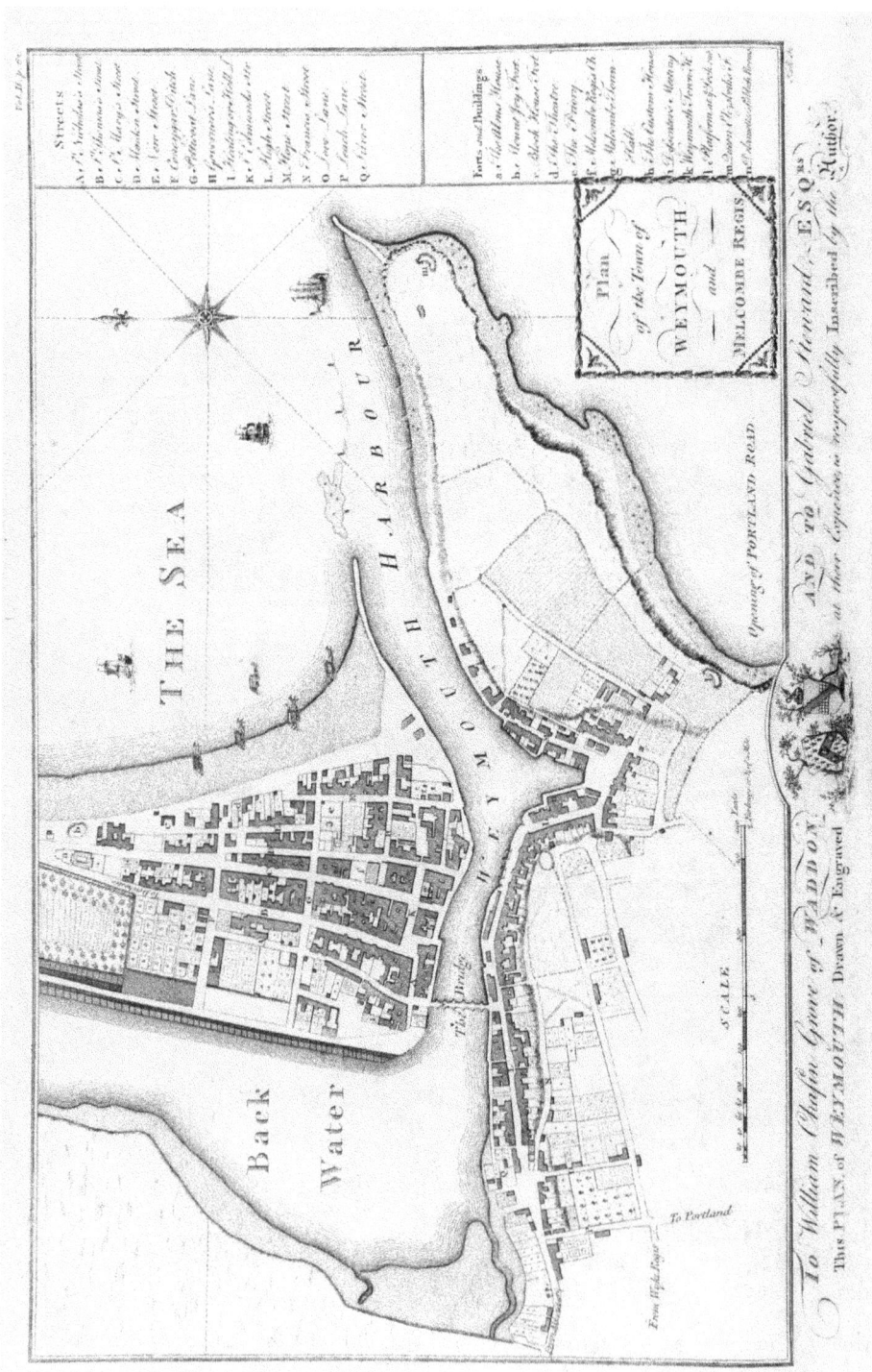

3 *Map of Weymouth and Melcombe Regis commissioned by William Chafin Grove, Recorder of Weymouth and Melcombe Regis 1774–1786. From J. Hutchins History of Dorset, 2nd edition, v.2, p.62.*

4 Crane for unloading ships at the quay, early 20th century

5 Customs house and warehouses on the Melcombe Regis quay, late 20th century

6 *The Armada Chest, which reputedly came from the Spanish Armada ship the San Salvador, was used for secure storage in the Customs House. It is now kept at the Weymouth Museum. A similar chest housed the town documents and the Minute Book.*

7 *Melcombe Regis town hall, on the site of the seventeenth century building, late 20th century*

8 Weymouth town hall, converted from three cottages with extensive modifications in the 18th and 19th centuries

9 *Minute Book, page 55, the start of the Weymouth rental*

10 Minute Book, page 58, the start of the Melcombe Regis survey

11 Minute Book, page 102, quarantine of a plague ship

12 Minute Book page 248, sale of stones from the Civil War forts, 1653

13 Minute Book page 257, leases of the bridge, market and customs, 1655

THE BOROUGH AND TOWN OF WAYMOUTH AND MELCOMBE REGIS IN THE COUNTY OF DORSET

An assembly held in the Guildhall of Melcombe Regis within the borough and town of Waymouth and Melcombe Regis aforesaid in the said county of Dorset by the mayor, aldermen, bailiffs and capital and principal burgesses of the said borough and town, the ninth day of October 1617 and in the year of the reign of our sovereign lord James by the grace of God of England, France and Ireland King, defender of the faith, etc, the fifteenth and of Scotland the one and fiftieth.

Whereas it is fit that the mayor and bailiffs of this borough and town have assistance of the aldermen and capital and principal burgesses of the said borough and town in causes of his Majesty and matters concerning the state and government of the same borough and town it is therefore ordered and constituted and agreed by and with a full assent and consent of the said mayor, aldermen, bailiffs and capital and principal burgesses of the said borough and town that if any of the said aldermen or capital and principal burgesses be sufficiently required and warned from the mayor and bailiffs, or any of them in causes concerning the King or the state and government of this borough and town, or otherwise and shall not give his attendance accordingly without some reasonable excuse that then every alderman shall forfeit for every default 3s 4d. And every one of the capital and principal burgesses shall forfeit for every default 12d to be levied to those of this Corporation upon the goods and chattels of every of them which shall so make default, by way of distress to be taken by the mayor's warrant and the same distress to be sold by the like warrant. And if any surplus above the sum forfeited shall be made upon the sale of the same distress that then the same surplus shall be delivered to the party or parties from whom the same distress shall be so taken.

[Signed by] John Pitt, mayor; William Holman, bailiff; John Roy, bailiff; Robert Whit, William Waltham, Robert Knight; Henry Russell, Edward Roy, Thomas Giear, John Pytt, John Reynolds, Peter Neale [his mark], William Bonfield, Matthew Allin, Henry Blickell, Roger Fry [his mark], Robert Vall [his mark], John Ellis [his mark], William Martell [his mark], James James, Thomas Lockier, Edward Hodder, Robert Major, Henry Waltham, William Williams.

[page 2] An assembly held in the Guildhall of Melcombe Regis within the borough and town of Weymouth and Melcombe Regis in the county of Dorset by the mayor, aldermen, bailiffs, burgesses and capital and principal burgesses of the said borough and town the ninth day of October 1607.

At this assembly it was and is fully and generally agreed and ordered that the greater book of the two books shall serve for the entering of the last and the new charter both in Latin and English and of the record of the sessions of the peace, court leets and view of frankpledge and of all matters of Justice and that the lesser book shall serve for the entering of all the names of the freemen, enrolling of apprentices and of all constitutions agreed upon by this Corporation and of all other matters which concern this borough and town and the Corporation the most.

At this assembly it was and is also fully and generally agreed and ordered that all freemen of this Corporation shall come into some one court held within this borough and town either in his and their own person or persons or by his or their friends or deputies upon or before the tenth day of November next following and shall pray that his and their name and names may be entered and enrolled amongst other freemen of this Corporation in the book appointed for that purpose. Or else his or they which shall neglect the same shall take no benefit of his and their freedom until he and they shall challenge the same.

At the same assembly it was and is also fully and generally agreed and ordered that all tradesmen, handicrafts artificers and others that do use any manual occupation shall upon or before the twentieth day of this instant month come unto the town clerk of this borough and town who shall receive a catalogue of their names and trades to the end that at the next assembly then after to be held the mayor, aldermen, bailiffs and capital burgesses of this borough and town may consider who are fit to use their trades here and who are not.

At the assembly aforesaid it was and is also agreed and ordered by and with a full and general consent that the old constitutions and orders shall be viewed and considered by Mr William Holeman and Mr John Roye, bailiffs, Mr Thomas Gier, Mr Matthew Allin, aldermen, Henry Michell and Mr Robert Vaule who shall make request at the next assembly here to be held which of them are to be confirmed and enrolled in the new book of constitutions and which are not and this to be done within fourteen days next following.

[Signed by] John Pitt, mayor; William Holman, bailiff; John Roy, bailiff, Robert Whit, alderman; Henry Russell, alderman, William Mansell, John Reynolds, John Pytt, Thomas Giear, Robert Vall [his mark], Roger Fry [his mark], Thomas Lockier, Henry Blickell, Henry Waltham, Robert Major, John Ellis [his mark], William Williams, James James, Edward Hodder.

[page 3] 13 October 1617

At this day it was and is fully agreed by a general consent of the mayor, aldermen, bailiffs and capital and principal burgesses of this borough and town of Waymouth and Melcombe Regis, by and with the assent of William Waltham, late mayor of this borough and town that Mr Bailiff Holeman and Mr Bailiff Roy, Mr John Pitt, the elder and William Williams, Thomas Gardner and Thomas Wallis shall be auditors of the accounts of the said William Waltham touching all such monies, rents, revenues and other things belonging unto this Corporation as he has received or disbursed unto or for the use of the said Corporation in the time of his late mayoralty and that as the said auditors five or four of them shall determine of the said accounts so it shall bu[manuscript damaged, remainder of word illegible] as well this Corporation as the said William Waltham to stand unto the same.

3 November 1617

At this day upon a meeting of Mr Mayor, the aldermen, bailiffs, burgesses of this borough and town it was and is agreed by them to and with Thomas Lovelis and the said Thomas Lovelis did agree with them that he the said Thomas Lovelis before the feast of the Purification of the Virgin Mary next shall build up a house at the west end of Melcombe Hall in manner and form following viz, in breadth by the ground nine foot and at least eleven foot westwards and in length the whole breadth of the town hall and over of the *line* of the butchers shambles upon five turned pillars of twelve inches square with five windows, each of three lights and one window towards the north of the whole breadth and to cover the upper room with two inch plank with battlement of two foot with a pair of stairs with boards and *braz* of convenient height and two hatch doors to the lower room and one door to the upper room. And in consideration thereof the Corporation are to pay him fifteen pounds ten shillings. There must be two lofts the lower loft of good deal *boomed* and the upper loft of two inch plank as aforesaid and if the Corporation will have battlements 4 foot high then Thomas Lovelis is to have £16 10s.

10 November 1617

An assembly held in the Guildhall of Melcombe Regis within the borough town of Waymouth and Melcombe Regis in the county of Dorset by the mayor, aldermen, bailiffs and capital and principal burgesses of the said borough and town.

Upon this present day Thomas Ledoze coming to desire his freedom and submitting himself to the censure of the bench for the taxing of his fine was by general consent of the same court taxed to pay the fine of £10 and to pay all petty customs until Michaelmas next and so is to be admitted a freeman and to receive his oath. And at that time it was and is generally agreed by the same court that from henceforth no man shall be admitted as freeman of this Corporation by way of fine nor the mayor, aldermen, bailiffs and capital and principal burgesses for the time being shall give any voice or consent of admitting of any man to be a freeman by way of fine under the sum of £5. And upon the fourteenth day of the same month of November aforesaid the said Thomas Ledoze did pay his fine and did take the oath of a freeman.

14 November 1617

An assembly held in the Guildhall of Melcombe Regis within the borough and town of Waymouth and Melcombe Regis in the county of Dorset by the mayor, aldermen, bailiffs and capital and principal burgesses of the said borough and town the fourteenth day of November 1617.

Upon this present day upon a motion made unto this assembly on the behalf of Thomas Wallis touching the granting of his freedom it was and is agreed by the same assembly that upon the payment of forty shillings unto the Corporation he shall have his freedom of this town as a lawful freeman by way of redemption always provided that he shall pay all such petty customs as shall grow due until the feast of St Michael the Archangel next coming. And this was granted unto the said Thomas Wallis for forty shillings the former order not withstanding in respect of Mr Mayor's special respect and in respect that he the said Thomas Wallis has been a long time a town inhabitant and always behaved himself well.

[page 4] It was and is also fully and generally agreed by this assembly that from henceforth no freeman of this town shall take any apprentice whom he shall intend to make a freeman by his service but only such as he may lawfully took to be an apprentice according to the statute made 5 Elizabeth [1562-1563] and such as he shall from time to time enrol the indenture of his apprenticeship within one year next after the date of the same indenture and that such freemen of this town as have apprentices which have served them some time already and do intend to make such apprentice free by the service shall enrol the indentures of their apprenticeship within one year next ensuing. And if any master of any such apprentice shall neglect to do the same that then every such master of any apprentice shall in either of those cases forfeit and loose to this Corporation two shillings and six pence for every quarter after the end of the year that he shall neglect the enrolment of his apprentice indenture and that the same master shall pay all such forfeitures and the arrears (*tharrerage*) thereof if any shall be before such time as his apprentice shall be admitted freeman and that the common clerk of this town shall have the making of all such apprentice indentures and shall do it in reasonable time and shall have two shillings for his pains and that the master of such apprentice shall pay for enrolling of every such apprentice indenture three shillings in manner and form following viz. to the mayor twelve pence and to each of the bailiffs six pence and to the town clerk twelve pence. And that the apprentice which is to be admitted a freeman of this Corporation shall pay to the same Corporation three shillings and four pence at the time of his admission.

[Signed by] John Pitt, mayor; William Holman, bailiff; John Roy, bailiff; Robert Whit, Henry Russell, William Manfeld[?], John Reynolds, John Pytt, Thomas Giear, Thomas Lockier, Henry Waltham, Henry Blikell, Robert Major, Roger Frye [his mark], James James, John Ellis [his mark], Edward Hodder, William Williams.

[page 5] Constitutions and orders made and fully agreed upon by the mayor, aldermen, bailiffs and capital and principal burgesses of the borough and town of Waymouth and Melcombe Regis in the county of Dorset the fourteenth day of November the years of the reign of our Sovereign Lord James by the grace of God of England, France and Ireland, king, defender of the faith etc. the fifteenth and of Scotland the one and fiftieth 1617.

First it is constituted ordered and agreed that there shall be yearly chosen by the mayor, alderman, bailiffs and capital and principal burgesses or the greater part of them upon the feast day of St Matthew the apostle one honest and discrete man being either an alderman or a capital or principal burgess of this borough and town who shall receive [by] virtue of his office to the use of the same Incorporation all and all manner of rents, petty customs, duties, revenues, issues, profits and commodities whatsoever which shall grow due or payable unto the said Corporation from the feast of St Michael the Archangel next after he shall be chosen receiver as aforesaid for one whole year then next following. And that the same receiver being so chosen shall within one month next after he is so chosen enter into bond unto the said Corporation in a reasonable sum to be appointed by the mayor and bailiffs of the said Corporation for the time being or any two of them whereof the mayor to be with a condition there unto annexed that the same receiver shall from time to time render yield up unto the said Corporation or unto some other selected persons named and appointed by the said mayor, aldermen, bailiffs, capital or principal burgesses or the greater part of them for that purpose a honest and true account of all the receipts which he shall receive in time wherein he shall be receiver as aforesaid upon pain that the said receiver refusing, neglecting to enter into bond to forfeit ten pounds unto the said Corporation and it is further constituted, ordered and agreed upon that the said receiver shall not at any time or times disburse or pay or cause to be disbursed or paid any sum or sums of money onto his receipt aforesaid to any intent or purpose about any of the affairs of the said Corporation otherwise without having a warrant for the payment thereof in manner and form following. That is to say that if it be for the payment of 40s or under then a warrant signed by mayor only for the time being but if it be for the payment of ten pound or any sum under ten pounds and above 40s then a warrant signed by the mayor, bailiffs, two aldermen and two of the capital or principal burgesses and that no greater sum than ten pounds shall be disbursed by the said receiver without a warrant and under the town seal with the consent of the said mayor, aldermen, bailiffs and capital or principal burgesses or the greater part of them in which several cases every warrant made in form aforesaid shall be a sufficient discharge unto the same receiver of and for so much as is contained and mentioned in any such warrant. And it is also constituted, ordered and agreed that in all those several cases the same receiver shall pay any sum of money that shall be contained in any such warrant if he has money sufficient of the stock of this Corporation in his hand keeping upon pain to forfeit unto the Corporation double the sum which he shall neglect to pay as aforesaid.

Item it is constituted, ordered and agreed that no man shall cast any manner of filth or dirt the same or other annoyance out of any house or from any quay or wharf of the same town into the haven of the same town whereby the said haven may be annoyed or impaired upon pain to forfeit for each such offence the sum of 2s 6d.

It is constituted and agreed that no man shall lay or cause to be laid any manner of filth or other ordure upon any of the *staund* or *stronds* of either side or part of the haven within the extent of the full sea mark of the said haven upon pain to forfeit for such offence 2s 6d.

It is constituted and agreed that no man shall cast out of ship, crayer, barge or boat any scarpe ballast to say: sand, gravel, earth or the like on any side or part of the said haven within the full sea mark nor any oyster shells, oyster *scroffe* or oysters, but one in caves above David Guyer his corner in Melcombe side and the hive by John Ellys house in Weymouth side, upon pain for forfeit for every such offence 3s 4d.

It is constituted, ordered and agreed that no man shall cast or lay any ballast, stone ballast or any other stones upon either part or side of the said haven within the full sea mark of the same but shall remove the same the next low water following without above the precinct of the said full sea mark upon pain to forfeit for every such offence 3s 4d

It is constituted, ordered and agreed that no man shall dig or break any ground upon any the stronds of either side or part of the said haven for the *grating* or dressing any ship or barque or other vessel but shall the next low water following fill up and level the said ground so broken upon pain to forfeit for every such offence the sum of 5s.

[page 6] It is constituted and ordered that no man shall cast any scoope ballast that is to say sand, gravel, earth or the like out of any ship barque or other vessel upon the quay, or land, or into any boat or lighter, or out of any boat or from the quay into any ship, barque, creyer or other vessel without bringing some *bonnet* or *sayle* upon the side of every such ship or *barque* or other vessel whereby none of the same ballast may fall into the said haven to the impairment of the same upon pain to forfeit for each such offence the sum of 3s 4d.

It is constituted, ordered and agreed that no man shall cast any manner of ballast out of any ship, or *barque*, or other vessel into the channel of the said haven or any part thereof, or into the road of the said haven, or any part thereof upon pain to forfeit for every such offence 10s.

It is constituted and agreed that no man shall lay or cause to be laid any filth or other ordure in any street, lane or other usual way of the said town, or upon any quay, or wharf of the same town but shall carry the same to such place or places as is appointed for the same whereby the said town, nor any part thereof, may be annoyed upon pain of forfeiture for every such offence the sum of 12d.

It is constituted, ordered and agreed that no man shall lay or encumber any the streets, lanes or other usual way or ways of the said town or any quay or wharf of the same town with any timber, stones or other encumbrance upon pain of forfeiture of five shillings if he move not the same by the end of three days after the landing or laying of it in any such place

It is constituted, ordered and agreed that no man being a brewer shall cast any grains or other filth into any the streets of the said town upon pain of forfeiture for every such offence 2s 6d.

It is constituted, ordered and agreed that if any alderman, burgess or freeman of this borough and town do revile or seek to discredit by word or otherwise any other of the said aldermen, burgesses or freemen do strike or hurt any other of the said aldermen, burgesses or freemen whereby the King's Peace may be broken he or they so offending for every such offence in any the case so remembered shall pay such fine as by the mayor, aldermen and capital or principal burgesses of the said town or the greater part of them shall be assessed or adjudged the same offence being lawfully proved by the testimony of two sufficient witnesses before the mayor, bailiffs and two alderman of the said town.

It is further constituted, ordered and agreed that if any of the said aldermen, burgesses or inhabitants do assemble themselves together and make any conference for the breaking or disallowing of any constitutions heretofore made, now made, or hereafter to be made by the mayor, aldermen, bailiffs and capital or principal burgesses of the said borough and town without the consent and order of the mayor and bailiffs of the said borough and town that every such offender or offenders shall pay such fine and abide such imprisonment as by the discretions of the said mayor, aldermen, bailiffs and capital or principal burgesses or the greater part of them shall be thought meet the offence not being lawfully proved by the testemony of two sufficient witnesses before the mayor and bailiffs and two of the aldermen and two capital and principal burgesses of the aforesaid borough and town.

Item it is also constituted, ordered and agreed that there shall be attorneys belonging to the court of record of the said borough and town which shall be sworn that they shall minister no foreign plea except they will depose in their consent their said pleas to be true and that no stranger shall be allowed to plead his own case in the said court or any other for him without retaining some one or more of the attorneys of record of the said court and only freemen taking upon him to plead his own case without retaining some one of the said attorneys except he will depose that his plea is true shall pay such fine and suffer such punishment as by the decision of the mayor, aldermen, bailiffs, burgesses and capital or principal burgesses of the said borough and town for the time being or the greater part of them shall be thought fit.

[page 7] It is constituted ordered and agreed that no man shall make any affray upon any officer which with good demeanour doth his messuage by the commandment of the mayor, recorder, bailiffs or alderman of this town and that no man shall misbehave himself in railing upon the mayor, recorder, bailiffs or aldermen of this town or against any officer which shall by commandment be sent to bring or carry any breaker of any of the laws or constitutions of the town or to levy any distress upon the forfeiture and breach of all law or constitution of the borough and town upon pain to suffer imprisonment for the space of two days and payment of such fine as by the discretion of the mayor, aldermen, bailiffs and capital burgesses of the said borough and town or the greater part of them shall be thought fit.

And it is lastly fully constituted, ordered and agreed that all pains and forfeitures imposed upon the breach of any constitution or order made at this assembly shall be levied by the common sergeants of this borough and town or by any one of them upon warrant under the hand and seal of the mayor of the said borough and town for the time being by way of distress and sale of the goods of the same person or persons which shall break any of the Constitutions or orders aforesaid. Which distress shall be sold by the same sergeant or sergeants for the raising and levying of any such forfeiture to the use of the said Corporation and the surplus thereof rendered unto the said party so distrained.   Provided always that the warrant which shall be made forth for the levying of the forfeitures aforesaid shall be under the mayor and bailiff's hand and seals for the time being, or under the hand and seals of two of them whereof the mayor always shall be one or else the warrant shall not be held good. And if any of their forfeitures shall be let to farm, the same warrant shall be made unto the farmer or farmers thereof in form aforesaid.

[Signed by] John Pitt, mayor; William Holman, bailiff; John Roy, bailiff; Robert Whit, alderman; Henry Russell, alderman; William Mansell, John Reynolds, John Pytt, Thomas Giear, Robert Vaul [his mark], Thomas Lockeire, Henry Waltham, Henry Michell, James James, Robert Major, Roger Frye [his mark], Edward Hodder, William Williams, John Ellis [his mark].

[page 8] First it is constituted, ordered and agreed that the water bailiffs, if there be any, or the farmer or farmers of the forfeitures upon the constitutions made, or to be made, for the preservation of the harbour and keeping clean of the quay as for the time being shall give order and direction for and touching the placing and displacing of ships, barques and other vessels at the quays to laid or unlaid, or for any other purpose and for the removing of any ship, barque or vessel from the quays if there be cause. And that if any owner, master or company of any ship or vessel having lawful warning by the water bailiffs or farmer or farmers above said to remove his or their ship, barque or other vessel from the quay shall refuse or neglect to do the same at the next tide next after warning so to be given, he or they shall forfeit 3s 4d for every tide that the said ship shall remain there after warning so to be given to be levied by the water bailiffs, or farmer or farmers aforesaid of and upon the same ship, barque or vessel, or of or upon some part of the apparel or furniture of the same ship, barque or vessel. Provided always that Mr Mayor for the time being or Mr Bailiffs for the time being or any one of them (in his absence) shall have a superior authority touching this constitution to overrule all things according to his, or their, best discretion. And it is further ordered constituted and agreed that the water bailiffs, or farmer or farmers aforesaid for the time being, shall forfeit for every time that he or they shall refuse or neglect to levy the forfeitures aforesaid if he or they have warning from Mr Mayor for the time being, he doing the thereof.

It is constituted, ordered and agreed that the water bailiffs or the farmer or farmers of the Ballast shall have all the ballast which shall be cast upon the quay on either side of the water by any stranger and shall take for it four pence the ton and for all other ballast which any stranger shall fetch himself he shall take two pence the ton as heretofore has been 4d. And the same farmer or farmers shall appoint the stranger where he shall fetch his ballast and where he shall lay it upon the quay and shall see that such ballast as the same stranger will cast out of his ship or barque to lie six foot from brink of the quay at the least. And the same farmer or farmers shall have care that all such persons as do fetch any ballast shall fetch the same upon shackles and pullys as often and at such times as conveniently he or they may. And it is provided and agreed that such ballast as any townsmen shall cast upon the quay shall lay it also six foot at the least from the brink of the quay. And if any townsmen shall suffer his ballast to lie upon the quay above fifteen days together then it shall be lawful unto the farmer or farmers of the ballast to take it to his or their own use as he may take stranger's ballast. And that no townsman shall sell or dispose his ballast to any person or persons if it be landed upon the quay. And it is also agreed, constituted and ordered that no person or persons shall from henceforth cast any ballast upon the jetty nor shall take any ballast on any side of the same jetty within twenty foot of the same jetty if the farmer or farmers of the ballast in his or their discretion shall not hold it necessary to take it within twenty foot. And it is also fully constituted, ordered and agreed that whoever shall offend in any of the premises contrary to the true meaning hereof shall forfeit for every time 5s.

It is also constituted, ordered and agreed that from henceforth there shall be an assembly and appearance of the mayor, aldermen, bailiffs, burgesses and capital or principal burgesses at the Guildhall of Melcombe Regis within the borough and town of Waymouth and Melcombe Regis if Mr Mayor shall not appoint to sit elsewhere upon every Friday by eight of the clock in the fore noon without any summons or warning thereof to be given unless there shall be other appointment and order given by the mayor and bailiffs or two of them whereof the mayor to be one beforehand. And that whosoever shall neglect to assemble and appear accordingly without some reasonable excuse according to a Constitution heretofore made for the attendance at assemblies shall forfeit for every time of such neglect in manner and form following viz: if he be an alderman 3s 4d, if he be a capital or principal burgess then 12d.

[page 9] It is also constituted, ordered and agreed that the Corporation shall be at the charge of pitching and paving of the quays and ground joining unto the quays which do belong unto the Corporation so broken as and where it shall be thought convenient by the mayor and bailiffs the for time being. And that after such time as the same quays and grounds shall be so pitched and paved no cart with iron bound wheels shall be suffered to come or unload upon the same ground so pitched and paved except it shall be for the allowing of such goods as of necessity must be laden by and with the crane and in such case the cart to take the direct way to and from the same crane and not to go upon the same quay upon pain that he which doth own the same cart or the cart that doth drive, haul or pull the same cart shall forfeit for every time so offending the sum of 12d.

It is also constituted, ordered and agreed that this Corporation shall with all convenient speed buy and provide a drag for the scouring of the harbour or haven. An also shall procure men and boat to use the same drag about the purpose aforesaid according to the discretion of the mayor and bailiffs for the time being. And there shall be done from time to time at the charge of the Corporation. And it is agreed that the forfeitures shall be levied according to the former order.

It is lastly constituted, ordered and agreed that all pains and forfeitures imposed upon the breach of any constitution or order made at this assembly shall be levied by the common sergeant of this borough and town, or by any one of them upon a warrant under the hand and seals of the mayor and bailiffs of the said borough and town for the time being or of any two of them whereof the mayor to be one by way of distress and sale of the goods of the same person or persons which shall break any of the Constitutions aforesaid which distress shall be sold by the same sergeant or sergeants to the use of the said Corporation and the surplus rendered unto the party so distrained. Provided always that this Constitution shall no way touch the execution of the forfeiture set upon the first constitution made at this assembly. But that the water bailiffs or farmer or farmers of the forfeitures upon constitutions made or to be made for the preservation of the harbour and keeping clean of the quays shall by warrant made unto him or them in form aforesaid execute the same warrant and take the forfeiture upon the same Constitution to his and their use if it be done by the farmer, and to the use of the Corporation if it be done by the water bailiffs

[Signed by] John Pitt, mayor; William Holman, bailiff, John Roy, bailiff; Peter Neale [his mark], William M, Robert Whit, Henry Russell, John Reynolds, John Pytt, Robert Knight, Roger Frye [his mark], Robert Vaule [his mark], Matthew Allin, Thomas Lockeir, Edward Hodder, M. Banfild, Henry Michell, James James, Richard Allin junior, Henry Waltham, Robert Major, John Ellis [his mark].

The names of the mayor, aldermen and capital burgesses of the borough this which is begun is to be set by reason of the date to page 11 being executed the first of December.

[page 10] Constitution made and fully agreed upon by the mayor, aldermen bailiffs and capital or principal burgesses of the borough and town of Waymouth and Melcombe Regis in the county of Dorset the first day of December in the year of the reign of our Sovereign Lord James by the grace of God of England, France and Ireland King, Defender of the faith etc. the fifteenth and of Scotland the one and fifty 1617.

First it is constituted, ordered and agreed that there shall be procured a reformed and proficient and learned preacher of God's word to be lecturer and preacher here within this borough and town of Waymouth and Melcombe Regis aforesaid who shall be reputed and taken to be the preacher of this Corporation. and that the same preacher shall be allowed and paid towards his maintenance the sum of £20 per annum out of the revenues of the said Corporation which £20 shall be paid quarterly by even pounds.

It is constituted, ordered and agreed that Mr William Holman, Mr John Roy, bailiffs, Mr John Pitt the elder, William Williams, Thomas Gardener and Thomas Wallis shall be auditors of the account for the town's revenues to continue from the time of making of this Constitution unto the feast of St. Matthew the Apostle next ensuing and that such accounts as shall be audited by the said five or four of them shall stand in force according as they shall audit the same. And it is further ordered, constituted and agreed that at all times hereafter on the feast day of St Matthew the Apostle at the time of the choice of the mayor for the said borough and town there shall be elected and chosen six auditors, the two bailiffs then chosen and two of the capital and principal burgesses and two of the commonality and that they six, five or four of them shall, for one year after such choice audit all the accounts touching and concerning the revenues and profits of the same town then unaudited. And it is further constituted, ordered and agreed that every mayor and other receiver of the town's revenues and profits shall from henceforth within one month next after the end of his and their office deliver unto the mayor for the time being a perfect account of all such sum and sums of money as he or they have received to the use of the Corporation in the time of his and their office which mayor for the time being shall with all convenient speed deliver such account and accounts to the auditors for the time being, or to some or one of them. And the said auditors or the greater part of them shall within one month next after the receiving of the same account or accounts audit the same. And that such money as shall be due unto this Corporation upon the auditing of the same account and accounts, shall be paid over unto the receiver for the time being or to some other person or persons appointed to receive the same upon reasonable demand thereof upon pain that every person offending any way to the contrary of this order in any part thereof shall for every such offence forfeit ten pounds to the use of this Corporation.

Whereas before this time diverse persons have procured and gotten themselves to be admitted freemen of this borough and town of Waymouth and Melcome Regis being at the time of their admittance inhabiting and co-resident (*comorant*) within this same borough and town and shortly after or since the same have departed out of the said borough and town and inhabited elsewhere by means whereof they are not charged with any tax or tallage, nor called to any office for the government of the said borough and town and notwithstanding they are so departed and do inhabit elsewhere as aforesaid yet they do continually take and enjoy the benefit of freemen by trading and transporting of merchandise into and from the same town without paying any of the petty customs not only to the great decaying of the petty customs and revenue of the same town but also to the very great impoverishment of the inhabitants thereof. It is therefore at this present assembly constituted, ordered and agreed that if any such person or persons which is, or are, free of this borough and town shall depart and dwell out of the same notwithstanding do or shall use the trade of merchandise within this town and do not commit to inhabit and dwell within this town before the feast of St Michael the Archangel next coming and from thenceforth do not remain and continue inhabitants of the same borough and town whereby they may be charged with taxes and tallage and called to bear office with the said borough and town, for the government thereof, as other freemen inhabitants of the said town are, that then every such person as do not so come to inhabit and dwell within the said town before the said feast or after the said feast shall not continue inhabitants there shall be utterly dismissed of his and their freedom and never after shall receive or take the benefit of a freeman with the said [page 11] borough and town until he be newly admitted a freeman by the general consent of the mayor, aldermen, bailiffs and capital or principal burgesses of the said borough and town or greater part of them. And it is further constituted, ordered and agreed that if any freeman of this borough and town which now is, or at any time hence after shall be inhabiting and inhabit out of the same by the space of one whole year and notwithstanding that he do so inhabit out of the same town shall use to trade and deal in merchandise within the same borough and town, that then every such freeman so inhabiting out of the said town by the space of one whole year and trading in merchandise as aforesaid shall be likewise utterly dismissed of his freedom and never after shall receive or take the benefit of freeman within this said town until he shall be newly admitted a freeman as aforesaid.

That whereas there is a bridge made over the haven of this borough and town of Waymouth and Melcombe Regis at the great charge of the inhabitants of the same town which bridge in short time will decay if special care be not taken for the maintenance and continuance thereof. And whereas the drawbridge up of the drawbridge of the said bridge is a great decaying to the same bridge and likewise the passing of the carts and wains (*waynes*) over the same bridge. It is therefore ordered, constituted and agreed that from henceforth there shall be paid by the owners or owner of every ship, barque or other vessel that shall pass through the said drawbridge and shall have one or both leaves drawn for every time twelve pence at the time of his going up and at the time of her return nothing. And that likewise there shall be paid by every owner, carter or driver of any cart or wain having wheels bound with iron that shall pass over the said bridge for every time that any such cart or wain shall pass over the same bridge forward four pence and at the return thereof back nothing. An it is also constituted, ordered and agreed that from henceforth the farmer of the bridge shall keep the drawbridge when and so long as it is undrawn locked and also from time to time shall cause the same bridge to be kept clean upon pain that the said farmer shall forfeit for every time that the said drawbridge shall not be locked or the said bride shall not be kept clean, the sum of 12d.

It is lastly constituted, ordered and agreed that all pains and forfeitures felt and imposed upon any the constitutions aforesaid shall be levied by the common sergeants of the said borough and town, or by any one of them upon a warrant under the hand and seals of the mayor and bailiffs of the said borough and town for the time being or by any two of them whereof the mayor shall be one by way of distress and sale of the goods of the said offenders which distress shall be sold by the same sergeant or sergeants to the use of the said Corporation and the surplus unto the parties which shall be distrained.

[Signed by] John Pitt, mayor; William Holman, bailiff; John Roy, bailiff; Henry Russell, Edward Roy, William Maunsell, John Reynolds, John Pytt, Richard Allin junior, Henry Blickell, Roger Fry [his mark], Thomas Giear, Thomas Lockeir, Edward Hodder, John Ellis [his mark], William Mansell [his mark], Robert Major, John Pearcey, Peter Neale [his mark], James James, Matthew Allin, Robert Vall, Henry Waltham.

The names of the mayor, aldermen and capital burgesses of the borough and town of Waymouth and Melcombe Regis in the county of Dorset present at the granting of a warrant unto John Bagg and Robert Parmiter, sergeants at the mace within the said borough and town for the inhibiting and forbidding of the enclosing of Clarks Hill parcel of Melcombe Common within the borough and town of Weymouth and Melcombe Regis aforesaid.

John Pitt, mayor; William Holeman and John Roy bailiffs, Robert White and Henry Russell aldermen, Robert Vaule, William Maunsell, John Reynolds, John Pitt senior, William Bondfield, Richard Allin junior, Thomas Luckier, Roger Fry, Henry Michell, Matthew Allin, James James, Robert Major, John Ellis, Edward Hodder and William Williams, capital burgesses.

James Hunt, William Baiyly, William Pears, Thomas Boult of Radipole, workmen forbidden by the sergeants aforesaid to dike any further.

Richard Burlenton of Stalbridge, Robert Ford of Sturminster, Nicholas Rogers of Wincanton, George Gayler of Dorchester, John Fowler and Giles Fowler of the town witnesses at the forbidding of them.

[page 12] Constitutions and orders made and fully agreed upon by the mayor, aldermen, bailiffs and capital or principal burgesses of the borough and town of Waymouth and Melcombe Regis in the county of Dorset the twelfth day of December in the years of the reign of our sovereign Lord James by the grace of God of England, France and Ireland King, defender of the faith etc. the fifteenth and of Scotland the one and fiftieth 1617.

First it is constituted, ordered and agreed that from henceforth every alien which shall come into this harbour with any ship, barque or other vessel shall have a pilot of this town to guide and bring his or their ship, barque or other vessel into and out of the same harbour and that the same pilot for himself and his three men and his boat shall take and have of the same alien for his and their pains, in that behalf, the sum of three shillings and four pence if the same alien's ship, barque or other vessel be twenty and four pence if the same aliens ship, barque or other vessel be twenty tons or under and if she be above the burden of twenty tons then they shall receive and take not only the said sum of three shillings and four pence but also so much more as it shall amount unto by way of increase after the rate of six pence for every five tons which the same ship, barque or other vessel shall be in burden over and above twenty tons until it shall come and amount unto the sum of ten shillings whereof the said pilot and his company shall be paid whether the said alien will be piloted or not. And that in case the said pilot and his company shall deserve more than is herein allowed for their pains then Mr Mayor for the time being if there be cause shall order and rate the same according unto his best discretion. And that as the same mayor shall order and rate the same it shall bind both the pilot and his company which are to have the same and also the alien which is to pay the same and that there shall be six sufficient and skilful persons allowed and appointed from time to time by the mayor, aldermen, bailiffs and capital or principal burgesses of this borough and town of Waymouth and Melcombe Regis aforesaid to attend that service who shall be called the town pilots and shall receive the duties and sums of money appointed for pilotage as aforesaid. Provided always that there shall be no pilotage paid in case the said pilots or some one of them shall not be ready and offer to do their pain in that behalf and that that pilot which shall first be on board or come near the aliens ship, barque or other vessel shall receive and have the wages and hire. And it is also agreed that William Bondfyeld, Laurence Brooke, Henry Hought, Robert Dillicke and Thomas Elkins shall be the first six pilots ordained and appointed to be the town pilots and to attend that service and to receive the wages and hire appointed for their pains and pilotage as aforesaid. And that they or any of them six shall continue or be altered from time to time at the will and pleasure of the said mayor, aldermen, bailiffs and capital or principal burgesses or the greater part of them.

It is also ordered, constituted and agreed that from henceforth there shall be two scavengers appointed for the carrying away of the dirt and filth of the streets and quays of this borough and town who shall carry away the same once every week viz: upon every Saturday and shall lay the same at such several places as shall be from time to time appointed for the laying thereof by the mayor and bailiffs for the time being and by two aldermen and two of the capital burgesses or principal burgesses of this borough or town or by the five or four of them whereof the mayor and bailiffs for the time being shall be always three. And that there shall be £10 per annum allowed unto the same scavengers for their pains to be taken in this behalf and shall also have the benefit of the soil which they shall so carry away. And that if the said scavengers or either of them shall neglect to carry away the same dirt and filth weekly as aforesaid then such scavenger or scavengers so neglecting shall forfeit 12d. And that every householder, tenant or inhabitant within this borough and town shall upon every Saturday or some time in the forenoon make clean and sweep up together all the dirt and filth which shall be before their several houses or land towards the street upon pain that every one neglecting the same shall forfeit, for every time of such neglect, the sum of 4d.

[page 13] It is also constituted, ordered and agreed that from henceforth the farmers of the ballast shall not lay nor suffer to be laid any ballast upon any of the quays of this borough and town, or in any place near the harbour, other than in such place or places as shall be appointed for that purpose by Mr Mayor and Mr Bailiffs for the time being, or by any two of them whereof the mayor to be one. And in such case not within five foot of the brink of the quay or of the haven upon pain that the same farmers shall forfeit for every offence therein the sum of 12d.

It is further constituted, ordered and agreed that according to the direction of Mr Mayor and Mr Bailiffs for the time being, or of any two of them, whereof the mayor to be one, there shall be a gutter made in or about the middle of the streets of this borough and town of Waymouth and Melcombe Regis which gutter, at the charge of this Corporation, shall be paved so broad as in the discretion of the said mayor and bailiffs, or any two of them, whereof the mayor to be one shall be thought fit.

It is likewise constituted, ordered and agreed that Mr Mayor for the time being, shall from henceforth, from time to time, appoint a beadle for the punishing of rogues, vagabonds and wandering and idle persons coming hither within this borough and town and for the doing of such other service as in other towns and places beadles are accustomed to do. And that the same beadle shall be allowed yearly, out of the revenues of this town for his pains to be taken on that behalf the sum of 20s per annum which shall be paid quarterly by even portions.

It is lastly constituted, ordered and agreed that all pains and forfeitures set and imposed upon any the constitutions aforesaid, shall be levied by the common sergeant of the said borough and town, or by any of them, upon a warrant under the hand and seals of the mayor and bailiffs of the said borough for the time being, or by any two of them, whereof the mayor always to be one, by way of distress and sale of the goods of the offenders which distress shall be sold by the same sergeant and sergeants to the use of the said Corporation and the surpluses rendered unto the parties which shall been distrained.

[Signed by] John Pitt, mayor; William Holman, bailiff; John Roy, bailiff; John Reynolds, William Maunsold, John Pytt, Peter Neale [his mark], Robert Vaule [his mark], W. Banfild, Edward Roy[?], Henry Blichell, James James, Thomas Lockier, Matthew Allin, Edward Hodder, Robert Major, John Ellis [his mark], John Pearcey.

3 December 1617
Upon the day and years aforesaid Robert Dillicke, farmer of the forfeitures upon the constitutions made for the preservation of the harbour and keeping clean the quays, did say upon his oath that he having a warrant from Mr Mayor and Mr Bailiffs for the levying of 3s4d upon the barque of William Minterne or upon some of her apparel or furniture for so much forfeited for that the said barque was not removed from the quay according to a constitution in that behalf provided and he this testator going on board the said barque to execute the said warrant the said William Mintern came on board after him this testator and did withstand this testator and would not suffer him to execute his warrant whereupon the said William Minterne was committed upon his good behaviour. But upon his submission and acknowledging of his error to be done by ignorance he was released.

[page 14] **10 November 1617**
The names of such persons as are found to be freemen of this borough and town of Waymouth and Melcombe Regis by charter, patrimony, service or fine together with such as shall be found or allowed until Michaelmas next or after.

By charter
John Pitt, the younger, mayor
William Holeman, bailiff
John Roye, bailiff
Aldermen:
Richard Pitt
John Mockett
John Bond
Robert White
William Waltham
Matthew Pitt
Robert Knighte
Barnard Michell
Henry Russell

Capital and principal burgesses, common council
Peter Neale
William Mounsell
William Bonfyeld
Robert Vaule
Edward Roye
Roger Frye
Matthew Allin
John Ellis

Stephen Dennis
William Williams
William Martell
Hugh Pearsy
Richard Allin senior
John Reynolds
John Pitt Senior
Richard Allin junior
Thomas Guyer
Thomas Lockier
Henry Waltham
Henry Michell
James James
Robert Major
James Sirrey
Edward Hodder
By Patrimony
John Michell
Thomas Waltham
Owen Holeman
William Pitt
Benjamin Pitt
Giles Greene
Thomas Bagg
Elias Bond
Henry Russell junior

John Waltham
Arthur Holman
July 16th 1630 Henry Knight
July 19th 1630 Robert White

[Page 15] *By Service*
Gabriel Cornish
John Casse
Richard Champion
Marmaduke Pitt
John Bray
William Godbere
John Gallott
John James
George Flirry
12 August 1631 Thomas Rose apprentice to Mr Edward Roy sworn a freeman
6 August 1632 Robert Davye alias Pydle apprentice to Edward Hodder sworn a freeman

By Fine	William Cade	Henry Cuttance
Philip Alexander	Joyce Vandergozen	Robert Pitt
John Shattock	Thomas Ledoze	Nicholas Cornne
Edward Lynsey	Thomas Wallis	Gregory Babbidge
John Lockier	Thomas Lovelis	John Thorneton
Richard Harrison	David Gyer	John Cade
Jeremy Babbag	Edward Cuttance	John Senior
Henry Rose		

19 July 1630 Robert Gyer

6 April 1632 James Gier sworn a freeman who paid five pounds but by a general consent out of the respect the Company bear to Mr Mayor the said James Giear being his son in law three pounds was given him back again forthwith.

26 October 1632 Francis Tuthill sworn a freeman, who paid five pounds but by a general consent (in respect that he served Mr Henry Waltham by the space of five years) forty shillings was forthwith delivered him again.

[page 16] 5 January 1620, Sworn freemen, John Freke esquire, Christopher Erle esquire

23 September 1623, Sworn freemen, Edmond Windham esquire, Arthur Pyne esquire

29 April 1625, Sir John Strangwayes, knight, sworn a freeman

16 October 1629, Sworn freemen, Jonas Denis, Thomas Wallis

4 December 1632, George Pitt of Weymouth sworn a freeman by inheritance or by descent from his father who was anciently a freeman.

25 Jan 1632, William Holmes an inhabitant of Waymouth sworn as a freeman of this borough by fine and for his fine paid five pounds which was delivered to the treasurer.

3 September 1632, John Hodder the son of Edward Hodder of Melcomb Regis sworn a freeman of this borough by fine, and for his find paid five pounds, but by a general consent forty shillings was given him again, the rest delivered to the treasure.

9 August 1633, Thomas Waltham son of Henry Waltham of Melcomb Regis sworn a freeman of this borough by descent his father being a freeman.

5 September 1633, John Pitt the son of John Pitt senior of Melcomb Regis sworn a freeman of this borough by descent his father being a freeman of the same

13 January 1634, William Charity of this borough sworn a freeman by fine.

20 January 1634, Thomas Chapple of this borough sworn a freeman by fine.

27 January 1634, Francis Edwards late apprentice to George Florry of this borough sworn a freeman of the same borough by service.

27 January 1634, James Strangwayes son to Sir John Strangways, knight, sworn a freeman of this borough ex gratia.

21 July 1634, Roger Rose son of Henry Rose of this borough sworn a freeman of the same borough by descent.

2 October 1634, Sir George Moreton Baronet and Sir George Horsey Knight sworn freemen ex gratia.

[page 17] 2 October 1634, John Horsey, eldest son of Sir George Horsey, knight, sworn freeman of the borough ex gratia.

3 October 1634, George Moreton, eldest son of Sir George Moreton, knight, sworn a freeman of this borough ex gratia.

17 August 1635, John Gardiner, son of John Gardiner of this borough, admitted and sworn a freeman of the same borough, by fine.

17 August 1635, Richard Odye the elder of this borough admitted and sworn a freeman of the same borough by fine.

30 October 1635, John Arthur of this borough, merchant, admitted and sworn a freeman of this borough by fine.

30 October 1635, John Maynwaring of this borough, merchant, admitted and sworn a freeman of the same borough by fine.

19 February 1636, George Churchey, merchant, sworn a freeman of this borough by fine.

19 February 1636, Hugh Persie, late apprentice to Henry Russell the younger, sworn a freeman of the borough by service.

13 May 1636, Edmond Bermier late apprentice unto James James of this borough, merchant, sworn a freeman of the same borough by service.

23 September 1636, George Freke esquire, son and heir of John Freke esquire, sworn a freeman of this borough, ex gratia.

14 October 1636, Robert Richards, son of Damaris the wife of Nicholas Cornew sworn a freeman of this borough by fine.

29 October 1636, John Swettenham, woollen draper, sworn a freeman of the borough by fine.

12 March 1640, Giles Strangways esquire, son and heir apparent of Sir John Strangeways knight, sworn a freeman of this borough ex gratia whereupon the said Mr Strangwayes freely gave five pounds to the use of the poor of both sides, which was forthwith delivered to the overseers to be disposed of accordingly.

[page 18] Constitutions, orders and agreements made and fully agreed upon by the mayor, aldermen, bailiffs and capital or principal burgesses of the borough and town of Waymouth and Melcombe Regis in the county of Dorset, the ninth day of January in the years of the reign of our Sovereign Lord James by the grace of God of England, France and Ireland the fifteenth and of Scotland the one and fiftieth 1618.

First it is constituted, ordered and agreed that Robert Stone, clerk of the parish church of Radipoll in Melcombe Regis within this town of Waymouth and Melcombe Regis shall have and be allowed out of the revenues of the said town, forty shillings per annum to be paid unto him quarterly for keeping of the clock the whole year and for ringing of the bell every evening at eight of the clock and every morning at four of the clock from the feast of St Michael the Archangel until the feast of Easter then next following.

Item, it was and is agreed by a general consent of the mayor, aldermen, bailiffs and capital or principal burgesses here assembled on the behalf of this Corporation, and by Mr Bailiffs Holman, Mr Richard Pitt, Mr John Bond, Mr William Waltham, Mr

Matthew Pitt, Mr Peter Neale, Mr John Reynolds, Mr William Mounsell, Mr Robert Vaule, Mr John Pitt the elder, Mr William Bondfield and Mr John Ellis on their own behalves respectively and severally. That all matters of difference between this Corporation and the said several parties aforenamed concerning the loan of money towards the building of the bridge and monies stopped up concerning the same loan, shall be referred unto the arbitration of Mr John Roy, bailiff and Mr John Gould the younger who making an end therein upon or before the five and twentieth day of March next coming, their end shall bind all parties whom it shall concern. And if they cannot make an end by that time then they the said arbitrators shall make choice of an umpire who making an end thereon before the feast of Easter then next following his end shall fully conclude and bind all parties whom it shall concern as aforesaid.

Whereas Peter Johnson, Master of a barque or pink of Flushing in Zeland did sell here within this town, two bags of hops containing about five hundredweight unto one Henry Lee of Dorchester, a foreigner and not freeman of this town. And therefore the same two bags are forfeited unto this Corporation for goods foreign bought and foreign sold within this town contrary to the ancient liberties and privileges of the town, Now at this assembly upon the humble submission of the said Peter Johnson and upon his protestation made unto this court, that he knew not the custom of the town, in that behalf it was and is agreed by a general consent of the mayor, aldermen, bailiffs and capital and principal burgesses here assembled, that in consideration of ten shillings by the said Peter to be paid unto the use of this Corporation, the forfeiture of the said two bags of hops shall be remitted and forgotten.

[Signed by] John Pitt, mayor; William Holman, bailiff; John Roy, bailiff; Peter Neale [his mark], William Mounsell, John Reynolds, Robert Knight, W. Banfild, John Pitt, Henry Russell, James James, Richard Allin junior, Roger Fry [his mark], Edward Roy, Matthew Allin Thomas Lockier, Robert Vaule [his mark], Robert Major, Henry Waltham.

[page 19] An assembly held in the Guildhall of Melcome Regis in the borough and town of Waymouth and Melcombe Regis in the county of Dorset by the mayor, aldermen, bailiffs and capital or principal burgesses of the said borough and town the sixteenth day of January in the year of the reign of our sovereign Lord James by the grace of God of England, France and Ireland the fifteenth and of Scotland the one and fiftieth 1618.

At this assembly it was and is agreed by a general consent of the mayor, aldermen, bailiffs and capital or principal burgesses of this borough and town here assembled that from henceforth so long as they shall think requisite, there shall be a watch kept within this borough and town of four men, or more if there shall be occasion of more in the discretion of Mr Mayor and Mr Bailiffs for the time being, every night as well in the winter time, as in the summer time. And that every householder within this borough and town resident, or not resident, in the discretion of Mr Mayor for the time being, either in his own person or by his sufficient deputy, shall provide a watchman for and towards the performance of that service so often as it shall come to his turn by course. And it was and is further agreed by the said mayor, aldermen, bailiffs and capital or principal burgesses that if any householder within this borough and town, either resident or not resident, shall neglect to watch in person, or else to provide a sufficient deputy to watch in his stead, or else to pay the watchmen that shall be appointed by the constable or constables of this borough and town to watch in his stead so much as is ordinarily used to be paid unto a watchman in the like case, then every such householder that shall so neglect to watch in person or to provide a sufficient deputy to watch in his stead, or else to pay the watchman that shall be appointed to watch in his stead, as aforesaid, shall forfeit for every such offence 8d. To be levied by the constables and sergeants at the mace within this borough and town, or by some or any of them, who of their own authority by virtue of this Constitution and agreement shall have power to levy the same by distress and sale of the offender's goods rendering to each party the surplus which shall be made of his or their goods so distrained.

John Pitt, mayor; William Holman, bailiff; John Roy, bailiff; Robert Knight, alderman; Henry Russell, alderman; John Reynolds, Peter Neale [his mark], Robert Vaule [his mark], Thomas Giear, John Pytt, Henry Blickell, Edward Roy, Roger Fry [his mark], Edward Hodder, Matthew Allin, Thomas Lockeir, James James, Robert Major, Hugh Pearcey.

[page 20] Waymouth and Melcombe Regis: monies given by benefactors to the use of the poor and other good uses hereafter expressed

Sir Thomas Middleton, knight, gave ten pounds to remain in stock to buy wood and coal to the use of the poor of this Corporation which now doth remain in stock accordingly.

Mrs Rosamond Payne, late of Upway, widow, deceased, gave ten pounds to remain in stock to the use of the poor of this Corporation which was forthwith divided by equal portions unto the relief of the poor of both sides and now doth remain and always is to remain in stock accordingly.

Mr John White, alderman of this town deceased, gave five pounds to remain in stock to the use of the poor of this Corporation which doth remain in stock accordingly.

Mr Robert Middleton, late of London, merchant, deceased, gave one hundred pounds to the uses following, (that it to say) the same is to be lent unto four young merchants of this town for three years paying five pounds per annum for the loan thereof which £5 per annum is to be given weekly in bread to those of the poor. And at the end of every three years the same hundred pounds is to be paid in and then forthwith to be lent again unto other four young merchants upon the same condition as before. As appears by the express words of the will of the said Robert Middleton hereunder set down as follows.

I will and devise that the sum of one hundred pounds of lawful English money shall be paid and delivered by my Executors or some of them, within three months next after my decease unto the mayor and bailiffs of the town of Waymouth and Melcombe Regis in the county of Dorset where Margaret my late loving wife deceased, was born. To the end that the mayor, bailiffs and aldermen of the said town for the time being shall lend and deliver the same from three years to three years forever to poor young men of the said town of Waymouth and Melcombe Regis, using there the trade of merchandises if there shall be any such. And in default of merchants to four other young men of the said town at the discretion of the mayor, bailiffs and aldermen of the said town for the time being. That is to say to each man twenty five pounds a piece first entering Bond with sufficient securities to the mayor and bailiffs of the said town for the time being in the sum of fifty pounds for the repayment thereof at three years to be reckoned and accounted from the time of the lending thereof which allowance and consideration therefore after the rate of five pounds for a hundred pounds for a year which allowance and consideration I will shall be employed and given to the poor inhabitants of the said town by the discretion of the mayor and bailiffs for the time being, or other sufficient deputy, where most need to them shall appear.

[page 21] Provided always and my express mind and will is that if the mayor and burgesses of the said town of Waymouth and Melcombe Regis for the time being, shall be remiss and make default in lending and delivering the said one hundred pounds, or in distributing the interest or allowance therefore as aforesaid, contrary to the true intent and meaning of this my last will and testament, that then my gift and devise of the said one hundred pounds mentioned to the said mayor and bailiffs of the said town of Waymouth and Melcombe Regis for the time being, shall cease and be utterly void. And the same shall remain and come to the aldermen and bailiffs of the town of Denbigh for the time being by them to be distributed or laid out upon a purchase of lands, tenements or hereditaments in the said town or county of Denbigh of the clear yearly value of five pounds of lawful English money at the least, over and above all charges and reprises whereby the poor inhabitants of the said town [a number of words crossed through] of Denbigh may be relieved with five pounds *pench*: [the editor can find no suitable expansion for this abbreviation] for ever to be distributed by the aldermen and bailiffs of the said town for the time being, or their sufficient deputies, when and where most need to them shall appear.

Provided always and my express mind and will further is that if the aldermen and bailiffs of the said town of Denbigh for the time being, shall be remiss and make default in lending and delivering the aforesaid two hundred pounds, or in distributing the interest or allowance therefore or if they shall make default in lending or delivering the aforesaid one hundred pounds if the same shall come into their hands or possession as aforesaid. or in distributing the interest or allowance therefore as aforesaid, that then and from thenceforth, this my gift and devise of such of the premises wherein such neglect or default of the premises shall be, shall cease and be utterly void and of none effect to all intents and purposes.

The hundred pounds aforementioned and appointed to be paid and delivered unto the mayor and bailiffs of the town of Waymouth and Melcombe Regis was paid and delivered unto them according to the true intent and meaning of the last will and Testament of the said Robert Middleton and by them was lent unto four young merchants of the said town upon securities as follows.

The Corporation have given a writing under their seal unto Mr. Middleton, his executors for the employment of the £100 above mentioned according to the Will of the donor.

Henry Knighte has £25 for three years upon bond dated the fourth day of October 1616 wherein said Henry Knighte and Robert Knighte, William Waltham and Richard Allin the younger, of the same town merchants, do stand bound for the repayment thereof and of the interest and allowance.

Owen Holman has £25 for three years upon bond dated the fourth day of October 1616, wherein the said Owen Holman, William Holman, Henry Russell and James Siriye of the same town, merchants, do stand bound for the repayment thereof and of the interest and allowance.

William Pitt has £25 for three years upon bond dated the fourth day of October 1616 wherein the said William Pitt, John Pitt the elder, Robert Major of the same town, merchants and Robert Pitt of Wyke Regis, yeoman do stand bound for the repayment thereof and of the interest and allowance.

William Williams has £25 for three years upon bond dated the fourth day of October 1616 wherein the said William Williams, Robert White, John Roye and Edward Roy of the same town merchants, do stand bound for the repayment thereof and of the interest and allowance.

[page 22] Constitutions and orders made and fully agreed upon by the mayor, aldermen, bailiffs and capital or principal burgesses of the borough and town of Waymouth and Melcombe Regis in the county of Dorset, the thirtieth day of January in the years of the reign of our sovereign Lord James by the grace of God of England, Scotland, France and Ireland King, defender of the faith etc. That is to say of England France and Ireland the fifteenth and of Scotland the one of fiftieth 1618.

First it is constituted, ordered and agreed that every inhabitant within this borough and town of Waymouth and Melcombe Regis or the precincts thereof shall from time to time from henceforth take such special care to have the chimneys of his house continually swept and made clean that through the neglect thereof any of the chimneys of his house may not be set or fall on fire either to the damage of his neighbours houses standing near, or to their disturbance about the quenching of the same fire upon pain that every householder neglect to have and keep the chimneys of his house swept and made clean as aforesaid so that by means thereof any of his chimneys may happen to fall or become on fire as aforesaid shall forfeit for every time that any chimney shall become on fire if it be between sun setting and sunrise then the sum of 6s 8d but if it be between sun rising and sun setting then only the sum of 3s 4d.

It is constituted, ordered and agreed that no man, woman or child, or any other person or persons of what degree, or condition, whatsoever be or shall be being above the age of seven years shall from henceforth filth, or do his or her easement of body in or upon any of the quays, streets or lane of this borough and town upon pain of every person so offending therein to forfeit 6d to be levied upon the goods of the offenders if they have any. And if they have none then to be levied upon the goods of the offenders parents, or master. And if any mother, nurse or keeper of any child under the age of seven years shall set forth into the street or lanes of this borough or town any child under the age of seven years to the end to have such child to filth or do his or her easement of body in the said street or lane then every such mother, nurse or keeper of child shall forfeit for every such offence the sum of 3d to be levied of the offenders goods if he or she has any, or otherwise upon the goods of the husband or master of such offenders. And it is further agreed that every householder before whose house any person shall so filth or do his or her easement, shall cause the same filth to be carried away every day before nine of the clock in the morning upon pain to forfeit 3d.

It is also agreed that all forfeitures upon either of these Constitutions above written shall be levied by warrant under the hands of the mayor and bailiffs for the time being, or any two of them whereof the mayor to be one, in such manner and form as is formerly appointed for the levying of forfeitures upon other Constitutions.

[Signed by] John Pitt, mayor; William Holman, bailiff; John Roy, bailiff; Robert Knight, Henry Russell, Peter Neale [his mark], John Reynolds, Matthew Allin, Roger Fry [his mark], William Mounsell, Henry Waltham, Robert Major, James James, Thomas Giear, Edward Hodder, Thomas Lockier, Edward Roy.

[page 23] Deodands, goods seized by Mr John Roy, bailiff, to the use of this Corporation upon the unnatural and untimely death of John Dry for the felonious injuring and killing of himself, and approved by John Pope and John Pearcey the fourth day of March 1618.

> Firstly, one bedstead 3s 6d
> One mattress of sedge 4d
> One coverlet 1s
> One table board and form 1s
> Two stools 6d
> Two empty chests 1s 4d
> Two plates of earth 2d
> Two saucers 4d
> Three drinking glasses 4d
> One Emery 1s 6d
> One cradle 6d
> One pillow 1s
> One salt and one glass case 6d
> 6 February 1618

A book of the names of all such as do voluntary contribute towards the bettering of the maintenance of a lecturer to be procured from Oxford for this Corporation of Waymouth and Melcombe Regis with the several sums promised to be paid quarterly from the five and twentieth of March 1618 to continue one whole year and so from year to year, so as it stand with the good liking of the greater part of the inhabitants within named whereof five pounds shall be paid quarterly unto the lecturer of the Corporation and the over plus shall be given and bestowed upon such preacher of god's words as shall be thought fit by the mayor, aldermen, bailiffs and capital or principal burgesses of the said borough and town or by the greater part of them.

The several names and sums of money which each man promised to pay is in a paper book made for that purpose. This should have been set down before the deodand goods above said.

An assembly held in the Guildhall of Melcombe Regis within the borough and town of Waymouth and Melcombe Regis in the county of Dorset by the mayor, aldermen, bailiffs and capital burgesses of the said borough and town the third day of April 161 [manuscript damaged, presumably 1618]

At this assembly it was and is agreed by the said mayor, aldermen, bailiffs and capital burgesses to and with Thomas Lovelis, carpenter. And the said Thomas Lovelis did agree with them that he the said Thomas Lovelis in the north side of the town hall of Melcombe before the feast of the Nativity of St John the Baptist next coming shall set up six turned pillars answerable to the pillars of the new house standing at the west end of Melcombe town hall and shall joist and plank the same and set up battlements thereunto as there is upon the same house and at the east end, the roof shall set up a house in the form of so much of the same new house as standing northward towards St Mary's Street without the north west corner of the wall of the same town hall. In consideration whereof the said Thomas Lovelis shall be paid ten pounds in money and shall take to his own use all the timber and slate of the present house now fixed unto the north wall of the said town hall and shall also have his freedom and be admitted a freemen of this town.

30 April 1618

It was and is agreed by a general consent that the mayor, aldermen, bailiffs and capital or principal burgesses of this borough and town of Waymouth and Melcombe Regis that upon the eighth day of May next there shall be another meeting of them and that at that time they shall conclude of the preacher whom they will make a choice to entertain amongst them.

[page 24] An assembly held in the Guildhall of Melcombe Regis within the borough and town of Waymouth and Melcombe Regis in the county of Dorset, the mayor, aldermen, bailiffs and principal burgesses of the said borough and town the twentieth day of March 1618.

Whereas it appears as well by the confession of Harvy Legall of Ushant, master of the barque called the Michael of Ushant. As also the the confession of Henry Cuttance of this town being both foreigners and neither of them a freemen of this town. That the said Henry Cuttance has bought here within this town the said barque's lading of salt of the said Harvy Legall and for the same salt was foreign bought and foreign sold contrary to the ancient privilege and custom of this town whereupon according to the same privilege and custom of this town the same salt is absolutely lost and forfeited by this Corporation. It is now therefore ordered by the said mayor, aldermen, bailiffs and principal burgesses of this borough and town that there shall be a warrant granted and made forth unto the sergeants at the mace for the forfeiting of the same salt to the use of this Corporation where and in whose house soever it shall be found. But afterwards the said Henry Cuttance, coming into this court and submitting himself unto the said court for the assessing and taxing of his fine for offending the liberties and privileges of this town as aforesaid, was therefore assessed and ordered by the same court to pay unto the use of this Corporation the sum of three pounds and thereupon the same salt was remitted so as the said Henry Cuttance do pay the same money unto Mr Mayor, to the use of this Corporation by ten of the clock in the forenoon of this present day or else the warrant to be made forth as aforesaid which money was accordingly paid and twenty shillings thereof given back unto him by a general consent of this court.

Whereas upon examination it appears that Edward Lynsey a freeman of this town knowing that there was a barque's lading of salt here bought and sold between Harvy Loyall, a Frenchman, and Henry Cuttance a townsman but not freeman did not only conceal the same buying and selling as aforesaid but also did join with him the said Henry Cuttance in taking part of the same bargain whereas he ought to have discovered it unto Mr Mayor, or some other magistrate of this town being bound thereunto by his oath of a freeman, It is therefore ordered that he shall pay for his neglect in that behalf, twenty shillings which he laid down in the court, but upon his plaint (*playne*) or declaration of the truth, and his submission to the censure of this court then following thereof by a general consent of this court, was given back unto him again.

[Signed by] John Pitt, mayor; John Roy, bailiff; Robert Knight, Henry Russell, John Reynolds, William Mansell, Richard Allin junior, John Pytt, Richard Allin the elder, Edward Roy, Thomas Giear, Edward Hodder, Thomas Lockier, [illegible], James James, Robert Major, Henry Blickell

[page 25] An assembly held in the Guildhall of Melcombe Regis within the borough and town of Waymouth and Melcombe Regis in the county of Dorset the mayor, aldermen, bailiffs and principal burgesses of the said borough and town the two and twentieth day of May 1618.

Upon this present day it was and is agreed by a general consent of the mayor, aldermen, bailiffs and capital or principal burgesses of this borough and town that there shall be a hundred marks taken up by Mr Mayor to the use of this Corporation until St Andrew's day next following which hundred marks shall be employed to the payment of such moneys as this Corporation doth owe and unto the enrolment of the new charter both in the Crown Office and in the Exchequer and unto such other business as this Corporation shall think fit. And that a lease of the petty customs, anchorage, quayage, wharfage and other things used to be let with the petty customs shall be granted unto the party of whom the money shall be taken up for his security for one year to begin from the said feast of St Andrew next coming with a proviso that if the same hundred marks with the use and interest from henceforth until the said feast of St Andrew shall be truly paid at the same feast that then the same grant shall be void etc.

Upon the day and year above said Mr Thomas Giear, Mr Edward Roy, Mr Robert Major and William Williams entreated to take a view and an inventory of all implements and other moveable things whatsoever belonging to this Corporation and to return the same into this Corporation at the next meeting of this assembly.

Upon this day the jury are enjoined to return their parchment touching the survey and rental of this Corporation in Melcombe side before the feast of the Nativity of St John the Baptist next coming. This order was continued until the first day of August next.

[Signed] John Pitt, mayor; John Roy, bailiff; Robert Knight, Henry Russell, John Reynolds; William Maunsell, Richard Allin, junior; John Pytt, Richard Allin the elder, Edward Roy, Thomas Giear, Thomas Lockeire, Henry Blickell, [illegible name], Edward Hodder, James James, Robert Major.

The names of the mayor, bailiffs, aldermen, common council assembled in the Guildhall of Waymouth and Melcombe Regis for the choice of a lecturer and other business for the Corporation the 8th day of May 1618.

John Pitt mayor, William Holeman and John Roy, bailiffs.

Robert White, William Waltham, Matthew Pitt, Robert Knight, and Henry Russell aldermen.

Peter Neale, William Mounsell, William Bondfield, Robert Vaule, Edward Roy, Matthew Allin, John Ellis, William Martell, William Williams, Hugh Pearcy, John Reynolds, John Pitt senior, Richard Allin junior, Thomas Gier, Thomas Lockier, Henry Waltham and John James, common council.

At this assembly when it was put to voices for a lecturer for this Corporation they rose out of the court of the above said assembly seven or eight who went forth of the doors and of the remainder being seven or eight and there next twelve of them who gave their voices for Mr John Ball and Mr Mayor's double voice made thirteen voices and there was only Mr Richard Allin for Mr Williams and the remainder would not give their voices to either side for the greatest number was to Mr John Ball as appears in the margin of the names of the said assembly.

[page 26] Enrolment of apprentices by Indentures with freemen and Inhabitants of this borough and town and the days and times of their inclement according to a Constitution heretofore made by the mayor, aldermen, bailiffs and capital or principal burgesses of the said borough and town to that end and purpose by the same Constitution more at large appears.

The two and twentieth day of May 1618 are enrolled as follows:

Angel Lawrence, son of Richard Laurence of Steepleton in the county of Dorset gentleman, Apprenticed unto Henry Waltham, merchant, a freeman and inhabitant of this borough and town by indenture dated the tenth day of August in the years of the reign of our Sovereign Lord James and Kings Majesty that now is, that is to say, of England, France and Ireland the twelfth and of Scotland the fourth and fortieth 1614, for eight years from the feast of the Annunciation of our Lady Mary the Virgin last past before the date of the said indenture.

John Luer son to William Luer, gentleman, deceased of Penzance in the county of Cornwall, apprentice to Henry Waltham, merchant, freeman and inhabitant of this borough and town by the indenture dated the second day of August in the years of the reign of our sovereign lord James the Kings Majesty that now is, that is to say of England, France and Ireland the fourteenth and of Scotland the fiftieth 1616 for seven years from the feast of St Michael the Archangel next after the date of the said indenture.

14 August 1618. Thomas James the younger son of Thomas James, the elder, of Chepnoll in the county of Dorset, gentleman, Apprentice unto James James, merchant, a freeman and inhabitant of this borough and town by indenture dated the twentieth day of March in the years of the reign of our Sovereign Lord James the Kings Majesty, that now [is missing]. That is to say of England, France and Ireland by the fifteenth and of Scotland the one and fiftieth 1617 for seven years from the feast of the Annunciation of our blessed Lady St Mary the Virgin net after the date of the said indenture.

11 September 1618. Charles Hardy son of John Hardy late of Dorchester in the county of Dorset gentleman, deceased, apprentice unto John Pitt the younger, merchant, a freeman and inhabitant of this borough and town by indenture dated the last day of April in the years of the reign of our Sovereign Lord James, the Kings Majesty that now is, that is to say of England, France and Ireland the fifteenth and of Scotland the fiftieth 1617 for twelve years from the feast day of the Annunciation of our blessed Lady St Mary the Virgin last past before the date of the said indenture.

[page 27] Robert Hayse son of John Hayse of Wescombe in the parish of Batcombe in the county of Somerset, yeoman, apprentice unto John Pitt the younger, a freeman and inhabitant of this borough and town by indenture dated the first day of November in the year of the reign of our Sovereign Lord James the Kings Majesty that now is. That is to say of England, France and Ireland the fifteenth and of Scotland the one and fiftieth 1617 for nine years from the feast day of the Annunciation of our blessed Virgin Mary next ensuing the date of the said indenture.

2 October 1618. John James the younger, son of John James the elder, of Waymouth and Melcombe Regis, yeoman. Apprentice unto James James, a freeman and inhabitant of this borough and town by indenture dated the second day of October in the year of the reign of our Sovereign Lord James the King's Majesty that now is. That is to say of England, France and Ireland the thirteenth and of Scotland the nine and forty for eight years from the feast of St Michael the Archangel last past before the date of the said indenture.

Fabian Hodder, son of Edward Hodder of Waymouth and Melcombe Regis in the county of Dorset, merchant. Apprentice unto John Pitt the younger, a freeman and inhabitant of this borough and town by indenture dated the nine and twentieth day of September in the years of the reign of our Sovereign Lord James the King's Majesty that now is. That is to say of England, France and Ireland, the sixteenth and of Scotland the two and fiftieth 1618 for seven years from the date of the said indenture.

Thomas Ford alias Simes, son of Edward Ford alias Simes of Lye in the parish of Yeatmister in the county of Dorset, husbandman. Apprentice unto John Roy and Edward Roy, freeman and inhabitants of this borough and town by indenture dated the tenth day of May in the year of the reign of our Sovereign Lord James, the King's Majesty that now is. That is to say of England, France and Ireland the Sixteenth and of Scotland the one and fiftieth 1618 for seven [years] from the date of the said indenture.

George Byshopp, son of Thomas Byshopp of Woth Frances within the parish of Netherbury in the county of Dorset, gentleman, apprentice to John Roy and Edward Roy, freemen and inhabitants of this borough and town by indenture dated the two and twentieth day of March in the years of the reign of our Sovereign Lord James the King's Majesty that now is. That is to say of England, France and Ireland the eleventh and of Scotland the seven and fortieth 1613 for nine years from the date of the said indenture.

[page 28] John Skynner son of Elizabeth Skinner of Newport in the Isle of Wight in the county of Southampton, widow. Apprentice unto John Roy and Edward Roye, freemen and inhabitants of this borough and town by indenture dated the first day of July in the years of the reign of our Sovereign Lord James the King's Majesty that now is. That is to say of England, France and Ireland, the twelfth and of Scotland the seven and fortieth 1614 for eleven years from the date of the said indenture.

Orpheus Dunkin son of Robert Dunkin of Penzance in the county of Cornwall, merchant. Apprentice unto John Roy and Edward Roye, freemen and inhabitants of this borough and town by indenture dated the sixth day of October in the years of the reign of our Sovereign Lord James the King's Majesty that now is. That is to say of England, France and Ireland the fifteenth and of Scotland the one and fiftieth 1617 for seven years from the date of the said Indenture.

7 April 1619. George Flirry son of Henry Flirry of Wyke Regis in the county of Dorset, shepherd. Apprentice unto Edward Hodder, freeman and inhabitant of this borough and town by indenture dated the twentieth day of September in the years of the reign of our Sovereign Lord James the King's Majesty that now is. That is to say of England, France and Ireland the sixteenth and of Scotland the two and fiftieth 1618 for seven years from the date of the said indenture.

28 May 1619. Thomas Wallis the younger, son of Peter Wallis of Yevill in the county of Somerset, husbandman. Apprentice unto Thomas Wallis the elder, freeman and inhabitant of this borough and town by indenture dated the twelfth day of May in the years of the reign of our Sovereign Lord James the King's Majesty that now is. That is to say of England, France and Ireland the seventeenth and of Scotland the two and fiftieth 1619 for nine years from the date of the said indenture.

10 November 1620. William Cade the younger, son of William Cade the elder of this borough and town of Waymouth and Melcombe Regis in the county of Dorset. Apprenticed unto the said William Cade the elder his father, a freeman and inhabitant of the same borough and town, by indenture dated the twentieth day of September in the years of the reign of our Sovereign Lord James the King's Majesty that now [is missing]. That is to say of England, France and Ireland the eighteenth and of Scotland the four and fiftieth 1620 for seven years from the feast of St Michael the Archangel next ensuing the date of the said indenture.

13 April 1621. Thomas Hussey, son of Joseph Hussey of Stower Paine in the

county of Dorset, gentleman, Apprentice unto Richard Harrison of Waymouth and Melcombe Regis aforesaid, freeman and inhabitant of this borough and town by indenture dated the five and twentieth day of March last past for the term of eight years from the date of the said indenture.

[page 29] 19 October 1621. William Simpson, son of John Simpson, late of the town and county of Poole, gentleman deceased. Apprentice unto Henry Waltham, freeman and inhabitant of this borough and town by indenture dated the nineteenth day of May in the years of the reign of our Sovereign Lord James the King's Majesty that now is. That is to say of England, France and Ireland the eighth otherwise 1620 for eight years from the day of the date of the said indenture.

5 March 1623. Thomas Rose, son of John Rose of West Ellworthe within the parish of Abbotsbury in the county of Dorset, yeoman. Apprentice unto Edward Roye, freeman and inhabitant of this borough and town by indenture dated the six and twentieth day of September in the year of the reign of our Sovereign Lord James the King's Majesty that now is. That is to say of England, France and Ireland the seventeenth and of Scotland the three and fiftieth 1619 for seven years from the feast of St Michael the Archangel next ensuing the date of the said indenture.

12 March 1623. Richard Justice, son of Mary Justice of Waymouth and Melcombe Regis in the county of Dorset, widow. Apprentice unto David Gyer and Mary his wife, a freeman and inhabitant of this borough and town by indenture dated the ninth day of December in the year of the reign of our Sovereign Lord James the King's Majesty that now is. That is to say of England, France and Ireland the one and twentieth and of Scotland the seven and fiftieth 1623 for nine years from the feast of the Nativity of our Saviour Christ next ensuing the date of the said indenture.

22 October 1624. Edmund Vernen son of Robert Venner, late of Roseash in the county of Devon, gent deceased. Apprentice unto James James and Dorothy his wife, a freeman and inhabitant of this town by indenture dated the twelfth day of October in the years of the reign of our Sovereign Lord James the King's Majesty that now is of England, France and Ireland the two and twentieth and of Scotland the eighth and fiftieth 1624 for the term of eight years from the feast of St Michael the Archangel last past before the date of the said indenture.

4 May 1627. George Gawdye, son of Thomas Gawdy of Charmeswell within the Isle of Purbeck, husbandman. Apprentice unto James James a freeman and inhabitant of this town by indenture dated the eighth day of March in the years of the reign of our Sovereign Lord Charles the King's Majesty that now is the second 1626 for the term of seven years from the feast of the Annunciation of our blessed Lady St Mary the Virgin the next following the date of the said indenture.

18 May 1627. Francis Tuthill son of Richard Tuthill of Bridgwater in the county of Somerset, linen draper. Apprentice unto Mr Henry Waltham, a freeman and inhabitant of the town, by indenture dated the fifteenth day of this instant month of May for the term of eight years from the feast of the Nativity of St John the Baptist next ensuing the date of the said indenture.

[page 30] 5 December 1628. Francis Edwards the son of Madeleine Edwards of Waymouth and Melcombe Regis in the county of Dorset, widow. Apprentice unto

George Flirry, a freeman and inhabitant of this town by indenture dated the thirtieth day of March the year of our Lord 1627 for the term of seven years from the day of the date of the said indenture.

7 August 1629. Humphry Phillippes, late of Bridport in the county of Dorset. Apprentice with Mr Edward Roy, a freeman and inhabitant of this town, by indenture dated the two and twentieth day of January in the year of our Lord 1629 for the term of seven years from the day of the date of the said indenture. [margin note. Not confirmed by Mr Mayor and Mr Bailiffs]

20 May 1630. Richard Jordaine, son unto Anthony Jordaine, late deceased of Waymouth and Melcombe Regis in the county of Dorset, mariner. Apprentice with John Michell and Henry Michell, merchants, freemen and inhabitants of this town, by indenture dated the three and twentieth day of November, the year of Our Lord 1626 for the term of eight years from the date of the said indenture.

2 July 1630. Raymond Anthony, son of Thomas Anthony of Bridgwater in the county of Somerset, merchant. Apprentice with Henry Waltham, merchant, a freeman and inhabitant of this town by indenture dated the tenth day of June, the year of Our Lord 1639 for the term of eight years from the date of the said indenture.

8 February 1631. William Mynson, son of Thomas Mynson of Baunton in the county of Dorset, fisherman. Apprentice unto Richard Gardiner of Waymouth, shipwright by indenture bearing date the 29th day of March the sixth year of Charles now King of England for the term of eight years from the day of the date of the said indenture.

10 September 1632. Hugh Percy of the town bound apprentice unto Henry Russell the younger by indenture bearing the date the first day of May the fourth year of Charles now King of England, 1628, from the day of the date of the said indenture for and during the full term of seven years but before the said Percye be sworn a freeman it is ordered that he must pay or his master for him, all such monies as an forfeit for not enrolling him sooner.

20 May 1640. Edward Allin son of Alice Allin of Uplyme in the county of Devon, widow, bound apprentice to John Hodder of this borough, mercer, by indenture bearing date that last day of May 1639 to serve for seven years from the first day of February last past before the date of the said indenture.

Petty customs and town duties

A

Alum the hundred shall pay 2d

Aniseed the bale or bag 4d

Apples the quarter 1/2d

Anchorage for every ship or barque 4d

Anchors great the piece 4d

Anchors small the piece 2d

B

Bolt thread the ballett containing 100 Bolts 12d

Brimstone the barrel 2d

Black soap the hundred 2d
Blockwood the hundredweight 1 1/2d
Burrs for millstones the hundred 4d
Beer the tun 4d
Ballast for every tun 2d
Brazell the hundredweight 3d
Boomage for every ship or barque 4d
Bottles the dozen 1/2d
C
Calf skins the dozen 1d
Cassia fistula the sack or chest 2d
Cups the *Maude* [wicker basket] 4d
Copperas the butt 4d
Claypole the hundred 2d
Cochineal [*Cuchineale*] the pound weight 1d
Conger [eels] the hundred 4d
Cabbages the hundred 1d
Canvas called Normandy canvas the hundred ells 4d
Canvas called *vittrye* canvas the fardell 6d
Coals and chaulder 1d
Cotton wool the hundred 4d
Currants the butt 8d
D
Dowlais [coarse linen] the piece or treager 2d
Deal boards the hundred 6d
Drinking glasses the case 2d
Dry lyng the pack 1d
Dry rugging the hundred 1/2d
F
Feathers the hundred 2d
French nuts the puncheon 2d
Figs the *sorte* 2d
French wines the ton 6d
Foreigners for every tonne for quayage 1d
[page 35]
G
Green wood the hundred 1/2d
Glass for windows the case 2d
Gold the ounce 2d
Grain of all sorts transported the quarter 1d
H
Herring the last 4d
Holland the piece 1d
Hops the sack 4d

Hops the packet 2d
Hides called Indian hides the piece 1/2d
Hides called Irish hides the piece 1/4d
Horses the piece 4d
Hemp the hundredweight 1d
I
Iron called Spanish Iron the ton 4d
L
Lead the ton 8d
Lemons the thousand 2d
Licorice the bale 2d
M
Money the pound 1d
Mather [madder] the hundredweight 2d
Millstones the piece 4d
Middermex the piece 1d
Muscadell and Maulsy [Muscatel and Malmsey] the ton 12d
[page 36]
N
Nails of all sorts the barrel 2d
Nuts called walnuts the barrel 1d
O
Oranges the thousand 1d
Oil called *civill* [presumably civit oil] the ton 12d
Oil called rape oil the ton 8d
Oil called train oil the ton 6d
P
Pilchards the barrel 1/2d
Poldavis the piece 1d
Pitch and tar the last 4d
Paper called brown paper the hundred bundles 4d
Playing cards the gross 2d
Perle [pearl] the ounce
Prunes the hundredweight 1d
Plaster of Paris the *mounte* 1d
R
Raisins the piece 1/2d
Rice the hundred 1d
Raisins of the sun the hundred 1d
S
Spices of all sorts the hundred pound weight 12d
Sugar the hundredweight 2d
Sack and Bastard [wines] the ton 12d
Silver bullion the pound weight 2d

Salt the quarter 1d
Sider [cider] the ton 6d
Smith's coal the chaulder cont. thirty and two bushels 1d
Salsa Perilla [sarsaparilla root] the hundredweight 6d.
[page 37]
Tynne [tin] the hundred 2d
Thread the bale 12d
Towlas oade [probably a type of woad] the bag 2d
V
Wolle [Wool] cloth of all sorts for every cloth 4d
Vinegar the ton 6d.
W
Woollen cloth of all sorts for every cloth entered 4d
Writing paper and chap paper the ream 1/2d
White soap the hundred 4d
Woolcard the dozen 1d
Wet rugging the hundred 1d

Memorandum that all foreigners and strangers are to pay unto this Corporation for the petty customs and town duties of all such goods and merchandises as shall be here either imported or exported by them and which are not set down in the table of rates before written after the rate of 1d of the shilling for every shilling more or less with the great customs, otherwise called the kings customs, for the same goods and merchandises shall come unto as heretofore always have been accustomed to be paid.

[page 38 blank]
[page 39] An assembly held in the Guildhall of Melcombe Regis within the borough and town of Waymouth and Melcome Regis in the county of Dorset by the mayor, aldermen, bailiffs and capital or principal burgesses of the said borough and town the third day of July 1618. In the year of our Lord James of England etc. seventeenth of Scotland fifty one.

At this assembly it was and is fully agreed by a general consent of the said mayor, aldermen, bailiffs and capital or principal burgesses that every person which has any deeds of any land or house southward from the brewhouse between the same brewhouse and the way that leads from the highest roof in Hope eastward unto a place in the manor of Wyke Regis, called the looking place, shall have the same land there lying severally confirmed unto them by the Corporation upon condition that every of them shall make and leave and forever maintain a gutter where there is necessary cause for a gutter to be made and left for the passage of the water from the hills into the haven as it doth now pass under the house of Robert Wilshiere and upon condition that every of them do also make the way of the street on the west part of their said several lands so far as every of their several lands particularly doth extend itself in length north and south.

Upon the same day it was and is also agreed that every person that doth challenge any land in Hope northward from the house of Richard Pitt unto the house of John Pitt the elder, shall bring into this court here to be held upon this day fortnight all their several deeds and that every person that shall challenge any land in Hope in the west side of the street there shall also then show their deeds.

10 July 1618

Upon this present day it was and is agreed in manner and form aforesaid that there shall be two scoops made at the charge of the town each of which shall contain a just peck of water measure one of which shall be always be used in measuring of salt from the stranger upon the measuring of which salt there shall be only one of the same scoopful allowed unto the buyer upon every quarter.

Upon the same day it was and is also agreed that there shall be always allowed unto the mayor for the time being, according to the ancient custom of this borough and town out of whatsoever grain, salt or other thing that is bought or sold by the bushel or any other measure and brought in hither in any ship, barque or other vessel, only one bushel of the same grain, salt or other thing of the said ship, barque or other vessel shall have no top or but one top but if the said ship, barque or other vessel shall have two tops or more then two bushels and not above.

Whereas Giles Greene, gentleman, has laid out about the procuring of a new seal unto the town charter and about the enrolling of the said charter in the King's Bench and in the Exchequer twenty two pounds, nine shillings and six pence it is now agreed by a general consent that Mr Mayor shall pay unto him the same money out of the monies of this Corporation.

[Signed by] John Pitt, mayor; William Holman, bailiff; John Roy, bailiff, Robert Knight, Henry Russell, William Maunsell, Thomas Giear, John Reynolds, Henry Blithell, Richard Allin junior, Henry Waltham, Thomas Lockeir, Matthew Allin, James James, John Pearcey, Robert Major, Edward Hodder.

[page 40] An assembly held in Melcombe Regis within the borough and town of Waymouth and Melcombe Regis in the county of Dorset by the mayor, aldermen, bailiffs, and capital or principal burgesses of the said borough and town the seventh day of August 1618. In the year of our Lord   James of England etc. sixteenth and Scotland the fifty second.

At this assembly it was and is agreed by a general consent of the said mayor, aldermen, bailiffs and capital or principal burgesses that Mr Mayor shall pay Richard Hills for the ironwork used and employed about the new house adjoining to the town hall.

It is was and is also agreed by the like consent that the masons shall proceed in their work about the making of the wall between the town hall and Mr Mayor's house with a stone window and a stone door. And that Mr Mayor shall pay them for their labour, viz: for the stone windows door 28s and for the residue of the work by the day with 6s allowance for the pillars.

[Marginal annotation] The warrant in the other side should have been set here.

An assembly held in the Guildhall of Melcombe Regis within the borough and town of Waymouth and Melcombe Regis in the county of Dorset by the mayor, aldermen, bailiffs and capital or principal burgesses of the said borough and town the fourth day of September 1618. In the year of our Lord James of England etc. sixteenth and Scotland fifty second.

At this assembly it was and is agreed by a general consent of the said mayor, aldermen, bailiffs and capital or principal burgesses that the sergeants at the mace shall forthwith admonish the tradesmen and artificers (which are to be admitted to keep shops and use their trades within this borough and town according to a former agreement) that they pay their composition monies before the 11th day of this instant month or else they shall not be suffered from thenceforth to keep open their shops nor use their trades within this borough and town without new composition.

At the same assembly it was and is agreed by the like general consent that the stairs into the new house adjoining to the west end of the town hall shall be set up at the south end of the same new house; with this further agreement that if the same shall fall out to be hurtful, or to do any damage, or annoyance unto the cellar of Mr Barnard Michell unto which the said stairs shall be adjoining that then the same stairs shall be taken down again.

At the same assembly it was and is also agreed by the like general consent that Mr Mayor shall pay twenty and one shillings unto Robert Turbervile, David Fyppen and the other constables of this borough and town for their charges spent about their attendance at the two last assizes and sessions of gaol delivery. The consent of paying the constables charges shall not be a precedent hereafter that the like allowance shall be made unto the succeeding constables without a general consent.

[page 41] At the aforesaid assembly it was and is ordered by the like general consent that the town clerk upon this day fortnight shall bring hither to this Guildhall all such books as he has of the records of the court of this town there to be put and safely kept in a chest.

[Signed by] John Pitt, mayor; William Holman, bailiff; John Roy, bailiff; Thomas Giear, Robert Whit, Henry Russell, Robert Vaule [his mark], William Banfild, Edward Hodder, Edward Roy, John Reynolds, Thomas Lockeir, William Maunsell, Henry Waltham, John Ellis [his mark], Roger Fry [his mark] James James.

19 August 1618

The names of the mayor, aldermen, bailiffs and capital burgesses of the borough and town of Waymouth and Melcombe Regis in the county of Dorset present at the granting of a warrant unto John Bagg and Robert Parmiter, sergeants at the mace within the said borough and town for the willing and requiring of Thomas Powlett gent and all and every other person and persons to lay open the enclosed land called Oldarcke Hill and that neither he nor they, nor any of them, do come upon the said land to inter meddle with or carry away the corn there, cut or growing, or to be cut or growing, or to do any other trespass there.

John Pitt, mayor; Robert Knighte and Henry Russell, aldermen.

John Reynolds, Henry Michell, Richard Allin junior, Thomas Giear, James James, Peter Neale, Henry Waltham, John Pitt the elder, Roger Fry, Robert Major, Edward Hodder, Hugh Pearcey, William Martell, Richard Allin, senior, Edward Roye, William Mounsell and Thomas Lockier Common Council.

John Hardy, Thomas Hill of Rodipoll, Margaret Paulfrey, Elizabeth Clearcke and Alice Bacaban of this town witnesses who were present at such time as Robert Parmyter did execute this warrant to the above named Thomas Powlett, gentleman.

The execution of this warrant should have been brought in the other side.
[page42] An assembly held in the Guildhall of Melcombe Regis within the borough and town of Waymouth and Melcombe Regis in the county of Dorset by the mayor, aldermen, bailiffs and capital or principal burgesses of the said town and borough the eighteenth day of September 1618.   In year of our Lord James of England etc. seventeenth and Scotland the two and fiftieth.

At this assembly it was and is agreed by a general consent of the said mayor, aldermen, bailiffs and capital or principal burgesses of the said borough and town, that from henceforth all and every stranger or foreigner that is not a freeman of this town who shall either bring into this harbour to land here, or shall lade here to carry out of this harbour any beer, almonds (*maunds*) of any things, currants, wines of any sort, herrings, hops, madder, millstones, oils of any sort in cask, pilchards in cask, pitch and tar, prunes, raisins in cask, sugar, cider, vinegar, timber of any sort landed upon the town quays, any sort of ordnance, cotton wool, grinding stones, hemp, sumac (*shumacke*), wool or any other goods or merchandises which is to be taken into or out of any ship, barque or other vessel, shall pay unto this Corporation, or unto the farmer or farmers, assign or assigns of this Corporation for and in the name of cranage after and according to the several rates hereunto particularly set down and expressed all be it the same goods or merchandises or any part thereof shall not be craned by the town crane. Victuals to be craned unto the seas for fishermen's provision only excepted.

Beer the tonne 4d
Almonds (*allamudes*) greater 4d
Half almonds (*maundes*) 2d
Quarter almonds (*maundes*) 1d
Currants the tonne 13d
Wines of all sorts the tonne 4d
Herrings the last 6d
Hops the hundred 1/2d
Madder the tonne 4d
Millstones whole per piece 8d
Oil of all sorts the tonne 4d
Pilchards in cask the tonne 4d
Pitch and tar the tonne 4d
Prunes the tonne 4d
Raisins in cask the tonne 4d
Sugar a chest 2d

Cider the tonne 4d

Vinegar the tonne 4d

Timber of all sorts landed upon the town quays the tonne 6d

Ordnance the tonne 4d

Cotton wool the hundred ½d

Grinding stones the tonne 4d

Hemp the tonne 6d

Shumacke the tonne 4d

Wool of all sorts the hundred ½d

[page 43] 21 September 1618

Upon this present day Mr Thomas Gyer is elected mayor of this borough and town for the year following

Upon the same day Mr Robert White and Mr Barnard Michell are elected bailiffs of this borough and town for the year following.

Upon the same day Thomas Gardiner alias Ledoze, John Drye, Henry Rose and Richard Odye are elected constables of this borough and town for the year following.

Upon the same day Mr Thomas Lockier is chosen receiver of the rents, revenues and profit of this borough and town for the year following according to the form, intent and purpose of a constitution thereof heretofore made etc.

Upon the same day it was and is agreed by a general consent of the mayor, aldermen, bailiffs and capital or principal burgesses of this borough and town that the mayor for the time being and the mayor elected shall now name four persons for the election and choice of the receiver of the town rents, revenues and profits (*provenues*) of this borough and town belonging unto this Corporation for the year to come and that out of the said four, one shall be chosen by the said mayor, aldermen, bailiffs and capital or principal burgesses of the said borough and town, or by the greater part of them, who shall take upon him to execute the same office according to the form of a constitution heretofore made in that behalf and that from henceforth the like course shall be observed in the choosing of every receiver hereafter.

Upon this present day Mr Robert White and Mr Barnard Michell, bailiffs elected Mr Edward Roy, Mr Richard Allin junior, Joyce Vandorgozen and Thomas Curding alias Lodoze are chosen auditors of the accounts for the town revenues for this year following according to the form of a former constitution thereof heretofore made.

28 September 1618

Upon this present day the petty customs, anchorage, quayage, wharfage, boomage and the moiety of the king's beams are granted by increase of twenty shillings or more upon every several offer during the burning of the wax candle unto John Pitt the elder at the rent of one hundred twenty and one pounds for one year from the feast of St Michael the Archangel then next following.

Upon the same day the bridge rates, operates and drawing of the bridge are granted for this year following unto Jeremy Babbidge at the rent of six pounds and five shillings.

Upon the same day the cartage was granted unto William Mounsell for this year following at the rent of fourteen pounds.

Upon the same day the profits of the market was granted unto John Read for this year following at the rent of six pounds.

Upon the same day the ballast and forfeitures of the constitution made touching the harbour were granted unto Robert Parmiter for this year following at the rent of seven pounds.

[page 44] An assembly held in the Guildhall of Melcombe Regis within the borough and town of Waymouth and Melcombe Regis in the county of Dorset by the mayor, aldermen, bailiffs and capital or principal burgesses of the said borough and town the three and twentieth day of October 1618 in the year of our Lord James of England etc. seventeenth and Scotland fifty second.

Whereas it is manifest by too much expenditure that cart wheels and other wheels with storts and dowels without iron bonds do much more annoy both the bridge and streets of this borough and town then wheels with iron bonds do. Against the using of which wheels with storts and dowles without iron bonds it is requisite and necessary for provision should be had and taken, it is therefore ordered, constituted and agreed by a general consent of the said mayor, aldermen, bailiffs and capital or principal burgesses of the said borough and town that there shall be from henceforth paid by every owner, carter or driver of any cart, wain or other carriage having wheels with iron sticks or dowles without iron bonds that shall pass or be drawn either over the bridge, or in the streets of this borough and town, for every time four pence which shall be levied in such manner and form as pains and forfeitures for and imposed upon former constitutions and ordained and appointed to be levied. And it is also agreed that the former constitution touching the passing of iron bound cart wheels and wain wheels over the bridge shall stand in force as it has been heretofore (anything in this Constitution to the contrary not withstanding).

[Signed by] Thomas Giear, mayor; William Holman, bailiff, Robert Whit, Robert Knight, John Roy, Edward Roy, William Mounsell, John Reynolds, Henry Michell, Thomas Lockeir, Richard Allin junior, James James, Peter Nother [his mark] Robert Valle [his mark], Edward Hodder.

[page 45] An assembly held in the Guildhall of Melcome Regis within the borough and town of Waymouth and Melcombe Regis in the county of Dorset by the mayor, aldermen, bailiffs and capital or principal burgesses of the said borough and town the eighteenth day of January 1618 in the year of our Lord James of England etc. seventeenth of Scotland fifty second.

At this assembly it was and is agreed by a general consent that there shall be a penny raised upon every ton of such shipping as is to go for Newfoundland this year, either for fishermen or sack towards the charge of Mr William Niell, town clerk of Dartmouth which he has been at about for the obtaining of an order from the King and others of his Majesty's most noble Privy Council for reformation of the abuses of the now plantation at Newfoundland. And that a penny per ton be not sufficient to give content unto the said Mr Niell, then there shall be a half penny per ton more raised upon the same shipping to the purpose to give him content.

22 January 1619
At an assembly held as above said upon the last day aforesaid it was and is agreed by a general consent, that there shall be a warrant made unto Jeremy Babbidge and Henry Hiller for the collecting of the moneys which shall be due for the cranage from henceforth until the feast of St Michael the Archangel next coming, and then they are to yield their accounts and render up what they have received.

5 March 1619
At an assembly held as above said upon the last day aforesaid it was and is agreed by a general consent, that towards the raising of four hundred and fifty pounds required by the Lords of his Majesty's most honourable privy council from the merchants and owners of shipping of this town, there shall be paid by the owners of any ship and barque belonging unto any inhabitant of this town after the rate of six pence upon every ton, and that then half thereof shall be paid, at the first going outwards or coming in, of all ships or barques and the other half thereof at their next coming inwards or going outwards and that no ship or barque shall in the whole pay but after the rate of six pence per ton at two times as aforesaid. And it is also generally agreed, that if their lordships shall accept of £100 from the town in lieu of their whole demand and if their lordships shall require the whole sum of £450 that in either of these cases three selected persons of this Corporation shall be named and appointed (viz:) Mr Henry Russell, Mr Edward Roy and Mr Thomas Lockier who shall have full power and authority to rate every person of this town according to their best discretion for the raising of the £100 if it be accepted of, or for the raising of £225 for the payment of the first moiety of the £450 if the £450 be required, and that as they shall rate, so it shall bind every person to lay down accordingly which money so to be rated and laid down is intended but only to be lent until it may be raised upon the customs by one upon the hundred and upon the tonnage as aforesaid, and that the mayor, aldermen, bailiffs and capital burgesses or the greater part of them shall rate those selected persons above named. Provided always that if this money can be procured by loan upon interest then the revenues of the town shall be leased unto those that shall procure the same for their security of repayment.

[Signed by] Thomas Giear, mayor; Robert Whit, bailiff, Robert Knight, Peter Neale [his mark], Henry Russell, William Waltham, John Roy, Robert Vaule [his mark], John Pitt, Richard Ody[?], William Maunsell, John Ellis [his mark], Thomas Lockeire, Henry Blickell, Richard Allin, Richard Allin junior, Henry Witham, Steven Dennis, James James, Edward Hodder, Edward Roy, Robert Major.

[page 46] An assembly held in Melcombe Regis within the borough and town of Waymouth and Melcombe Regis in the county of Dorset by the mayor, aldermen,

bailiffs and capital or principal burgesses of the said borough and town the nineteenth day of March 1618 in the year of our Lord James by the Grace of God England etc. the sixteenth and Scotland the fifty second.

At this assembly by a general consent Mr Mayor of this town for the time being (upon the order of the Lords of his Majesty's Privy Council touching the receiving of one upon the hundred of all customs of goods and merchandises traded in or out of this port by the officers of his Majesty's customs house which by their Lordship's writs the said officers are enjoined to receive and deliver over) is now nominated and appointed to receive the same from time to time from the said officers. And that David Gyer shall have his freedom in respect of the loan of £50 which he is to have again of the first monies received.

An assembly held in form aforesaid by the aforesaid mayor, aldermen, bailiffs and capital or principal burgesses the last day of April 1619 in the year of our Lord King James by the Grace of God of England etc. the Seventeenth and Scotland the fifty second.

At this assembly by a general consent of the mayor, aldermen, bailiffs and capital or principal burgesses aforesaid it was and is agreed that Mr Mayor shall purchase timber and plank for the repairing and amending of the bridge with all the convenient speed it may be done. And that there shall be also stones purchased in readiness for the repairing of the town quays and lime and plaster of Paris for the finishing of the new building on the north and west part of Melcombe town hall. All which shall be provided and come at the charge of this Corporation and that the collectors of the town revenues upon warrant from Mr Mayor and Mr Bailiffs from time to time shall pay such monies as the doing thereof shall come unto.

An assembly held in form aforesaid by the aforesaid mayor, aldermen, bailiffs and capital or principal burgesses the eighth and twentieth day of May 1619 in the year of our Lord James by the grace of God of England etc. the seventeenth and Scotland the fifty second.

At this assembly it was and is agreed by a general consent of the said mayor, aldermen, bailiffs and capital or principal burgesses of the said borough and town that Mr Mayor shall pay threescore and thirteen pounds unto Mr Henry Waltham upon the first day of June next for the redeeming of a lease of the petty customs made unto him by this Corporation in mortgage for the payment of the same threescore and thirteen pounds, viz: fifty pounds out of the monies which were taken up of Mr John Pitt upon use and the other twenty three pounds out of the Corporation monies which are in stock and that the other hundred pounds taken up of Mr John Pitt upon use, shall be put out to use until Michaelmas Day next upon good security to be taken by Mr Mayor to the use of the Corporation.

[page 47] **27 August 1619**
Whereas at a court of survey of Melcombe Regis within the town of Waymouth and Melcombe Regis a Jury was impanelled for the making of a rental of all the rents

due unto this Corporation of the tenements of Melcombe Regis aforesaid which Jury notwithstanding diverse adjournments have neglected their duty in that behalf, it is therefore ordered and agreed by a general consent of the mayor, aldermen, bailiffs and capital or principal burgesses of the said town that the said Jury shall assemble themselves together and conclude and agree upon their verdict and make return thereof upon the thirteenth day of September next coming upon pain of every of them that shall not perform his duty in that behalf shall forfeit 3s 4d.

21 September 1619

Upon this present day Mr Matthew Pitt is elected mayor of this borough and town for the year following.

Upon the same day Mr Henry Russell and Mr Robert Vaule are elected bailiffs of this borough and town for the year following.

Upon this present day Thomas Gardner, Thomas Wallis, Henry Rose and John Drye are elected constables of this borough and town for the year following.

Upon the same day Mr Robert Major is chosen receiver of the Rents, Revenues and profits of this borough and town for the year following according to the form intent and purpose of a Constitution thereof heretofore made.

Upon this present day Mr Henry Russell and Mr Robert Vaule, bailiffs elected. Mr Edward Roye, Mr Henry Waltham, John Pope and Henry Rose are chosen auditors for the accounts for the town's revenues for this year following according to the form of a former Constitution thereof heretofore made.

27 September 1619

Upon this present assembly it was and is agreed by a general consent that the Corporation shall keep the petty customs, anchorage, quayage, wharfage, boomage and the one half of the weight and beams and weights of the town in their hands for this year following, or so long as the same Corporation shall think fit and that so long as the same Corporation shall detain and keep the same in their hands Mr John Pitt the elder shall collect and gather the same duties until there shall be a new mayor sworn and another collector appointed. And it is also agreed that all other duties of the town shall be let by a candle upon tomorrow next being Michaelmas Eve as it has been used heretofore about three of the clock in the afternoon.

At this assembly it was also agreed by a general consent of the mayor, aldermen, bailiffs and capital and principal burgesses of this borough and town of Waymouth and Melcombe Regis that Mr John Man, collector for the farmers of the King's Customs shall also receive and take up the one upon the hundred which is to be received and taken up here by order from the Lords of his Majesty's most noble privy council and shall pay over the same unto the mayor of this town for the time being according to the tenor of the same writ.

[page 48] 28 September 1619

Upon this present day the bridge groats (*bridggroates*), rope groats (*roapegroates*) and drawing of the bridge are granted for this year following to Mr James James at the rent of seven pounds and fifteen shillings.

Upon the same day the cartage was granted unto Mr Richard Allin the younger for this year following at their rent thirteen pounds fifteen shillings.

Upon the same day the profits of the market were granted unto John Read for this year following at the rent of five pounds ten shillings.

Upon the same day the ballast and forfeitures of the Constitution made touching the harbour were granted unto Richard Allin the younger for this year following at the rent of five pounds and fifteen shillings.

1 October 1619

Whereas upon the day last aforesaid the sums of £157 10s 0d are to be paid unto Mr John Pitt one of the aldermen of this town for the debt of this Corporation, which at this present accordingly was paid it is now to be remembered that £100 thereof was paid by Mr Thomas Gyer, mayor of this town out of the monies borrowed of Mr Pitt and £38 3s 10d more thereof was paid by the said Mr Mayor out of the monies received by him for the 50 per 100. And the residue being £19 6s 2d was paid out of the poor money remaining in Mr Edward Roy his hand which he paid unto Mr Pitt to make up the full payment of the said sum of £157 10s 0d which £19 6s 2d is to be paid back unto Mr Edward Roy his hand out of the town revenues of the first monies which shall be received to the town's use. Their being present Mr Thomas Gyer, mayor; Mr Robert White, bailiff; Mr John Pitt, alderman; Mr Thomas Lockier, Mr Edward Roy, Mr Henry Waltham, Mr William Mounsell, Mr Richard Allin the younger and Mr Matthew Allin.

29 October 1619

Upon this present day it was and is ordered and agreed by a general consent of the mayor, aldermen, bailiffs and capital and principal burgesses of this borough and town that Mr Henry Michell and Mr John Pitt the elder, shall peruse the rates of the petty customs and town duties belonging to this Corporation and shall cause the town clerk to set them down in this book according to the rates of the ancient table.

At the same time it was and is also agreed by the like assent and consent that Mr William Mounsell shall have one month's time longer from this time for the payment of his rent for the cartage, which is behind and was due at Michaelmas last.

[page 49] Edward Roy and Robert White the elder, do stand bound by their obligation dated the eight and twentieth day of September 1619 unto this Corporation in the sum of fifty pounds for the payment of twenty five pounds twelve shillings and four pence to the use of the poor of Waymouth side upon the feast Day of St Michael the Archangel which shall be in the year of our Lord God 1620.

The said Edward Roye and Robert White the elder do likewise stand bound by their obligation dated the said 28th day of September 1619 unto this Corporation in the sum of forty marks for the payment of fourteen pounds, ten shillings and four pence to the use of the poor of Melcombe Regis upon the said feast Day of St Michael the Archangel which shall be in the year of Our Lord God 1620.

Matthew Allin alias Belpitt and Richard Allin alias Belpitt the younger do stand bound by their obligation dated the said 28th day of September 1619 unto this Corporation in the sum of 88 pounds for the payment of £44 to the use of the poor of Melcombe Regis aforesaid upon the said feast Day of St Michael the Archangel which shall be in the year of Our Lord God 1620.

William Pitt has £25, parcel of Mr Midleton's gift upon bond dated the 4th day of October 1619 wherein the said William Pitt, John Pitt the elder, Robert Major and Edward Hodder of this town, merchants, do stand bound for the repayment thereof at the end of three years and for the interest and allowance in the mean time.

Owen Holeman has £25 parcel of Mr Midleton's gift upon bond dated the 4th day of October 1619 wherein the said Owen Holeman, William Holman, Henry Russell and James Sirry of this town, merchants, do stand bound for the repayment thereof at the end of three years and for the interest and allowance.

Henry Knighte has £25 parcel of Mr Midleton's gift upon bond dated the 4th day of October 1619 wherein the said Henry Knighte, Robert Knighte, William Waltham and Thomas Gyer of this town, merchants, do stand bound for the repayment thereof at the end of three years and for the interest and allowance.

William Williams has £25 parcel of Mr Middleton's gift upon bond dated the 4th day of October 1619 wherein the said William Williams, Edward Roy, Robert White and Robert Vaule of this town, merchants, do stand bound for the repayment thereof at the end of three years and for the interest and allowance.

[page 50] 3 November 1619

Upon this present day it was and is agreed and ordered that Mr John Pitt, alderman, William Mounsell, Mr Thomas Lockier, Mr Robert Major, Mr John Ellis, Mr James James shall view as well the ground where Mr Bailiff Russell doth desire to set up his windmill as also the ground where Mr Giles Greene doth desire to set up a quay before his house and to make report what they shall think fit to be done therein at the next assembly to be held upon Friday next.

Upon the same day Edward Lynsey one of the freemen of this town was chosen one of the capital and principal burgesses of the same town in the room and place of Mr Thomas Gyer now one of the aldermen of the same town.

5 November 1619

Memorandum that a lease was made by this Corporation unto Richard Allin alias Belpitt the younger, and Matthew Allin alias Belpitt, of the town ward, dated the 6th day of April 1615 to begin at the feast of the Annunciation of the Blessed Lady St Mary the Virgin last past before the date of the same lease and to continue for the term of twenty and one years from thence next following under the yearly rent of ten pounds of current English money to be paid yearly at the feast of St Michael the Archangel and the Annunciation of Our Blessed Lady St Mary the Virgin or within ten days next after either of the said feasts by equal portions.

Memorandum that the Petty customs hereof was let unto Mr Richard Wrighte customs of the port of Poole so long as it shall be to the liking of this Corporation and of the said Richard Wright under the rent per annum of 26s 8d to be paid quarterly whereof three quarters rent was due at the feast of St Michael the Archangel last past that is to say 20s.

Upon the same day it was and is agreed by a general consent of the mayor, aldermen, bailiffs and capital and principal burgesses of the said borough and town that all those persons which were amerced or pained at the Law Days of either side of this borough and town for the last year and their amercements extracted that if they will sue unto Mr Mayor for abatement of the same amercement and pain then it shall be lawful unto Mr Mayor to abate them the one half of whatsoever they were amerced or pained.

Upon the same day it was and is agreed by the like consent that the cellar under the town hall of Melcombe Regis shall be let and granted by a candle who will give most for it by yearly rent for seven years to begin at the feast of the Nativity of Our Lord God next coming and that the lease shall covenant that neither he or his assigns shall lay anything there that shall make any noisome or offensive smell or savour into the said town hall nor shall carry away or remove any paving, pitching, enter close or door that he or his assigns shall their make or set up and thereupon it was let and granted unto Richard Harryson at the rent of 43s per annum to be paid half yearly that is to say at Midsummer and Christmas.

[page 51] Memorandum that whereas John Pitt the elder farmer of the petty customs and other duties belonging unto this Corporation was behind in payment of his rent due at the feast of St Michael the Archangel last past it was and is agreed by a general consent of the mayor, aldermen, bailiffs and capital or principal burgesses of the said Corporation that for some several considerations he shall be forgiven £10 parcel of the monies behind in payment as aforesaid and that twenty one pounds 10s more which is behind he shall pay £11 10s thereof forthwith and the other ten pounds of the sum 20s shall be given unto him in respect and regard that he shall take the pains to collect and gather the petty customs and other duties there which used to be let for this year following. That is to say until the feast of St Michael the Archangel next coming and in respect and regard he shall give security to the Corporation to pay the same monies which he shall so collect and gather unto this Corporation within ten days next after every of the feasts of the Birth of Our Lord God, the Annunciation of Our Blessed Lady St Mary the Virgin, the Nativity of St John the Baptist and St Michael the Archangel in the said year whereupon the said John Pitt did forthwith satisfy the same eleven pounds and ten shillings unto the receiver of this Corporation for the time being.

Memorandum it is and was also agreed by the like general consent that there shall be a new clock bought to be set up in Melcombe Church and that there shall be given for the same the old clock which stands there and four pounds in money of this Corporation.

8 November 1619

Memorandum that upon the day and year above said it was and is agreed by the general consent of the mayor, aldermen, bailiffs and capital or principal burgesses of this borough and town that there shall be a bench and ceiling so high at a man's head set up in the room under the Custom House against the wall and that there shall be a partition and room with a table board and bench made in the Custom House for the farmer of the petty customs. All which shall be made and done at the charge of this Corporation.

Upon the same day and year it was and is also agreed by the like consent that this Corporation shall grant to Mr Henry Russell and his heirs forever a certain piece of ground lying without the Cuniger on the west side of the highway towards the narrows containing in length from the east to the west three score foot and in breadth three score foot. That is to say: from the south to the north for which he is to pay £40 fine and £5 yearly rent at the feast of St Michael the Archangel or within ten days after the said feast and at his and their own charges it to maintain the east bank and they are not to molest the same piece of ground at any time without composition and consent of this Corporation.

14 November 1619

Memorandum that upon the day and year aforesaid it was and is agreed by a general consent of the mayor, aldermen, bailiffs and capital or principal burgesses of this borough and town that so much as shall be wanting of two hundred twenty and five pounds to pay towards his Majesty's intended expedition and is not collected upon one of the hundred according to the order of the Lords of His Majesty's most Honourable Privy Council shall be taken upon interest and that the petty customs and other things, used to be let with the petty customs, shall be leased to secure the same for such a term as shall be thought fit according to the sum of money which shall be so taken up.

3 December 1619

Memorandum that the day and year aforesaid it was and is agreed by a general consent of the mayor, aldermen, bailiffs and capital or principal burgesses of this borough and town that the Corporation do give security unto Edward Cuttance and Henry Cuttance, or unto one of them, for the payment of one hundred pounds which they are to lend unto this Corporation until midsummer next. Then there shall be a lease made unto such a person as Mr Mayor will nominate of all the petty customs etc. for the term of two years to begin from midsummer day next with a proviso that if this Corporation shall pay the sum hundred pounds to the party to whom the same lease shall be made upon Midsummer Day next then the same lease shall be void.

Upon the same day and year it was and is also agreed that upon the payment of one hundred pounds unto Mr Mayor by the above named Edward Cuttance and Henry Cuttance to be lent unto this Corporation until Midsummer next, they the said Edward Cuttance and Henry Cuttance, shall be admitted freemen of this Corporation.

7 December 1619

Upon this day Edward Cuttance and Henry Cuttance did pay unto Mr Mayor the hundred pounds last above mentioned and at an assembly of the mayor, aldermen, bailiffs and capital or principal burgesses of this town held the tenth day of the said month of December were admitted and sworn freemen of this Corporation according to a former agreement.

[page 53] An assembly held in the Guildhall of Melcombe Regis within the borough and town of Waymouth and Melcombe Regis in the county of Dorset by the mayor, aldermen, bailiffs and capital or principal burgesses of the said borough and town the last day of December 1619.

At this assembly for the better keeping and observing of the Lords holy Sabbath and for the better performance of that worship and divine service, which ought to be done unto God by all persons upon that day, and for the taking away of all vain and idle excuses in buying and selling and taken of occasions to break the Lords Commandments concerning that day, it was and is constituted established and agreed by a general consent of the mayor, aldermen, bailiffs and capital or principal burgesses here assembled that no shoemaker, butcher, or any other artificer or shopkeeper within this borough and town, shall at any time from henceforth upon the Sabbath Day utter or sell any commodity whatsoever out of his or their shop or shops, unless it shall be in case of necessity which necessity shall be considered and allowed by Mr Mayor and Mr Bailiffs for the time being, or by two of them whereof the mayor to be one, upon pain of every person offending or doing to the contrary, to forfeit for every time twelve pence which forfeiture shall be levied by warrant from the mayor and bailiffs for the time being or two of them where the mayor to be one in such sort as other forfeitures are ordained and provided to be levied.

[Signed by] Matthew Pitt, mayor; Henry Russell, Robert Knight, John Bond, John Pitt, Thomas Giear, Robert Whit, William Holman, Peter Neale [his sign], William Banfild, John Pytt, Thomas Lockeir, Edward Roy, Roger Fry [his mark], Henry Waltham, Henry Blickell, John Ellis [his mark], James James, Robert Major, William Williams, Edward Hodder, James Serrey.

[page 54] An assembly held in the Guildhall of Melcombe Regis within the borough and town of Waymouth and Melcombe Regis in the county of Dorset by the mayor, aldermen, bailiffs and capital or principal burgesses of the said borough and town the 4th day of February 1620.

Memorandum that at this assembly it was and is agreed by a general consent of the mayor, aldermen, bailiffs and capital or principal burgesses of the said borough and town that there shall be a warrant under the town seal made unto John Pitt the elder for the collecting and levying of the petty customs, anchorage, quayage, wharfage, boomage and town beams and the profits and duties thereof, from the feast of St Michael the Archangel last past until the feast of St Michael the Archangel then next coming, that is to say, for one whole year.

At this assembly it was and is constituted, established and agreed by a general consent of the mayor, aldermen, bailiffs and capital or principal burgesses of the said borough and town that Mr John Pitt, Mr Thomas Gyer, Mr Henry Waltham, Mr Henry Michell, Mr Edward Roy and Mr James James shall set and make an indifferent rate as well for the porter's fees and wages, as also for the salt carriers from the quays to the harbour of this town unto every several person's house within this town and such rate as they shall make shall bind as well the porters, salt carriers and the sergeants at the mace touching their duties and fees what they shall demand of merchants. As also the merchants what they shall pay them.

[Signed by] Matthew Pytt, mayor; Henry Russell, bailiff; Robert Vaule, bailiff [his mark]; John Bond, John Pitt, John Pytt, Robert Whit, Peter Neale [his mark], Edward Roy, William Waltham, Roger Fry [his mark], Robert Knight, Henry Blickell, [illegible] Ellins, James James, Robert Major, William Williams.

[page 55] A survey of the rents of the burgage tenements and lands in Waymouth within the borough and town of Waymouth and Melcombe Regis in the county of Dorset taken the eighteenth day of June 1617 upon the oath of those tenants whose names are here under written.

Matthew Allin	Hugh Percey	Thomas Kneller
Peter Neale	Henry Cuttance	Edward Allin
Robert Vaule	Henry Haught	Thomas Ledoze
William Martell	William Williams	Thomas Bigges
John Ellis	Richard Brooke	Reynold Kelway

In the east side of Hope
John Pitt the elder 6d
the same John Pitt 6d
George Pitt of Hope 1s 8d
Robert Vaule 5d
Peter Neale 5d
John Saunders 2s 6d
Luke Jordaine 8d
Joan Whites 2s 4d
The widow Gould 4d
Roger Wades' heirs 8d
Mary Wades 6d
Joan Whites 2d
Anthony Bennett 4d
John Cotton 2d.

In the west side of Hope
John Pitt the elder 6d
John Hamon 2d
John Pitt the elder [blank]
Thomas Turkey 1s
William Maby 6d
John Johnson 6d
Henry Jesopp 6d
John Huchinson 6d
William Simonds 1s

Philip Allexsander 1s
Peter Applebee 4d
Thomas Bagg 1s 4d
Richard Bird 1s
George Pitt 1s
Richard Pitt 1s
Mr Napper 6d
John Saunders 1s
William Richardson 1s
Brandinn Growte, John Cotten and John
    Growte 10d
Hugh Marten 4d
Richard Marten 4d
Christopher Batter 2d
William Morgan 4d
Richard Abram's heirs 4d
William Richardson 4d
Phillip Bishopp 4d
Thomas Nichols 1s
Gabriel Cornish 8d
Humphry Moore 8d
[Total for the first column page 55]
    £1 8s 4d
Susan Betterly 8d
Gabriel Cornish 1s
The same Gabriel Cornish 1s.

Mr Napper 1s
George Pitt 1s
Mr Napper 1s.

In the south side of the High Street
Edward Johnson 6d
Mr Royes 1s 8d
Robert Wilshiere 2½d
James Codd 2½d
William Avery, John Tanner, Nicholas
    Clatworthy 7d
Snelling's heirs 6d
Lord Russell's heirs 11d
Matthew Allin 1s 6d
John Early 1s
John Wall 10d
John Wall 6d
Mary Wades 5d
Robert Vaule 4d
Joan White's widow 4d
Hugh Abbott's heirs 6d
John Kowly 8d
Thomas Ledoze 6d
Stephen Denis 6d
Thomas Biggs 4d
William Collins and Richard White 10d
William Clement's heirs 10d
John Randall 1s
Henry Randall 1s
Thomas Favell's heirs 1s 10d
widow Andney 1s
Jeffrey Preston 6d
John Case 6d
Joan Bryer 9d
The widow Goulde 1s 10d
Edward Bush 1s 4d
John Percey 1s 3d
Hugh Peircy 1s 3d
Edward Allin 2s 6d
George Browne 1s 3d
William Keate 1s
[Total for the second column page 55]
    £1 16s 4d
[page 56]

Mr Roger Keate 4s 6d
Phillip Alexander, Phillip Alexander 1s
Robert Bishopp 1s 4d
Thomas Barnes 1s 6d
Richard Brooke 1s 4d
James Serrey 1s 4d
William Danser's heirs 8d
Laurence Boyte 9d
Jeffrey Hardy 2s
James Ledoze 1s 3d
William Mounsell 1s
John Mann 1s 8d
Robert Knott's heirs 1s
Thomas Bagg 1s
John Peltote's heirs 1s
William Mounsell 6d
William Vallance 1s 6d
Thomas Best's heirs 2s
Robert Hedgcocke 1s 2d
John Cookery 10d
Robert Milpley 1s 2d
Thomas Chappell 8d
William Maye 4d
John Samwayes 1s
Thomas Chappell 8d
Robert Knott's heirs 9d
William Kneller 3d
James Hopkins 3d
Richard Ash his heirs 3d

In the north side of High Street
Matthew Allin 2s
Mr Royes 1s 8d
Robert White 4d
Henry Hebbert 4d
Stephen Denis 1s
William Bonvill 1s
Robert White 1s
Peter Neale 1s
The widow Gould 4d
William Martell 1s
David Gyer 8d
John Laurence's heirs 9d
John Samways 1d

Martin Keech 2s
Justinian Hingston 5s
Richard Hill 1s 4d
William Bonvill 9d
Thomas Favell 2s 8d
Henry Haught 1s 3d
Robert Randall
Henry Cuttance 2s
Robert Kenning, Edward Cuttance,
    William Williams 2s
John Ellis 1s
William Poye's heirs 6d
[Total for the first column page 56]
    £3 4s 4d
Thomas Samwayes 10d
Robert Byatt's heirs 4d
Christopher Simond's heirs 6d
John Keeles 1s 6d
John Bartlett 1s 3d
Thomas Kneller 10d
Thomas Kneller 6d
John Ford 1s 6d
Thomas Best's heirs 1s 7d
Thomas Chappell 1s
William Hebberd's heirs 1s
William Clements 9d
Mary Russell widow 6d
John Deanis 6d
Roger Chipp 9d
Henry Peach 2s 3d
Thomas Bagg, Thomas Bagg 2s 9d
Roger Page 1s 8d
John Cade's heirs 1s 3d
Henry Nichols 1s 6d
Thomas White 8d

In the north side of the West Street
Thomas Bagg 4d
William Martell 6d
Roger Page 4d
Edward Cuttance 4d
Roger Fry 4d
John Chipp 6d
John Cade's heirs 9d

John Hill's heirs 4d
The widow Sanger 1d
Thomas Devenish 4d
Henry Hawkins 6d
Thomas Bagg 3d
Thomas Bagg 6d
John Combes 3d
John Ford 9d
Andrew Buckler 1s 6d
Robert Gibbens 6d
Henry Gawdin 6d
Grindum's heirs 1s
Wiffen's heirs 1s
John Peltote's heirs 8d
William Mounsell 2s
William Waltham 2s 4d
Thomas Best 2s 4d
Robert Pitt 7d.

In the South side of West Street
Thomas Gyer 9d
Lord Russell's heirs 2s 4d
William Waltham 2s 6d
Andrew Buckler 1s
Robert White 1s 2d
Robert White 2s 6d
James Serrey 2s
Andrew Buckler 5s
Thomas Best's ~~heirs~~ 1s 6d
[Total for the second column page 56]
    £3 1s 8d
[page 57]
John Ford 1s
Ricatt's heirs 1s 10d
Andrew Buckler 5s
Thomas Best 1s 6d
Henry Hawkins 2d
Bryan Buck 2d
John Williams 9d
William Bonfield 4d
Robert White 10d
Widow Whites 1s 4d

In Saint Nicholas Street

The widow Gould 1s
Mary Taylor 1s 2d
John Brich 10d
John Brich 1s 2d
Joseph Ponnte 8d
Lord Russell's heirs 1s 4d
Hugh Martin and Richard Martin 4d
John Keeles 4d
Peter Barger 9d
Thomas Best 1s
Robert Knott's heirs 8d
William Valence 8d
Richard Ford 8d
William Williams 10d
John Lyne 8d
Edward Allin 1s 4d
Jeffrey Hardy 1s
Matthew Allin 1s
Matthew Allin 4d
Roger Frye 4d
Richard Martin 4d

In Newbury
Lord Russell's heirs 2s 6d
John Randall 2s

John Randall 1s
John Cotten 1s
Lord Russell's heirs 1s
Richard Ford 9d

In the south side of Francis Street
Robert Hayward 8d
Porter land 6d
William Mounsell 6d
Phillip Alexander 3d
Thomas Favell's heirs 3d
Henry Holman 6d
Robert Randall 1s 6d
Thomas Bagg 8d
[Total for the column of page 58]
    £2 3s 5d
[Arabic numerals providing corrected
    totals for the five columns]
£1 18s 4d
£1 16s 4d
£3 4s 4d
£3 0s 7d
£2 3s 5d
£12 3s 0d The whole of the foregoing
    rent

[page 58] A survey of the rents of the burgage tenements and land in Melcombe Regis within the borough and town of Waymouth and Melcombe Regis in the county of Dorset taken upon the sixth day of ~~January~~ August 1617 upon the oath of those tenants whose names are hereunder written.

John Pitt Senior	James Sirrey	John Hodge
Richard Allin Junior	Robert Major	Simon Godfrey
Thomas Lockier	Jeremy Babbidge	Henry Backwell
Henry Michell	Richard Hill	John Darby
James James	Richard Odye	Roger Ossett

In the south part of St Edmund Street
[Plot 1] John Pitt the younger for the north part of his dwelling house sometime John Mounsell's first bought of the town bounded on the east on Mayden Street, in the west on the town lands, the grounds purchased of Owen Reynolds on the South. Rent 1s.

[Plot 2] And for the south part of his said house whereof the land was purchased of Owen Reynolds, bounded on the east on Mayden Street the land sometime of Amy Reynolds on the south The town hall with a room built over the meal house on the east end of the same and a backside belonging to the town hall on the south part.

Rent 6d

[Plot 3] One plot of ground belonging to Richard Allin junior and Nathaniel Allin bounded in the east on St Mary's Street, the west on St Thomas Street leading to the Bridge, in the South on the town quay three foot broad. Rent 3s

[Plot 4] Thomas Powlett's dwelling house bounded on the east on St Thomas Street leading to the Bridge, in the west on the heirs of Robert Morris dwelling house, in the south on the sea or haven. Rent 1s

[Plot 5] The heirs of Robert Morris their dwelling house bounded in the east on Thomas Powlett's house, in the West on Sir John Brown's house in the south on the haven. Rent 6d

[Plot 6] Sir John Browne's house now in the tenure of Edward Lynsey bounded in the east on the house of the heirs of Robert Morris, in the west in the house of Alice Hodge sometimes Thomas Burley's, in the sea on the south part. Rent 2d

[Plot 7] Alice Hodge wife of John Hodge her dwelling house bounded in the east on Sir John Browne's house, in the west on a stable of John Hodge, in the south on the sea. Rent 2d

[Plot 8] John Hodge's stable bounded in the east on Alice Hodge's house in the west on a cellar of John Pitt the younger, in the south on a backside of the above said Alice Hodge. Rent 1d

[Plot 9] John Pitt the younger his cellar bounded on the east on John Hodge's stable and Alice Hodge's backside, in the west on the wharf of Nicholas Street, in the south on the sea. Rent 1d

[Plot 10] David Gyer's plot of ground bounded in the east on the wharf of St Nicholas Street, on the west and in the south on the sea. Rent 2s 6d

In the north of St Edmund Street

[Plot 11] The house of the heirs of Bartholomew Allin, bounded in the north on a house of Thomas Gould's sometimes Holton's land, in the east on Mayden Street, in the west Edward Hodder's house. Rent 1s 3d

[Plot 12] Edward Hodder's dwelling house sometimes Thomas Pitt's, bounded in the north on John Pitt the elder's house, in the east on the heirs of Bartholomew Allin's house, in the west on St Mary's Street. Rent 1s 3d

[Plot 13] Richard Major his dwelling house bounded in the north on a shop and stable of John Reynolds, in the east on St Mary's Street, in the west on the house of Matthew Pitt. Rent 1s 2d

[Plot 14] Matthew Pitt his house bounded in the north on a stable and backside of John Reynolds, in the east of Richard Major's house, in the west of John Pitt the younger's house. Rent 4d

[Plot 15] John Pitt the younger his house bounded in the north on a house of Henry Waltham's in the east on Matthew Pitt's house, in the west on a cellar of the said Matthew Pitt's and of one other cellar bought of John Gregory and now in the occupation of the said John Pitt. Rent 6d.

[Plot 16] Matthew Pitt his cellar sometimes Thomas Samways bounded in the east on John Pitt the younger's house, in the west on St Thomas Street, in the north on the cellar of John Pitt the younger which was bought of John Gregory as above said. Rent 6d

[Plot 17] Thomas Lockier his dwelling house and backside sometimes Thomas Membrims bounded in the east on St Thomas Street and in the west on Henry Russell's cellar and in the north on the dwelling house of Henry Russell. Rent 3d.

[page 59]

[Plot 18] Henry Russell's cellar bounded in the east on Thomas Lockier's land now a backside, in the west on a house of the heirs of John Oats in the north on a garden of the said Henry Russell. Rent 6d

[Plot 19] The heirs of John Oats a house, in the east on Henry Russell's cellar, in the west on a cellar of John Pitt the younger in the north in the land of Michael Browne. Rent 1d

[Plot 20] John Pitt the younger his cellar bounded in the east on the house of the heirs of John Oats in the west on St Nicholas Street, in the north on Michael Browne's house. Rent 2d

[Plots 21 and 21a: it has not been possible to establish the exact location of the places mentioned in the following text with two plots marked 21 on the map produced by Miss Weinstock to accompany the survey] The heirs of Henry Walker one burgage bounded in the north on the tenement of James Barton and Henry Cox, in the east on St Nicholas Street, in the west on the Sea, in which are two slaughterhouses some part toward St Edmond Street on Thomas Barnes house and the heirs of Henry Cox house within which circuit is a tenement in the occupation of Anthony Jordaine, a cellar and stable in the occupation of Thomas Powlett gentleman, a tenement in the occupation of Clement White all in St Nicholas Street and a tenement in the occupation of Richard Cosens, a tenement in the occupation of Margot Cavede and a tenement in the occupation of Justinian Hingston all which doth pay 10d rent of which Thomas Powlett pays 4d. Rent 6d.

[Plot 22] Richard Allin the younger his land sometime Knaplock's land bounded in the east on the way leading into Richard Cox house, in the west on the Sea and in the north on the land of the above said Henry Walker. Rent 1d.

[Plot 23] Thomas Barnes house sometime Knaplock's land bounded in the east on the heirs of Walker's house, in the west on a way leading into Richard Cox his house, son of Henry Cox and on the north on the house of the above said Richard Cox. Rent 1d.

[Plot 24] Richard Cox his house and a way leading to it bounded in the north and east on the heirs of Walker's land and Thomas Barnes house lying in the east of the way and on the south of Coxe's house and in the west on the land of Richard Allin the younger. Rent 1d.

In the West Street

[Plot 25] Richard Somerset alias Cox tenement, sometime Thomas Trenche's bounded in the east on James Barton's garden, in the south on the heirs of Henry Walker's land, in the north on the house of the said Richard Cox and in the west on the sea. Rent 6d.

[Plot 26] Richard Somerset alias Cox his house bounded on the east on a tenement of Thomas Wayman's, in the north on Sea and town ground, in the south on his land bought of Thomas Trench and in the west on the sea. Rent 3d.

[Plot 27] Thomas Wayman's house bounded in the east on the heirs of Robert Morris garden and James Barton, in the north on the town ground, in the west and south on Richard Somerset alias Cox his house and land. Rent 3d.

[Plot marked as Town Land] The town land being north and south about 109 foot and in the east bounded on the heirs of Robert Morris garden and William Waltham's garden and in the west into the sea. [No rate shown].

[Plot 28] John Pitt junior, in the west side of the West Street a tenement bounded in the north on a tenement of Matthew Pitt in the south and west by the sea. Rent 6d

[Plot 29] Matthew Pitt a tenement bounded in the north on William Waltham's house, in the south on John Pitt junior his tenement and in the west on the sea. Rent 6d

[Plot 30] William Waltham his dwelling house bounded in the north and west on the sea and in the south on the tenement of Matthew Pitt. Rent 1s.

In the west part of St Nicholas Street
[Plot 31] Thomas Pollett gentleman, his stable and cellar bounded in the north on Anthony Jordaine tenement and in the south on a tenement in the occupation of Clement White and in the west on the backside and ground in the occupation of the said Clement White. Rent 4d

[Plot 32] Anthony Jordaine a tenement and backside parcel of the heirs of Walker's land bounded in the north on James Barton's tenement and in the south on the stable or and cellar of Thomas Powlett gent and in the west on the heirs of Walker's land which rent is comprehended in Walkers land.

[Plot 33] James Barton's tenement bounded in the north on the land of the heirs of Robert Morris and in the south on the tenement of Anthony Jourdaine and in the west on the land of the heirs of Walker. Rent 3d.

[Plot 34] The heirs of Robert Morris one tenement and garden bounded in the north on a garden of William Waltham's and in the south on James Barton's tenement and in the west on Thomas Wayman's land and the town land. Rent 6d.

[Plot 35] William Waltham his garden and stable bounded in the north on the tenement and garden of John Pitt junior, in the south on the garden of the heirs of Robert Morris and in the west on the town ground. Rent 6d.

[Plot 36] John Pitt junior his cellar and garden backward bounded in the north on a cellar and garden of Matthew Pitt in the south on a stable and garden of William Waltham and in the west on the West Street. Rent 1s 6d.

[page 60]

[Plot 37] Matthew Pitt his cellar and garden backward bounded in the north on a garden of Thomas Powlett, gentleman, in the south on a cellar and garden of John Pitt junior and in the west on the West Street. Rent 1s.

[Plot 38] Thomas Powlett, gentleman, a garden bounded in the north on a garden of John Pitt junior, in the south on a cellar and garden of Matthew Pitt and in the west on West Street. Rent 1s.

[Plot 39] John Pitt junior a garden bounded in the north on a lane, in the south on a garden of Thomas Powlett, gentleman, and in the west on West Street. Rent 1s.

[Plot 40]

Richard Allin junior, Nathaniel Allin and Matthew Allin a garden divided in equal thirds between them, bounded in the north on a garden of Richard Major's in the south on a lane and in the west on the sea. Rent 2s

[Plot 41] Richard Major a garden bounded in the north on the land of Sir John Browne, in the south on the garden of Richard Allin, Nathaniel and Matthew Allin and in the west on the sea. Rent 2s 6d

[Plot 42] Sir John Browne a house and garden ground bounded in the north on a lane called Cuniger ditch and in the south on a garden of Richard Major's and in the west on the sea. Rent 5s.

In the east part of St Nicholas Street
[Plot 43] Michael Browne a tenement bounded in the north on a tenement of Henry Russell and in the east on a garden of Henry Russell's and in the south on John Pitt's cellar and John Oates' backside. Rent 1d.

[Plot 44] Henry Russell a house and garden bounded in the south on Michael Browne's house in the north on John Pitt junior's garden, in tenure of Edward Gibson and in the east on the land of the said Henry Russell. Rent 3d.

In the west side of St Thomas Street
[Plot 45] John Barfoote a garden ground bounded in the north on the sea and town ground, in the south on a garden of John Mockett and in the west butting to the sea. Rent 3s.

[Plot 46] John Mockett a garden plot bounded in the north on John Barfoote's garden and in the south on John Pitt senior's garden and in the west butting to the sea. Rent 1s.

[Plot 47] John Pitt senior a tenement and garden plot bounded in the north on John Mockett's garden and in the south on Jeremy Babbidge garden and in the west butting to the sea. Rent 1s.

[Plot 48] Jeremy Babbidge a tenement and garden plot which were several gardens bounded in the north on John Pitt Senior's garden and house and in the south on John Bond's garden and in the west butting to the sea. Rent 2s. 6d.

[Plot 49] John Bond a garden plot bounded in the north on Jeremy Babbidge's garden and in the south on Richard Hill's garden and in the west butting to the sea. Rent 1s.

[Plot 50] Richard Hill a garden plot bounded in the north on John Bond's garden and in the south on a garden of William Holman's and in the west butting to the sea. Rent 1s.

[Plot 51] William Holman a garden plot bounded in the north on Richard

Hill's garden and in the south on the land called the Cunigar ditch and in the west butting to the sea. Rent 1s.

[Plot 52] Thomas Loveles a plot of ground bounded in the north on a lane called Cuniger ditch and in the south on a tenement in the occupation of Robert Godwin sometime Peter Soper's and in the west of St Nicholas Street. Rent 1s 6d.

[Plot 53] Robert Godwin half a burgage and garden plot sometime Peter Soper's in the north on Thomas Lovelis and in the south on John Notlye's garden and in the west of St Nicholas Street. Rent 4d.

[Plot 54] John Notley half a burgage and garden plot sometime Peter Soper's bounded in the north on Robert Godwin and in the south on John Hodge stable and garden and in the west on St Nicholas Street. Rent 4d.

[Plot 55] John Hodge stable and garden sometime Susan Pitt's bounded in the north on John Notley and in the south on a garden of Henry Michell and in the west of St Nicholas Street. Rent 8d.

[Plot 56] Henry Michell a garden plot bounded in the north on a stable of John Hodge and in the south on a garden of John Mockett and in the west on St Nicholas Street. Rent 1s 4d.

[Plot 57] John Mockett a garden plot bounded in the north on Henry Michell and in the south on Robert Major's house and garden and in the west on St Nicholas Street. Rent 4½d.

[Plot 58] Robert Major a house and garden bounded in the north on John Mockett's garden in the south on a garden plot of John Martin's and in the west on St Nicholas Street. Rent 7d.

[Plot 59] John Martin a house and garden bounded in the north on Robert Major's house and garden and in the south on another house and garden of the said John Martin's and in the west on St Nicholas Street. Rent 4d.

[Plot 60] More a house and a garden plot bounded in the north on the said house and garden of the said John Martin and in the south on a lane and in the west on St Nicholas Street. Rent 6d.

[Plot 61] John Bond his dwelling house and garden purchased of Thomas Clyfox bounded in the north on the lane, in the south on another tenement of the said John Bond and in the west of St Nicholas Street, the house at 8d, the garden at 6d. Rent 1s 2d.

[Plot 62] John Bond one tenement sometime the land of [blank] Samways and garden plot to the same bounded in the north on his dwelling house and in the south of John Mockitt's tenement and in the west on St Nicholas Street. Rent 1s 2d.

[Plot 63] John Mockett the northern part of his dwelling house bounded in the north on John Bond's tenement and in the south on the rest of his dwelling house and in the west on St Nicholas Street. Rent 1½d.

[Plot 64] More the south part of his said house bounded in the south on Henry Waltham's house and in the west on St Nicholas Street. Rent 7½d.

[Plot 65] Henry Waltham for his dwelling house sometime part of Thomas Flavell's land bounded in the north on a tenement of John Mockett, in the south on the other part of Thomas Flavell's land in the occupation of John Pitt junior, in the west on St Nicholas Street. Rent 1s 6d.

[page 61]

[Plot 66] John Pitt junior the other part of the said piece of ground now built to a cellar bounded in the south on another land of the said John Pitt's, sometime Thomas Flavell's. Rent 6d.

[Plot 67] John Pitt junior for a house and garden sometime Thomas Flavell's bounded in the north on the ground of the said John Pitt and in the south on the tenement of Henry Russell and in the west of St Nicholas Street. Rent 7½d.

[Plot 68] Henry Russell a tenement sometime Thomas Samways' bounded in the north on John Pitt junior and in the south on a tenement of Thomas Lockier and in the west on a garden plot of the said Henry Russell. Rent 5d.

In the east side of St Thomas Street

[Plot 69] John Pitt junior a cellar purchased Ro. Gregory bounded in the north on a tenement of Henry Waltham's and in the south on a tenement, of Matthew Pitt sometime the widow Samways' and in the east on a house of the said John Pitt. Rent 4d.

[Plot 70] Henry Waltham one tenement bounded in the north on his stable and ground sometime part of an orchard of Mr Owen Reynolds and in the south on a tenement of John Pitt junior and a cellar sometime John Gregory's and in the west on John Reynolds land. Rent 4d.

[Plot 71] Henry Waltham one stable and ground part of an orchard sometime Owen Reynolds on the land of James James in the north, of John Reynolds in the east and his tenement in the occupation of John Richard in the south. Rent 3½d.

[Plot 72] James James the other part of the orchard sometime Owen Reynolds bounded on a garden of James James on the north, the land of Henry Waltham on the South and the land of John Reynolds on the east. Rent 2d.

[Unidentified plot] James James one garden plot bounded between the tenement of the heirs of John Martin on the north and part of the above said orchard, on the south one brewhouse and cellar of John Reynolds and part of James James' house on the east. Rent 9d.

[Plot 73] The heirs of John Martin one tenement bounded on the north on the garden of Mary Pearce and Henry Hopkins, sometime John Samways, on the east of the lands of James James and Mary Pearce and in the south the above named garden of James James. Rent 7d.

[Plot 74] Mary Pearce sometime the wife of Thomas Samways one garden plot bounded in the north of the lands of Thomas Gyer, on the east on the land of Owen Samways and Henry Hopkins and in the south on the land of John Martin. Rent 7d.

[Plot 75] Thomas Giear one garden plot bounded in the south on Mary Pearce garden, in the north on another tenement of the said Thomas Giear in the east on the land of Bartholomew Preston and the heirs of Roger Damon. Rent 3d.

[Plot 76] Thomas Giear for one house and garden bounded on a lane in the north and his own garden in the south and the land of Robert Brine in the east. Rent 6d.

[Plot 77] Elizabeth Russell wife to Joseph Russell a tenement bounded in the east on the land of Mary Harrison wife to Richard Harrison, in the north on a stable of Thomas Gyer's and in the south on a lane. Rent, part of 4d. [The entries for Elizabeth Russell, Mary Harrison and Thomas Gyer are bracketed together with the rent 4d and followed by the text "all three pay", but with no indication as to how this rent was distributed between the holdings].

[Plot 78] Mary Harrison wife to Richard Harrison a tenement bounded in the west on the land of Elizabeth Russell in the north on the land of James Sirrey, in the east on the land of Alice Allin widow and Barbara Randall, in the south on a lane. Rent, part of 4d.

[Plot 79] Thomas Gyer a stable bounded in the north on a stable of James Serrey, in the south on a tenement of the said Elizabeth Russell's and in the east on a backside of Richard Harrison's. Rent part of 4d.

[Plot 80] James Serrey a stable sometime in the tenure of old Gillman, bounded in the north on the land of the said James Serrey, in the South on Thomas Gyer's stable and in the east on the land of Richard Harrison. Rent 2d.

[Plot 81] James Serrey a tenement bounded in the north on the land of Robert Godfrey, in the south and east on his own stable and land. Rent 4d

[Plot 82] Robert Godfrey one tenement bounded in the north on a garden of Richard Allin the elder in the south on a tenement of James Serry and in the east on the land of Richard Hill and James Serry. Rent 6d.

[Plot 83] Richard Allin senior. One garden bounded in the north on a garden of Richard Odye's, in the south on a tenement of Richard Godfrey in the east on the land of the heirs of John Feaver. Rent 4d.

[Plot 84] John Chount and Justinian Hingston one tenement being two dwelling houses bounded in the north on Henry Rose's house, in the south on Alice Allin's garden and in the east on the lands of the heirs of William Whetcombe. Rent 7½d

[Plot 85] Henry Rose one house bounded in the north on a lane by the Cuninger ditch in the south on the tenement of Justinian Hingston and in the east on the land of Henry Backwell. Rent 7½d

[Plot 86] Richard Hill a garden plot bounded in the north on the land of Henry Waltham, in the south on the lane by the Cuniger ditch and in the east on the land of William Bayly part of the same burgage. Rent 2s.

[Plot 87] William Bayly a house and garden being part of Richard Hill's aforesaid in the lane by Cuniger ditch, bounded in the west on the garden of Richard Hill and in the north on the land of Henry Waltham and in the east on the land of William Minterne other part of Richard Hill's aforesaid. Rent 3s.

[Plot 88] Henry Haughte a house bounded in the north on the land of Thomas Lovelis in the south on Henry Waltham's land and in the east on the heirs of Bartholomew Clarke. Rent 5s.

[Plot 89] Thomas Lovelis a tenement bounded in the north on a tenement of his own, in the south on Henry Haught's house and in the east on William Hopkins. Rent 5s

[Plot 90] Thomas Lovelis his dwelling house bounded in the north on a house of Henry Favell's in the south on his own land above said and in the east on the land of William Wilcox. Rent 5s.

[Plot 91] Henry Favell his dwelling house bounded in the north on the land of Thomas Wallis in the south on the house of Thomas Lovelis and in the east on the land of Richard Bolte. Rent 5s.

[page 62]

[Plot 92] Thomas Wallis his dwelling house bounded in the north on a garden of Joyce Vandergassen, in the south on Henry Favell and in the east of the land of the widow Boyte. Rent 5s

In the west of St Mary's Street

[Plot 93] James Frampton, gentleman, a plot of ground bounded in the north on the land of the town's, in the west on St Thomas Street, in the south on a garden of Joyce Vandergassen. 2s.

[Plot 94] Joyce Vandergassen a garden bounded in the north of James Frampton's ground in the west on St Thomas Street and in the South on the land of Thomas Wallis and the widow Boyte. 2s.

[Plot 95] The widow Boyte's house and garden bounded in the north on Joyce Vandergassen's garden in the west of the land of Thomas Wallis and in the south on Richard Boult's house. 5s.

[Plot 96] Richard Boult his dwelling house and garden bounded in the north on the widow Boyte's house, in the west on the land of Henry Clarke and in the south on the land of William Wilcox. 5s.

[Plot 97] William Wilcox his house and garden bound in the north on Richard Boult's tenement, in the west on Thomas Lovelis and in the south on William Hopkins sometime Zachary Martin's. 5s.

[Plot 98] William Hopkins a tenement sometime Zachary Martin's bounded in the north on the tenement of Wilcox in the west on Thomas Lovelis's land, in the south on a tenement of Henry Cox. 1s 8d.

[Plot 99] Henry Cox a tenement sometime Zachary Martin's bounded in the north and south on two tenements of William Hopkins and in the west on Thomas Lovelis's land. 1s 4d.

[Plot 100] William Hopkins a tenement sometime Zachary Martin's bounded in the north on a tenement of Henry Cox, in the south on a tenement of the said William Hopkins and in the west on Thomas Lovelis's land. 2s.

[Plot 101] William Hopkins a tenement sometime John Knapp bounded in the north on his tenement above said, in the south on a tenement of the heirs of Bartholomew Clarcke, on the west on Henry Haught's land. 2s 6d.

[Plot 102] The heirs of Bartholomew Clarcke a tenement bounded in the north on William Hopkins' tenement, in the south on a burgage of Henry Waltham and in the west on Henry Haught's land. 2s 6d.

[Plot 103] Henry Waltham a tenement bounded in the north on Henry Haught's tenement of the heirs of Bartholomew Clarcke, on the west St Thomas Street and in the south on the land of William Minterne, William Bayly and Richard

Hill. 10s.

[Plot 104] William Minterne his dwelling house and garden being sometime part of Richard Hill's garden plot, bounded in the north on a burgage of Henry Waltham's, in the west of William Baylive's house and garden, in the south on a land called Cuniger ditch. 5s 0½d.

[Plot 105] Henry Backwaye one tenement bounded in the north on a lane called Cuniger ditch in the west on the land of Henry Rose, in the south on the heirs of William Whetcombe. 7½d.

[Plot 106] The heirs of William Whetcombe one tenement bounded in the north on a tenement of Henry Backway, in the west on a tenement of John Chount and Justinian Hingston, in the south on a house and garden of Alice Allin widow. 7½d.

[Plot 107] Alice Allin, widow, a burgage bounded in the north on a tenement of the heirs of William Wetcombe and John Chount's tenement and in the west on St Thomas Street and in the south on a tenement of Richard Ody. 1s 8d.

[Plot 108] Richard Odye a tenement sometime John Allin's senior bounded in the north on the tenement of Alice Allin widow, in the west on St Thomas Street, in the south on a tenement of the heirs of Barbara Randall and a garden of Richard Allin senior. 1s 4d

[Plot 109] The heirs of Barbara Randall one tenement sometime John Feaver's bounded in the north on the house and garden of Richard Odye, in the west on Richard Allin's garden, in the south on a garden of Richard Hill. 4½d

[Plot 110] Richard Hill a garden plot sometime Jo. Bryer's bounded in the north on the heirs of Barbara Randall, in the west on a tenement of the heirs of Robert Godfrey in the south on the house and backside of James Serry. 4½d.

[Plot 111] James Serry a house and backside sometime William Holman's bounded in the north on a garden plot of Richard Hill's, in the west on his own land, in the south on the land of the heirs of Barbara Randall. 4½d.

[Plot 112] The heirs of Barbara Randall her dwelling house and backside sometime a garden of John Feaver's, bounded in the north on the dwelling house of James Serry, in the west on the land of Richard Harryson and in the south on a dwelling house of Alice Allin widow. 7d.

[Plot 113] Alice Allin widow a dwelling house and a cellar sometime John Feaver's shop, bounded in the north on the tenement of the heirs of Barbara Randall, in the west on the land of the heirs of Richard Harryson and in the south on a lane. 7½d.

[Plot 114] The heirs of William Bryne one burgage bounded in the north on a lane, in the west on the house and part of garden of Thomas Gyer in the south on a tenement of Thomasin Damon, widow. 4½d.

[Plot 115] Thomasin Damon a dwelling house and backside bounded in the north on the land of the heirs of William Bryne, in the south on the land of the heirs of Daniel Gregory and Bartholomew Preston, in the west on part of Thomas Gyer's land. 4d.

[Plot 116] The heirs of Daniel Gregory one tenement and backside bounded in the north on the house and part of a backside of Tamson Damon, in the south on a tenement of Owen Samwayes and in the west on a tenement of the heirs of Bartholomew Preston and part of Thomas Gyer's garden. 6d.

[page 63]

[Plot 117] The heirs of Bartholomew Preston one tenement and backside late parcel of the land which was Daniel Gregory's, bounded in the east on St Mary Street and part of on the backside of the said Daniel Gregory in the north of the land of Thomasin Damon, in the west on a garden of Thomas Gyer and in the south on the land of the said Daniel Gregory the rent [illegible word] is paid in the heirs of Daniel Gregory's land.

[Plot 118] One tenement backside and garden sometime John Samwayes and now divided into three parts viz: to Owen Samwayes, Henry Hopkins and Mary Pierce widow, bounded in the north on the heirs Owen Gregory's land and part of Thomas Giear's garden, in the south on a tenement of James James and Anthony Martin and in the west on the land of the said Mary Peers. All three paid 9½d.

[Plot 119] James James dwelling house and two backsides bounded in the north on Mary Pearce and part on the heirs of John Martin and in the south on John Reynolds house, backside and cellar and in the west on the end of John Martin and his own garden. 10d.

[Plot 120] John Reynolds dwelling house and backside bounded in the north on the dwelling house and stable of James James, in the south on a shop of the said John Reynolds, in the west on the land of James James. 1s 1d.

[Plot 121] More one shop in the occupation of William Comfry bounded in the north on John Reynolds, in the south and west on the said John Reynolds land and garden. 6d.

[Plot 122] More one shop, garden and stable bounded in the north on his dwelling house and Comfry's shop and in the south on Richard Major, Matthew Pitt and Henry Waltham and in the west on James and Henry Waltham. 1s.

In the east side of St Mary's Street.

[Plot 123] John Pitt junior for the long cellar bounded in the north on the town hall yard and part on Barnard Michell's cellar and in the east on the land of the said John Pitt sometime John Mounsell's. 1s.

[Plot not numbered] A room built over the walk now the Custom House being the town land bounded on the west on the end of the town hall which is let out for £1 6s 8d.

[Plot 124] Barnard Michell a cellar bounded in the south on John Pitt junior's long cellar and in the north on the town hall and in the east on the town hall's backside. 1s.

[Plot 125] John Pitt the elder his dwelling house and backside bounded in the south on the house and backside of Edward Hodder, in the north on the churchyard, in the east on the land of George Holliday and Thomas Gould. 1s 3d

[Plot not numbered] The church and churchyard bounded in the south on the land of John Pitt senior and George Holliday and in the north on the land of William

Holman and in the east into Mayden Street.

[Plot 126] William Holman, a tenement and backside bounded in the north on his dwelling house, in the south on the churchyard and in the east on Mayden Street. 4d.

[Plot 127] More his dwelling house and backside bounded in the south on his other tenement and backside and in the north on Robert Knight's dwelling house and backside and in the east on Mayden Street. 7½d.

[Plot 128] Robert Knight's dwelling house and backside bounded in the south on William Holman's dwelling house and backside and in the north on a lane and in the east on Mayden Street. 7d.

[Plot 129] Richard Allin junior his dwelling house bounded in the north on a tenement of Richard Hill and the heirs of Richard Shepham, in the south on a lane and the west on Madon Street. 8d.

[Plot 130] Richard Hill one tenement bounded in the south part on Richard Allin's dwelling house and backside and the other part on the heirs of Richard Shepham's house bought of the said Richard Hill and in the north part on the land of John Roodwort and part on the land of the heirs of Roger Barnes and in the east part on Maydon Street and part on Richard Shepham's house. 3½d.

[Plot 131] John Redwood part of a tenement sometime Richard Chown's bounded in the south on Richard Hill's tenement and the heirs of Roger Barnes part of Richard Chowne's and in the north on Richard Chowne's part of the same and in the east on Mayden Street and on the heirs of Roger Barnes part. 4½d.

[Plot 132] Richard Chowne for an other part of his father's tenement bounded in the south on John Redwood's sometime part of this tenement and in the north on a tenement of the widow Godsould's and in the east on Mayden Street. 1½d.

[Plot 133] William Godsole one tenement and garden plot bounded in the south on Richard Chowne's tenement, in the north on a tenement of John Wheadon and in the east on Mayden Street. 7½d.

[Plot 134] John Weadon one tenement bounded in the south on widow Godsole's, in the north on a garden plot of David Tompson's, in the east on Mayden Street. 6s 8d.

[Plot 135] David Tompson one garden plot bounded in the south on John Wheaden in the north on the heirs of Jo. Lyle and in the east on Mayden Street. 5s.

[Plot 136] The heirs of Jo. Lyle a garden plot bounded in the south on Davy Tompson's garden plot and in the north on the land called Cuniger ditch and in the east on Mayden Street. 1d.

[Plot 137] Simon Godfrey a plot of ground bounded in the south on the lane called Cuniger ditch and in the north on his dwelling house and in the east on his own land. 1s.

[Plot 138] Simon Godfry his dwelling house being two tenements bounded in the north on Edward Chappell house, in the south on the above said plot of ground and part of a lane and in the east on New Street. 6s 8d.

[Plot 139] John Keeche's tenement bounded in the south on Simon Godfrey's house, in the north on the burgage of the heirs of Jacob Procter, in the east on New

Street. 5s.

[Plot 140] The heirs of Jacob Procter a burgage bounded in the south on John Keeche's house and garden and part on St Mary's Street, in the north on French Catherine's heir's house and garden and in the east on New Street. 5s.

[Plot 141a] Bernard Stone for part of a burgage bounded in the south on the heirs of Jacob Procter's land, in the north on Thomas Adam's tenement, in the east on New Street. 1s 8d.

[Plot 141b] John Read for one other part of the said burgage. 1s 9d.

[Plot 141c] John Justice for one other part of the aforesaid burgage. 1s 9d.

[page 64]

[Plot 142] Thomas Adam's tenement bounded in the south on the tenement of French Catherine, in the north on the land in the west on the New Street. 3s 4d.

[Plot 143] Thomas Lockyer a plot of ground bounded in the south on the land to the blockhouse, in the north on the land of the heirs of Lodwin, in the east on New Street. 5s.

[Plot 144] Heirs of Lodwin bounded in the south on Thomas Lockyer's land, in the north on a tenement of William Chubb's, in the east on New Street. 1d.

[Plot 145] William Chubb a house and backside bounded in the south on the heirs of William Lodwin, in the north on John Warr, in the east on New Street. 1s 8d.

[Plot 146] John Warr his house and backside sometime Marshall's land bounded in the south on William Chubb on the said John Warr and in the east in New Street. 1s 8d.

[Plot 147] John Warr a plot of ground bounded in the south on his other land, in the north on John Hingston, in the east on New Street. 3s 4d.

[Plot 148] John Hingston half of a burgage bounded in the south on John Warr, in the north on William Smith, in the east on New Street. 1s 8d.

[Plot 149] William Smith the other half of a burgage bounded in the south on John Hingston, in the north on William Hopkins, in the east on New Street. 1s 8d.

[Plot 150] William Hopkins a house and backside bounded in the south on William Smith, in the north on a piece of ground sometime John Keyes, in the east on New Street. 3s 4d.

[Plot 151] John Keyes a void piece of ground bounded in the south of William Hopkins, in the north on Peter Joy and in the east on New Street. 3s 4d.

[Plot 152] Peter Joy his house and backside bounded in the south on John Keyes, in the north on his new plot of ground, in the east on New Street. 3s 4d.

[Plot 153] More one new plot of ground in the south on his old tenement, in the north on the town land and in the east upon the sands. 1s.

In the west side of Mayden Street

[Plot 154] The heirs of Roger Barnes, sometime part of a burgage of Richard Chowne, bounded in the north and west on John Redwood and in the south on Richard Hill's house. 1½d.

[Plot 155] The heirs of Richard Shepham sometime part of Richard Hill's burgage bounded in the north and west in the south on Richard Allin junior. 4d.

[Plot 156] George Holiday a tenement bounded in the north on the churchyard, in the south on Thomas Gould, in the west on John Pitt senior. 5s.

[Plot 157] Thomas Gould his tenement, sometime Holton's land bounded in the north on George Holliday, in the south on Alice Allin, in the west on John Pitt senior and exchanged with the town for the south part of the churchyard. 3d.

In the east side of Mayden Street

[Plot 158] Richard Allin now Elizabeth Mico his tenement bounded in the south on the quay, in the north on Mr Churchill's garden, in the east on a void plot of Samuel Allin's and in the west part on a tenement of the said Meco and part on the town quay. 6d.

[Plot 159] More one plot of ground bounded in the south on the town quay, in the north on John Churchill's cellar, in the east on the said Elizabeth Mico. 6d.

[Plot 160] John Churchill his cellar sometime Rives' cellar and garden plot bounded in the south on Elizabeth Mico's land, in the north on a lane, in the east on John Pitt junior's yard, the cellar paid 7d, and the garden 4d. [Total] 11d.

[Plot 161] Barnard Michell his dwelling house bounded in the south on the lane, in the north on his garden, in the east part on a tenement of Giles Greene called hell and part on a tenement of his own. 6d.

[Plot 162] More a tenement in the said lane bounded in the west on his said dwelling house, in the east on Giles Greene's, in the north on his backside. 3d.

[Plot 163] More a garden plot bounded in the south on his dwelling house and backside, in the north on his land purchased of Holton, in the east on the land of the heirs of William Pocum which was sometime Martin's. 6d.

[Plot 164] More his house and land bought of Holton bounded in the south on his own land and Pocum's land, in the north on another tenement bought of Holton on the east. 1s 7½d.

[Plot 165] More one other tenement bought of the said Holton sometime Newtons bounded in the north on the friary land, in the south on the land of the said Barnard Mitchell bought of Holton and in the east on [space left for missing word]. 6d.

[Plot 166] For the friary land purchased of the King 2s 6d.

[Plot not numbered] For Milton Hould, 7½d.

[Plot 167] For a plot of ground that Mitchell's pigs house stood on. 4½d.

[Plot 168] For all the ground land and tenements lying behind the said priory directly eastwards to the low water mark. 3s 2½d.

[Plot 169] The heirs of Richard Peers a burgage bounded in the south on a lane, in the north on William Bryne sailor's house and in the east on New Street. 6d.

[Plot 170] William Bryne sailor, a burgage in the right of his wife, bounded in the south on the heirs of Richard Peers alias Gooddard's land, in the north on the heirs of Catherine Watson's by Davy Tompson their house and in the east on New Street. 3d.

[Plot 171] The heirs of Katherine Watson by Davy Tompson her second husband, their house and backside bounded in the south on William Bryne's land, in the north on Margery Pullen's house and in the east on New Street. 3d.

[page 65]

[Plot 172] Margery Pullen's a tenement bounded in the south on Katherine Watson's heirs above said, in the north on a tenement of Richard Allin junior and in the east on New Street. 6d.

[Plot 173] Richard Allin junior a tenement bounded in the south on Margery Pullen's land, in the north on Grace Wilford's tenement and in the east on New Street. 3d.

[Plot 174] Grace Wilford a tenement bounded in the south on Richard Allin junior's tenement and in the north on the heirs of Bellinger Preston, in the east on New Street. 7d.

[Plot 175] The heirs of Bellinger Preston a burgage and garden plot being two burgages bounded in the south on the heirs of Justinian Wilford's tenement, in the north on a tenement of John Redwood and in the east on New Street. 1s 4d.

[Plot 176] John Ridout [possibly Redwood] part of a garden plot bounded in the south on the heirs of Bellinger Preston's land, in the north on the other part being Tamsy Damon's and in the east on New Street. 1s 3d.

[Plot 177] Tamsey Damon the other part of the garden plot bounded in the south on John Roodword's garden, in the north part on a garden plot of Thomas Parkins and part on Joyce Vandergasen's garden and in the east on New Street. 1s 3d.

[Plot 178] Thomas Parkins a garden plot bounded in the south on Tamsey Damon's garden and in the north and east on Joyce Vandergooson's land. 6d.

[Plot 179] Joyce Vandergoosen his dwelling house and backside bounded in the south on Thomas Parkins and Tamsey Damon, in the north on Jacob Vandergosen part on the lane and part on Leonard Hillard's house and in the east on Leonard Hillard's and part on New Street. 1s.

[Plot 180] Jacob Vandergoosen his dwelling house bounded in the south and east on Joyce Vandergoosen's land and in the north on the lane. 6d.

[Plot 181] The heirs of Leonard Hillard their dwelling house bounded in the south and west on Joyce Vanderoosen's land, in the north on the lane and in the west of New Street. 6d

In the East of New Street

[Plot not numbered] The blockhouse containing 45 foot north and south, 45 foot east and west, westland on south of the block house containing [blank] foot north and south being the town's land. No rate.

[Plot 182] Jacob Proctor a plot of void ground bounded in the north on the void ground of the town's, in the south on Simon Godfrey's stable and backside, in the east upon the sand. No rate

[Plot 183] Simon Godfrey a stable and backside bounded in the north on the heirs of Jacob Proctor's land, in the south on the heirs of Nicholas Hunt's house and backside and in the east on the sands. 5s.

[Plot 184] The heirs of Nicholas Hunt's house and backside bounded in the north on Simon Godfrye's stable, in the south on a lane and in the east on the sands. 5s.

[Plot 185] Simon Hickman a tenement bounded in the north on the lane, in the south on a tenement of Mark Palfry, in the east on the sand. 2s 6d.

[Plot 186] Mark Palfry's tenement bounded in the north on Simon Hickman's, in the south on John Hannon's tenement, in the east on the sand. 2s 6d.

[Plot 187] John Hamon a tenement bounded in the north of Mark Palfry in the south on the parsonage house, in the east on the sand. 5s.

[Plot 188] The Parsonage house bounded in the north on John Hamon's tenement, in the south on widow Woodd's tenement, in the east on the sands. 5s.

[Plot 189] Widow Wood's tenement bounded in the north on the parsonage house, in the south on Edith Clarck's tenement, in the east on the sands. 5s.

[Plot 190] Edith Clarck's tenement in the occupation of Robert Short bounded in the north on the widow Wood's tenement, in the south on John Derbye's tenement, in the east on the sands. 5s.

[Plot 191] John Derby one tenement bounded in the north on Edith Clarck's tenement, in the south on the town's land in the occupation of Thomas Welman and Nicholas Jarvis, in the east on the sands. 5s.

[Plot 192] The town a tenement in the occupation of Thomas Welman and Nicholas Jarvis, bounded in the north on John Darbye's tenement, in the south on John Clarck's tenement, in the east on the sands. 5s.

[Plot 193] John Clarcke a tenement bounded in the north on the town's tenement, in the south on William Holman's garden, in the east on the sands. 2s.

[Plot 194] William Holman a garden bounded in the north on John Clarck's tenement, in the south on a stable of Matthew Allin's, in the east on other land of his. 1s.

[Plot 195] Matthew Allin's part of a stable bounded in the north on William Holman in the south on Richard Allin junior, in the east on Richard Allin's land, sometime Gooddance. 8d.

[Plot 195] Richard Allin junior the other part of the stable bounded in the north on Matthew Allin, in the south on a garden and a house of the heirs of Richard Scott, in the east a tenement sometime Edward Gooddance. 8d.

[Plot 196] Ann Hawkins a tenement and garden bounded in the north on a garden of the heirs of Richard Scott, in the south on a lane by the Friary, in the east on a tenement of the heirs of Henry Lyne in the west on West Street. 1s.

[Plot 197] The heirs of Henry Lyne one tenement bounded in the west on Ann Hawkins' tenement, in the east on a tenement of Roger Ossett's, in the north on Richard Scott's heir's land and in the south on the lane. 6d.

[Plot 198] Roger Ossett a tenement bounded in the west on the heirs of Henry Lyne, in the south a lane and in the east on East Street, in the north on Richard Scott's heir's house and garden. 6d.

In the East Street

[Plot 199] Richard Scott a house and garden on west side bounded [sic] , in the south on a tenement of Roger Ossett, the heirs of Henry Lyne and Ann Hawkins, in the north on a stable and garden of Richard Allin junior, in the west on New Street. 1s 4d.

[Plot 200?] A tenement sometime Edith Gooddance, bounded in the west of Richard Allin junior and Matthew Allin, in the north on a plot of ground of William Holman's, in the east on the sands and in the south on the end of East Street. [No rate provided].

[Plot 200?] William Holman a plot of ground bounded in the west on his own garden, in the north and east on the same and in the south on the [word missing] sometime Edward Gooddance. [No rate provided].

[Plot 201] Robert Knight a tenement bounded in the north and east on the sands, in the south on a lane and in the west on East Street. 5s.

[Plot 202] Thomas Gould a garden plot bounded in the north on Mayden Lane [Friary Lane on map], in the south and west on Mr Michell's land, sometime Holton's and in the east on the land which rent is contained in Thomas Gould's rent for his house in Mayden Street. [No rate provided].

[Plot 203] Heirs of William Pocum. A tenement bounded in the east on a lane towards the sea, in the north on the land of Barnard Michell, sometime Holton's and in the west on the land of Barnard Michell, in the south on the land of Giles Greene. 6d.

[Plot 204] Giles Green a tenement called hell bounded in the east on the lane towards the sea, in the south on a lane called hell, in the north on the land of the heirs of Barnard Michell, the heirs of William Pocum and in the west on the land of Barnard Michell. 1½d.

[page 66]

[Plot 205] John Pitt junior part of a plot of ground now paled in bounded in the east on the sea, in the north on a lane, in the west of John Churchill's land and in the south on the haven and part on the other part of this plot of ground belonging to Samuel Allin. 1s 4d.

[Plot 206] Samuel Allin the other part of this plot of ground bounded in the north on that part of the same ground belonging to John Pitt, in the south on the haven, in the west of the dwelling house of Elizabeth Mico. 8d.

Matthew Pitt for the rent of the Upper Mill at Causway and of the ground thereunto belonging, sometime in the tenure of John Buckler. Forty shillings to be paid quarterly. £2 os od.

The names of such tradesmen and artificers as have liberty for them, their children and apprentices to use only their trade within this town being no freeman within the same.

Tailors	John Pettye	William Williams
Thomas Bigge	Richard Ody	John Deane
Thomas Andrewes	William Comfry	Ship carpenters
John Notley	Hugh Trewin	Roger Marques
Thomas Samways	Laurence Sanger	John Justice
Roger Gill	Jerome Locke	Robert Brunstone
Henry Backway	Coopers	Robert Wilson
Richard Harvest	Thomas Cornish	John Frampton
Robert Parmyter	John Rickman	George Pitt

Roger Ossett
Thomas Ledoze
John Damon
John Watercombe
Francis Motyer
Thomas Kneeler
William Valence
[the division between
    Ship carpenters and
    weavers is not clear.
    The following seven
    apprentices could be
    in either category].
Thomas Parmyter
Robert Bennett
Weavers
Thomas Crane
Edmund Scriven
Edmund Warren
Richard Boult
Joiners
David Fippen
Henry Cox
John Derby
Henry Hedmore
William Cox
Abel Fippen

Bakers
John Wheaden
Edward Allen
Robert Locke
Simon Godfry
Richard Brooke
Henry Taunton 20
    October 1626
Shoemakers
James Ledoze
John Bagg
Henry Gregory
Reynold Vervill
John Pope
James Chappell
Robert Fudge
Joseph Mannders 12
    October 1626
Blacksmiths
Nicholas Boult
Thomas Webber
Surgeons
Edward Gibson
William Hunt
Wheeler
William Browne

Butchers
Maximilian Loader
Thomas Barnes
Thomas Hingston
Richard Hicke
Edward Harvy
Henry Hopkins
John Hingston
Justinian Hingston
Walter Bythewood
Tanners
John Dry
Thomas Gardner
John Samwayes
Samuel Tackell
John Combes
John Ford
William Clarke
William Tackle
Chapman
John Shute
Brazier
John Warr
Hellier
James Spicer
William Brighte
William Smith
Bartholomew Payne

[page 67] An assembly held in the Guildhall of Melcombe Regis within the borough and town of Weymouth and Melcombe Regis in the county of Dorset by the mayor, aldermen, bailiffs and capital or principal burgesses of the borough and town aforesaid the tenth day of March 1620.

At this assembly it was and is agreed by a general consent of the mayor, aldermen, bailiffs and capital or principal burgesses aforesaid that Roger Growte now prisoner in this town Prison shall be allowed two pence every day out of the town stock towards his relief during the time of his imprisonment.

Memorandum That it was agreed at this assembly that Mr Mayor and some of the aldermen of this town may repair at the next assizes unto Mr Recorder with the town charter and entreat him to go with them unto the Lord Chief Baron and move an allowance of the town charter and a dismissal of the constables from their attendance at the assizes according to the same charter and that what charge shall be laid forth by Mr Mayor therein shall be hence forward allowed and paid by the town.

Memorandum that at the same assembly it was also agreed that the constables of this town shall be allowed 13s 4d of their bill of charges spent at the last assizes and that at the next assizes they shall have nothing.

12 April 1620

At an assembly held the day and year last aforesaid by a general consent of the mayor, aldermen, bailiffs and capital or principal burgesses aforesaid it was and is agreed that Jeremy Babbidge from henceforth until the feast day of St Michael the Archangel next coming shall collect and gather the ballast monies and duties upon forfeits of constitutions touching the cleansing and keeping clean of the quays and haven, to the use of the Corporation.

Upon the same day and year it was and is likewise agreed by a general consent of the mayor, aldermen, bailiffs and capital or principal burgesses aforesaid that Henry Hillerd from henceforth until the feast Day of St Michael the Archangel next coming shall collect and gather the profits duties and fees which shall be due for the cartage etc. to the use of this Corporation.

Upon the same day and year it was and is likewise agreed by the like general consent that the law shall be executed against William Mounsell's refusal upon his last year's bond as upon this year's bond.

14 April 1620.

At an assembly held the day and year last aforesaid it was and is agreed by a general consent of the mayor, aldermen, bailiffs and capital or principal burgesses aforesaid that the writs already penned concerning the release of shipping under the purveyors auspices shall be sent unto the Lords of His Majesty's Most Honourable Privy Council by John Pope or some other messenger to be gotten by Mr Mayor and that the charge shall be borne as well by the Corporation as by the owners of ships now bound forth in their voyage unto the Newfoundland and that Mr Mayor shall agree with the messenger for his pains and shall deliver him two pieces to be given to Sir Clement Edmonds, clerk of the Council to solicit the content of those Lordships unto their God.

[page 68] 5 May 1620

At an assembly held in the Guildhall of Melcombe Regis within the borough and town of Waymouth and Melcombe Regis in the county of Dorset by the mayor, aldermen, bailiffs and capital or principal burgesses of the said borough and town it was and is ordered and agreed by a general consent that James James, now farmer of the profits and duties of the bridge, shall set a workman on work about the roping of the bridge and that the receiver of the town duties shall pay the workman his wages.

14 June 1620

At an assembly held by the mayor, aldermen, bailiffs and capital or principal burgesses of this borough and town of Waymouth and Melcombe Regis it was and is agreed by a general consent that if Mr Mayor be compelled by the Lords of His Majesty's

Most Honourable Privy Council to make present payment of the two hundred and twenty five pounds for the second payment towards His Majesty's intended expedition against the Turks, then upon taking up of the same monies the revenues of this town shall be engaged for the repayment thereof and of the interest for the forbearing thereof for so long time as it shall be taken up.

28 July 1620

At an assembly held by the mayor, aldermen, bailiffs and capital or principal burgesses of this borough and town of Waymouth and Melcombe Regis it was and is agreed by a general consent that Mr Mayor shall give entertainment unto such Lords with their followers as are appointed to and shall come to view the quarry of Portland and that the same entertainment shall be borne at the charge of this Corporation.

27 September 1620

At an assembly held by the mayor, aldermen, bailiffs and capital or principal burgesses of this borough and town of Waymouth and Melcombe Regis it was and is agreed that the petition drawn by Mr Recorder to be exhibited to his Majesty concerning a benevolence towards the erecting and building of the mouldhead at the north shall be engrossed and sent up unto Mr Recorder with a writ where on it shall be signified to him that he shall have fifty pounds from the Corporation if he can procure such allowance as is petitioned.

At the same assembly it was and is agreed by the said mayor, aldermen, bailiffs and capital or principal burgesses that Mr John Pitt the elder, shall collect the petty customs, anchorage, quayage and other duties (which he collected this last year) from the feast of St Michael the Archangel next coming for one whole year then following and shall enter into bond for the true collecting, gathering and answering of them quarterly as he did this last year. And for his pains to be taken therein he shall be allowed ten pounds for the whole year that is to say fifty shillings every quarter.

[page 69] 21 September 1620

Upon this present day Mr John Bond is elected mayor of this borough and town of Waymouth and Melcombe Regis for this year following.

Upon the same day Mr Giles Green and Mr James James are elected bailiffs of the same borough and town for the year following.

Upon the same day Thomas Wallis, Thomas Gardner, David Gyer and William Charitie are elected constables of the same borough and town for this year.

Upon the same day Mr Edward Lynsey is chosen receiver of the rents, revenues and profits of this borough and town for the year following according to the form, intent and purport of a constitution thereof heretofore made.

Upon the same day Mr Giles Green, Mr James James, bailiffs elected, Mr Edward Roy, Mr Henry Waltham, David Gyer and William Charitie are chosen auditors for the accounts for the town's revenues for this year following according to the form of a former constitution thereof heretofore made.

28 September 1620

Upon this present day it was and is agreed by a general consent of the mayor, aldermen, bailiffs and capital burgesses of this borough and town that the rope groats shall be collected by Mr John Pitt the elder for this year following for which he shall be answerable as he is for the petty customs and other duties which he is to collect for the town.

Upon the same day the profits of the market were granted unto John Reade for the year following at the rent of five pounds and ten shillings.

Upon the same day the cartage, bridge groats and drawing of the bridge were granted unto Henry Hillerd for this year following at the rent of fifteen pounds and five shillings upon this condition, that he shall not make any composition with any person touching the passage of carts of iron bound wheels over the bridge but shall take the ordinary rate of four pence for every time any shall pass over.

Upon the same day the ballast and forfeitures of the Constitutions touching the quays and harbour were granted unto Mr John Pitt the younger for this year following at the rent of six pounds.

Upon the same day Matthew Allin alias Belpitt and William Hopkins entered into bond unto this Corporation in £20 for the payment of £48 8s to the use of the poor of Melcombe side upon the feast of St Michael the Archangel 1621.

Upon the same day Edward Roy and Robert White the elder, entered into bond unto this Corporation in £30 for the payment of £15 10s 4d to the use of the poor of Melcombe side upon the feast Day of St Michael the Archangel 1621.

Upon the same day the said Edward Roy and Robert White the elder, entered into bond unto this Corporation in £56 for the payment of £30 5s 6d to the use of the poor of Waymouth side upon the feast Day of St Michael the Archangel 1621.

[page 70] An assembly held in the Guildhall of Melcombe Regis within the borough and town of Waymouth and Melcombe Regis in the county of Dorset by the mayor, aldermen, bailiffs and capital or principal burgesses of the said borough and town the thirteenth day of October 1620 in the year of His Majesty James of England etc. the eighteenth and Scotland 54th.

At this assembly it was and is agreed by a general consent of the said mayor, aldermen, bailiffs and capital or principal burgesses that there shall be a pound at the charge of the Corporation near unto Melcombe Blockhouse. And that Mr Edward Hodder and Mr Edward Lynsey shall have the oversight of the doing thereof and that they shall not neglect their pains in the overseeing thereof to be done by Allhallowtide next upon pain of either of them to forfeit unto this Corporation 10s.

At this assembly it was and is also agreed by the like general consent that Thomas Welman shall hold the house wherein he dwells for the term of his life paying yearly to this Corporation the rent or sum of two shillings and six pence of current English money at the feast of St Michael the Archangel or within ten days then next following, and keeping the said house sufficiently repaired from time to time during the said term. And it is provided that he shall not make any fire in the same house until he has made a sufficient mantle there.

An assembly held in the Guildhall of Melcombe Regis within the borough and town of Waymouth and Melcombe Regis in the county of Dorset by the mayor, aldermen, bailiffs and capital or principal burgesses of the said borough and town the twentieth day of October 1620 In the year of Our Lord Majesty James, England etc. twenty eighth and Scotland 54th.

At this assembly is was and is constituted, ordered and agreed by a general consent of the said mayor, aldermen, bailiffs and capital or principal burgesses of the said borough and town that from henceforth so much of a former Constitution heretofore made and agreed upon the first day of December in the year of our Lord 1617, and in the year of the reign of our sovereign lord James the King's Majesty that now is. That is to say of England, France and Ireland the fifteenth and of Scotland the one and fiftieth before entered in the tenth page, as doth concern the election and choice of auditors touching the accounts of the revenues and profits of the said borough and town. That is to say the election and choice of the two bailiffs elected, two capital and principal burgesses and ten of the commonalty shall herein be utterly void and of none effect to all intents, considerations and purposes. And that from henceforth always and from time to time on the feast Day of St Matthew the Apostle at the time of the choice of the mayor and bailiffs for the said borough and town for the year following, there shall be elected and chosen by the said mayor, aldermen, bailiffs and capital or principal burgesses six auditors, that is to say, the two bailiffs then elected, one alderman and three of the said capital or principal burgesses, and that they six, five or four of them shall, for one year after such choice, audit all the accounts touching and concerning the revenues, profits of the same town unaudited and it is further ordained constituted and agreed that all things else contained in the said former Constitutions shall stand in force to all intents and purposes, according to the true intent and meaning thereof, under such pains and penalties as in the same Constitution are limited and expressed, anything herein contained to the contrary thereof notwithstanding.

[page 71] 27 October 1620

At an assembly held the day and year above said it was and is agreed by the mayor, aldermen, bailiffs and capital or principal burgesses of the borough and town of Waymouth and Melcombe Regis aforesaid that the receiver of the town's revenues shall pay Margaret Payge, widow, 20s for the jurors dinners at the last Law day held in Waymouth.

At the same assembly held by the said mayor, aldermen, bailiffs and capital or principal burgesses it was and is ordered and agreed that every of the porters shall give and deliver unto Mr Mayor for the time being and so from time to time yearly for a yearly fine, one good fat capon or eighteen pence in money, at the choice of the mayor which capon or 18d shall be paid yearly upon St Thomas Day before Christide. And that the same porters shall be bound upon their oaths that they would impound all such pigs as they shall see abroad in the streets of this town and that they shall take for their pains therein according to a rate made by a former order in that behalf provided.

27 November 1620
At an assembly held the day and year above said it was and is agreed by the mayor, aldermen, bailiffs and capital or principal burgesses of the borough and town of Waymouth and Melcombe Regis aforesaid that the water coming down from St Thomas Street and St Edmonds Street shall from henceforth be carried above ground and no more to have her course underground between Mr Powlett's' house end and Jeremy Babbidge his yard if it can be so conveniently carried above ground. And that Mr Thomas Lockier and Mr Edward Linsey shall oversee the work and that Mr Linsey shall pay the charge out of the town revenues.

19 March 1621
At an assembly held the day and year above said it was and is agreed by the mayor, aldermen, bailiffs and capital or principal burgesses of the borough and town of Waymouth and Melcombe Regis aforesaid. That there shall be forty pounds laid forth of the Corporation money about the repairing of the town boat and harbour with all convenient speed and that Mr Robert White, Mr Henry Russell, Mr John Pitt senior and Mr Matthew Allin, Jeremy Babbidge and John Pope shall be the overseers and directors of the same work. And that there shall be a proceeding in the work of the mould head and jetty and that the same shall be done by contribution of labour of all persons, freeholders, tenants, inhabitants and residents within the same. And that every of them shall provide so many workmen from time to time, to work by turn towards the doing thereof as the said Mr White, Mr Russell, Mr Pitt, Mr Allin, Jeremy Babbidge and John Pope or the greater number of them shall rate and assess them at. And that the same labourers shall be provided by every of them severally at such days as they shall be summoned and warned for that service by the sergeants of the same town, or by any one of them. And that whosoever shall neglect to provide his labourer or labourers according to their order, shall forfeit 12d for every fault to be levied by distress upon warrant of the mayor for the time being to be made unto the sergeants in that behalf. Provided that the mayor and bailiffs or two of them at the least, whereof the mayor to be one, shall ratify and confirm the same rate before it be put in execution.

Upon the day and year above said Robert Pitt, by a general consent, is admitted to be a freeman of this town for 20s fine which he is appointed to pay upon tomorrow and then to receive the oath of a freeman.

[page 72] An assembly held in the Guildhall of Melcombe Regis within the borough and town of Waymouth and Melcombe Regis in the county of Dorset by the mayor, aldermen, bailiffs and capital and principal burgesses of the borough and town the twentieth day of July 1621 in the year of our lord King James of England etc. the nineteenth and Scotland the 54th.

At this assembly it was and is agreed by a general consent of the said mayor, aldermen, bailiffs and capital and principal burgesses that there shall be paid by the receiver or receivers of the revenues of this town, the sum of twenty pounds out of the stock of this town before the feast of St Michael the Archangel next coming towards the building of Waymouth Chapel, and the like sum of twenty pounds out of the same stock before the feast of Easter next coming towards the building of Melcombe Church which monies so to be paid by the same receiver or receivers shall be allowed unto him or them upon his or their account or accounts.

10 August 1621

At an assembly the day and year above said it was and is agreed by the mayor, aldermen, bailiffs and capital or principal burgesses of the borough and town of Waymouth and Melcombe Regis aforesaid that Joseph Maunders paying unto the receiver of this town ten shillings upon the 17th day of this instant month shall be admitted to use his art or mystery or manual occupation of a shoemaker and to keep open shop within this town.

Upon the same day Mr David Gyer is nominated and chosen to be one of the capital and principal burgesses of this borough and town in the stead and place of Richard Allin alias Belpitt the elder, deceased, and upon the 21st day of September then next following he was sworn a burgess.

Upon the same day it was and is agreed by a general consent of the mayor, aldermen, bailiffs and capital or principal burgesses that Mr William Mounsell shall from henceforth be dismissed from being one of the society of the capital and principal burgesses of this borough and town for diverse special causes and respects best known unto this assembly and thereupon Mr Giles Greene is nominated and chosen a capital and principal burgess of this borough and town in the stead and room of the said William Mounsell.

21 September 1621

Upon this present day Mr Edward Roye is elected mayor of this borough and town of Waymouth and Melcombe Regis for the next year following.

Upon the same day Mr Robert White the elder, and Mr John Pitt the younger, are elected bailiffs of the same borough and town for the next year following.

Upon the same day David Gyer is chosen receiver of the rents, revenues and profits of this borough and town for the year following according to the form, intent and purpose of a Constitution thereof heretofore made.

Upon this same day Mr Robert White and Mr John Pitt, bailiffs elected Mr Matthew Allin, Mr Robert Mawe, John Lockier, Henry Cuttance are chosen auditors of the accounts for the town revenues for the year following according to the form of a Constitution thereof heretofore made.

[page 73] 18 September 1621

Upon this present day the profits of the market are granted unto John Reade for this year following at the rent of five pounds and ten shillings.

Upon the same day the cartage, bridge groats and drawing of the bridge were granted unto John Pope for this year following at the rent of fifteen pounds and ten shillings upon the condition set down the last year.

Upon the same day the ballast and forfeitures of the Constitution touching the quays and harbour were granted unto Mr Henry Russell at the rent of £5 15s.

Upon the same day it is agreed that the petty customs and rope groats shall be let to farm for this year following and that the party which shall take the same shall upon Monday next (if he will pay the rent for the same quarterly) tender unto Mr Mayor and Mr Bailiffs of this town only one sufficient security, but if he will pay the rent half yearly then he shall upon that day tender unto them two sufficient securities for the payment of the rent, or else making default shall forfeit unto this Corporation forty shillings to be levied according to the form of the Constitution provided for the levying of forfeitures. And the Corporation to refund the same petty customs and other things so to be left into their own hands. And thereupon the same was granted unto John Pitt the elder at the rent of one hundred, twenty and one pounds.

15 October 1621

Upon this present day Mr Edward Roye was sworn mayor of the borough and town of Waymouth and Melcombe Regis for the year following.

19 October 1621

Upon this present day Henry Cuttance is chosen to be one of the principal burgesses of this borough and town of Waymouth and Melcombe Regis.

Upon this present day Mr Robert White the elder and Mr John Pitt the younger now bailiffs of the borough and town and Mr Henry Russell one of the aldermen of the same town are appointed to have the keeping of the keys of the Corporation chest.

Upon the same day Mr Robert White the elder and Mr Robert White the younger entered into bond unto this Corporation in £30 for the payment £17 12s 8d or 3d to the use of the poor of Melcombe side upon the feast Day of St Michael the Archangel 1622.

Upon the same day Mr Robert White the elder and Mr Robert White the younger entered into bond unto this Corporation in £60 for the payment of £32 4sod to the use of the poor of Waymouth side upon the feast Day of St Michael the Archangel 1622.

Upon the same day Matthew Allin alias Belpitt and William Hopkins entered into bond unto this Corporation in £100 for the payment of £53 4s 8d to the use of the poor of Melcombe Regis upon the feast Day of St Michael the Archangel 1622.

22 October 1621

Upon this present day it was agreed by a general consent of the mayor, aldermen, bailiffs and capital and principal burgesses of this borough and town that Mr Mayor should write unto Mr Mayor of Exeter to understand from him what they at Exeter intend to do touching Sir Ferdinando Gorge aforesaid about the plantation and fishing at New England.

[page 74] **26 October 1621**

Upon this present day it was agreed by a general consent of the mayor, aldermen, bailiffs and capital burgesses of the borough and town of Waymouth and Melcombe Regis that John Cavesline a Frenchman, of late an elder of the Church at Newhaven, coming over into England upon the *Broylis* in France and bringing with him diverse pieces of cloth and stockings and other things, upon several requests made on his behalf, shall be admitted and licenced to keep open a shop for the sale of those commodities within this town and to continue the same so long as the Corporation shall think good and no longer.

Upon the same day it was likewise agreed by the like consent that the bridge and the town hall and prison in Waymouth side shall be repaired at the charge of this Corporation and monies to be disbursed by the receiver of the Revenues of this Corporation.

2 November 1621

Upon this present day it was agreed by a general consent of the mayor, aldermen, bailiffs and capital burgesses of this borough and town of Waymouth and Melcombe Regis, that Mr Giles Greene according to the directions and advice of the town council shall take out prosecutions against the bailiffs which did break the liberty of the town and that he shall prosecute against them with effect.

21 December 1621

Upon this present day it was and is agreed by a general consent of the mayor, aldermen, bailiffs and capital burgesses of this borough and town of Waymouth and Melcombe Regis that there shall be four barrels of new powder, twelve land pikes and two dozen of leather *burrratts* provided and bought at the charge of this Corporation to the use of the same Corporation. And that the monies to pay for the same shall be disbursed and paid by the receiver of the Revenues of this Corporation. And that one dozen of the same burratts shall from time to time be hanged up in Melcombe Church and that the other dozen shall from time to time be hanged up in Weymouth Chapel for the necessary use of the whole town upon all occasions.

11 January 1622

Upon this present day Mr Matthew Pitt did promise to pay unto this Corporation after the rate of five pounds per annum per cent for all such monies as are in his hands of the monies collected upon and of the hundred by order of the Lords of His Majesty's Honourable Privy Council which is, as appears by his accounts, £105 14s 6d.

[pages 75 and 76 blank]
[page 77] The rental of the lands in Melcombe Regis by alphabet

A
Bartholomew Allin, alderman 1s 3d
Alice Allin 2s 3 1/2d
Richard Allin senior 1s 4d

Richard Allin junior 3s 10
Matthew Allin 2s 2d
Samuel Allin ? 8d
Thomas Adams 3s 4d

B
Sir John Browne knight 5s 0d
John Bond alderman 3s 4d
John Barfoote 3s 0d
Jeremy Bavidge 2s 6d
Michael Browne ? 4d
Richard Bolte 5s 0d
Thomas Barnes 1d
James Barton 3d
William Bayly 3s 0d
Henry Backway 7 1/2d
Roger Barnes 1 1/2d
The widow Boyte 5s 0d
William Brnie 4 1/2d
C
Chistristrum Howse 6s 8d
John Churchil gent 11d
Richard Cox, mason 10d
Henry Cox 1s 4d
John Clarck 2s 0d
Bartholomew Clarck 2s 6d
Richard Chowne 1s 0 1/2d
William Chubb 1s 8d
Edith Clerck 5s 0d
D
John Darby 5s 0d
Thomusin Damon 1s 7d
F
Friary land 2s 6d
Friary land eastward 3s 2d
James Frampton 2s 0d
Henry Favell 5s 0d
G
Thomas Gyer alderman 9d
Giles Greene gent 1 1/2d
David Gyer 2s 6d
Simon Godfrye 11s 8d
Robert Godfrye 6d
John Godsole 8 1/2d
Daniel Gregory 6d
Robert Godwin 4d
Thomas Gould 3d
H
William Holman alderman 2s 11 1/2d

Richard Harryson £2 3s 0d
Edward Hodder 1s 3d
William Hopkins 9s 6d
George Halliday 5s 0d
Richard Hill 3s 8d
Henry Haughte 5s 0d
Nicholas Hunt 5s 0d
John Hamon 5s 0d
Simon Hickman 2s 6d
John Hingston 1s 8d
Justinian Hingston 7 1/2d
Ann Hawkins 1s 0d
John Hodges 11d
Henry Hopkins 9 1/2d
Bernard Hillerd 6d
J
James James 1s 9d
Peter Joy 4s 4d
John Justice 1s 9d

K
Robert Knighte alderman 5s 7d
John Keech 5s 0d
John Keys 5s 4d
L
Thomas Lockier 3s 7d
Edward Linsey 2d
Thomas Lovelis 11s 6d
Henry Lyne 6d
John Lyle 1d
William Lodwin 1d
M
John Morkett alderman 2s 1 1/2d
Bernard Michell alderman 4s 9d
Henry Michell 1s 4d
Robert Major 4s 3d
William Minterne 5s 2 1/2d
Mary Morris widow 1s 0d
John Martin 1s 5d
Melcombe held 7 1/2d
N
John Notlye 4d
O
Richard Odye 1s 4d

Roger Ossex 6d
John Oats 9d
P
John Pitt alderman 8s 6 1/2d
Matthew Pitt alderman 2s 4d
John Pitt senior 2s 3d
Jacob Proctor 5s 6d
Thomas Pawlett gent 2s 4d
Mark Palfrye 6d
William Percombe 6d
Bellingham Preston 1s 4d
Richard Peersey 6d
Margery Pullen 6d
Mary Peers 6d
Thomas Parkins 6d
[Page 78] R
Henry Russell alderman 6s 2d
John Reynolds 2s 7d
John Rydoute 1s 7 1/2d
John Reade 1s 9d
Henry Rose 7 1/2d
Barbara Randall 11 1/2d
Elizabeth Russell 4d

S
James Serrye 10 1/2d
Richard Scott 1s 4d
William Smithe 1s 8d
Barnard Stone 1s 8d
Richard Sheppard 4d
T
David Tompson 5s 0d
V
Joyce Vandergozen 3s
Jacob Vandergozen 7d
W
William Waltham alderman 1s 6d
Henry Waltham 11s 4d
Thomas Wallis 5?
William Wilcocks 5?
John Whoudon 6s 8d
John Warr 5?
Thomas Welman and Nicholas Jurvis 5?
Widow Wood 5?
Whetcombe's heirs 7 1/2d
Thomas Waymon 3d
Katherine Watson 3d
Grace Wilford 6d
Henry Walker 6d

[page 79] **1 February 1622**

At an assembly held in the Guildhall of Melcombe Regis within the borough and town of Waymouth and Melcombe Regis in the county of Dorset upon the day and year above said it was and is agreed by a general consent of the mayor, aldermen, bailiffs and capital or principal burgesses of the said borough and town. That out of this Corporation stock and monies there shall be thirty pounds bestowed and laid forth upon piles, planks and work for and about the repairing of the bridge. And that there shall be also, out of the same stock and monies disbursed and laid forth, fifty pounds about the making and repairing of the mouldhead, harbour, jetties and quays. And that Mr Robert White and Mr John Pitt, bailiffs, Mr Henry Russell, Mr John Pitt the elder, Mr Robert Vaule, Mr Thomas Lockier, Jeremy Babbidge and John Pope shall be overseer and overseers of the same work and shall direct and order the same business at their best discretion. And that there shall be a help and furtherance given towards the proceeding in the same work of the mouldhead, harbour, jetty and quays by contributions of labour of all persons, freeholders, tenants, inhabitants and residents within this borough and town. And that every of them shall provide so many workmen from time to time to work by turn towards the doing thereof as the said

Mr Robert White, Mr John Pitt, bailiffs, Mr Henry Russell, Mr John Pitt the elder, Mr Robert Vaule, Mr Thomas Lockier, Jeremy Babbidge and John Pope or the greater number of them shall rate and assess them at. And that the same labourers shall be provided by every of them severally to work upon and at such days as they shall be summoned and warned for that service by the sergeants at the mace of the said town or by any one of them. And that whosoever of the same freeholders, tenants, inhabitants or residents shall refuse or neglect to provide his labour or labourers according to this agreement shall forfeit 12d for every default to be levied by distress upon warrant of the mayor for the time being to be made unto the sergeants in that behalf. Provided always that the mayor, bailiffs or two of them at the least, whereof the mayor to be one shall ratify and confirm the same rate before it be put in execution. And that a warrant from the same overseers or from any six or five of them whereof Mr Bailiff White and Mr Bailiff Pitt shall be two, shall be a sufficient warrant from time to time unto the collectors or receivers of the revenues of the town for the payment of those monies appointed for the use aforesaid.

At the same assembly it was and is agreed by the like consent that Mr Mayor shall pay twenty shillings unto John Pope for the taking of Lancelot Growte the son of John Growte the younger to be his apprentice for eight years which money shall be allowed unto Mr Mayor out of the monies which he is bound to pay unto this Corporation to the use of the poor of Waymouth.

8 March 1622
At an assembly held the day and year above said by the mayor, aldermen, bailiffs and capital and principal burgesses of the borough and town aforesaid it was and is agreed by a general consent. That no person or persons whatsoever shall take the town boat to employ and use without the leave and consent of Mr Mayor and bailiffs for the said town or of two of them at the least, whereof the mayor to be one, upon pain of any person doing to the contrary to forfeit 6s 8d to be levied of his or their goods and chattels in such manner and form as other forfeitures upon Constitutions and appointed to be levied.

[page 80] **15 March 1622**
At an assembly held the day and year above said by the mayor, aldermen, bailiffs and capital or principal burgesses of the borough and town of Waymouth and Melcombe Regis it was and is agreed by a general consent of the said mayor, aldermen, bailiffs and capital or principal burgesses. That Mr Giles Greene shall have by the way of gift from this Corporation the sum of thirty three shillings and four pence towards the charge of the making of a quay and slip which he has built upon the town ground on the east side of his house and in Hell Lane. And there shall be eight pounds six shillings and eight pence more paid unto the said Mr Greene which in the whole amounts to the sum of ten pounds and the said eight pounds, six shillings and eight pence are allowed unto him for and in respect of the charge by him laid forth about the delivery of the letters unto the Lords of His Majesty's Most Honourable Privy Council concerning the papist sermon and for and in respect of charges of suits in law against William Mounsell and

the sergeant at the mace for their two terms last past. And it is also agreed by the mayor, aldermen, bailiffs and capital or principal burgesses that this their agreement shall be a sufficient warrant unto the receiver of the revenues of this Corporation to satisfy and pay unto the said Mr Green the said sum of ten pounds before mentioned.

At the same assembly it was and is also agreed by the said mayor, aldermen, bailiffs and capital or principal burgesses that the east part of the building against the town hall shall be now finished and that Mr Robert White, Mr John Pitt bailiffs, Mr Henry Russell, Mr John Pitt the elder, Mr Robert Vaule Mr Thomas Lockier, Jeremy Babbidg and John Pope shall be overseers of the same work and as they, or any five of them, whereof one of the bailiffs to be one, shall direct the same building so it shall proceed without any contradiction and that the charge thereof shall be paid by the receiver of the revenues of this town.

29 March 1622
At at assembly held the day and year above said by the mayor, aldermen, bailiffs and capital or principal burgesses of the borough and town of Waymouth and Melcombe Regis it was and is agreed by a general consent of the said mayor, aldermen, bailiffs and capital or principal burgesses that there shall be £20 of the poor stock taken out to be employed in flax to set the poor on work whereof Mr Matthew Allin shall have £10 for the poor of Weymouth and Richard Harrisson shall have the other part for the poor of Melcombe and either of them to be answerable at the year's end for the several sums by them received whereof Mr Edward Roy, mayor shall disburse out of the monies of the poor stock for Waymouth side £10 and Mr Matthew Allin shall disburse out of the monies of the poor stock for Melcombe side the other £10.

5 April 1622
Upon this present day it was agreed and ordered by the mayor, aldermen, bailiffs and capital and principal burgesses of this borough and town of Waymouth then assembled that Mr Bailiff White, Mr Henry Russell, John Pope and Jeremy Babbidge shall oversee the work of the haven for this month and Mr Bailiff Pitt, Mr John Pitt the elder, Mr Robert Vaule and Mr Thomas Lockier for the next month. And that £20 shall be paid by the receiver of the revenues of this town unto Mr Henry Russell to pay charges of the workmen and otherwise concerning the same work, and that he shall be accountable for the same at the end of this month.

[page 81] **3 May 1622**
Upon this present day it was ordered by the mayor, aldermen, bailiffs and capital or principal burgesses of the borough and town of Waymouth and Melcombe Regis then assembled, that the carriages for the town piece at the north shall be viewed by Richard Hill, Thomas Lovelis and David Phyppen.

Upon the same day Mr Mayor and Mr Bailiffs did nominate and appoint Mr William Waltham, James James and John Lockier, overseers for the poor of Melcombe side and John Ellis, William Cate alias Keate and Thomas Ledoze alias Cardinge for Waymouth side.

7 May 1622

Upon this present day it was ordered and agreed by the mayor, aldermen, bailiffs and capital and principal burgesses of the borough and town of Waymouth and Melcombe Regis then assembled. That Mr Russell shall dispose of the ballast landed and laid on shore out of the town lighter and that he shall have 2d per ton out of the monies which he shall make thereof and for the residue that he shall make thereof he shall be accountable to this Corporation.

Upon the same day it was likewise ordered and agreed that the carriages for the piece at the north and of the piece at the bulwark shall be newly made at the charge of this Corporation and that Mr Russell, Mr David Gyer and Richard Champion or any two of them shall have the oversight of the work and compound with the workmen for the doing thereof and likewise for the platform. And that the two *Murtherers* [small cannons] belonging to this Corporation shall be also mounted at the charge of this Corporation and that a new beacon shall be also forthwith made at the charge of this Corporation.

14 June 1622

Upon this present day it was ordered and agreed by the mayor, aldermen, bailiffs and capital or principal burgesses of the borough and town of Waymouth and Melcombe Regis then assembled. That the piece of ordnance lying near Mr Matthew Pitt's cellar and of late brought out of the blockhouse by him, or his assigns, without order of this Corporation, shall be forthwith carried back unto the same blockhouse and shall be there mounted upon his carriage for the defence of the town.

Upon the same day Mr Mayor and Mr Bailiffs did give leave unto John Kinge to make a cobblers shop under the stairs going up into Mr Michell's loft adjoining unto the town hall for which he doth promise to pay unto this Corporation 12d per annum to the use of the same Corporation, and to leave the shop to the town's use if the said John Kinge doth not use it himself.

Upon the same day Mr Mayor and Mr Bailiffs did likewise give leave unto Edward Gibson, surgeon, that his shop called the barber's shop shall stand between Mr Barnard Michell's his cellar and Mr Bailiff Pitt his door next adjoining unto it, for which licence and leave the said Edward Gibson doth promise to pay unto this Corporation 12d per annum to the use of the same Corporation.

Memorandum that it is agreed the action commenced against Mr John Bond by John Gardner shall be defended and that the charges to be disbursed about the defence of the same action, which shall be over and above five pounds, shall be borne by this Corporation.

[page 82] **2 August 1622**

Upon this present day it was and is ordered and agreed by a general consent of the mayor, aldermen, bailiffs and capital or principal burgesses of the borough and town of Waymouth and Melcombe Regis in the county of Dorset that upon and after the cancelling of a deed with Mary Richardson upon this day brought into the court concerning a void piece of ground with the appurtenances situate lying and being in Waymouth in a certain place called the Hope between the void land of Constance Knott on the north and the street on the south and the sea on the north and west and the way leading to the north on the east which void ground contains in length thirty foot and in breadth forty foot. The the said Mary shall have of the Corporation 30s for the same which immediately was performed accordingly on both sides.

Upon the same day it was and is ordered and agreed by the like general consent of the mayor, aldermen, bailiffs and capital or principal burgesses of the said borough and town that all such persons as will cancel and deliver up their deeds of any part of the void ground in Hope shall have, every of them, 30s not in respect of any right or interest they have because their deeds are void in law but in respect of their need and necessity.

Upon the same day Mr Bailiff White did acknowledge that he borrowed of the Corporation powder one barrel at the last going forth of the Thomasin to the seas which barrel of power is as yet owing to the Corporation.

21 September 1622

Upon this present day Mr Henry Waltham is elected mayor of the borough and town of Waymouth and Melcombe Regis for the next year following.

Upon the same day Mr Thomas Gyer and Mr Edward Roy are elected bailiffs of the said borough and town for the same next year following.

Upon the same day David Gyer is again chosen receiver of the rents, revenues and profits of the same borough and town for the said year next following according to the form, effect, intent and meaning of a Constitution thereof heretofore made.

Upon the same day Mr Thomas Gyer and Mr Edward Roy, bailiffs elected William Williams, Edward Hodder, William Cade and Richard Harryson are chosen auditors for the accounts of the town's revenues for this next year following according to the form of a constitution thereof heretofore made.

Upon the same day William Cade, Robert Lock, John Lockier and Owen Holman are chosen constables of the said borough and town for the is year following.

[page 83] 28 September 1622

Upon this present day it is agreed that the petty customs and rope groats shall be let to farm for this year following, but not under one hundred and twenty pounds. And that the person which shall take the same shall upon Monday next (if he will pay the rent quarterly tender unto Mr Mayor elect and Mr Bailiffs elected or unto two of them only) one sufficient security, but if he will pay the rent half yearly then he shall, upon that day, tender unto them two sufficient securities for the payment of the same rent or else making default shall forfeit unto this Corporation ten pounds to be levied according to the form of the constitution provided for the levying of forfeitures. And the town to resume the petty customs and other things so to be let into their own hands, further agreed that from henceforth the farmers of the same petty customs shall not at the end of his term take the benefit of any goods entered outwards unless the same be shipped before his term to ended nor of any goods entered inwards until the same be landed, but that it shall remain unto the succeeding farmer. And thereupon it is granted unto Mr John Pitt the elder, at the rent of one hundred and twenty one pounds.

Upon this present day the profits of the market are granted unto John Read for this year following at the rent of five pounds, ten shillings.

Upon the same day the cartage, bridge groats and drawing of the bridge were granted unto Henry Hillard for this year following at the rent of fifteen pounds ten shillings.

Fabian Hodder has £25 parcel of Mr Robert Midleton's gift upon bond dated the fourth day of October 1622 wherein the said Fabian Hodder, John Pitt the younger, Edward Hodder and Andrew Kelway do stand bound for the repayment thereof at the end of three years and for the interest and allowance of twenty five shillings per annum in the meantime.

John Kennyge has £25 parcel of Mr Robert Midleton's gift upon bond dated the fourth day of October 1622 wherein the said John Kennynge, Robert White, Edward Roy and Robert Vaule do stand bound for the repayment thereof at the end of three years and for the interest and allowance of 25s. per annum in the meantime.

John Russell has £25 parcel of Mr Robert Midleton's gift upon bond dated for fourth day of October 1622 wherein the said Joseph Russell, Henry Russell, Owen Holman and Jeremy Babbidge do stand bound for the repayment thereof at the end of three years and for the interest and allowance of 25s per annum in the meantime.

Richard Allin has £25 parcel of Mr Robert Midleton's gift upon bond dated the fourth day of October 1622 wherein the said Richard Allin, William Waltham, Henry Michell and Edmund Smithe do stand bound for the repayment thereof at the end of three years and for the interest and allowance of 25s per annum in the meantime.

4 October 1622
Upon this present day Mr John Pitt, alderman, did declare and make known unto Mr Mayor, Mr Bailiff Gyer and the other aldermen of this town then present, that Mr Richard Pitt deceased, the late father of the said John Pitt, has devised and given by his last will and testament, the sum of fifty pounds unto this Corporation to the use of the poor of this town.

11 October 1622
Upon this present day Mr Edward Roye had the oath ministered unto him by Mr Henry Waltham, mayor, which is used and accustomed to be ministered unto the bailiffs of this town and so was sworn one of the bailiffs of this town for the year following.

18 October 1622
At an assembly held the day and year above said by the mayor, aldermen, bailiffs and capital and principal burgesses of the borough and town of Waymouth and Melcombe Regis it was and is agreed and ordered that William Bayly, mason, builder of the stone wall of the new building at the east end of Melcombe town hall shall before

this day seven night bring and restore unto this Corporation the water tables and window stuff that he took out of the old building, or else bring five of the overseers appointed for that work, their hands to signify that it was allowed unto him upon the agreement made with him about that work upon pain to forfeit 30s. to be levied upon his goods and chattels according to the form of the constitution made for the levying of forfeitures upon constitutions.

At the same assembly Mr John Lockier and Mr Richard Harryson were chosen two of the capital and principal burgesses of this borough and town of Waymouth and Melcombe Regis.

At the same assembly it was and is ordained, constituted and agreed that henceforth no butcher within this town shall kill, open or unbowel any sheep, calf, pig or other beast in any of their shops upon pain to forfeit for every sheep, calf, pig or other beast so killed 2d to be levied in form aforesaid.

At the same assembly it was and is agreed that the town prison shall be strengthened and made strong at the discretion and direction of Mr Henry Russell, Mr David Gyer and Mr Richard Harrison who are appointed overseers of the same work to be done with all convenient expedition at the charge of this Corporation.

1 November 1622

At an assembly held the day and year last aforesaid by the mayor, aldermen, bailiffs and capital and principal burgesses of this borough and town of Waymouth and Melcombe Regis it was and is ordered that the pain of 30s shall be levied of the goods and chattels of William Bayly for the he has not brought and restored unto this Corporation the water tables and window stuff which he took out of the old building of the wall at the east end of Melcombe town hall and nor brought five of the overseers appointed for that work, their hand to signify that it was allowed unto him the agreement made with him about that work according to a former constitution thereof made the eighteenth day of October last past.

Upon the same day at the same assembly Mr Edward Roy now bailiff and late mayor did deliver unto Mr Henry Waltham now mayor, four letters formerly sent unto the mayor of this town from the Lords and others of His Majesty's Honourable Privy Council concerning the receiving and collecting of one per cent etc. and three other letters from the same Lords concerning other matters.

[page 85] 13 December 1622

At an assembly held the day and year above said by the mayor, aldermen, bailiffs and capital and principal burgesses of the borough and town of Waymouth and Melcombe Regis it was and is agreed that Mr John Pitt, the elder, shall bring in and pay unto the receiver of the revenues of this town the sum of forty pounds of current English money, which was due unto this Corporation at the feast of St Michael the Archangel in the year of our Lord 1621, upon this day fortnight or else that his bond shall be put in suit.

At the same assembly it was and is likewise ordered and agreed that Mr Henry Russell shall in like manner pay unto the said receiver by the said day such monies as he doth owe unto this Corporation or else that his bond shall be put in suit.

At the same assembly it was and is also ordered and agreed that from henceforth no person shall either fill or empty any cask whatsoever of water upon any of the quays within this town upon pain that every person which shall offend therein shall forfeit for every cask so filled or emptied 4d to be levied according to the form of the constitution provided for forfeitures.

At the same assembly it was and is also ordered and agreed that the receiver of the town's revenues shall deliver unto the churchwarden of Melcombe the sum of ten pounds towards the finishing of Melcombe Church. To be paid back again unto the said receiver at Our Lady Day next, out of such monies as in the meantime shall be collected towards the building of the same Church and that this order and grant shall be the receiver's warrant for the doing thereof.

At the same assembly it was and is further agreed and ordered that the windows of the town hall in Melcombe shall be glazed forthwith at the town charge.

[Signed by] Henry Waltham, mayor; Thomas Giear, bailiff; Edward Roy, bailiff; John Bond, Robert Whit, William Waltham, Giles Grene, William Holman, James James, Robert Knight, Edward Hodder, Henry Russell, Edward Linze, Robert Vaule [his mark], John Lockier, Thomas Lockeire, William Willyams, William Martell [his mark], Henry Blithell, David Geare, Richard Harrisone, Richard Allin.

[page 86] 30 December 1622
At an assembly held upon this present day Mr John Pitt the elder, did offer unto this Corporation the house and grounds in the Cuniger now in the occupation of the said John Pitt, or his assigns, in mortgage for his assurance of paying of the forty pound which he doth owe unto this Corporation to be paid at the end of one year, together with the interest for the forbearing thereof for that time. Which offer was accepted by the Corporation and it was agreed upon that the assurance should be made unto Mr Thomas Gyer, Mr Henry Michell and Mr David Gyer to the use of this Corporation.

6 January 1623
At an assembly held upon this present day Mr John Man, being not freeman of this town is by a general consent, upon his own submission, fined for that he did sell two butts of sack within this town unto a stranger which being foreign bought and foreign sold is by the privilege and custom of the town utterly lost and forfeited at [blank]

20 January 1623
Upon this present day it was ordered by Mr Mayor and Mr Bailiffs that the common brewers of this town shall not make or brew any beers above the rate of ten shilling the hogshead.

27 January 1623
Upon this present day it was and is agreed by a general consent of the mayor, aldermen, bailiffs and capital and principal burgesses of this borough and town here assembled that this Corporation shall execute with effect their action against Jasper Dadridge

for intruding into and breaking of their liberties in arresting of Mr William Holman upon a writ [*capias ad satisfaciendum*] at the suit of Judith Parkins, widow and that Lionel Cooke being drawn in by the said Dodridge to offend in the same business (upon his submission and protestation that his name was set down in the warrant without his *privitie* or knowledge) shall be therefore remitted. And it is agreed that the Corporation shall bear all the charges in prosecuting the same action.

28 February 1623
Upon this present day it is ordered and agreed that Mr David Gyer shall pay out of the town stock unto the workman and maker of the king's arms, prince's arms and town arms the sum of three pounds. And that this order shall be Mr Gyer's warrant and discharge for the same.

[page 87] **14 March 1623**
At an assembly held in the Guildhall of Melcombe Regis within the borough and town of Waymouth and Melcombe Regis in the county of Dorset upon the day and year above said it was and is agreed and ordered by a general consent of the mayor, aldermen, bailiffs and capital and principal burgesses of the said borough and town. That Mr Bailiff Gyer, Mr Robert White, Mr Robert Knight, Mr Robert Vaule and Mr Robert Major shall be overseers to view and see what shall be requisite and necessary to be done about the building of the molehead, repairing of the town lighter, quays, harbour and jetties and to view and see the same to be accordingly repaired and done at the charge of this Corporation so as the same charge shall not exceed the sum of forty pounds. And that there shall be a help and furtherance given towards the proceeding in the same work by the contribution of labour of all persons, freeholders, tenants, inhabitant and residents within this borough and town. And that every of them shall provide so many workmen from time to time at several days and times as the said overseers, or the greater number of them, shall rate and assess them at. And that the same labourers shall be provided by every of them severally by the sergeants at the mace of the said borough and town, or by any one of them. And that whosoever of the freeholders, tenants, inhabitants or residents shall refuse or neglect to provide his labourer or labourers to work according to this agreement, shall forfeit 12d for every default to be levied by distress upon warrant of the mayor for the time being, to be made unto the sergeants in that behalf provided always that the mayor of this town shall ratify and confirm the same rate before it be put in execution. And it is also ordered and agreed by the said mayor, aldermen, bailiffs and capital or principal burgesses that a warrant from the same overseers or any four or three of them, whereof Mr Bailiff Gyer shall be one, shall be a sufficient warrant from time to time unto the collector or receiver of the revenues of this town, for the payment of such monies as shall be necessarily employed about the reparations and occasions aforesaid not exceeding the sun aforesaid.

[Signed by] Henry Waltham, mayor; Thomas Giear, bailiff, Edward Roy, bailiff; William Waltham, John Pitt, John Pytt, William Holman, Robert Knight, David Giare, John Bond, Henry Russell, Edward Linze, Richard Allin, John Lockier, Robert Whit,

Peter Neale [his mark], Robert Maior, William Willyams, Edward Hodder, Richard Harrisone, Robert Vaule [his mark], Henry Blickell, Thomas Lockeir, Steven Dennis

[page 88] 9 May 1623

At an assembly held in the Guildhall of Melcombe Regis within the borough and town of Waymouth and Melcombe Regis in the county of Dorset by the mayor, aldermen, bailiffs and capital and principal burgesses of the said borough and town upon the day and year above said. It was and is agreed, ordered and appointed that Mr John Pitt the younger, Mr Robert Knight, Mr Thomas Lockier and Mr Henry Michell shall view the house of Mr Richard Allin whether it be a convenient house for the setting of the poor on work, and if they shall find it to be, then they shall consider what the inheritance thereof is worth to be bought and thereof to certify their opinion at the next assembly.

Upon the same day Mr David Gyer was appointed to provide a necessary and fit woman to keep the poor children of this town at work.

Upon the same day it was and is agreed, ordered and appointed by a general consent that the churchwardens and overseers of the poor on either side of this town shall take view and notice what poor children there are in this town on either side and at the next assembly to certify this Corporation of their names and ages that thereupon course may be taken for the putting of such as are able for the[m] to be apprentices and for the setting of the residue on work.

4 July 1623

Memorandum that upon this present day it was agreed by a general consent of the mayor, aldermen, bailiffs and capital burgesses of this borough and town that Mr William Niell shall be paid five pounds for his pains taken about the suit unto the Lords of His Majesty's Council concerning the Lizard light and the bringing in of the commodities of the Baltic seas, which five pounds it is agreed that Mr David Gyer, receiver of the town revenues shall pay unto the said William Niell out of the town's money and this order shall be discharge for the same.

Memorandum that upon the same day it was agreed by Mr Mayor, Mr Bailiff Gyer and others the aldermen and principal burgesses of Melcombe side that they would take of Mr John Pitt, one of the aldermen of that side, his house next adjoining at the west end of John Hodges house at the yearly rent of three pounds of current English money to make a house to set the poor people of that side on work. And thereupon it was agreed by the said Mr John Pitt that they should have the same house at the yearly rent of three pounds per annum.

7 July 1623

Memorandum that upon this present day it was agreed and ordered by a general consent of the mayor, aldermen, bailiffs and capital burgesses of this borough and town that Mr Richard Allin shall upon the morrow travel towards Exeter there to meet with Mr William Niell upon Wednesday next to confer with him about the poor captives in Angier [Algiers] and that his charge in the time of his travels shall be borne by the Corporation.

[page 89] **25 July 1623**
Memorandum that upon this present day it was agreed by a general consent of the mayor, aldermen, bailiffs and capital burgesses of this borough and town here assembled that John Peers, mariner, shall have eight pounds out of the revenues of this town from the receiver of the same revenues. And that in consideration of the same eight pounds John Keyes shall make over all his estate in the burgage and house wherein the said John Peers now dwells unto this Corporation, which estate the said Corporation shall grant over unto the said John Peers if he shall pay the same eight pounds back unto this Corporation within three years next following, or at any time before upon payment of the said eight pounds

3 September 1623
Memorandum. That upon this present day it was and is agreed by a general consent of the mayor, aldermen, bailiffs and capital burgesses of this borough and town here assembled. That for the enlarging of the thirteen persons hereunder named out of the captivity and slavery of the Turks the interest of the monies remaining in the hands of Mr John Bond and Mr Matthew Pitt shall be employed. And that what else shall be requisite shall be raised by the town. And that in the meantime the monies shall be disbursed out of the town stock with this caution, that the charge exceed not above three pounds a man.

Henry Neale
John Frampton
Matthew Knott
Henry Browne
John Kinge
Thomas Cookery
John Rogers
William Wilcoxe
William Seymer
Robert Watts
William Cooke
Edward Keymer
Robert Langden

[signed by] Henry Waltham, mayor; William Waltham, alderman; John Pitt, alderman; William Holman, alderman; Robert White, alderman; Henry Russell, alderman; Matthew Alline, Thomas Giear and Edward Roy, bailiffs; Henry Cuttance, Peter Neale [his mark], Robert Vaule [his mark], Thomas Lockeir, James James, Edward [illegibe surname], David Giare, John Pytt, Robert Major, John Lockier, Edward Hodder, William Willyams, Richard Harrisone, William Martell [his mark].

[page 90] **21 September 1623**
Upon this present day Mr Matthew Allin was and is elected mayor of the borough and

town of Waymouth and Melcombe Regis for the year following.

Upon the same day Mr Matthew Pitt and Mr Henry Cuttance are elected bailiffs of the said borough and town for the year following.

Upon the same day Mr David Gyer is again elected receiver of the rents, revenues and profits of the said borough and town for the next year following according to the form of a Constitution thereof heretofore made.

Upon the same day Mr Matthew Pitt, Mr Henry Cuttance, bailiffs, Mr Barnard Michell, Mr James James, Owen Holman and John Thorneton are chosen auditors for the accounts of the revenues of this Corporation according to the form of a Constitution thereof heretofore made.

23 September 1623
Upon this present day Edmond Windham and Arthur Pynot esquires are admitted and sworn freemen of this town.

24th day of September 1623
Upon this present day Mr Thomas Waltham and Mr Owen Holman are chosen to be two of the capital and principal burgesses of this Corporation.

Upon this present day Nicholas Cornent and Gregory Babbidge are admitted and sworn freemen of this town and Corporation. And either of them gave for his admittance the sum of five pounds. But the Corporation give back unto the said Gregory Babbidge out of his £5 the sum of forty shillings.

28 September 1623
Upon this present day it was and is agreed by a general consent of the mayor, aldermen, bailiffs and capital burgesses of this borough and town then assembled that the petty customs and the other things used to be let and granted with the petty customs shall not be let for this year following under the rent of one hundred and thirty pounds and that the person which shall take it shall forthwith bring and deliver into Mr Mayor's hands the sum of five pounds which shall rest in his hands as forfeited to this Corporation if he shall not name sufficient security unto Mr Mayor for the payment of the rent by, or before tomorrow's court and shall not produce the same security to enter into bond accordingly on Friday next. And that the same rent shall be paid quarterly if he produce but one security then the rent to be paid quarterly. If he produce two securities then half yearly or within ten days from next following. And that none shall offer by way of increase less than 20s. And it was afterwards granted unto Mr Henry Russell, Mr James James and Gregory Babbidge for the rent of £139.

[page 91] Upon the day and year aforesaid the cartage, bridge groats and drawing of the bridge were granted unto Jeremy Babbidge at the rent of seventeen pounds for the year following.

Upon the same day the profits of the market were granted unto John Reade at the rent of six pounds for the year following.

Memorandum that at this assembly it was and is agreed by a general consent that Thomas Lovelis at the charge of the Corporation shall make up the partition in the hall according to the directions given him and shall also make up a *skellinge* in the little court within the hall of Melcombe in such manner as he is directed.

30 October 1623
At an assembly held in Melcombe Regis within the borough and town of Waymouth and Melcombe Regis upon the day and year aforesaid by the mayor, aldermen, bailiffs and capital and principal burgesses of the said borough and town it was and is agreed by a general consent. That the farmers of the petty customs shall distrain the goods of Denis Bond of Dorchester, merchant if he shall refuse to pay petty customs for his goods either imported or exported. And that if the said Denis Bond shall commence any suit against him or them that shall take the distress then the Corporation shall defend and save harmless the petition (against whom the same suit shall be commenced) from all damage and charges whatsoever rising or growing by reason of the same suit.

7 November 1623
Upon this present day Mr Henry Waltham, alderman, is elected named and appointed to have the keeping of one of the keys of the town chest for this year following.

14 November 1623
At an assembly in Melcombe Regis within the borough and town of Waymouth and Melcombe Regis upon the day and year aforesaid by the mayor, aldermen, bailiffs and capital and principal [burgesses] of the said borough and town it was and is ordered and agreed that from henceforth every person which shall take any thing by grant from the town shall pay for the making of his writing concerning the same.

Upon the same day it was and is further ordered and agreed that from henceforth the constables of this borough and town shall bear their own charges in and about the execution of their Office.

[page 92] 29 November 1623
A survey and audit of the accounts of David Gyer, treasurer and collector of the revenues of the said borough and town for two years past that is to say in the mayoralties of Mr Edward Roy and Mr Henry Waltham their being auditors that is to say Mr Matthew Pitt and Mr Henry Cuttance, bailiffs, Mr Barnard Michel, John Thorneton and Owen Holman.

Firstly they find Richard Allin and William Mounsell to rest behind for cartage and ballast 1619 as by Robert Major's account appears is £9 17s 0d

Item more owing by John Pitt senior upon a mortgage of his land in the Cuniger in the hands of Mr David Gyer payable at Christide next for the sum of £44

Item more owing by Mr Robert Major as by his account appears, £3 3s 5d

Item owing by Mr Henry Waltham as by his account appears £1 7s 10d

Item owing by John Peers upon a mortgage of his house being lately in the occupation of John Keyes. £8

Item Benjamin White his wife owes for wool, coal and money £1 7s 4d

Item Henry Hillard owes for rest of cartage for the last year the sum of 7s

Item Mr Henry Waltham owes for money paid Mr Kellway for John Small the sum of 13s 4d

Item Mr Henry Waltham owes for the Lieutenants of the County their charges £1 7s 6d

Item Mr Henry Waltham owes for money paid John Small for making of John Pitt of Lanehouse his writings. 15s

Item Mr Edward Roy owes for monies charged to the treasurer his account for entertainment of the Justices at the Muster the sum of 14s

Item Mr Edward Roy owes for Mr Recorder's charges at the time of his feast charged to the treasurer's account. 18s.

Item Mr Russell owes for 85 tons of ballast at 2d per ton. 14s 2d

Item Jeremy Babbidge owes which he is to repay at Our Lady Day next which was lent to the church of Melcombe. £30

Item Mr Henry Waltham for so much surcharged on Mr Recorder's entertainment not thought fit to be allowed. 13s 4d.

Item Mr David Gyer owes to balance his account to this Corporation being audited and perfected the day and year above written for the two years past the sum of. £76 0s 4d

Item it doth not appear unto us how £3 can be due unto Mr William Waltham for the bridge and therefore we do not allow it. £3

Total £186 8s 3d

Item Mr Robert White the elder owes a barrel of powder lent him out of the town provision to be repaid.

Item Mr John Lockier owes another barrel of powder.

Item William Bayly owes 75 stones lent him.

[page 93] 12 December 1623

At an assembly held at the Guildhall of Melcombe Regis within the borough and town of Waymouth and Melcombe Regis in the county of Dorset by the mayor, aldermen, bailiffs and capital or principal burgesses of the said borough and town it was and is agreed by a general consent of the said mayor, aldermen, bailiffs and burgesses that with all speed there shall be twenty frames provided for the making of *yuckle*. And that Mr David Gyer, receiver of the town's revenues shall have the charge and care of the delivery of the thread for the making of the same yuckle unto the overseer of the poor children which shall be set on work therewith. And it was and is further likewise agreed that [blank] White, wife of Benjamin White shall be the overseer of the same poor children for the teaching and setting of them to work and shall yield a weekly account from time to time unto the said collector of such yuckle as shall be made by the poor children over whom she has the oversight. And that the said collector shall have into his hands all the poor stock which the Corporation has now abroad upon interest. And therewith shall provide the thread, pay for the frames and work and for such other things as shall be necessary for the setting of the same poor on work, and shall convert such work as shall be so made to the best profits for the benefit of the poor and maintenance of the stock.

[Signed by] Matthew Allin, mayor; Matthew Pitt, bailiff, Henry Waltham, bailiff.
This Constitution before it was full subscribed unto was by a general consent made void.

19 January 1624

At an assembly held at the Guildhall of Melcombe Regis within the borough and town of Waymouth and Melcombe Regis in the county of Dorset by the mayor, aldermen, bailiffs, burgesses and freeholders, then assembled together about the choice of burgesses for this town to serve at the next Parliament. It was then and there agreed by a general consent of the said assembly that Mr Matthew Pitt and Mr Thomas Gyer being chosen two burgesses to serve for this town shall be allowed and paid for their fees and wages three shillings and four pence a piece for every day during the time of Parliament and for four days before the beginning of the Sessions and for four days after the end of the Sessions.

30 January 1624

At an assembly held at the Guildhall of Melcombe Regis within the borough and town of Waymouth and Melcombe Regis in the county of Dorset by the mayor, aldermen, bailiffs and capital or principal burgesses it was and is agreed by a general consent that there shall be £20 laid forth of the town's monies for the satisfying of so much which is to be paid for the discharge of this town against the monies charged upon English merchants in France. And that the receiver of the revenues of this town shall collect and gather up the same monies upon the merchants of the town upon all goods entered in the King's Custom House here from the feast of the Purification of Our Blessed Lady St Mary the Virgin next coming at the rate of 12d per £ as well upon custom as imposition [*impost*].

And that the same collection shall continue until the same £20 be fully raised and levied.

[Signed by] Matthew Allin, mayor; Matthew Pitt, bailiff, Henry Cuttance, bailiff, Robert Knight, Henry Russell, Thomas Giear, Edward Roy, Henry Waltham, Robert Major, Thomas Waltham, William Willyams, Richard Harrisone, Owen Holman, David Giair, John Pytt, Richard Allin, Henry Birchell, James James, Edward Hodder.

[page 94] 1 February 1619

Item paid into the exchequer by Mr Edward Lechland according to order to him given. £225
    Item for post of letters 2s 8d
    Item for two sugar loaves given unto Sir Julius Casar by order £1 9s 10d
    Item for writing the book to Mr Man's boy and Cozen Pitt the sum is 11s od
    10 January 1620
    Rest to level this amount which according to Mr Mayor's order is ready to be paid in London £105 14s 6d
    [Total] £332 18s od
    to pay half interest from my mayoralty. [Signed by] Matthew Pitt

29 November 1619
Item received of Henry Waltham for yards laden in Poole by John Parkins and John Blachford

> £12 13s 2d
> 9 December Received of John Man £70
> 24 December Received by Robert Major £38 3s 10d
> 30 December Received of John Man £22 1s 2d
> 20 April Received of John Man £59 10s 11d
> 29 June Received of John Man £53 18s 0d
> 3 October Received of John Pitt £76 10s 11d
> [Signed by] Matthew Pitt [Total] £332 18s 0d
> Mr Bond's account
> Received from Mr Gardner and gave him a bill £130 17s 8d
> Henry Waltham owes £40
> Rests in my hands £90 17s 8d
> So that in Mr John Bonds hands there is £90 17s 8d
> and in Mr Henry Waltham's there was £40 which is promised to Mr Bond.
> [Total] £130 17s 8d
> to pay half interest for it from the time of my mayoralty.
> 6 February 1624
> Upon this day Mr John Bond did acknowledge the account afore written and

that there did remain in his hands the whole sum of £130 17s 8d.

[page 95] **12 March 1624**
At an assembly held in the Guildhall of Melcombe Regis within the borough and town of Waymouth and Melcombe Regis in the county of Dorset upon the day and year above said it was and is agreed by a general consent of the mayor, aldermen, bailiffs and capital and principal burgesses of the said borough and town. That out of this Corporation stock and monies there shall be fifty pounds bestowed and laid forth upon and about the making and repairing of the bridge, molehead, harbour, jetty and quays; and that Mr John Pitt, alderman, Mr Henry Russell, alderman, John Lockier, David Gyer, Owen Holman and John Thornton shall be surveyors and overseers of the same work, and shall direct and order the same business at their best directions. And that there shall be a help and furtherance given towards the proceeding in the same work of the molehead, harbour, jetty and quays by contribution of labour of all such persons, freeholders, tenants, inhabitants and residents within this borough and town. And that every of them shall provide so many workmen from time to time to work by turn and course towards the doing thereof as the said Mr John Pitt, Mr Henry Russell, John Lockier, David Gyer, Owen Holman and John Thorneton or the greater number of them of them shall rate and assess them at. And that the same labourers shall be provided by every of them severally to work upon and at such days and times as they shall be summoned and warned for that service by the sergeants at the mace of the same town, or by any one of them. And that whosoever of the same

freeholders, tenants, inhabitants and residents shall refuse or neglect to provide his labourer or labourers, according to this agreement, shall forfeit 12d for the default of every labourer to be levied by distress upon warrant by the mayor for the time being, to be made unto the sergeants at the mace of the said town in that behalf. Provided always that the mayor and bailiffs,or two of them at the least whereof the mayor to be one, shall ratify and confirm the same rate before it be put in execution. And that a warrant from the same overseers or any five or four of them, whereof the said Mr John Pitt and Mr Henry Russell shall be two, shall be a sufficient warrant from time to time unto the collector or receiver of the revenues of this town for the payment of the said sum of fifty pounds for the use aforesaid.

18 June 1624

Upon this present day Roger Taunton in consideration of five shillings paid unto Mr David Gyer, receiver of the revenues of this town is admitted to use the trade of a baker freely within this town.

25 June 1624

Upon this present day it was and is agreed by a general consent that Mr Mayor shall retain Counsel at the charge of the Corporation about the Constitution for disfranchising of such freemen as shall inhabit out of the town and notwithstanding shall take the benefit of freemen within the town, and about such other business as do concern the town.

Upon the same day it was and is agreed by a general consent that Mr Mayor shall provide at the charge of the Corporation, so many piles for four piles or otherwise, for the bridge as are wanting and three or four planks.

[page 96 blank]
[page 97] An assembly held in the Guildhall of Melcombe Regis within the borough and town of Waymouth and Melcombe Regis in the county of Dorset by the mayor, aldermen, bailiffs and capital and principal burgesses of the said town the sixth day of October 1624.

Whereas about six years last past, there were letters from the Lords of His Majesty's Most Honourable Privy Council diverted unto the mayor of this town for the time being, for the levying of four hundred and fifty pounds upon the goods, wares and merchandises of such persons as should enter any goods either inwards or outwards in His Majesty's Custom House here. To be taken after the rate of one percent over and above His Majesty's customs which monies were so appointed to be raised and levied towards His Majesty's charge in setting forth His Highness's fleet against the Turks of Algier, and were to be paid to His Majesty's use in two several years when the same should be called for. And whereas Mr Thomas Gyer, one of the aldermen of this town, being mayor of this town at the time when the same letters were so diverted as aforesaid the for performance of a sudden payment of £225 of the £450 (which was then required) did to the great cost, loss and damage of this Corporation take up the same £225 upon interest and otherwise. And whereas upon the end of the mayoralty of the said Mr Gyer he did deliver over unto Mr Matthew Pitt deceased, his succeeding mayor, as well the said letters as also an account of the monies which he had received upon the same letters, together with such monies as did remain in his hands upon the same account. Whereupon the said Mr Matthew Pitt did collect and gather in the time of his mayoralty diverse sums of money out of which the £225 received to His Majesty's use as aforesaid was paid, and there rested in his hands upon his account over and beside the same £225 so paid as aforesaid, the sum of £105 14s 6d as by his account appears, which £105 14s 6d has not been paid over unto the next mayor of this town, for the time being, nor unto any other mayor for the time being since that time, although he was often times in his lifetime requested thereunto. And whereas Mr John Bond being the next successor of the said Mr Matthew Pitt in the office of mayor of the said town, did also in his time of mayoralty receive by four of the said letters the sum of £130 17s 8d as by his account appears, which he has not paid over neither to His Majesty's use, nor unto his next successor mayor of the said town, nor unto any other mayor since that time, albeit he has likewise often times been requested thereunto. Now for as much as by the same his being so directed unto the mayor of this town, for the the the time being, it is evident and manifest to be understood that the Lords of His Majesty's Council will require the other £225 which is behind of the sum of £450 at the hands of the mayor which is or shall be, for the time being, and not at the hands of the executor or executors of the said Mr Matthew Pitt, nor at the hands of the said Mr John Bond. It is therefore at this assembly fully agreed, ordered, constituted and appointed that warning shall be given unto the executor or executors of the said Mr Matthew Pitt, to bring in and pay the said monies so received by the said Mr Matthew Pitt, as aforesaid, within twenty days next after such warning given, or else shall forfeit to this Corporation the sum of ten pounds of lawful English money to be levied of their goods and chattels to the use of this Corporation. And it is further at this assembly fully agreed, ordered, constituted and ordained, that the said Mr John Bond shall bring in and pay unto the mayor for the time being, the same £130 17s 8d by him received and remaining in his hands as aforesaid, upon Wednesday next being the thirteenth day of this instant month of October, between the hours of nine and eleven of the clock in the forenoon, of the said day, at the Guildhall of Melcombe Regis aforesaid, or else shall forfeit to this Corporation the sum of forty pound of lawful English money to be levied of his goods and chattels to the use of this Corporation.

[Signed by] Henry Blichell, mayor; John Lockier, bailiff; Edward Linze, bailiff; Robert Whit, Thomas Giear, William Holman, Edward Roy, Matthew Allin, Robert Knight, Giles Grene, James James, William Martell [his mark], Henry Cuttance, Richard Allin, Henry Russell, David Giar, John Pytt, Robert Vaule [his mark], Thomas Lockeir, John Ellis [his mark], Peter Neale [his mark], Richard Hansford, Edward Hodder, William Willyams.

[page 98] 15 October 1624

At an assembly held in the Guildhall of Melcombe Regis within the borough and town of Waymouth and Melcombe Regis in the county of Dorset by the mayor, aldermen, bailiffs and capital and principal burgesses of the said borough and town it was and is agreed by a general consent of the said mayor, aldermen, bailiffs and capital and principal burgesses. That David Gyer, receiver of the town revenues shall pay unto Henry Browne, late captive in Turkey, out of the revenues of this town the sum of forty shillings to make him a new suit of apparel and that this agreement shall be the said receiver's sufficient warrant and discharge for the same.

16 October 1624

At an assembly held in the Guildhall of Melcombe Regis within the borough and town of Waymouth and Melcombe Regis aforesaid in the county of Dorset upon the day and year last above said by the mayor, aldermen, bailiffs and capital and principal [burgesses] of the said borough and town it was and is agreed by a general consent of the said mayor, aldermen, bailiffs and capital and principal burgesses that the solicitation of the town's petition unto His Majesty and the Lords of his Council shall be commended unto Mr Barnard Michell and that he shall be paid all such charges as there shall be occasion to lay forth in or about the soliciting thereof. And that such monies as he shall take up to be employed about the same business upon his Bill of Exchange shall be satisfied here by the receiver of the revenues of this town out of the same revenues and this agreement shall be sufficient warrant and discharge in that behalf.

12 November 1624

At an assembly held in the Guildhall of Melcombe Regis within the borough and town of Waymouth and Melcombe Regis in the county of Dorset upon the day and year last above said by the mayor, aldermen, bailiffs and capital and principal burgesses of the said borough and town by a general consent of the said assembly Mr Thomas Gyer, Mr Matthew Allin, Mr Thomas Lockier, Mr Richard Allin, Mr Henry Cuttance, Mr Thomas Waltham, John Thorneton and William Charitie are elected, named and appointed overseers for and about the repairing amending and making up of the molehead, harbour, jetty and quays of and belonging unto the borough and town of Waymouth and Melcombe Regis aforesaid. And it is agreed by a general consent that the same overseers, or the greater number of them, shall rate and assess all and every freeholder, burgess, tenant, inhabitant and resident unto what number of labourers every of them shall provide to work about the same premises. And that the same freeholders, burgesses, tenants, inhabitants and residents shall from time to time provide their several labourers there to work upon and at such several days and times as they shall be summoned and warned by the sergeants at the mace of the said borough and town for that purpose, or by any one of them. And that whosoever shall refuse or neglect to provide his or their labourer or labourers according to this agreement shall forfeit 12d for the default of every labourer not provided or not attending to do his service accordingly, to be levied by distress upon a warrant of the mayor, for the time being, to be made unto the said sergeants at the mace who by virtue of the said warrant shall have power to levy the same forfeiture. Provided always that the mayor and bailiffs or two of them (whereof the mayor to be one) shall ratify and confirm the same rate before it be put in execution.

[page 99] **26 November 1624**
Upon this present day Mr Henry Waltham one of the aldermen of this town in a public assembly at the Guildhall of Melcombe Regis within this borough and town of Waymouth and Melcombe Regis did deliver up unto Mr Mayor's hands and keeping ten several letters which have been heretofore at several times sent unto the mayor of this town for the time being, from the Lords of His Majesty's Most Honourable Privy Council.

3 December 1624
Upon this present day Mr John Pitt the younger, one of the aldermen of this town, in a public assembly at the Guildhall of Melcombe Regis within this borough and town of Waymouth and Melcombe Regis, did deliver up into the hands of Mr Henry Michell, mayor of the said borough and town, the sum of five pounds of current English money given unto the poor of this town by Mr Richard Pitt deceased, one of the aldermen of the town and father of the said Mr John Pitt.

Upon the same day it was ordered by a general consent of the mayor, aldermen, bailiffs and capital and principal burgesses of the borough and town of Waymouth and Melcombe Regis then assembled that there shall be a warrant made unto the hands and to and for the use of this Corporation three cauldrons of sea coal which were sold by one George S. Robins of Swansey, mariner, unto John Hill of Dorchester, merchant, being both foreigners and neither of them a freeman of this Corporation and so foreign bought and foreign sold, whereby it is become forfeited to this Corporation which warrant was accordingly made by Mr Mayor and executed by the sergeants.

8 December 1624
Upon this present day Mr Mayor made a warrant unto the sergeants at the mace within this borough and town of Waymouth and Melcombe Regis for the seizing of sixteen pieces of raisins unto the hands and to and for the use of this Corporation which were sold by John Gardner for and in the behalf of one Abraham Rutter, a merchant of Exeter unto John Major of Blandford, grocer, being all foreigners and not one of them a freeman of this Corporation and so foreign bought and foreign sold whereby it became forfeited to this Corporation and this warrant was executed whereupon the said John Gardner upon the tenth day of the same month came into the Guildhall of Melcombe Regis within the borough and town aforesaid unto the mayor, aldermen, bailiffs and capital and principal burgesses of the said borough and town then there assembled and did compound and agree with them as well for the same sixteen pieces of raisins so forfeited as aforesaid as also for free leave to sell such other raisins and commodities as the said Abraham Rutter has more to sell, extant within this Corporation, upon which composition and agreement the said John Gardner did affirm and promise to pay unto this Corporation upon the first day of January next coming the sum of ten pounds of lawful money of England.

10 December 1624

Upon this present day Mr John Bond, at the Guildhall, in a public assembly did pay unto Mr Mayor for himself £130 17s 8d and for Mistress Philip Pitt £105 14s 6d being the monies which the said Mr John Bond and Mr Matthew Pitt did receive in the time of their mayoralties and should have been paid in to His Majesty's Officers towards the charge of His Majesty's fleet against Angier, but remaining in their hands they upon a petition made unto His Majesty and the Lords of His Majesty's Most Honourable Privy Council, now ordered to pay unto the said mayor towards the building of the mouldhead at Waymouth Northe. Out of which monies Mr Dennis Bond was allowed five pounds for his charge in travelling unto London.

[page 100] **25 January 1625**

Upon this present day it was and is agreed by a general consent of the mayor, aldermen, bailiffs and capital and principal burgesses of this borough and town of Waymouth and Melcombe Regis that the overseers already appointed and named for the work about the molehead, jetty, quays etc. shall have the power and authority by virtue hereof from time to time to charge Mr Henry Michell mayor of the said borough and town to disburse the monies which shall be laid forth about the same molehead, jetty, etc. so long as the monies which he has received by order of the (Letters) of his Majesties most honourable Privy Council shall behold and continue which monies he shall so disburse upon a warrant under the hands of any five of the same overseers whereof Mr Thomas Gyer, Mr Matthew Allin and Mr Thomas Lockier shall be always one.

4 February 1625

Upon this present day it was and is agreed by a general consent of the mayor, aldermen, bailiffs and capital and principal burgesses of the said borough and town that the suit commenced in the Star Chamber by Mr James Hanam against Mr Mayor and others of this town shall be defended at the charge of this Corporation.

Upon the same day it was and is agreed by the like consent that there shall be four new bushels made for the measuring of salt at the charge of this Corporation which shall remain from time to time to the use of the mayor of the said Corporation for the time being for the measuring of salt and not otherwise.

At an assembly held at the Guildhall of Melcombe Regis within the borough and town of Waymouthe and Melcombe Regis in the county of Dorset by the mayor, aldermen, bailiffs and capital and principal burgesses of the said borough and town the 11th day of March in the year of our Lord God 1624 it was and is ordered constituted ordained and agreed by a general assent and consent of the said mayor, aldermen, bailiffs and capital and principal burgesses then and there assembled that for as much as the suffering of carthorses and of other horses and horse beasts to eat their hay and meat and to stand tied in the streets or lanes or upon the quays of this borough and town either in the market time or at any other time is found very offensive and annoying (noysom) both to the inhabitants of this borough and town and others which come into the same borough and town and also to the harbour; therefore from henceforth no carter or other person or persons whatsoever shall suffer any horse or horse beast whereof he or they have either the riding, driving or leading to stand eating, feeding or tied in the streets, lanes or upon the quays of the borough and town at any time upon pain to forfeit for every horse or horse beast 8d. to be levied by the distress in such manner and form as other forfeitures upon constitutions are appointed to be levied and the same shall be so levied by the sergeants at the mace, the porters or scavenger and the executioner to have the one half of the same forfeiture for his pains taken in the behalf.

19 April 1625
Upon this present day it was and is agreed by a general consent of the mayor, aldermen, bailiffs and capital and principal burgesses of this borough and town that there shall be but one inhabitant of this town chosen for a burgess of this town at the next parliament. And that he which shall be so chosen shall have such allowance for his wages as any other of the burgesses of this town at the last Parliament was allowed.

[page 101] 22 April 1625
Upon this present day it was and is agreed by a general consent of the mayor, aldermen, bailiffs and capital and principal burgesses of this borough and town of Waymouth and Melcombe Regis that the poor's monies which are in the hands of Mr Edward Roy and Mr Matthew Allin shall be brought in at Midsummer next and from thence forth employed about the setting of the poor on work.

At an assembly held at the Guildhall of Melcombe Regis within the borough and town of Waymouthe and Melcombe Regis in the county of Dorset by the mayor, aldermen, bailiffs and capital and principal burgesses of the said borough and town the first day of July in the year of lord Charles by the grace of God of England, Scotland, France and Ireland king, defender of the faith, etc. the first, 1625, it was and is agreed by a general consent if the said mayor, aldermen, bailiffs and capital and principal burgesses of the said borough and town here assembled that from henceforth so long as they shall think it requisite there shall be a watch kept within this borough and town of four men or more if there shall be occasion of more in the discretion of Mr Mayor and Mr Bailiffs for the time being every night throughout the whole year as well in winter as in summer. And that every householder within this borough and town resident and not resident in the discretion of Mr Mayor for the time being either in his own person or by his sufficient deputy such one as by the mayor for the time being shall be approved and accepted be a sufficient watchman shall watch so often as it shall come to his turn by course and it was and is further agreed by the said mayor, aldermen bailiffs and capital and principal burgesses of the said borough and town that if an householder within this borough and town either resident or not resident shall neglect to watch in person or shall not provide a sufficient deputy to watch in his stead to be ready to attend the constables on the bridge by eight of the clock every night when it shall come to his turn. Then every such householder neglecting his stead watch in person or not providing a sufficient deputy to watch in his stead such one as is aforesaid shall forfeit for every such offence and neglect eight pence to be levied by the constables and sergeants at the mace within the said borough and town or by some or one of them who of his and their own authority by virtue of this constitution and agreement shall have power to levy the same by distress and sale of the offenders and neglecter's goods rendering to each party the over plus which shall be made of his or their goods so distrained and sold. And it is further ordered and agreed by the like general consent that the sergeants for the time shall give warning unto every person at his house that is to provide a watchman in every forenoon of the same day in which he shall be appointed to provide and have a watchman the night following upon pain that the same sergeants in the default shall provide a watchman in the stead of him or them that shall be absent for want of warning as aforesaid.

Item, it was and is further agreed by a general consent of the said mayor, aldermen, bailiffs and capital and principal burgesses of the said borough and town that the two hogsheads of Gascoigne wines which were here foreign bought and foreign sold by one Thomas Combes of Southampton merchant to one Thomas Meryfield of Bridport, vintner, being neither of them freeman of this borough and town and therefore forfeited and seized to the use of this Corporation of this borough shall be sold to the best profit and advantage of the said Corporation. And that if either of the said Thomas Combes or the said Thomas Meryfield shall commence to bring any action or suit against the person or persons for or concerning the same two hogsheads of wine or any part thereof then the same action or suit shall be defended at the general charge of this Corporation. Edward Linze.

Signed: Henry Michell, mayor, Edward Linze, John Lockier, William Holman, Robert Knight, Henry Russell, Thomas Giear, Robert Vaule [initials], William Martell [initials], John Pytt, Thomas Cockinge, Richard Allin, James James, Henry Cuttance, David Giear, Edward Hodder, Thomas Waltham, Owen Holman, Richard Harrisone

[page 102] 15 July 1625

Upon this present day it was and is agreed and ordered by a general consent of mayor, aldermen, bailiffs and capital and principal burgesses of this borough and town of Waymouthe and Melcomb Regis that the barque whereof William Langer is master under God which lately came from London shall not land any part of the goods now on board of her within the liberties of this town until the same be thoroughly aired and it is also further agreed and ordered by the like consent that as well the said William Langer as all other masters of ships, barques which shall come from London with any goods brought from thence at any time during the time of God's visitation of plague in London and shall give occasion whereby there shall be a watch and ward appointed and set for the keeping of them out of the town, shall bear and pay the same watch and ward at his and their own proper costs and charges.

Upon the same day it was and is further agreed and ordered by the like general consent that Mr Robert White and Mr Matthew Allin shall bring in and pay to the recorder of the revenues of this town at the next assembly and meeting of the said mayor, aldermen bailiffs and capital and principal burgess all such monies and stock of the poor as are in their or either of their hands. To this end the same may be employed and converted to the setting of the poor to work.

Upon the same day it was and is also agreed and ordered by the like consent of the said mayor, aldermen, bailiffs and capital and principal burgesses That the coals lying in the yard of John Gallott which were heretofore seized to the use of this Corporation being foreign bought and foreign sold within this town between John Hill of Dorchester and George S. Robin of Swansey in Wales shall be not taken into the hands and possession of the Corporation out of the yard of the said Gallott.

29 July 1625
Upon this present day it was and is agreed and ordered by the general consent of the mayor, aldermen, bailiffs and capital and principal burgesses of the said borough and town of Waymouthe and Melcombe Regis that Mr David Gyer, receiver of the revenues, of this town shall buy and take from Mr Bailiff Lockier three barrels of powder and shall pay for the same as they shall agree.

Upon the same day it was and is also agreed and ordered by the like general consent of the said mayor, aldermen, bailiffs and capital and principal burgesses of the said borough and town that if any overseer of the work or workmen about the work of the molehead shall be molested troubled or fined for fetching of any stones unto that work from convenient places that then this Corporation at their proper costs and charges shall defend and keep harmless any person and persons which shall be so molested troubled or fined.

4 August 1625
Upon this present day at an assembly held by the mayor, bailiffs and of this borough and town Thomas Blackford one of the burgesses of this town in consideration of the four pence put unto him given and paid by Mr Henry Michell, mayor of the said town, did affirm and promise unto him the said Henry Mitchell that if Mr Giles Greene should be then chosen burgess to serve in the high court of parliament for this town in the place and stead of Thomas Middleton the younger, knight, lately chosen one of the knights of the county of Denbeigh and also chosen one of the burgesses for this town. Then he and the said Thomas Blackford would give unto the said Mr Henry Michell one hundred pounds if the said Giles Greene shall not attend that service or shall demand or require any wages for his attendance upon that service.

[page 103] 2 September 1625
Upon this present day it was and is agreed by a general consent of the mayor, aldermen, bailiffs and capital and principal burgesses of this borough and town of Waymouth and Melcombe Regis that if any question of suit in law shall be made either by Mr John Hill or Edward Bayly touching two bars of iron containing in weight [blank] being seized by order of Mr Mayor for that the same iron was foreign bought and foreign sold contrary to the privilege of this town Then the same suit shall be defended at the charge of this Corporation.

Signed:

Henry Mitchell, mayor	William Waltham	Robert Maier
Edward Linze, bailiff	Henry Russell	John Elis (his mark)

John Lockier, bailiff	Thomas Gier	Neald (his mark)
John Pytt	Edward Roy	James James
Henry Waltham	Edward Hodder	Matthew Allins
David Giare	Richard Harrison	Owen Holman, esquire
Thomas Waltham		

[page 104] 6 October 1625

Upon this present day it is agreed by a general consent of the mayor, aldermen, bailiffs and capital and principal burgesses of this borough and town of Waymouth and Melcombe Regis in the county of Dorset that the walls of the Blockhouse shall be built up with stone and that a platform for the two pieces of ordnance at and upon the north shall be made of Purbeck stone. All which shall be done at the charge of the Corporation.

25 November 1625

Upon this present day it was and is agreed by a general consent of the mayor, aldermen, bailiffs and capital and principal burgesses of the borough and town of Waymouth and Melcombe Regis in the county of Dorset that there shall be delivered and made good unto the churchwarden of Waymouthe side for the building of Weymouth chapel the sum of thirty pounds for so much likewise unto the churchwarden of Melcombe side for the furnishing of Melcomb Church heretofore allowed and paid.

Item, that the five pounds which were given unto the poor of Melcombe side by Mr John Pitt late an alderman of this town were delivered over by Henry Rose churchwarden unto James James as part of the thirty pounds lent unto him to the use of the poor of Melcombe side aforesaid.

20 January 1626

Upon this present day it was and is agreed by a general consent of the mayor, bailiffs and burgesses of the borough and town of Waymouthe and Melcombe Regis that there shall be two burgesses chosen out of the inhabitants of this town to serve for this town at the next session of Parliament to be held at Westminster upon the sixth day of February next coming which two burgesses so chosen shall bear their own charges having each of them 2s 6d per day from the town. And thereupon forthwith the burgesses proceeding to their election did make the choice of Sir John Strangwayes, knight, Arthur Pyne, esquire, Barnard Michell one of the aldermen of this town and Giles Greene, gentlemen, to be their four burgesses to serve for the said town at the said next session of Parliament.

24 January 1626

Upon this present day it was and is agreed by a general consent of the mayor, aldermen, bailiffs and capital burgesses of the borough and town of Waymouthe and Melcombe Regis that the treasurer of the revenue of this town shall pay unto the overseers of Waymouth side to and for the use of the chapel the £30 formerly ordered, and likewise £20 more to be employed by the inhabitants of Waymouthe for the obtaining of an act of Parliament for the making their said chapel a free chapel of ease for the use of the inhabitants and that there shall be the like sum allowed for the use of the church of Melcombe at the next occasion.

29 January 1626
Upon this present day it was and is agreed by a general consent of the mayor, aldermen, bailiffs and capital and principal burgesses of this borough and town that Richard Harrison shall have a new lease of the shop under the town hall now in his occupation to begin at Christide next and to continue from then for the term of 21 years under the rent of three pounds per annum and the said Richard Harryson is to covenant to seal the same shop over head and paved or planked under foot and so to leave it in the end of the term.

[page 105] 10 March 1626
Upon this present day it was and is agreed by a general consent of the mayor, aldermen, bailiffs and capital and principal burgesses s of the borough and town of Waymouthe and Melcombe Regis in the county of Dorset that Mr Arnold Bassett shall have leave freely to sell all the Gascoigne wines which he now has within this town without any forfeiture or consideration for being foreign sold and foreign bought. In Consideration whereof the said Mr Bassett did affirm and promise to give to this Corporation the sum of ten pounds of current English money to be paid the first day of April next coming.

25 April 1626
Upon this present day it was and is agreed by a general consent of the said mayor, aldermen, bailiffs and capital and principal burgesses of the borough and town that from hence forth the sergeants at the mace [of] this borough and town shall have and take of every freeman of this town every quarter of salt and every quarter of quarter of grain whatsoever coming into this town at his own adventure the sum of one half penny if they or their deputy do give attendance to strike the measure being requested there unto and from aliens and such as are not free the sum of one penny for every quarter, and it was likewise agreed at the same assembly that the porters of the town shall have and take the like fees as the sergeants are to take.

21 September 1626
Upon this present day Mr Edward Linsey was chosen mayor of this town for the year following.
Upon the same day Mr Henry Waltham and Mr Henry Cuttance were chosen bailiffs of this town for the year following.
Upon the same day Mr David Gyer was chosen collector and treasurer of the town revenues for this year following.
Upon the same day Mr Bailiffs elected Mr Henry Michell, Mr Robert Major, Jeremy Balbridge and Thomas Ladoze were chosen and appointed auditors to audit all accounts concerning this Incorporation for the year following.

28 September 1626

Upon this present day it was and is agreed by a general consent that Mr John Pitt shall have the collection of the petty customs and other things for this year following giving the town sufficient securities for answering thereof.

Upon the same day the cartage and bridge rates are granted unto Henry Hillerd for the year following at £19 10s rent per annum.

Upon the same day the profits of the market are granted to John Read for the year following at £6 rent per annum.

[page 106] 10 October 1626

Upon this present day it was and is agreed by a general consent of the mayor, aldermen, bailiffs and capital and principal burgesses of the borough and town that such persons as gave entertainment to the soldiers shall have 3s 6d per week for every soldier and that the constable shall collect it according to the rate made for one whole month.

Upon the same day it was also agreed by the like consent that there shall be like pain inflicted upon those that are appointed to round the watch if they shall neglect their duty as there is inflicted upon the watchmen.

Upon the same day it was likewise agreed by the like consent that the treasurer of the town revenues shall go forward with the work at the town's end so far as twenty pounds shall extend no further until there shall be a further order by consent of this court.

27 October 1626

Upon this present day it is agreed by a general consent of the mayor, aldermen, bailiffs and capital and principal burgesses of the borough and town that Mr Henry Russell and Mr James James shall be overseers to see the jetty repaired with all expedition at the town's charges.

3 November 1626

Upon this present day it was and is agreed by a general consent of the mayor, aldermen, bailiffs and capital and principal burgesses of the borough and town that Mr Henry Russell and Mr James James shall be overseers to see the jetty repaired with all expedition at the town's charges.

16 November 1626

Upon this present day it was agreed by the general consent of the mayor, aldermen, bailiffs and capital and principal burgesses of the borough and town that there shall be a new crane built and set up at the town's charge.

1 December 1626

Upon this present day Mr Robert Vaule, Mr Thomas Waltham, Thomas Ledoze and Henry Rose by a general consent of the mayor, aldermen, bailiffs and capital and principal burgesses of the borough and town are chosen, named and appointed surveyors about the repairing of the quays, jetties and other necessary repairs to be done about the water. And it is agreed by the like general consent that their warrant unto the collectors and receivers of the town's revenues for the payment of doing of the same repairs shall be his sufficient warrant for the disbursing of the same charge.

[page 107] **2 April 1627**
Upon this present day it was and is agreed by a general consent of the mayor, aldermen, bailiffs and capital and principal burgesses of this borough and town that if any action or suit at any time here after shall be commenced or brought against any town's man for coming or going upon the ground at the north that then the same action and suit shall be defended at the charge of this Corporation.

29 May 1627
Upon this present day it was ordered by a general consent of the by a general consent of the mayor, aldermen, bailiffs and capital and principal burgesses of the borough and town that John Hamon shall give this Corporation thirty shillings of current English money for the redeeming of the Gatcombe which he being not freeman of this town did sell where within this town to John Clarke of Dunhead, being also no freeman, and so it became forfeited for being foreign bought and foreign sold.

   Upon this same day it is agreed by the like general consent of the said by a general consent of the mayor, aldermen, bailiffs and capital and principal burgesses that if Mr John Blachford shall at any time hereafter commence or bring any action or suit against Mr Mayor or any other men of this town for or concerning one butt of wine, seized to the use of this Corporation as foreign bought and foreign sold, that then the same action and suit shall be defended at the charge of this Incorporation.

   Also at the same day it was and is agreed by a like general consent of the by a general consent of the mayor, aldermen, bailiffs and capital and principal burgesses of the borough and town that the molehead shall be repaired at the town charges and that Mr Matthew Allin shall pay the same charges out of such of the town's monies as are in his hands.

4 June 1627
Upon this present day John James, John Keeles, Simon Godfrey, John Casse, William Dryer and Leonard Hillard were sworn by Mr Mayor to sell (*viend*) the wood brought hither to be sold and to present whether it were agreeable unto the assize limited and appointed by the statute made in that behalf.

21 September 1627
Thomas Lockier was chosen mayor of this borough and town for the year following.

   Upon the same day Mr John Thorneton and. Mr Thomas Waltham were chosen bailiffs of this borough and town for the year following.

   Upon the same day Mr David Gyer was chosen treasurer for the revenues of this town for the year following.

[page 108] **28 September 1627**
Upon this present day the profits of the market are granted unto John Read for the year following at £8 per annum and to be paid quarterly.

Upon the same day the cartage and bridge rates are granted unto Mr Edward Linsey now mayor for the year following at £21 per annum and to be paid quarterly.

The petty customs and ballast are in the town's hands to dispose.

16 November 1627
Upon this present day Mr Richard Blachford Mr John Blachford of Dorchester, merchants, by James James of this town did submit themselves to be fined for selling of one butt of fortified wine (*sack*) within this town to Edward Romyn alias Foxe a country vintner, being foreign bought and foreign sold, where upon they were fixed at 20s.

Upon the same day John Rashley is admitted to use the trade of a fuller within this town and did give for his admittance 5s.

Upon the same Day it was agreed by a general consent of the mayor, aldermen, bailiffs and capital and principal burgesses of this town that bailiffs and Mr Matthew Allin shall have the keeping of the keys of the town chest for this year following.

Upon the same day it was agreed by the like consent that Mr Bailiffs, Mr Matthew Allin, Richard Harrison, Mr William Cade and Gregory Bubbage are chosen and appointed auditors to audit all accounts concerning this Incorporation for this year following.

Upon this same day it was agreed by the like consent that Mr John Pitt shall have £6 for the collecting of the last years petty customs and that he shall have the collection of the petty customs for this year following and 12d of every pound allowed for his pains. And shall give security to make payment of his collection at the end of every month.

19 May 1628
Upon this present day it was agreed by a general consent of the mayor, aldermen, bailiffs and capital and principal burgesses of this borough and town that Mr Mayor shall write unto Mr Henry Waltham to entreat him to make petition to the lords of the counsel on the behalf of this Corporation to grant powder, shot and carriages to serve for such ordnance as their lordships have granted for the fortification of this town according to the first order of their lordships. And that if it can not be procured at the King's charge that then he do buy and send down with the ordnance fifteen hundred weight of shot.

[page 109] **2 June1628**
Upon this present day it was agreed by a general consent of the mayor, aldermen, bailiffs and capital and principal burgesses of this borough and town that there shall be a £20 rate for the making and furnishing of the bulwark already made and to be made for the defence of this town and that Mr Bailiff Thornton, Mr Henry Michell, Mr David Gyer and Mr William Cade or any three of them shall make the same rate.

29 August 1628

At an assembly held by the mayor, aldermen, bailiffs and capital and principal burgesses of this borough and town of Waymouth and Melcombe Regis in the county of Dorset at the Guildhall there the day and year above said it was ordained, constituted, established and agreed upon by a general consent of the mayor, aldermen, bailiffs and capital and principal burgesses that if any person interested in any burgage, cottage or house within this borough and town shall from henceforth receive or take the same burgage or house any tenants or under tenants to inhabit or dwell therein which have not formerly been inhabiting and dwelling within this town by the space of three years rules such tenants or under tenants shall before hand give to this Corporation sufficient security, such as shall be to the liking of the mayor and bailiffs of the said borough and town, for the time being that neither he nor his wife, children, nor family shall be any way chargeable to this Corporation upon pain that every person so receiving or taking, any tenants or under tenants contrary to the true intent and meaning of this constitution shall proscribe £50 forfeit £20 to this Corporation to be levied according to the form of the levying of the forfeitures of this Corporation.

[Signatures of:] Thomas Cockinge, mayor, John Thornton, bailiff, Thomas Waltham, bailiff, Henry Michell, Henry Russell, John Pytt, Thomas Giear, John James, Henry Cuttance, David Giare, William Wylliams, Richard Harrisone.

[The marks of:] William Martell, Thomas Wallis, John Ellis

[page 110] **21 September 1628**

Upon this present day Mr David Gyer is chosen mayor for this borough and town for this year following.

Upon the same day Mr Matthew Allin and Mr Edward Lynsey are chosen bailiffs of this borough and town for this year following.

Upon the same day Thomas Waltham was chosen receiver of the town revenues for the year following.

Upon the same day John Gallott, George Flirrye and Christopher Hall are chosen constables for the year following.

14 November 1628

At an assembly held at the Guildhall of Melcombe Regis within the borough and town of Waymouth and Melcombe Regis by the mayor, aldermen, bailiffs and capital and principal burgesses of the said borough and town it was and is agreed by a general consent that Mr Richard Marwell, parson of Radipole, where unto Melcombe Regis is incident and belonging shall have receive and enjoy to his proper use and behalf four pounds per annum out of the rent of the shop under the town hall now in the possession of rent of Richard Harrison and out of the rent of the custom house in Melcombe Regis aforesaid for and towards the payment of the rent of the house wherein he dwells in Melcombe Regis aforesaid so long as he shall continue an inhabitant and dwelling in the said house.

[Signatures:] David Giare, mayor, Edward Linze, Henry Waltham, Henry

Russell, Thomas Giar, Henry Michell, Thomas Cocking, John Pytt, Thomas Waltham, Edward Hodder, James James, Richard Harrisone, Henry Rose, Owen Holman.
   The mark of Thomas Wallis.

[page 111] 5 October 1628

Upon the present day the hundred pounds given by Mr Robert Middleton to this town was divided between four young merchants of this town according to the will of the said Robert Middleton by them to be repaid the fifth day of October which shall be in the year of our lord God 1631.

6 October 1628

Upon this present day in consideration of five pounds paid into this Corporation by John Senior son in law to John Small, town clerk of this town, he is admitted and sworn a freeman of this town which five pounds now forth with by a general consent of the mayor, aldermen, bailiffs and capital and principal burgesses of this borough and town given to the said John Small in lieu and respect of his long service done to this town.

   Upon the same day Mr Matthew Allin, Mr Edward Linsey, bailiffs, Mr John Cade, Mr Thomas Ledoz, John Casse and Jeremy Babbidge are chosen and appointed auditors for the auditing of this Corporation..

   Upon the same day Henry Hillerd, Richard Chowne, Henry Winter, John Samways, Thomas Bascombe and Richard Smithe are re-sworn [as] porters and to make a true account of such monies, as they shall collect for the duties of the bridge.

   Upon the same day Henry Hillerd is appointed to receive and collect the duties of the bridge for this year following.

   Upon the same day Mr Henry Waltham took the ballast and forfeitures of the quays of this Corporation for this year following. And is to pay for the same £5 15s at Lady Day and Michaelmas as by even portions.

   Upon the same day Mr John Pitt is appointed to collect the petty customs and is to have for his pains as he has had the last year.

   Upon the same day it was agreed that Henry Gibson shall set up a new shop in the place of where his old shop doth stand making the same two feet longer than the old shop and broader paying unto this Corporation yearly during the term of 21 years for the grounds whereupon the the same shop shall stand being for so long since granted unto him the yearly rent of four shillings of current English money per annum and he is to keep the shop to his own use in the end of the term.

5 December 1628

At an assembly held in the Guildhall of Melcombe Regis within the borough and town of Weymouth and Melcombe Regis in the county of Dorset by the mayor, aldermen bailiffs and capital and principal burgesses of the said borough and town upon the day and year aforesaid Nicholas Minard, carpenter, an inhabitant of this town but no freeman having wronged the privilege of this town in buying of timber of one Watts of Dorchester who is likewise no freeman of this town did submit himself to the censure of this assembly for the rating and assessing of his fine for the same wrong where upon the said assembly did assess and rate his fine at ten shillings.

Upon the same day the said Nicholas Minard humbly submitting himself to this assembly did entreat that for the fine for forty shillings he may be admitted from henceforth to use his occupation within this town and to buy and sell freely within this town timber and other things belonging to his trade which for the same fine upon his earnest suit was granted unto him.

12 December 1628
Upon this present day Mr David Gyer, Mr Edward Roy, Mr Henry Michell and Mr John Thornton or any three of them are entreated and appointed for the making of a rate for the raising of £20 to finish and end the bulwark already began and to be made for the defence of this town And Mr Edward Cuttance, Richard Champion and John Pope are appointed overseers of the same work.

[page 112] 22 December 1628
Upon this present day it was agreed by a general consent of the mayor, aldermen, bailiffs and capital and principal burgesses here assembled that the sergeants of the mace shall set up the town beam and scales and bring forth the weights into the streets for the weighing of Mr Henry Russell, Mr John Gardner and Mr John Blachford their sugars. And that if they shall refuse to have it weighed at the town beam then the sergeants shall notice at the beam where they shall weight it what the weight of it shall come to, to the end they may distrain for the town's duty for the weight thereof.

4 February 1629
Upon this present day Richard Kinge esquire was chosen recorder of this borough and town in the place and in the stead of Hugh Ryne esquire deceased.

6 February 1629
Upon this present day it is agreed by a general consent of the mayor, aldermen, bailiffs and capital burgesses here assembled that Mr Thomas Wallis and the two constables of Melcombe side shall collect the rates of Melcombe side made for the finishing of the bulwark and that Mr Edward Cuttance and the two constables of Waymouth side shall collect rates of Waymouth side for the finishing of the same work. And that the same collection on either side shall be made and the monies delivered unto the treasurer of the revenues of this town by the last day of this present month upon pain of such collectors before named as shall make default in that behalf to forfeit 20d. And upon pain of such persons as be rated towards the same collection and shall refuse to pay the same rate every of them to forfeit double his rate.

13 March 1629
Upon this present day Joseph Andrewes is chosen and sworn one of the sergeants at the mace in the stead and place of Henry Rendall deceased.

13 April 1629

Upon this present day it is agreed by a general consent of the mayor, aldermen, bailiffs and capital and principal burgesses here assembled that the watch shall be continued this year following as it was the last year that Mr John Pitt and Mr Edward Hodder with the constable, George Flurye, for Melcomb side and Mr John Thornton and Mr William Cade with the constable, John Gallott, for Waymouth side shall prescribe a course for the appointing of the watchmen and rounders from time to time and that the sergeants at the mace shall from time to time summon and warn the watchmen and rounders upon that day by ten of the clock in the forenoon in which they are to watch the night following and whosoever that shall be summoned to watch or round the watch if any of them shall neglect to perform the service in his own person or by a sufficient man in his stead shall forfeit for every default 12d. to be levied upon his goods by any one or more of the constables.

Upon the same day by the like consent Thomas Baldwin is granted licence and leave to keep open shop for his trade and occupation of a tailor and to buy and sell such things as concern his trade upon condition that he take no apprentices but only such as shall be born within the town and upon condition that he pay forty shillings to the treasurer of this town within one month next following.

Upon this day John Hicks, tailor, has the like licence granted to him upon the like condition touching the taking of apprentices as aforesaid and upon condition that he pay twenty shillings as aforesaid.

Upon the same day John Reynolds, tailor, has the like licence granted to him upon the like condition touching the taking of apprentices as aforesaid and upon condition that he pay fifteen shillings as aforesaid.

[page 113] 19 June 1629

Upon the present day John Hickes, tailor, has paid his fine of twenty shillings for using his trade according to the former licence granted to him.

Upon this present day Nicholas Mynard has paid as well the fine of ten shillings for usurping the liberty of this town in buying of timber and selling of it again being no freeman of the town. As also forty shillings for licence to use his trade of a carpenter within this town. And for buying and selling of such things as he shall have occasion of for his own use.

28 September 1629

Upon this present day the ballast and forfeitures upon the constitution for keeping clean of the quays and cleansing of the harbour are granted to Mr Henry Waltham at the rent of ten pounds for this year following. The cartage and profits of the bridge are granted to Mr Thomas Waltham for the year following at the rent of £18 5s.

The duties and profits of the market are granted to John Read for this year following at the rent of £11.

The petty customs and other town duties Mr John Pitt is to collect as he has done heretofore.

9 October 1629

Upon this present day Mr Henry Rose and Mr, William Caide by a general consent of the mayor, aldermen, bailiffs and capital burgesses of this borough and town are chosen and appointed to have the oversight of the repairing of the jetty at the charge of the Corporation. And that the monies for doing therefore shall be disbursed by the treasurer upon their warrant which shall be his discharge for the same.

30 October 1629
Upon this present day it was agreed by a general consent of the mayor, aldermen, bailiffs and capital burgesses of this borough and town that Roger Devenishe, a glazier, shall have liberty to keep open his glazier's shop in this town upon condition that he pay weekly towards the relief of the poor of this town one penny, provided that if he bring his wife and children hither to dwell there his licence shall be void.

5 February 1630
Upon this present day it was and is agreed by a general consent of the mayor, aldermen, bailiffs and capital and principal burgesses of this borough and town that whosoever is behind in payment towards the making of the bulwarks and shall not pay the same within six days after demand shall not only pay so much money as they are rated at but also so much more as their rate amounts to which shall be levied by distress of their goods and chattels by the constables and sergeants at the mace of this borough and town or by some or one of them by warrant from the mayor and bailiffs of the said town.

5 March 1630
Upon this present day it was and is constituted, ordained and agreed by a general consent of the mayor, aldermen, bailiffs and capital and principal burgesses of this borough and town that what ship or bark soever shall shoot any piece of ordnance, or blow of any piece of ordnance, within the jetty head, the owner or master of the said ship or bark shall forfeit and pay to this Corporation the sum of twenty shillings and also to every party grieved such damage as shall appear to be done by the same shot which shall be levied upon the said ship or bark by warrant made by the mayor for the time being to the sergeants at the mace.
Upon the day and year last above written Thomas Baldwin, tailor, did pay unto the treasurer ten shillings in part of payment of his fine.

[page 114] 14 May 1630
Upon this present day it was and is agreed by a general consent of the mayor, aldermen, bailiffs and capital and principal burgesses of this borough and town that Mr David Gyer, Mr Henry Cuttance, Mr Robert Major and Mr William Cade shall make a rate for the porters' fees and that the porters shall not demand greater or other fees then according to the rate which they shall make.

21 May 1630
Upon this present day it was and is agreed by a general consent of the mayor,

aldermen, bailiffs and capital and principal burgesses of this borough and town that the Corporation shall pay John Pope the charges of the man which was hurt by the Fleming. And that the constables at the next sessions of the peace shall be fined for not doing their end, viz. to have apprehended the Fleming.

Upon the same day it was and is agreed by the like general consent that Mr Mayor of this town for time being shall in his best discretion appoint the placing of the town ordnance and carriages.

Upon the same day it was and is also agreed by the like general consent that Mr Bailiffs for the time being Mr Henry Russell, Mr John Thornton, Mr John Cade and Mr William Cade shall make a rate for the raising of monies to make platforms for the said ordnance. And that the rate as they or any five or four of them shall make shall bind the persons rated to make payment accordingly.

4 June 1630

Upon this present day William Ashe, tailor, by a general consent of the mayor, aldermen, bailiffs and capital and principal burgesses here assembled is admitted to use his trade within this town for the fine of forty shillings whereof he paid ten shillings in hand and the other 30s. he is to pay quarterly that is to say a 10s. every quarter provided always that he take his apprentices of the town.

Upon this present day Clement Bayly, a Frenchman of Sherbroke [Cherbourg] did pay forty shillings for making of two shot out of his ordnance on board his ship within the jetty, contrary to a constitution thereof made, but with a general consent he was restored 35s. back because he was an alien and knew not the constitution.

Upon this present day Mr John Lockier, Mr William Cade, Mr Henry Rose and Mr John James are chosen and appointed to view the decayed places of the quays on both sides of the harbour and to take order and see the same repaired at the town charges.

28 July 1630

Upon hearing of the difference between Mary Lock, widow, and her servant Joan Parmiter before Mr Mayor, Mr Bailiff Lodoze, Mr William Holman and Mr Henry Waltham, aldermen, for as much as it appeared to them that the said Mary had unreasonably beaten her said servant without any just cause. It was therefore ordered by them that the said servant should be at liberty to depart from and out of the said dame's service.

[page 115] 21 September 1630

Upon this present day Mr Thomas Gyer was chosen mayor for this year following there being named within the said choice Mr Henry Cuttance, Mr Thomas Waltham, Mr John Thorneton.

Upon the same day Mr John Lockier and Mr John Cade were chosen bailiffs for this year following.

Upon the same day Mr Thomas Waltham was chosen clerk and treasurer of the town revenues for this year following.

Upon the same day Mr Bailiffs elected Mr Matthew Allin, William Holmes and Arthur Holman are appointed auditors of the treasury and town's accounts.

28 September 1630

Upon this present day the petty customs were granted for this year following to Mr Thomas Waltham for the rent of £167 to be paid quarterly.

Upon this present day the profits of the market are granted to John Reade for this year following at the rent of £12 to be paid quarterly.

Upon this present day the cartage and the fees and duties of the bridge were granted to Thomas Ledoze for this year following at the rent of £20 to be paid quarterly.

Upon this present day the ballast and forfeitures upon constitutions for keeping clean the quays and cleansing the harbour are granted to Nicholas Corune for this year following at the rent of £10 to be paid quarterly.

18 October 1630

Upon this present day it was and is agreed by a general consent of the mayor, aldermen, bailiffs and capital burgesses then assembled that Mr Matthew Allin and Mr David Gyer should travel to London about the soliciting of the town business against crossing of Exeter and that the treasurer should deliver them ten pounds out of the town's money to bear their charges. And that if they should disburse any more it should be allowed to them upon their account. [A case was brought to the Exchequer in 1630 by Weymouth and Melcombe Regis and Jeremiah Babbidge, merchant, against Thomas Crossinge, alderman of the city of Exeter, determining whether the merchants, citizens or freemen of the city of Exeter were liable to pay petty customs in the port of Weymouth. See The National Archives, E 134/5Chas1/Mich7.]

Upon the same day it was also agreed by the like general consent that the use of the poor's money shall be brought in and new bonds shall be given for the principal.

30 December 1630 [This entry is inserted into the text between the entries for January and February 1631].

Upon this present day Francis Gape, gentleman, was by general consent of the mayor, aldermen and bailiffs there assembled, elected and sworn common clerk for this borough in the room and stead of John Smalle, gentleman, deceased; who is to have and receive all fees and duties belonging to the said office in as ample a manner as the said John Small had and enjoyed the same.

7 January 1631

Upon this present day it is agreed and assented to by a general consent of the mayor, aldermen, bailiffs and capital burgesses then in the Guildhall assembled that the full sum of five pounds per annum shall be paid to [blank] Small widow the relict of John Small, gentleman, deceased, late town clerk of this borough by the receiver of the town's revenues for the time being. The said sum to be paid to her quarterly by even portions and to be continued so long as she shall remain an inhabitant of this borough.

Upon the same day it is also agreed on by the like general consent of the same assembly that the receiver of the town's revenues shall pay to the sergeants at mace for this borough the sum of twenty shillings towards the payment for their cloaks for this year.

[page 116] Upon the same day Mr John Lockier and Mr John Cade, bailiffs, Mr, David Clear and John Thornton are by the same assembly desired to view the plot of ground allotted to William Bright to build, and to make certificate how many feet in breadth and length he has taken in.

21 February 1631

Upon this present day Mr Mayor caused 700 weight of bread bought and shipped by certain Frenchmen in a ship of Burdeaux in Gascoign called Shup Challibett in which John Ronpin went under God's mercy to be seized and fetched on shore. And upon view of their company, which were in number 7, and for their victuals homewards it was thought fit they should have allowed them 300 weight of the same bread, which was done accordingly. And the other 400 weight remains in the Guildhall seized until order shall be given by the lords of the council how the same shall be disposed of.

Upon this present day on the confession of George Flerry that he is to sell the deal boards remaining in his yard by retail for John Hill of Dorchester a foreigner who bought the same of Richard Bury of Dorchester aforesaid another foreigner. It is thought fit and agreed on by a general consent that the deal boards be seized on as forfeited to the town in being foreign bought and foreign sold, which was performed accordingly by Mr Mayor, Mr Bailiff Cade and Francis Gape the town clerk.

3 June 1631

Upon this present day Arthur Holman, Nicholas Cornew and Gabriel Cornish are elected to be three of the capital and principal burgesses of this Corporation at which time Nicholas Cornew and Gabriel Cornish took their oaths accordingly.

Upon the same day by a general consent of the mayor, aldermen, bailiffs and capital burgesses it is agreed upon that Mr Thomas Waltham, treasurer for this town, shall deliver to Andrew Keilway, gentleman, the sum of forty shillings to be by him delivered to the Justices of Peace for the county of Dorset as a free gift given by this town towards the repair of Moon's Bridge near Dorchester.

Upon the same day by a like general consent it is agreed that Mr Thomas Waltham shall deliver unto Francis Gape, gentleman, the town clerk, the sum of ten pounds towards the soliciting of the cause in the Exchequer chamber between this town and the City of Exeter, and that he likewise deliver unto him all such sums of money as he shall disburse in this said cause upon his account for the same.

[page 117] Upon the same day the watch house is by the like general consent let to James Chapple to make a shop to work in at the yearly rent of two shillings to be by him paid quarterly to the treasurer for the time being and he [is] to leave the same to the town again when he shall be thereunto required.

3 April 1631
Upon this present day Mr Mayor in the name of this whole Corporation made an entry upon the waste grounds lying in the High Street in Waymouth between the lands of Richard Brooke on the East part, and the lands of [blank] on the West having been an ancient burgage and fallen in decay, and proclamation having been made publicly for the owners or possessors thereof to rebuild the same, which they not having done it became forfeited to the town by the statute. In the presence of Mr John Cade, bailiff, Mr Robert Whyte, Mr Matthew Allin, Mr David Giear, Mr Henry Cuttance, Mr William Cuttance, Mr, William Cade, the town clerk and the two sergeants.

31 May 1631
It is agreed that the town clerk shall go to London in solicitation of the cause depending between the town and the city of Exeter, and that Mr Thomas Waltham deliver to him ten pounds to be by [him] expended in the solicitation thereof, and likewise to pay him such other sums of money as he shall disburse about the said business upon his account given for the same.

[page 118] **24 August 1631**
It is agreed on by a general consent in a full assembly this present day that, by reason the bridge in this town is decaying and stands in need of of prompt repair, threescore tonnes of choice timber shall be with all convenient speed bought, either in the New Forest or in the Isle of Wight to be employed in repair thereof; and that David Fippen shall be desired to undertake the buying thereof, and for that purpose to go thither forthwith. And the treasurer shall deliver him £10 in hand for buying of the said timber, and shall pay him 2s 6d for every day he shall be employed therein for his pains and expenses, and all such other sums of money as he shall lay out or agree for either for the timber or for carriage of the same both by sea and land or any other ways about this business upon his account given in for the same.

21 September 1631
Upon this present day Mr John Thornton was elected mayor of this borough for the year next ensuing, there being named with him for the same choice Mr Henry Cuttance, Mr Thomas Waltham and Mr Thomas Wallis the elder.

On the same day Mr Edward Roye and Mr Richard. Harrison were elected bailiffs for this year following within this borough.

Upon the same day Mr Thomas Giear the last mayor is elected collector and treasurer of the rents and revenues of this town for this next year.

Upon the same day Mr Bailiff elected Mr David Giear, William Cade, John James, Thomas Snowden and William Charity are appointed auditors of the treasurer's and town's accounts.

[page 119] **28 September 1631**
Upon this present day the petty customs were let to Jeremy Babbidge for this year following at the rent of £190 to be paid quarterly.

Upon the same day the profits of the market are let to John Reade at the rent of £13 for this year following, the said rent to be paid quarterly.

Upon the same day the cartage is let to Mr John James for this next year at the rent of £15 10s, and it is agreed that the bridge shall remain in the town's hands, and Mr Mayor to appoint some one to collect duties payable on it.

Upon the same day the ballast and forfeitures upon the quays and harbour are granted to the said John James for the year ensuing and at the rent of £10 10s to be paid quarterly.

It is agreed upon this present day by the whole assembly that four shillings shall be paid to John Pope the elder for carrying away the soil from the quay against his house.

Upon this present day the lighter that belongs to this town being unfit for service is sold to Henry Rose for £3 2s.

Upon this present day 'it is agreed on that the town clerk shall go to London in solicitation of the cause depending between this town and the City of Exeter, and that the sergeant, Justinian Bagg, being served by a messenger to appear before Sir Robert Heath, the King's Attorney, shall go up with him. And that Mr Treasurer shall deliver to the town clerk ten pounds and to the sergeant forty shillings, and to pay such other monies as shall appear upon account to be disbursed in both the said businesses.

[page 120] 23 December: 1631

Upon this present day it is agreed by the mayor, aldermen, bailiffs and capital and principal burgesses at a general assembly, that the treasurer for this borough shall deliver to Justinian Bagg, one of the sergeants at mace for this borough, the sum of forty shillings which this town doth freely give him for his loss of time and his hindrance thereby in his journey to London.

Upon the same day by the same assembly Mr, Russell and Mr Lyndsey are desired to take a view of the timber that David Pippen has bought and brought home for the town's use, and whether he has brought home the full quantity that he was appointed to buy. And the said Pippen is appointed to bring in to them his notes as well of the said timber bought, as of the moneys disbursed about the same.

Upon the same day it is agreed by the like general consent that the town shall relinquish the forfeiture of the void land in the High Street in Waymouth between the land of Richard Brook on the East and the land of [blank] on the West, into which an entry was lately made. And to confirm the lease that Joan Serry widow has of the same land.

23 December:1631

Upon this present day it is agreed by a general consent of the mayor, aldermen, bailiffs and capital or principal burgesses at a general assembly that a crane with a house over it shall be made at the town's charge and erected in a fit place upon the quay in or near the place where the old crane stood, and that Luke Wilson of Portland be by Mr Mayor desired to confer with Mr Russell about the framing thereof, and it be set by the first day of May next.

[page 121] It is likewise agreed on this present day that a Rundlett of the best wine which shall contain about eight or ten gallons shall be bought and presented to Sir Francis Ashley, knight of Counsel with this town as a gratuity for his love and readiness to pleasure this Corporation.

30 March 1632

Upon this present day at a general assembly Gilbert Loder of Dorchester within this county, gentleman, executor of the last will and testament of Joan Gold of Dorchester aforesaid widow, deceased, paid to Mr Mayor of this borough the full sum of £20 sterling being a legacy given by the same Joan Gold to this Corporation to be employed to the relief of the poor therein according to her last will and testament, the tenor of which gift in her will follow in these words, viz:

Item 1 give and bequeath unto the mayor, aldermen, bailiffs, burgesses and communality of the town of Waymouth and Melcomb Regis in the county of Dorset the sum of twenty pounds to be by them and their successors employed and used to and for charitable uses for the better relief of the poor within the same town as in their discretions they shall think most fit and convenient, which money to be paid one year after my decease.

Upon the receipt of which money Mr Mayor with a general consent gave a release to the said Gilbert Loder, sealed with the town seal, which monies by like consent are to remain in Mr Mayor's hands until the same may be put forth to the best benefit of the poor of both towns which is desired may be speedily effected.

6 April 1632

Upon this present day at a general assembly Mr John Lockier, Mr John Cade, Henry Rose and Gabriel Cornish are appointed overseers of the defects of the harbour, and desired to procure lighters and labours to work in the water for the cleansing thereof, so many as they shall think necessary, to agree with such workmen for their wages which shall be paid them by the treasurer for this borough upon their note. And they are likewise desired (if the shall be occasion) to warn such inhabitants within this borough as are of ability to send each man a workman to work in the dry for the removing and carrying away of stone and rubbish that stops the said harbour, they giving them warning to provide such workman or labourers the day before he shall work, upon which notice given it is agreed that every inhabitant of ability shall procure and send an able workman or labourer for doing thereof or more if need shall require.

[page 122] Upon this present day it is by a a general consent agreed that Mr Matthew Allyn, alderman, and the now town clerk shall ride to London this next Term about the solicitation of the town's business against Exeter, and in all the passages thereof to be directed by these gentlemen that are of Council for this town against them; to go on either to a public hearing or else to send the businesses by way of arbitration. And the treasurer is likewise desired to deliver to the said town clerk money to for council and to bear their charges in the journey upon the town's account.

Upon the same day it is by a general consent agreed to that the treasurer for this borough shall deliver to this town clerk twenty shillings to be given to John .Foyle, servant to Mr Humphrey Jolliffe, for his pains and care about the town's affairs.

9 July 1632

Upon this present day it is agreed by a general consent that if Captain Prust, muster master, for this county, shall make any complaint for that the fees which he demands are not paid him by this town, as he desired, the same shall be answered by the town at the general charge thereof.

Upon the same day Mr Henry Waltham is by a general consent elected captain of the trained soldiers in Melcomb side in the stead of Mr Thomas Giear now Captain, who by reason of his age desires to be discharged from the said office; and Mr John Cade is chosen to be his Lieutenant, and Owen Hollman to be assistant, which they all accepted of at a meeting the 9th day of August 1633.

[page 123] 26 July 1632

Upon this present day at a general assembly, in the town hall, Mr Recorder being present, upon a consultation and long debate whether it were better for those of this town to proceed in reference of the cause between them and the City of Exeter, or to go to [a] hearing, in the Exchequer chamber. It is thought fit and agreed by the general consent that it will be the safest and best to go to [a] hearing, and not to end the same by reference, and for that purpose the town clerk with others to be nominated to go to London this next term to retain and instruct our council again, and to provide for [a] Hearing. There being present at this assembly Mr Mayor, Mr White, Mr William Holman, Mr Thomas Giear, Mr Henry Mitchell, Mr Lynsey, Mr Thomas Lockier, Mr David Giear, Mr Russell, Mr Wallis, Mr Thomas Waltham, Mr Ledoze, Mr John Lockier, Mr John Cade, Mr Hodder, Mr Rose, Mr William Cade, Mr John James, Mr Arthur Hollman and Mr Gabriel Cornish. To which all did assent.

14 September 1632

Upon this present day Jonas Dennis and James Giear were elected to be two of the capital and principal burgesses for this Corporation and have taken their oaths accordingly.

21 September 1632

Upon this present day Mr Henry Cuttance was elected mayor of this borough for this year next ensuing, there being named with him Mr Thomas Waltham, Mr Thomas Wallis the elder and Mr Henry Waltham.

Upon the same. day Mr Matthew Allin and Mr David Giear were elected bailiffs of this borough for the year following.

Upon the same day Mr John Thornton being the last mayor is elected collector and treasurer of the rents and revenues of this borough for this next year.

Upon this present day Mr Bailiffs elected John Lockier, Arthur Holman, William Cade the younger, and George Flerry are appointed auditors of the last treasurer's accounts for this town.

[page 124] **26 September 1632**
Upon this present day it. is by a general consent agreed on that Francis Gape, gentleman, town clerk of this borough shall forthwith ride to London in solicitation of the town business, and to make what friends he can procure by Sir Robert Napier and others to prevent Mr Attorney general from bringing a *Quo Warranto* against this town for the privileges thereof [*Quo Warranto*, literally 'by what warrant', a writ requesting the the town demonstrate by what authority it held certain rights and privileges]. And that the treasurer for this borough shall deliver him pay to him twenty pounds in hand, and pay to him what other monies he shall disburse about the same upon his account at his return given in.

26 October 1632
By an unanimous consent it is this present day concluded on that a house or covering shall be made in the place adjoining to the bulwarks to shelter and keep dry the ordnance and carriage thereto belonging from all wet weather and rain. And Mr Henry Russell and Mr Thomas Wallis are desired to undertake the erecting thereof, and with all convenient speed to get materials ready, and workmen to do the same, and what they shall expend there about shall be paid to them by the treasurer for the borough upon their account given in the charges thereof.

23 November 1632
It is this present day ordered by a general consent of the mayor, aldermen, bailiffs and capital or principal burgesses of this borough at their assembly in the Guildhall there that unless William Skinner, alias Gillett of this borough doth remove John Bascombe and Thomas Bascomb, tailors, straight out of his house within ten days next coming and doth not permit them to lodge or work there any longer time, then the sum of twenty pounds (being a penalty for such an offence by a constitution heretofore made expressed) shall forthwith be by the sergeants at mace for this borough levied on the goods of the said William Skinner, according to the said former constitution.

Upon the same day Thamasyn Dennys, widow, and Thomas Ledoze are ordered to cause all the rubbish which they have laid on the quay and in the street in Waymouth side to be carried thence by Christmas next upon pain of fifty shillings apiece if they shall make default therein.

[page 125] **14 December 1632**
At a general assembly of the mayor, aldermen, bailiffs and capital or principal burgesses in the Guildhall there the day and year above said George Churchey, merchant, being no freeman of this borough and having bought of one William Osmond, a foreigner, 16 pieces of raisins is for the said offence fined at forty shillings. And Robert Pydle being a freeman and knowing the said George Churchey to have bought the said raisins of the said foreigner, and not revealing the same to Mr Mayor is likewise fines at ten shillings, which they are ordered to bring into court the next hall day.

21 December 1632

Upon this present day at a general meeting of the mayor, aldermen, bailiffs and capital and principal burgesses in the Guildhall of this borough George Churchey, merchant, brought in forty shillings at which he was the 14th day of this month fined for goods foreign bought and foreign sold, at which time, by a general consent, twenty shillings was given him back again, and the rest delivered to the treasurer of this borough.

25 January 1633

Upon this present day William Holmes, an inhabitant of this borough, upon payment of five pounds to the use of this Incorporation is admitted to be a freeman of the same; which money he, paying to the treasurer, did take the oath of a freeman.

Upon this same day William Holmes by a general consent is elected and sworn one of the capital and principal burgesses of this Incorporation.

Upon the same day, by a like general consent, leave is granted to Thomasyn Dennis, widow, to take in five foot northward from her quay in Waymouth side to extend in length Eastward so far as Mrs Bonfeild's quay.

[page 126] 15 February 1633

Upon this present day Robert Pydle alias Davyes being formerly fined at 10s for knowing George Churchey, merchant, being no freeman of this borough to have bought goods of a foreigner and not revealing the same to Mr Mayor brought the money into court, at which time 5s was given him back and the rest delivered to Mr Treasurer.

22 February 1633

At a general assembly held at the Guildhall in this borough upon receipt of letters from the mayor of Exeter for a meeting to be had there to treat of some course to be taken against the Turks, it is agreed that the now town clerk shall ride thither to give a meeting and to treat about the same, and to take a note of what courses shall be proposed, but to conclude of nothing without further advice; and his expenses to be paid by the treasurer upon bill given in.

5 April 1633

It being informed this court at a general meeting in the Guildhall this present day that one Christopher Burbidge, a foreigner, did buy of one Henry Wooller, a foreigner likewise, a butt of sacke, which was forfeited to this Corporation on being foreign and foreign sold, and that after the bargain and sale thereof made George Flerry, a freeman of this town, knowing the same did to *colour* it out and to prevent the knowledge thereof (as much as in him lay) colouredly and fraudulently buy the same sacke of the said Wooler, and sold it again to the said Burbidge with intent (as is conceived) to defraud this Corporation of its right; and the said Flerry being questioned therefore cannot absolutely deny the same, but refers himself to the censure of this assembly. This court does therefore think fit that the said George Perry shall pay to the treasurer of this borough forty shillings as .a fine imposed on him for the said offence.

[page 127] 22 March 1633
By a general consent this present day at a general assembly held in the Guildhall, upon consultation had whom this town would think fit to employ as an agent for them and on their behalf to petition his Majesty and the lords and the Honourable Privy Council concerning a speedy course to be taken against the Turks (according to a treaty at Exeter at a meeting there the last of February last past) it is agreed that Mr Bernard Mychell being now in London shall be employed in that business, and that letters shall be forthwith directed to him to request him to undertake the care thereof, and his expenses in following the same to be borne by this town.

12 April 1633
At a general assembly held in the Guildhall this present day it is agreed by a general consent that the treasurer for this borough shall deliver to Mr, Henry Mychell the sum of ten pounds by him to be returned to his brother Mr Bernard Michell in London to expanded (if need require) in solicitation of the business against the Turks, in which we are already employed, the said Mr Mychell being to give an account to this court how the same shall be expended and employed.

26 April 1633
Upon this present day at a general assembly by the mayor, alderman, bailiffs and capital or principal burgesses of this borough it is agreed and concluded on that part of the bridge next to Waymouth side shall with all expedition be repaired and that Thomas Lovelesse and David Fippen shall be Mr Carpenters in the same, and that other labourers and workmen shall be gotten, such as Mr Mayor shall think fit. And that John Pope shall have the oversight of the said work and workmen, and to be paid for his pains when the work is finished so much as this court shall judge him worthy of. And further that the treasurer shall pay all such sums of money as shall be expended about the said work upon sight of a note under Mr Mayor's hand which shall be his discharge.

[page 128] 9 May 1633
Upon this present day George Flerry paid to Mr Mayor, aldermen, bailiffs and capital and principal burgesses of this borough in the Guildhall then assembled the sum of forty shillings he was formerly fined at, as appears in the former lease, which money was forthwith delivered to the treasurer.

17 May 1633
At an assembly held at the Guildhall this present day by the mayor, aldermen, bailiffs and capital or principal burgesses of this borough it is agreed that David Pippen of this town shall go into the county of *Southton* [Hampshire] and buy, where he shall think fit six piles for the use of this Corporation to be employed about the repairing of the bridge. And he is allowed two shillings per the day for his labour and expenses, and the treasurer to pay it him, and deliver him three pounds in hand, and to pay for

the timber at the arrival of it here.

At the same assembly Mr, treasurer is desired to pay Thomas Lovelesse the sum of nine pounds for his timber work in railing in the ground at the North end of Melcomb's town's end.

At the same assembly John Cotton move to buy a void piece of ground near the Hope in Waymouth side adjoining to another void piece of land lately sold to Bryan Spycer; which is referred to Mr Edward Roy, Mr John Thornton, Mr Ledoze and Mr Cornish to view, and to report how much they conceive fit to be granted him.

[page 129] **6 June 1633**

At a general assembly of the mayor, aldermen, bailiffs and capital and principal burgesses of this borough in the Guildhall there this present day It is agreed that Mr, David Giear one of the bailiffs of this town shall ride to Sherbourne to Mr Recorder to have conference with him concerning the town affairs, but chiefly concerning a Quo Warranto brought by Mr Attorney General against this town, whereby their liberties are questioned, and to advise with him what course is fittest to be taken. And what monies he shall therein expend in his journey to be paid at his return home upon his note thereof given in.

Upon the same day by the same assembly John Keiles and Francis Sanders appointed overseers of the defaults of posts for mooring of ships on both sides of the harbour; and where they shall think fit to amend such defaults, and to get new posts (if occasion be), and workmen to set them in convenient places: and what money shall be expended about the same the treasurer for this borough is to pay upon their bill thereof given in.

At the same assembly Mr John Mann late an inhabitant of this borough moved to have delivered him a certain bond of his lying in the town chest for payment of monies when he formed the petty customs which monies were long since paid; whereupon it was generally agreed that the said bond should be delivered accordingly.

After the same assembly by the like general consent it is agreed on that a warrant of attorney shall be made under the town seal, under Mr Offley an attorney in the crown office, to appear on behalf of this Corporation to the *Quo Warranto* by the Attorney General brought against this town. And that Mr Humphry Jolliff shall solicit the same and that the treasurer for this borough shall deliver to the said Mr Joliffe the sum of five pounds to retain Counsel at London to advise upon the same.

[page 130] **5 July 1633**

At a general assembly by the mayor, aldermen, bailiffs and capital or principal burgesses of this borough in the Guildhall it being informed that John Lowth of this town, being no freeman, did buy of William Buckler a pipe of sacke (the said Buckler being a foreigner), whereby the same is become forfeited to this Corporation as being foreign bought and foreign sold, and that the sacke was in the possession of the said John Lowth. It was ordered that the sergeants at mace should forthwith seize the same forfeited, which they accordingly did perform, but left it in the custody of the said John Lowth he having first undertaken to keep it to the use of this Corporation. But afterwards, viz, at the same assembly the said William Buckler and John Lowth came into the court, and humbly submitted themselves to the censure thereof, praying their favour therein . Upon which it was generally agreed that the said William Buckler and John Lowth should (between them) pay to the use of this Corporation the sum of twenty shillings, and upon payment thereof the said John Lowth should have the power to dispose of the said pipe of sacke at his pleasure not withstanding the said seizure, and the said William Buckler should have leave to sell at his pleasure another pipe of sacke which he now has in his possession within this borough, without any danger of forfeiting the same.

At the same assembly, by the like general consent, it being moved on the behalf of Robert Hibbard of this borough that he being a poor man and that in labouring to quench the fire at Mr, Henry Waltham's, his house being then on fire, he received much hurt by reason of a fall he took from that house, the cure of which has cost him much besides his loss of time in not being able to labour in his vocation to get his living as he formerly did, that therefore some monies may be given him out of the Treasury of this town to pay his cure and in some part to satisfy his losses. It is agreed and concluded that the 'treasurer for this borough shall deliver to the said Robert Hibbard the sum of three pounds in lieu thereof.

At the same assembly, by the like general consent, Mr Treasurer is desired to deliver to John Pope the elder the sum of forty shillings which is given to him in recompense of his care and pains in looking to and overseeing the work and workmen in repair of the bridge, to which he was formerly appointed.

[page 131] At the same general assembly, it being openly shown that the ship called the Shuttle whereof Richard Wright, Thomas Wallis the elder, Henry Russell the elder, Gregory Babbidge are owners is by them sunk in the middle of the harbour above the bridge to the great damage and annoyance of the same harbour. It is ordered by a general consent that the said owners shall remove the said ship thence into some convenient place where she shall not be prejudicial to the said harbour by the fifth day of August next upon pain that the said owners shall pay if they make default thereof the sum of forty shillings to the use of this Corporation. And it being likewise informed that the ship called the Blessing, whereof Henry Russell the elder and Thomas Chapple are owners, is also sunk in the harbour, above the bridge to the great prejudice and annoyance thereof. It is likewise by a general consent ordered that the said owners do remove the said ship called the Blessing to some fit place, so that she be no more hurtful or annoying to the said harbour by the fifth day of August next, upon pain that said owners shall forfeit the some of five pounds to to the use of this Corporation in case they shall make default herein. And that the said several penalties shall be levied by the sergeants at mace for this borough upon warrant from Mr Mayor for that purpose upon the goods of the several owners, by distress and sale thereof, rendering to the several parties the over plus if (upon such sale) any shall happen to be. And further that Mr Mayor with the monies so levied shall cause the said several ships to be removed and placed as aforesaid.

9 August 1633

At a general assembly of the mayor, aldermen, bailiffs and capital or principal burgesses of this borough, in the Guildhall there, it is agreed that the town clerk ride over to Sherbourne to Mr Recorder to advise with him about the Quo Warranto by Mr Attorney General brought against this town, and to know what council he has taken about the same, and whether it be not the safest way to petition his Majesty therein, and to get a reference thereof (if it may be) from his Majesty to some lords of the Council or other. And what he shall lay out therein shall be paid by the treasurer of this borough upon his note thereof delivered in.

[page 132] At the same general assembly, it being moved on the behalf of John Gardiner, gentleman, controller of his majesty's customs, that he in Easter term last being informed against by Mr Attorney General for certain monies he received long since, and paid over by order from the right honourable the lords and others of his Majesty's most honourable Privy Council to the the mayor of this town to the use of this Corporation, has expended money therein, it being a business that concerns the whole borough, and not the said John Gardiner or any other private man. It is by the like general consent agreed that the said John Gardiner (upon his note delivered in) shall be paid all such monies as he has been enforced to disburse about the same by the treasurer of this borough.

[page 133] At a general assembly of the mayor, aldermen, bailiffs and capital or principal burgesses of this borough of Waymouth and Melcomb Regis, [in] the Guildhall there the fifth day of September anno domini 1633 and the ninth year of the reign of Charles now King of England, it is by a unanimous consent concluded on, ordered and constituted that every owner or master of any ship, bark or other vessel whatsoever, that at any time after this present day, have, or take occasion to *careen*, or *trimme* such his ship, bark, or other vessel at any of the posts placed upon the quays belonging to this harbour, for mooring and fastening ships and other vessels, shall pay to the use of this Corporation for every time that his ship, bark or other vessel shall be there *careened* or *trimmed* in manner and form following, viz. If the ship, bark or other vessel be under the burden the owner, or master shall pay the sum of twelve pence, of current English money; if the ship bark or other vessel be of the burden of three score tonnes or upwards onto one hundred tonnes, the master or owner shall pay the sum of two shillings; and if the said ship, bark or other vessel be of the burden of one hundred tonnes or above then the owner or master thereof shall pay the sum of three shillings of current English money; which several sums of money (as they shall happen to become due by virtue of this constitution) shall be paid to such person or persons as by the mayor, aldermen, bailiffs and capital and principal burgesses of this borough shall be thereto appointed, which if any owner or master of any such ship, bark or other vessel shall refuse, or neglect to pay (the same being demanded) shall be levied by the Water bailiffs, farmer [*fermor*] or farmers of the forfeitures, or by some other [of] the officers of this borough upon the goods of such owner or master or upon the tackle, apparel or furniture of such ship, bark, or other vessel by virtue of a warrant from the mayor, for the time being, for that purpose, upon complaint thereof to him made, to be granted. And it is further agreed on, ordered and constituted, that if any ship, bark, or other vessel shall be moored, or fastened at any of the two usual places to *careen*, or *trymme* at, (which shall be accounted one above the bridge at the house where John Pope the elder now dwells, and the other below the bridge against the house where [blank] Preston now lies) and any owner or master of any other ship, bark, or other vessel shall have occasion to careen or trim such his ship, bark, or other vessel at either of the said places, then the owner, master or company of that ship, bark, or other vessel upon notice to any of them to be given by the water bailiffs, farmer or farmers of the forfeitures for the time being, or, in their absence or default by any other person or persons by the then mayor to that purpose appointed, shall by the next tide after such notice given, remove thence such his ship, bark, or other vessel upon pain to forfeit, to the use of this Corporation for every time that he or they shall refuse, or neglect so to do, the full sum of twenty shillings of current English money, to be levied by the water bailiffs, farmer, or farmers aforesaid for the time being upon such ship, bark or other vessel, or upon some part of the apparel or furniture to the same belonging by virtue of a warrant from the mayor for the time being for that purpose, upon complaint thereof to him made, to be granted which forfeitures if the said water bailiffs, farmer or farmers shall refuse or neglect to levy, he or they so refusing or neglecting shall forfeit to the use of this Corporation the sum of forty shillings to be levied on his or their goods by like warrant from the mayor to the sergeants at mace to be directed.

[page 134] **28 September 1633**
Upon this present day Mr,Thomas Wallis was elected mayor of this borough for the year next ensuing. There being nominated on election with him Mr Thomas Waltham, Mr Henry Waltham and Mr John Lockier.

Upon this same day Mr Thomas Ledoze and Mr Edward Hodder were elected to be bailiffs of this borough for the next year following.

Upon the same day Mr Henry Cuttance (being the last mayor) was chosen to be collector and treasurer of the rents and revenues of this borough for the next subsequent year.

Upon the same day Mr Bailiffs elected Mr Edward Lynee, John Lockyer, Richard Harrison and William Williams are appointed to audit the last treasurer's account.

21 September 1633
Upon this present day the petty customs of this borough were let to farm for the year next ensuing to John Pitt the elder at the rent of £159 – to be paid quarterly

Upon the same day the profits of the market are let to farm for the next year to Mr Henry Cuttance at the rent of eleven pounds to be paid quarterly.

Upon the same day the ballast and the forfeitures upon the quays and in the harbour are granted to Jeremy Babbidge at the rent of £13 10s to be paid quarterly.

Upon the same day the cartage and the fees thereof (except duties of the bridge) are granted for the year next following to Mr David Lynee at the rent of £20 to be paid quarterly.

[page 135] At the same time the duties for the bridge were granted to Arthur Hollman for the whole year next ensuing at the rent of £5 15s to be paid quarterly.

1 October 1633

Upon this present day at a general assembly by a mutual assent it is agreed that the town-clerk shall ride to London in solicitation of the town business against the City of Exeter, and in petitioning his Majesty and soliciting Mr Attorney about the same, to advise with our counsel there about, and to do therein, what they shall direct, as also to get our charters confirmed or allowed by the court of King's Bench in the Crown office there, to the end the goods, chattels and moneys forfeited to his Majesty as deodands, *felones de se* [literally 'felon on himself', i.e. suicide] etc. and granted to the Incorporation may be by us received and retained according to the said grant, and the treasurer to deliver him twenty pounds in hand towards his charges and expenses therein, and to pay him such other monies as he shall disburse over and above that sum upon his note thereof delivered in.

4 December 1633

Upon this present day at a general assembly by a mutual consent of the mayor, aldermen, bailiffs and capital or principal burgesses of this borough agreed and concluded on that John Damon of this town shall on this side of the first day of March next ensuing erect and build to and for the use of this Incorporation one good and sufficient boat called a lighter to be employed in scouring and cleansing the harbour, and he to have for building and making her the sum of £45 the said money to be paid, and the boat to be built at such times and in such manner as in certain articles indented, made between the said mayor, aldermen, bailiffs, burgesses and commonality of the one part and the said John Damon of the other part, is contained and comprised the tenor of which articles follow, viz:

Articles of agreement indented had made concluded and agreed upon by and between John Damon of Waymouth and Melcomb Regis in the county of Dorset, shipwright, and the mayor, aldermen, bailiffs, burgesses and commonality of Weymouth and Melcomb Regis aforesaid in the 13th day of December in the ninth year of the reign of Charles now King of England, 1633.

Firstly it is covenanted and agreed on by and between the said parties to these presents And the said John Damon for himself, if his executors, administrators and assigns do covent and agree to and with the said mayor, aldermen, bailiffs, burgesses and commonality and their successors by these presents: that he the said John Damon his executors, administrators and assigns shall and will on this side the first day of March next ensuing the date hereof erect and build to and for the use of the said mayor, aldermen, bailiffs, burgesses and commonality and their successors one good and sufficient boat called a lighter ready prepared, furnished and made ready with good and sufficient timber and other materials such as are hereafter in these presents expressed, and all such other as shall be fit and necessary for a lighter to serve for the use of the said town of Waymouth and Melcomb Regis with a *dragg* in scouring and cleansing of the harbour, and the same to be of length breadth and depth following viz.

[page 136] The boat or lighter to be at the keel in length three and thirty foot, in breadth fifteen foot, and in depth four foot and half, the bottom planks to be of elm and the rest of good oak, the bottom to be made with three inch plank at the least, and to be sealed in the inside up to the *Portlesse* with good two inch planks, and all the rest of the planks to be [an] inch and half at the least. To make in her four beams *kneed* and bolted, two of which beams are to be placed in the mid-ship fitted with a *winke* and a *davytt* and all thing s else fit for a *crane* and a *dragg*. To put the ground timbers nine inches asunder, and they to be five inches and half deep and seven inches broad. To fit her with a foresheet and a stern sheet with two bulk-heads to both sheets, the foresheet to be *cawk-thwight* for lodging of men and to keep them dry.

The *futtockes* to have three or four foot *scarfe*, all the sides to be done with *rone* and *clench*, and the bottom to be *trenayl'd*. To make a bend in her broad stern to place the town arms on. To make a *killson* in her a foot broad and ten inches high fit to bear a mast. To make a rudder for her, and to make her *gunwall'd* fore and aft. All which with other thing necessary and fit for such a boat the said John Damon does covent to make ready at his proper costs and charges (great iron work only excepted) and by the time aforesaid to launch her and deliver her to the use of the said town.

In consideration whereof the said mayor, aldermen, bailiffs, burgesses and commonality covenant and promise to pay to the said John Damon the full sum of five and forty pounds of current English money in manner and form following, viz: ten pounds at the sealing and delivery of these presents, five pounds more when the said boat shall be *trenayl'd,* ten pounds more when she shall be boarded and twenty pounds more when she shall be made ready, launched, and delivered.

In witness whereof to one part of these articles remaining with the said mayor, aldermen, bailiffs, burgesses and commonality the said John Damon has set his hand and seal, and to the other part remaining with the said John Damon the said mayor, aldermen, bailiffs, burgesses and commonality have affixed the town seal of the said town the day and year first above written.

A true copy examined by me, Francis Gape

[page 137] Upon the same day by a like general consent it is concluded and agreed on that a ballast wharf shall be built next [to] Mr Pitt's land at the lower end of Hope in Waymouth side, and that masons and other labourers shall be with all convenient speed employed therein, and Mr William Hollman, one of the aldermen of this town, is desired to oversee the said work and workmen; and a constitution to be drawn to cause all to take their ballast there.

17 January 1634

Upon this present day upon the humble motion of Mr John Pitt by way of supplication to this assembly wherein he showed that he having taken the petty customs of this borough to farm from the feast of Michael the Archangel last past for a whole year from thence forth next ensuing at the rent of £159 to be paid quarterly, and to give good security of payment thereof, is now of so mean estate and weak ability that he is not able to procure such security promised, nor pay the rent agreed on, and therefore has prayed some commiseration of his estate, and that this assembly would not tie him to his bargain for that he is unable to perform the same; but has offered at his own charge and without any allowance from the town to collect the said petty custom, and to give security to pay the monies collected to the treasurer for this borough quarterly. It is by a general consent agreed on that the premises considered and the said Mr John Pitt to be freed from his said former contract, and to collect the same according as he prospers so as he give good security for performance of his said promise and payment of such money as he shall collect. This agreed on in the presence of Mr Mayor, Mr Bailiffs, Mr Holman, Mr Giear, Mr Russell, Mr Waltham, Mr, Michell, Mr Allen, Mr Lynze, Mr Thornton, Mr Cuttance, Mr Lockier, Mr Cade, Mr Rose, Mr Thomas Waltham, Mr Harrison, Mr Arthur Holman, Mr Owen Hollman, Mr Holmes.

25 January 1634
At a general assembly of the mayor, aldermen, bailiffs and capital or principal burgesses in the Guildhall of the said borough the day and year aforesaid John Elborne of this borough is by general consent elected to be one of the porters of the said borough in the room of Henry Hillard deceased, at which time he took his oath well and truly to execute that place; and the rest of the porters viz, Richard Chowne, Henry Winter, John Samwayes, Thomas Bascombe and Richard Smyth did then likewise severally take their oaths anew for the due execution of that place severally by each of them. And they all at the same were then enjoined to keep clean the quays of this borough at all times when so ever by loading or unloading of carts, carriages or goods the same should be made foul, and they to have twelve apiece yearly to be paid them by the treasurer for this borough to buy them brooms and *colerakes* for that purpose.

[page 138] 21 March 1634
At a general assembly of the mayor, aldermen, bailiffs, and capital or principal burgesses of this borough in the Guildhall there this present day it is by a general consent ordered and constituted as follows, viz: for as much as diverse nuisances and damages have in time past been done to this harbour, and the quays thereto belonging by laying ballast upon the same quays, and by throwing a great part thereof some negligently, and some wilfully into the said harbour, which have proceeded for the most part for that heretofore there has been no certain place appointed for laying of such ballast, and for fetching the same in time of need. And whereas the prevention of the like nuisances in time to come, this town has been at great charge to erect and build a quay, by them called a ballast wharf, next to the lands of John Pitt in Hope in Waymouth side. It is by a general consent in the Guildhall of this borough agreed on, ordered, constituted and decreed that all manner of persons whatsoever as well foreigners and strangers as freemen and inhabitants of this borough which shall in time to come have occasion to take in any ballast for any their ships, barques, crayers or other vessels within the harbour or the precincts thereof shall from the feast day of St John the Baptist next ensuing the date hereof take all such ballast as they shall use from the said new erected quay or ballast wharf; and that every such stranger or inhabitant, being no freeman of this borough shall pay for every tonne of such ballast the sum of twelve pence of English money, viz: eight pence to the use of

this Incorporation, and four pence for the boat that shall fetch the same; and every freeman shall pay only ten pence per tonne, viz: six pence to the use of this town and four pence for the boat. And if such ship, bark, *crayer* or other vessel shall fall down to the said quay or ballast wharf to take in his ballast thence himself, the owner or master thereof being an owner or no freeman shall pay only eight pence per tonne, and being a freeman only six pence per tonne to the use of this Incorporation. And that if any person whatsoever, whilst his ship, bark, *crayer* or other vessel is in *careening* or trimming within this harbour, shall have occasion to take out the ballast of such his ship, bark or crayer or other vessel, he shall lay the same at the said new erected quay or ballast wharf, and not elsewhere, and if he shall fetch the same thence within fifteen days next after, he shall take it freely the same, but if it shall remain there above or beyond the said space of fifteen days then he shall pay the rate aforesaid. And it is further ordered that no person or persons whatsoever shall from this day aforesaid fetch or take any ballast for any ships, barques, crayers, or other vessels from any other place save only from the said quay or ballast wharf And that no person or persons whatsoever shall from the time aforesaid lay any ballast at any time upon any of the quays belonging to this harbour, nor shall shall bring or cause to be brought any ballast called beach-ballast to or upon any of the said quays belonging to the said harbour to be put aboard any ships, or for any other use whatsoever, upon pain that every person offending therein shall pay for every offence the sum of ten shillings of current English money to the use of this Incorporation. And further it is ordered that every person or persons that shall put any ballast aboard his or their ship, bark, crayer, or other vessel shall during all the time of throwing the same into the holds, or other parts of such ship, bark, crayer, or other vessel use a sail or some other such sufficient safeguard to save and prevent such ballast from falling into the harbour. And that no person or persons whatsoever shall willingly throw or cast any ballast into the said harbour upon pain that every person offending in either of those kinds shall for every offence forfeit the sum of ten shillings of current English money to the use of this Incorporation, which forfeitures shall be levied by the sergeants at mace of this borough by virtue of a warrant under the hand and seal of the mayor of this borough for the time being by distress and sale of the goods of every several offender. And if any owner or master of any ship, bark, crayer, or other vessel being a stranger or an inhabitant and no freeman shall refuse to pay the aforesaid rate of eight pence per tonne, or if any owner or master of any ship, bark, crayer or other vessel being a freeman shall refuse to pay the said rate of six pence per tonne for ballast to the use of this Incorporation, according to the true meaning of this constitution, then the said several rates shall be levied by the sergeants at mace for this borough, or by the water bailiff, or farmer of the forfeitures for the time being by virtue of a warrant under the hand and seal, of the then mayor of this borough upon any of the tackle, apparel, furniture or provision of the ship, bark, crayer or other vessel of the party so refusing by distress and sale thereof. This Constitution was made in the presence and by the assent of Mr Thomas Wallis, mayor, Mr Thomas Ledoze, and Mr Edward Hodder, bailiffs, Mr William Holman, Mr, Henry Russell,. Mr Thomas Giear, Mr Edward Roy, Mr Edward Linze, Mr James James, Mr, John Thornton, and Mr, Henry Cuttance, aldermen, Mr John Lokier, Mr Thomas Waltham, Mr Richard Harrison, Mr Henry Rose, Mr Owen Hollman, Mr Arthur Holman, Mr Gabriel Cornish and Mr Jonas Dennys, burgesses.

Witnessed by me, Francis Gape, town clerk

28 March 1634

Upon this present day at a general assembly of the mayor, aldermen, bailiffs and capital or principal burgesses, it appearing to them that the rents of Melcomb Regis within this borough are much impaired and very uncertain by reason of much alteration of estates in recent years, many divisions of burgesses and tenements within the same town, the said mayor, aldermen, bailiffs, burgesses and commonality do desire Mr Edward Hodder, bailiff, Mr William Holman, Mr Henry Mitchell, Mr John Pitt, Mr John Cade, Mr Henry Rose, Mr Owen Hollman and Nathaniel Allen, or any six or four of them to survey the ancient rentals of the same town and to make and perfect a new rental by comparing the old, and by searching out and viewing the evidences of such burgesses of tenements as they shall find not to pay their ancient rent, and by adding such rents of such lands as since the last rental was made were granted to any person or persons to the end that this Incorporation may not lose their ancient rents.

[page 140] 6 June 1634

At a general meeting of the mayor, aldermen, bailiffs, and capital or principal burgesses of this borough in the Guildhall there it is generally assented to that John Frye, glazier (being a foreigner) shall have leave to open his shop windows and use his trade in Melcomb Regis in such manner as other tradesmen do on condition that he do forthwith amend the church windows in Melcomb aforesaid and to keep the same well glazed and in good repair so long as he shall continue an inhabitant, or shall use his trade there upon three days notice of any defects in the said windows.

2 June 1634

Upon this present day at a general assembly of the mayor, aldermen, bailiffs and capital or principal burgesses of this borough in the Guildhall there by a general consent [blank] Cotton, mason, for throwing stones into the harbour and for throwing ballast within the jetty is fined at three shillings four pence to be paid to the use of this Incorporation, and be ordered to take up the said stones which if he shall refuse or neglect to do Mr Treasurer is desired to get workmen to do the same, and Cotton to pay for it.

Upon the same. day by a like general consent Ralph Limbrey of this borough for throwing ballast off his boat into the harbour is fined at three: shillings and four pence to be paid to the use of this Incorporation.

Upon the same day George Florry for giving ill language to Mr John Lockier and Mr Richard Harrison in this court is by a general consent fined at three shillings four pence for the said offence, which he forthwith paid to Mr Treasurer in court.

[page 141] Upon the same day by a like general consent of the mayor, aldermen, bailiffs and capital or principal burgesses of this borough in the Guildhall there

Thomas Chapple of this borough upon payment of £5 to the use of this Incorporation is admitted and sworn a freeman of this town; which money he forthwith paid, upon payment whereof of fifty shillings by a like general consent was given him back again, and the residue was delivered to the treasurer.

At the same time by a like general consent the said Thomas Chapple was elected and sworn one of the capital or principal burgesses of this borough.

28 March 1634

Upon this present day at a general assembly of the mayor, aldermen, bailiffs and capital or principal burgesses of this borough in the Guildhall there Benjamin Devenish of Dorchester being no freeman of this town, and buying a certain quantity of hoops of a Wight man being a foreigner is fined at five shillings to the use of this Incorporation, which he presently paid to Mr Treasurer in court.

13 June 1634

Upon this present day by a general consent of the mayor, aldermen, bailiffs and capital and principal burgesses of this borough in the Guildhall there William Charity of this borough is upon payment of five pounds to the use of this Incorporation was admitted and sworn a freeman of this town, which money he forthwith paid, upon payment whereof twenty shillings thereof was given him back again, the residue was delivered to Mr Treasurer.

At the same time by a like general consent the said William Charity was elected to be one of the capital and principal burgesses of this borough, whereof he forthwith took the oath.

Upon the same day by a general consent forty shillings is given to John Demon of this borough as a free gift for that (as he alleged) he has been at some loss in building the town lighter, which money Mr Treasurer is desired to pay to him.

24 June 1634

Upon this present day Mr Thomas Giear and Mr Thomas Waltham entered into a hundred pounds. Bond to pay £50 with interest to use of this Incorporation upon the feast day of St John the Baptist next ensuing: it being the £50 given to this town about 4 years since by Sir John Strangwayes, knight, which was delivered to and kept in the custody of Mr David Giear until his decease, at which time enquiry being made for the same money Mr Thomas Giear confessed he had the same from Mrs Giear, and so entered into bond as aforesaid.

Memorandum: the said Mr Thomas Waltham and Mr Thomas Giear stand bound likewise in £100 by obligation dated 16 December 1630 for payment of £50 at the end of ten years, and in the mean time to pay £3 per annum interest for the same, which was the gift of the Lady Jane Browne late wife to Sir John Browne, knight, deceased, to be disposed of in manner following, viz: twenty shillings yearly to the repair of the Church of Melcomb Regis and forty shillings yearly to the relief of the poor of the same place.

[page 143] **21 September 1634**

Upon this present day Mr John Lockyer was elected to be mayor of this borough for this year next ensuing, at which time Mr Thomas Waltham, Mr John Cade and Mr Thomas Ledoze were nominated in election with him.

Upon the same day Mr Henry Michell and Mr John Thornton were chosen to be bailiffs of this borough for the year following.

Upon the same day Mr Thomas Wallis (being the last mayor) was elected to be collector and treasurer of the revenues of this borough for this next year, he giving caution to yield a true account of the same.

Upon the same day Mr Bailiffs elected, James James, alderman, Arthur Holman James Giear and John Dennys, three of the burgesses of this borough, were chosen auditors to audit the last treasurer's account.

21 September 1634

Upon the present day the petty customs and such other duties as usually theretofore have been let with them were let to farm to Jeremy Bubbidge of this borough at the rent of £135 for this year following, the rent to be paid half yearly.

Upon the same day cartage was let to farm to Francis Gape at the rent of £19 10s for the year ensuing, the rent to be paid half yearly.

Upon the same day the profits of the market were granted to Mr John Lockier, mayor, at the rent of .£11 5s for the year next coming, the said rent to be paid half yearly.

Upon the same day the bridge duties were let to Farm to Mr Matthew Allin for the next year at the rent of £7 5s to be paid half yearly.

Upon the same day it is agreed that the ballast and forfeitures shall be kept in the town's hands for the next year and that some discrete person be chosen to collect the same, and authorized to levy the money due by means thereof in case any shall refuse to pay the same; and to pay over such money as he shall receive to the treasurer for the time being.

[page 144] **9 October 1634**

Upon this present day the keys of the town chest were delivered to Mr Bailiffs and Mr Thomas Giear, to be by them kept for the next year, and the said chest delivered to the custody of Mr Mayor.

Upon the same day it is by a general consent agreed that a new pillory and cuckingstool shall be made at the town charges for the punishment of such offenders as shall deserve the same. And also that a letter be written to Mr Henry Cuttance (now in London) to buy two dozen of leather buckets which shall remain in the Guildhall for the use of the Corporation if need require; and likewise that the said Mr Cuttance will deliver money to Mr Jolliff to retain counsel to be advised upon the iron seized on as foreign bought and foreign sold being by Mr John Hill of Dorchester sold to Robert Fookes of Sutton, and which now remains in the town-hall, and further to be advised concerning the case in law drawn by the town clerk and sent to Mr Recorder and what monies he shall lay out about the same shall be allowed him by the treasurer upon his note delivered in.

Upon the same day Mr Robert Major is appointed to collect the money which shall be due to this Incorporation for, or by reason of, any ballast and for or by reason of the breach of any constitutions for keeping clean the quays and about the harbour; and that he shall have 2s 6d in the pound for his pains in gathering the same.

14 November 1634
Upon this present day John Synior paid in eight pounds remainder of £9 19s due from him upon bond for the market; at which time he said he paid the other 39s to Mr Cuttance the last treasurer, which eight pounds was forthwith delivered to Mr Wallis the now treasurer.

Upon the same day Jeremy Babbidge paid in 37s being the remainder of the money due for ballast this last year, which money was likewise delivered to the treasurer.

Upon the same day it is agreed on that in regard Mr Robert Major is absent at London and has taken no order for collection of the. ballast money and forfeitures, the same be gathered by Jeremy Babbidge for the residue of this year to come, and he to have 13d in the pound for collecting the same and to pay monthly the money he shall receive for the same to Mr Treasurer.

[page 145] **19 December 1634**
Whereas a writ has been directed to Mr Mayor of this borough and others for raising money for setting forth a ship of war for his Majesty's service, upon which, a meeting being had by the rest named in the writ Mr Mayor of this borough at which time £220 was thought fit to be raised here towards that service, which being conceived to be too high a proportion for this town to bear, it is agreed on by a general consent that the town clerk shall forthwith ride to London, there to petition either his Majesty or the Lords and Council for some abatement of that sum, and that he shall have ten pounds for his pains, and what he shall expend besides in petitioning and procuring an answer thereto shall be repaid him upon his note thereof delivered in.

10 April 1635
On this present day at a general meeting of the mayor, aldermen, bailiffs and capital and principal burgesses of this borough in the Guildhall there it is agreed that, whereas an action is is brought by Mr Hill of Dorchester against the sergeants of this borough for seizing certain iron of his which he sold to one Fooks, a foreigner, the said suit shall be defended at the town charge, and that the town clerk who is now to ride to London about other business for the town, shall advise with Mr Recorder and others and our counsel there concerning a lea to be given to that action.

20 May 1635
Upon this present day it is by a general consent agreed on that the town Clarke shall forthwith again ride to London to solicit Mr Attorney General for taking of the *Quo Warranto* by him brought against this Incorporation. And that the treasurer shall deliver him forty pounds to give such gratuities as Mr Recorder shall think fit of whom

he comes there, and what else he shall disburse shall be repaid him upon his account given in.

29 May 1635

Upon this present day Gabriel Cornish brought in twenty pounds, being money belonging to the poor of Waymouth, and two and thirty shillings for the interest of the same for the year past. Which sum of £20 was upon the last day of June following delivered to Mr Wallis, treasurer for this borough, to be by him employed about the town's occasions, which is to be made good to the poor's stock of Waymouth aforesaid at the feast of St Michael The Archangel next following with interest from that day until then. And the other 32s was delivered to James Giear, overseer of the poor of Waymouth.

[page 146] 20 July 1635

Whereas an action at law has been by Robert Fooks of Sutton, blacksmith, brought against the sergeants at mace of this borough for seizing about 1000lb weight of iron, which he bought of Mr Hill of Dorchester upon a market day, but at his seller remote from the market place, whereby it became foreign bought and foreign sold, to which (by advice of the Council) not guilty was pleaded. And thereupon issue joined, and Mr Hill who followed a cause called a *Nisi prius* [A catch all term for legal actions brought before the Court of King's Bench] to be brought down to Dorchester Assizes last to try the issue, where we being ready for trial, action was made to refer the matter to Mr sergeant Ashley, and our recorder, who purposefully came to this town. And upon hearing allegations on both parts, and viewing the place where the iron was sold, adjudged the sale was out of the market, and so the goods forfeited; But for amity's sake moved that the said Fookes coming in, and acknowledging before this assembly the offence committed , and paying something to the use of this Corporation in name of a fine to redeem his said iron, this town would be pleased to remit the offence, and deliver the iron. Upon which the said Pookes came this present day into the Guildhall of this borough before the mayor, aldermen, bailiffs, burgesses and communality then and there assembled, openly confessed that by reason of the bargain and sale in that place and manner his said good were forfeited, yet requested the said assembly to deal favourably with him, and so referred himself to them for his fine, who thereupon generally agreed that upon payment of five shillings in acknowledgement of the rights of this Incorporation, his iron should be redelivered, which he forthwith paid, and he received again his iron.

17 August 1635

Upon this present day at an assembly in the Guildhall of this borough John Gardiner, son of John Gardiner of this borough, gentleman, upon payment of five pounds to the use of this Incorporation was admitted and sworn a freeman of this borough, there being then present Mr Mayor, Mr Bailiff Michell, Mr Bayliff Thornton, Mr William Hollman, Mr Roy, Mr Russell, Mr Cuttance, Mr Allin, Mr Vaall, Mr Ledoze, Mr Major, Mr Hodder, Mr Harrison, Mr Owen Hollman, Mr Henry Rose, Mr Arthur Holman, Mr

Dennys, Mr Williams and William Charitye.

Upon the same day William Scamell of Dorchester being no freeman of this borough having brought a certain quantity of salt of another foreigner within this borough, and the same salt being seized to the use of this Incorporation as goods foreign bought, and foreign sold, came into this court; confessed his error in trespassing on the ancient privileges of this town, and prayed the favour of this assembly that the goods may be restored, submitting himself to them who upon consideration that the said Scamell was young, and not acquainted with the privileges of this town, should have the said salt redelivered to him, he paying ten shillings to the use of this Incorporation for his trespass committed; such he forthwith paid to the treasurer of the said borough, and thereupon the salt was restored him.

Upon the same day Richard Odye of this borough upon payment of five pounds to the use of this Incorporation was admitted and sworn a freeman of this borough, at which time (by a general consent of the persons before named) he being an ancient man, and having lived long within this borough and born many offices within the same, should have three pounds of the said money given him back again, which was accordingly done.

At the same time the said Richard Odye was by a general consent elected and sworn to be one of the capital and principal burgesses of this borough.

21 September 1635

Upon the present day Mr John Cade was elected to be mayor of this borough for the next year, there being then nominated with him Mr Thomas Ledoze, Mr Matthew Allynn and Mr Richard Harrison.

Upon the same day Mr Henry Russell the elder and Mr Jonas Dennys were chosen to be bailiffs of this borough for the year following.

Upon the same day Mr John Lockier (being now mayor) is elected to be treasurer of the revenues of this Incorporation for the next year ensuing, he giving security to yield a true account of all such monies as he shall receive in that time.

Upon the same day Mr Bailiffs elected Mr Henry Cuttance, alderman, Mr John Pitt, Mr Owen Hollman and Mr William Williams, three of the burgesses of this borough, are chosen to be auditors of the last treasurer's accounts.

[page 148] 2 October 1635

Upon this present day the petty customs with other duties heretofore accustomed to be let with them were granted to John Pitt of this borough at the rent of £123 for this next year, he giving good security to pay the rent quarterly.

Upon the same day the cartage was let to farm for this year ensuing to Mr John Lockier at the rent of £19 15s the rent to by paid half yearly.

Upon the same day the bridge duties were let to farm for the year following to Mr John Thornton at the rent of £7 5s to be paid half yearly.

Upon the same day the profit of the market was granted to Mr Henry Cuttance at the rent of £10 5s to be paid half yearly.

Upon the same day it is agreed that the duties payable for ballast, the forfeitures for not keeping clean the quays and harbour, and the duties for *carying* of ships shall be kept in the town's hands this next year and John Pitt is appointed to collect the monies due upon the same, and to have eighteen pence in the pound for collecting thereof, he first gave security to yield a true account, and to pay the money due thereupon when he shall be thereunto required.

9 October 1635

Whereas the petty customs and other duties were the second day of this month let to farm to John Pitt for the next year at the rent of £123 to be paid quarterly, and whereas the said John Pitt was then appointed to collect the monies due for ballast, forfeitures, *careening* of ships for the year following, and have 18d in the pound for his pains, he giving good security to pay the rent for the petty customs, and to yield an account and pay the money received for the other upon demand which security being now required of him, he has failed in performance thereof. It is therefore by a general consent agreed on that the former grant to him (being but conditional) be revoked, and that as well the said petty customs , as the duties for ballast, etc, [page 149] be kept in the town's hands, and that some able man (who will give good security to collect the same, and to yield a true account, and to pay the monies he shall receive for the same) be appointed collector thereof; whereupon Henry Rose one of the burgesses of this borough tending a good security, viz: Mr John Cade now mayor, and Roger Rose his son, with himself to be bound for performance of the promises is appointed collector of the same, from the feast of St. Michael the Archangel last past, for the space of one whole year from thenceforth next and immediately ensuing, and he to have for his pains twelve pence in the pound for collecting the petty customs and eighteen pence in the pound for gathering the rest.

23 October 1635

Upon this present day by a general consent it is agreed that Mr Mayor shall cause the town ladders and crooks to be mended and repaired, and (if he shall think fit) new to be made. And upon his note the treasurer is appointed to pay all such monies as shall be expended about the same.

Upon this present day by the like general consent the Strend on the East side of Melcomb from the jetty upwards to the bulwarks there, and Newberry in Waymouth are places appointed to lay the soil and filth of the streets, and ashes and other things that have been laid in the streets to the annoyance of the inhabitants. And it is ordered that no person laying any soil, filth, or other thing that may annoy in the streets or elsewhere, save only in the places before named, on pain to incur penalty of the former constitution to that purpose.

Upon the same day Mr John Thornton, who had formerly taken to farm the bridge duties for the next year, declaring openly that he took the same to the use of James Giear his son-in-law, desired a warrant might be granted to the said James Giear with power to collect the same under the common seal of this borough, which was accordingly performed, the said James Giear having first given security for payment of the rent reserved.

[page 150] **30 October 1635**
Whereas this Incorporation has lately been at great charges in new paving the gutters in many streets within this borough, and many of the inhabitants living in those streets have also been at great expenses in new paving the said streets before their several dwelling houses, which said streets and gutters were very much decayed by reason that brewers (as well townsmen as strangers) and others that use trade carts within this borough did bind the wheels of such their carts with iron bands, studs, and dowls, carying weighty carriages thereon through the said streets. And for that the said brewers and others that use trade carts do now again bind the wheels of their said carts with iron bonds, studs and dowls which will in short time much decay and impair again the said streets and gutters not only to the detriment and loss of this Incorporation in general, but also to the great damage of the said inhabitants in particular who have paved before their doors as aforesaid. For prevention whereof it is this present day by a general consent of the mayor, aldermen, bailiffs and capital or principal burgesses of this borough at a meeting in the Guildhall there agreed on, ordered and constituted, that from henceforth no brewer, townsman or strangers, or other person whatsoever using trade carts within the said borough shall drive any such carts whose wheels are bound with iron, or with dowls or studs of iron through any of the streets of this borough upon pain to forfeit for every time that he or they shall offend therein the sum of four pence to the use of this Incorporation, which shall be levied on him or them in such manner and by such persons as forfeitures on other constitutions have formerly been accustomed to be levied. Provided always that this constitution be not prejudicial to the porters of this town who have been allowed to bind their cart wheels with iron, so as the heads of their binding nails be smooth, and that they use no studs of iron, or dowls therein; but that they may do as heretofore they have been accustomed to do; nor to James Giear of this borough beer brewer until the feast of St Michael the Archangel next ensuing the date hereof, until which time (in regard he has farmed the profits of the town bridge) he has free liberty given him to make use of his iron bound wheels, so as forthwith cause the great nails, dowls and studs of iron to be beaten smooth, and even with the said bonds. This constitution was made in the presence of Mr John Cade, mayor, Mr Henry Russell, and Mr Jonas Denny, bailiffs; Mr William Holman, Mr James James, Mr John Thornton, Mr Henry Cuttance, Mr Thomas Wallis and Mr John Lockier, aldermen; Mr Ledoze, Mr Harrison, Mr Hodder, Mr Vaale, Mr Edward Cuttance, Mr Owen Holman, Mr Arthur Holman, Mr Giear, Mr Holmes, William Charity and Richard Ody, burgesses. Printed by me, Francis Gape, town clerk, at the date aforesaid.

[page 151] Upon this present day at the assembly aforesaid in the Guildhall of this borough by a general consent John Arthur, lately married to one of the daughters to Henry Waltham, one of the aldermen of this borough, is admitted and sworn a freeman of this borough upon payment of five pounds to the use of this Incorporation, which he forthwith paid to the treasurer of this town.

Upon the same day by a like general consent John Mainwaring, lately married to the daughter of John Lockier, one of the aldermen of this borough, is admitted and sworn a freeman of this borough upon payment of five pounds to the use of this Incorporation which he forthwith paid to the treasurer of this borough.

7 December 1635

At a general assembly of the mayor, aldermen, bailiffs and capital burgesses of this borough in the Guildhall there this present day, information being given that Peter Cornelius of this borough, being no freeman of the same, has bought of one Johnson, a Fleming, a certain bark loaded with oats within the precincts of this borough contrary to the liberties and privileges of the same borough. It is thought fit and ordered that the said bark and the oats in her be forthwith seized by the sergeants at mace to the use of this Incorporation as foreign bought and foreign sold; which being forthwith accordingly done by the sergeants, the said Peter Cornelius forthwith came into the court, and acknowledged his error and offence in breach of the liberties of this town, promising in time to come not to do the like, and pretending that this was by him done through ignorance, submitted himself to the judgement of this assembly praying their favour to him; whereupon it is thought fit and agreed that the said ship and oats shall be redelivered to the said Peter Cornelius, he paying the sum of forty shillings to the use of this Incorporation as a fine for that trespass by him committed as aforesaid; which sum of money the said Peter Cornelius forthwith paying in court to the treasurer of this borough had his said ship and oats delivered to him.

[page 152] Upon the same day, at the same general assembly, information being given that Fabian Hodder and John Maynwaring, two freemen of this borough, did know of the said bark and oats bought by the said Peter Cornelius of the said Johnson being two foreigners, and that they did not reveal the same to the mayor or the bailiffs of this borough, but concealed the same contrary to their oath, and to the infringement of the liberties and privileges of the same borough which they ought to uphold and maintain. It is ordered that they, the said Hodder and Maynwaring be forthwith sent for to appear before this assembly to answer the said information; whither when they came, and being charged therewith, they not denying, but confessing that they knew of the said bargain made by the said Peter Cornelius with the said Johnson for the said ship and oats and that they had not discovered the same as they ought to have done; upon which they were both severally fined at forty shillings apiece for such their offence; which they forthwith paid to the treasurer of this town and so were discharged.

19 February 1636

Upon this present day at a general assembly of the mayor, aldermen, bailiffs and burgesses of this borough in the Guildhall there, it is by a general consent agreed on that the marsh in Weymouth side whereof Mr Matthew Allin had a lease from this Incorporation for one and twenty years ending at our Lady Day next shall be left open for the sea to cover the same as heretofore it did, that by means whereof the harbour may be cleansed, and that more water may be in the same for ships to ride in. This was agreed on in the presence of Mr John Cade, mayor, Mr Henry Russell, one of the bailiffs, Mr William Hollman, Mr Henry Michell, Mr James James, Mr Edward

Lynze, Mr John Thornton, Mr Henry Cuttance, Mr Thomas Wallis, aldermen, John Pitt, Robert Major, Robert Vaale, Thomas Ledoze, Richard Harrison, Edward Hodder, Henry Rose, William Williams, Arthur Hollman, James Giear, Edward Cuttance, William Charity and Richard Odye, burgesses.

[page 152a, This page is incorrectly numbered by the clerk as a second page 152]

Upon the same day at the same general assembly it is agreed on that George Churchey, merchant, upon payment of thirty pounds to the use of this Incorporation shall be admitted a freeman of this borough which money he forthwith paying to Mr Mayor was incontinently sworn a freeman of the said borough.

At the same time by a general consent of the assembly aforesaid the said George Churchey is elected and sworne to be one of the capital and principal burgesses of this borough, etc.

Upon the same day Hugh Persie, late apprentice to Henry Russell the younger, a freeman of this borough, having served out his apprenticeship with the said Henry Russell is admitted and sworn a freeman of the same borough.

21 March 1636

Upon this present day, information being given that the quay near the widow Day's house is lately fallen into great decay, it is by a general consent of the, mayor, aldermen, bailiffs and burgesses then in the Guildhall assembled agreed on that the said decays of the said quay be forthwith viewed and amended and Mr Mayor is desired to get workmen to do the same.

Upon the same day, information being likewise given that the ballast wharf lately built near Hope in Waymouth side is likely to fall into great decay, except timely prevention be used for amendment thereof, it is thereupon ordered by the like general consent that the same be forthwith viewed, and that labourers and workmen be provided to amend the same. And Mr William Hollman, alderman, is desired to get such workmen and labourers as he shall think fit to work about the same; whom Mr Mayor is desired to pay for their work done in amendment thereof.

[page 153] 1 April 1636

Upon this present day at a general meeting of the mayor, aldermen, bailiffs, burgesses and commonality of this borough in the Guildhall it is agreed that in regard the Marsh formerly ordered to be laid open may yield some rent to this Incorporation for the pasture thereof during this summer season, the same shall be let by the candle to such person as will give most for the same. And then it was let to Mr John Thornton at the rent of fourteen pounds, and he is to have the pasture thereof until Michaelmas next, but the town (if they shall so cause) are to begin to work on it the 20th day of August next.

15 April 1636

Upon this present day it is agreed on that twenty pounds belonging to the poor of Melcomb Regis, lately paid in by Matthew Caseway, and now remaining in the town chest, be let to Fabian Hodder of this borough and Mr Mayor to give bond with him for repayment thereof.

13 May 1636
On this present day Edmund Benner, late apprentice to James James, alderman, is admitted and sworn a freeman of this borough.

10 June 1636
At an assembly this day in the Guildhall it is by a general consent agreed on that Mr Henry Rose of this borough (being now travelling towards London) shall there buy four barrels of gunpowder for the store of the town. And so much taffeta as shall make two ensigns for the use of this Incorporation, and what monies he shall disburse are to be allowed him upon his account.

On the same day by a like general assent it is agreed on that Thomas Lovelesse viewing the decays of the bridge can provide such timber and planks as shall be needful for repairs thereof, which shall be paid for out of the town stock.

16 September 1636
Upon this present day it is taken into consideration that many gutters in sundry streets in Melcomb Regis are in decay and annoying (*noysome*) to the inhabitants. It is by a general consent agreed on and ordered that Mr Henry Rose of this borough shall get a paviour, provide stones and other materials, and procure the same to amended. And he is to pay the workmen and for materials, which upon his account shall be allowed him. And that all persons before whose houses the said gutters shall be amended shall forthwith cause all the land before their said houses to be well and sufficiently paved.

[page 154] 21 September 1636
Upon this present day Mr Thomas Ledoze of Waymouth is elected to be mayor of this borough for the year following. At which time Mr Matthew Allin, Mr Richard Harison and Mr Henry Michell were nominated in election with him.

Upon the same day Mr Thomas Wallis the elder and Mr Edward Cuttance are chosen to be bailiffs of this borough for the year ensuing.

Upon the same day Mr John Cade, now mayor, is elected to be collector and treasurer of the revenues of this Incorporation for the year following. He giving security to yield a true account of all such sums of money as he shall receive.

Upon the same day Mr Bailiffs elect Mr Edward Lynze Mr George Churchey, Mr James Giear and Richards Odyer are appointed to audit the accounts of the receiver of the town's revenues the last year.

28 September 1636
Upon this present day the petty customs, etc, due to this Incorporation, are granted to Mr Thomas Ledoze, mayor elect, for this year ensuing at the rent of £100 10s to be paid half yearly.

Upon the same day the forfeitures, careening of ships, etc, are let to the said Mr

Ledoze for the year following at the rent of one and forty shillings, to be paid as the former.

Upon the same day the cartage is let to Mr Richard Hanson at the rent of eighteen pounds and fifteen shillings for this next year, the same to be paid as before.

Upon the same day the profits of the market are let to farm to Mr Henry Michell for this year following at the rent of nine pounds and fifteen shillings to be paid as before.

Upon the same day the bridge duties are let to farm to Mr James Giear for the next year at the rent of seven pounds to be paid as before.

[page 155] 14 October 1636

Upon this present day by a general consent of the mayor, aldermen, bailiffs and burgesses of this borough assembled in the Guildhall it is agreed that the Marsh belonging to this borough shall be let out to such person as will give most rent for the same, and that the walls .and banks thereof shall be forthwith repaired and amended. And that such tenant as shall rent the same shall covenant, to uphold the said walls and banks during his term, and at the end thereof to leave the same so sufficiently repaired and amended. And further that the rent thereof as also the profit of the ballast, and the forfeitures due to this Incorporation for or by reason of the breach of any constitution made and of the careening of ships shall be by the mayor for the time being yearly hereafter employed in keeping the lighter on work for dragging and cleansing of the harbour, which lighter shall constantly hereafter at all times convenient and fit for working be kept to work chiefly from our Lady Day to Michaelmas.

Upon the same day by a like general consent it is ordered that every inhabitant of this borough of ability of body and being at home shall in his person ward in the day time during this time of infection, except the mayor, bailiffs and aldermen, and that as well they, as all others that shall pretend inability of body or shall be absent shall. send a very sufficient man to ward in their rooms, such as they will answer for.

Upon the same day Robert Richards, son of Damaris the wife of Nicholas Cornew of this borough, is by a like general consent, upon payment of five pounds to be use of this Incorporation admitted to be a freeman of this borough, which money he forthwith paying to the treasurer and receiver of the town's revenues the said Robert Richards took his oath of a freeman.

21 October 1636

It is by a general consent of the mayor, aldermen, bailiffs and burgesses in the Guildhall of this borough assembled this present day agreed on that the Marsh shall be let to Mr James Giear for the term of seven years at the yearly rent of nineteen pounds, who is to repair the same, and so to leave it, provided that if at any time within that term it shall be thought fit and agreed to take the same into the town's hands to leave it open to the harbour, that then the said James Giear is to yield up the said marsh into their possession upon a years warning to him to be given so to do.

Upon the same day by a like general consent it is agreed on that George Florry shall collect the money that shall become due to this Incorporation for or by reason of the ballast taken and to be taken within the same, for the next year, and he is to give account of such monies as he shall receive for the same quarterly, and then to pay the said monies to the treasurer, and is to have for his pains therein as formerly has been allowed to others.

[page 156] Upon the same day by a like general consent Walter Bond, Martin Hamell, Richard Pitt, Henry Sparrow and Cardyn Abbott of this borough are appointed to pilots for the bringing in and carrying forth of all ships and other vessels that shall come to this harbour; for which they are to take such fees and duties as formerly have been appointed for pilots to take. And that the pilots shall go forth with sufficient *herrotts* or other boats able to carry and anchor and help a ship in extremity, and not with small *cock-boats* as usually they have done.

29 October 1636

At a general assembly of the mayor, aldermen, bailiffs and burgesses of this borough hereafter named, in the Guildhall of the same borough assembled, this present day It is concluded and agreed on that Mr Thomas Wallis now one of the bailiffs of this borough shall collect and gather the rents due to this Incorporation for the tenants of Melcomb Regis for this next year, and all that is in arrears, which he shall pay over to the receiver of the town revenues. And that in time to come the said rents shall yearly be collected by the bailiff of Melcomb side, who shall before his year expire always pay over the same to the treasurer or receiver of the town's revenues for the time being. Agreed on by Mr Mayor, Mr Bailiffs, Mr Russell, Mr Roy, Mr Allinn, Mr Linze, Mr Cuttance, Mr Thornton, Mr Cade, aldermen, John Pitt, Edward Hodder, Richard Harrison, Henry Rose, Arthur Hollman, William Williams, Jonas Dennys, William Holmes, George Churchey, Richard Odye and William Charity.

At the same time it is agreed on that Mr Mayor, Mr Henry Michell and Mr town clerk shall ride to Blandford, with one of the sergeants, to give a meeting to Mr Sheriff and the mayors and chief officers of other corporate towns in this county, about the rates to be made for collection of money throughout this county for setting forth a ship of war for defence of the Kingdom according to a writ lately received to that purpose. And their charges to be born by this Incorporation.

At the same day John Swettenham of this borough is admitted and sworn to be a freeman of the same borough upon payment of five pounds to the use of this Incorporation; which he forthwith paying to the treasurer, twenty shillings thereof was given him back again.

[page 157] 5 May 1637

Upon this present [day] by a general consent of the mayor, aldermen, bailiffs and capital or principal burgesses, in the said borough Guildhall there, at the humble request of [blank] Comfrey, widow, licence is granted for the said [blank] Comfrey to set the house she is now re-edifying one foot in breadth into the street adjacent to make the same a foot broader than it was, which is to be taken from the corner of John Reynolds' house, and to run the length sixteen foot and no more, for which she is to pay to this Incorporation twenty shillings in nature of a fine, and to pay one penny per annum rent for the same, provided that she erect no penthouse or shop window to hang over the street there.

Upon the same day it is ordered that the quays of the harbour shall be in all places needful amended, and that the two new posts are set near to Mr Russell's land in Melcombe side for the mooring of ships, one to be placed upon the quay there and the other under the quay.

Upon the same day it is ordered that Mr Bernard Michell who has for some time past made use of the town lighter shall pay 3s per day for every day that he has used the same, which payment he shall continue for all the time that he shall make use of the same; And that every other person who shall in time to come borrow the said lighter shall pay the like rate.

Upon the same day it is ordered that Mr Henry Russell (to which he also doth assent) shall erect and set up a boom in or near the ancient place where the boom heretofore stood, for the doing whereof the treasurer is to pay him twenty shillings in money, and to provide him a post and other timber necessary for that work, and he is to bear all the rest of the charge (if any be required) himself.

16 June 1637
Upon this present day by a general assembly in the Guildhall at the request of the mayor on the behalf of George Flory leave is granted to the said George Flory to set up two or more turned posts to rest on a penthouse before the shop of his new built house in Melcomb so as he place not the same posts to be a hindrance to carriages that way, nor annoy the street with the same. And so as he place no person to stand or sit there on any market day, but do leave the whole benefit of that to the town.

[page 158] 15 September 1637
At a general assembly this present day it is agreed on that three great Guns be provided to be discharged at the coming of the right Honourable Theophilus Earl of Suffolk to this borough towards his entertainment, and as many at his departure, which is to be done at the town charge.

On the same day Mr Michell paid thirty seven shillings and six pence to the treasurer for the use of the town lighter. And Mr Arthur paid ten shillings for the same, whereof 4s was allowed him for certain charges he had expended about her, the remainder was delivered to the treasurer.

21 September 1637
Upon this present day Mr Henry Michell of Melcomb is elected to be mayor of this borough for the year following, at which time Mr Matthew Allin, Mr Henry Russell, and Mr Richard Harrison were nominated in election with him.

Upon the same day Mr George Churchey and Mr William Holmes are elected to be bailiffs of this borough for the year following.

Upon the same day Mr Thomas Leddoz, now mayor, is chosen to be receiver and treasurer of the same for the year to come, he giving security to yield a true account of all such monies as he shall receive to the use of this Incorporation.

Upon this same day Mr Bailiffs elected Mr Henry Russell, Mr John Thornton and Mr William Williams and Fabian Hodder are appointed auditors to take the accounts of the receiver of the town's revenues the last year,

28 September 1637
Upon this present day it is ordered that the petty customs and other duties belonging to this Incorporation shall be kept in the town's hands the next year. And Mr John Pytt is appointed collector of the same who is to give in his account and pay such money as he shall receive to the treasurer at the end of every month and to give security for the same; And for his pains he is to have 12d in the pound of all the money he shall receive for Petty-Customs, etc, and 18d in the pound for the forfeitures.

[page 159] 28 September 1637
Upon the same day the duties and fees due to this Incorporation for and in respect of the cartage here are let to farm to Mr James Giear for the year following at the rent of seventeen pounds and ten shillings to be paid half yearly: the one moiety thereof at the feast of the Annunciation of our Blessed Lady St Mary the Virgin, and the other moiety at the feast of St Michael the Archangel next following.

Upon the same day the duties due for the market are let to farm to George Florry at the rent of eleven pounds to be paid as the former.

Upon the same day the duties due for the bridge are let to farm for the next year to Mr James Giear at the rent of five pounds and five shillings to be paid as before, with this restraint: that no soil be carried over the bridge in carts during that time; and if any be the parties are to pay for the same to the collector of the petty customs to the use of this Incorporation.

Upon the same day it is ordered that all fees and profits due by reason of any constitution made concerning the taking and laying of ballast be kept in the town's hands, and the same to be collected by the collector of the petty customs.

2 October 1637
Whereas Mr Henry Michell, being mayor elect of this borough, has absented himself, and does not come in at the court to take his oath duly to execute the said office, it is thought and agreed on by the whole court that he be amerced or fined at the sum of ten pounds for such his neglect, to the use of this Incorporation. And it is further ordered that if the said Mr Michell do not come in by Halloween [*Allhallowtyde*] next and take the said oath then he shall pay the fine of £100 more to the use of this Incorporation. And further it is by general consent ordered that if any person or persons whatsoever that in time to come shall be elected to be mayor of this borough shall refuse or neglect to appear at the next court leet held in Melcombe Regis (being the usual time and place) there to take the oath well and duly to execute the said office, that then each party so refusing or neglecting shall forthwith forfeit £10 to the use of this Incorporation, and shall be liable to such other and further fine and order as shall by this assembly be thought fit to be imposed on him.

[page 160] Mr Middleton's money:

> Twenty five pounds thereof lent to Mr Henry Cuttance
> Twenty five pounds thereof lent to Gregory Babbidge
> Twenty five pounds thereof lent to Robert Munday
> Twenty five pounds thereof lent to Owen Hollman

December 1637
Mr Henry Michell was upon this day sworn to execute the office of mayor of this borough he being elected before to that office.

9 March 1638
On this present day at a general assembly of the aldermen, bailiffs and burgesses of this borough in the Guildhall It is agreed on that the constitution made in the year 1620 for working at the *Molehead* be renewed, confirmed and continued for cleansing of the harbour by having labourers to work daily about the same. And Mr John Thornton, Mr John Cade, Mr Edward Cuttance, Mr Fabian Hodder, Mr Waale and George Florry or the greater number of them are by this court appointed to rate and assess every one of the inhabitants of this borough what and how many labourers he shall send and at what times, whereof they shall give a note in writing to the sergeants at mace, who are required to summon and give warning to each inhabitant appointed to labour to come in, or send in, his workmen at the time appointed. And whosoever shall neglect to come to work in person, or not send his labourer, or labourers to work at the days and times appointed shall forfeit 12d for each default the use of this Incorporation to be levied as other forfeitures have usually been levied. Which forfeitures shall be employed in hiring and paying other labourers about that work provided always that Mr Mayor and Mr Bailiffs, or any two of them, whereof Mr Mayor to be one, do allow of the said rates.

At the same assembly it is agreed on that Mr Mayor shall appoint some fit person to .execute the office of beadle who is to have a coat and staff provided for him at the town charge and have a stipend of twenty shillings per annum paid him by the treasurer.

[page 161] 18 May 1638
Upon this present day Mr Thornton and Mr Wallis are appointed to get workmen to view the defects of the carriages belonging to the great ordnances of this town, and to cause such as are in decay to be amended, and then to cause them all to be sufficiently tarred. And further to take care that a sufficient fence be made for preservation of the bulwarks and house at the town's end, the charges whereof the treasurer of this borough is appointed to pay upon a note of the expenses delivered to him under their hands.

6 July 1638
At a general assembly this present day by the mayor, aldermen, bailiffs and burgesses Nicholas Cooper is appointed to be the general scavenger of this borough, who is to keep clean the streets the bridge and the chapel stairs. And for that purpose Mr John

Pitt is desired to provide a wheel barrow and a shovel for him, and he is to have for his pains twenty shillings per annum to be paid him quarterly by the treasurer of [the] town's revenues.

Upon the same day Nicholas Sangar is appointed to be master of the town lighter, who does promise to look well to her, and to her tackle and provision, and it is agreed that if any man shall borrow the said lighter for his private use the said Nicholas Sangar shall be one of the company to work in her, as also at all times when she shall be employed about the town occasions, and then he is to have twelve [pence] by the day for his labour and to have five shillings by the quarter to be paid to him by the treasurer of this borough for his care and pains in looking to her.

10 July 1638

Upon this present day Thomas Lovelesse does covenant to drive five rows of piles about the bridge of four in a row, and three fence piles which make three and twenty in the whole; as also to take up the old planks of the bridge, and to lay new planks in their stead, to amend and new make the rails of the bridge and other things necessary, and to do the same sufficiently; And likewise to fit the engine and other things for driving those piles and reparation of the bridge, the town allowing him materials, for which he is to have four and twenty pounds to be paid to him by the treasurer.

[page 162] Upon the same day by a general consent of the mayor, aldermen, bailiffs and burgesses it is constituted and ordered as follows (viz.): whereas by a constitution made the 11th day of March in 1635 ordered that no carthorses, other horses or horse beasts, should be tied in any of the streets, lands, wharfs or quays of this borough there to eat meat or otherwise be offensive, on pain that every owner should forfeit 2d for every horse or horse beast to be levied by distress by the sergeants, porters or scavenger, now for that it appears that the said constitution has not been put in execution by reason that no penalty is set on the said sergeants, porters or scavenger for neglecting to levy the said pain, it is thereupon the present day ordered and constituted that the said sergeants, porters and scavenger or some or one of them do and shall from henceforth put the said constitution in execution by levying the said forfeiture due for each breach thereof upon pain to forfeit for every neglect the sum of four pence to be levied on the goods of such of them as shall be negligent therein by distress and sale thereof.

21 September 1638

Upon this present day Mr Edward Linze of Melcombe Regis is elected to be mayor of this borough for the year ensuing, Mr Matthew Allin, Mr Henry Russell and Mr George Churchey being nominated to be in election with him.

Upon the same day Mr John Cade and Mr James Giear are elected to be bailiffs of this borough for the next year.

Upon the same day Mr Henry Michell, now mayor, is chosen to be treasurer or receiver of the revenues belonging to this town for the year ensuing. He giving security to. yield a true account of all such sums of money as shall come to his hands to the use of this Incorporation.

Upon the same day Mr Bailiffs elected Mr Henry Cuttance, Mr Arthur Holman, Mr Jonas Dennys and Mr Henry Rose are appointed auditors to audit the accounts of the last treasurer for the year past:

[page 163] **28 September 1638**
Upon this present day it is ordered that the petty customs, forfeitures, duties payable for the careening of ships and ballast shall be kept in the town's hands this next year; and that Mr John Pitt shall collect the same, who is to give account and to pay such monies as he shall receive every month to the treasurer of this borough, and to give security so to do. And he is to have for his pains as he had last year.

Upon the same day the fees and duties due to this Incorporation for or by reason of the cartage of, in and within the same, are let to farm to Mr Henry Cuttance for the year following, at the rent of three and twenty pounds to be paid half yearly: the one moiety at our Lady Day, and the other moiety at Michaelmas following.

Upon the same day the profits of the market are let to farm to Mr Arthur Hollman for the year following at the rent of twelve pounds to be paid as before.

Upon the same day the fees and duties due for and in respect of the bridge and drawbridge are let to farm to Mr Arthur Holman for the year following at the rent of five pounds and ten shillings to be paid as before, with this restraint that if any shall carry soil over the bridge during that time in carts, the parties are to pay the same on to the collector of the petty customs; and it is desired that not any may be carried over in carts.

Upon the same day it is agreed on that the treasurer of this borough shall pay on to Mr John Foile, Mr Joliffe's man, forty shillings which is thought fit to be given on to him for his pains in assisting to soliciting about the town business in London.

[page 164] **12 October 1638**
It is on this day agreed on by a general assent that new tackles be made for the drawbridge, or the old to be amended and made to serve if they be fit.

On the same day it is agreed on that Mr Edward Cuttance shall cause the quays of this harbour to be new planked in the places where planks are wanting or decayed, and also that the said quays be new paved or pitched with stones in all places needful.

Upon the same day it is agreed that thirteen shillings be given unto Mr John Pitt upon the perfecting of his account.

8 February 1639
Upon this present day Mr Henry Michell, Mr Churchey, Mr Thorneton and John Allin the elder are appointed raters and assessors of both sides towards the money now assessed and required for setting out a ship of war for His Majesty's service, which is in all thirteen pounds.

10 May 1639
On this present day Mr Harison paid in ten pounds given by Mrs Mary Giear, widow, deceased, to this town of Melcomb Regis within this Incorporation (viz.) five pounds

thereof to the poor, and the other five pounds to the church there, which last five pounds by her directions was bestowed in a pulpit cloth, for the receipt whereof an acquittance is given to Doctor Morris, her executor.

23 August 1639
Upon this present day it is agreed on that Mr Edward Cuttance and Mr Gabriel Cornish are desired to take care that the quays be repaired on Waymouth side in all places where they are in decay.

21 September 1639
Upon this present day Mr George Churchey is elected to be mayor of this borough for the year ensuing. Mr Matthew Allin, Mr Henry Russell and Mr James Giear being nominated in election with him.

[page 165] Upon the same day Mr John Thornton and Mr Arthur Holman are elected to be bailiffs of this borough for the year following.

Upon the same day Mr Fabian Hodder is elected to be treasurer and receiver of the town's revenues for the year ensuing, he giving security to yield a true account at the year's end of all such monies as shall come to his hands for the use of this Incorporation.

Upon the same day Mr Bailiffs elect Mr Thomas Wallis, Mr Edward Cuttance, Mr Williams and Mr Rose are appointed auditors to audit the accounts of the treasurer for the year past.

27 September 1639
Upon this present day it is agreed and ordered that the petty customs, forfeitures upon breach of any constitution, monies due for careening of ships, for ballast, for use of the town lighter, town beams, etc, shall be kept in the town's hands this next year, and that Mr John Pitt shall collect the same , who is to give in his account and pay such monies as he shall receive monthly to the treasurer of this borough and to give security for performance thereof; And for his pains and care he is to have as formerly he has been paid.

Upon the same day the fees and duties due to this Incorporation for or by reason of the cartage of, in and within the same are let to farm for this year following to Mr Fabyan Hodder at the rent of four and twenty pounds and ten shillings to be paid half yearly, (viz.): the one half at Our Lady Day next and the other moiety at Michaelmas following.

Upon the same day the fees and duties due to this Incorporation for or by markets within the same are let to Mr James Giear at the rent of twelve pounds and five shillings to be paid half yearly as aforesaid.

Upon the same day the fees and duties due to this Incorporation for or by reason of the bridge and drawbridge within the same are let to Mr James Giear at the rent of six pounds to be paid each half year as aforesaid with the like restraint as in the precedent year.

11 October 1639

Upon this present day by a general consent of the mayor, aldermen, bailiffs and burgesses of this borough it is agreed on and ordered that the penalty of the breach of the constitution heretofore made for keeping clean the streets and lanes of the same shall be levied on every inhabitant within the same town that shall have any *mixon*, filth or dust lying before his doors on every Monday morning following, whether the party laid the same there or not.

[page 166] Upon this present day by a general consent of the mayor, aldermen, bailiffs and burgesses, in the Guildhall of the same borough assembled, it is concluded and agreed on that whereas every alehouse keeper within this borough did lately at the time of his licence granted to him of his owe consent agree and promise Mr Mayor and Mr Bailiffs that now are to pay four pence for every hogshead of beer which such alehouse keepers shall draw and utter during the continuation of such licence to the use of the poor of this Incorporation, and to pay the same monthly to such person or persons as the said Mr Mayor and Mr Bailiffs shall appoint to collect the same, which being now proposed to this assembly, they do not only approve thereof, but do conclude, agree and order (as much as in them lies) that hereafter in time to come Mr Mayor or Justice of Peace within this borough do give licence to any person to sell beer within the same borough except such person do first consent to pay the said sum of four pence for every hogshead of beer as he shall draw or utter by virtue of that licence, which sum shall be collected monthly by two persons to be nominated as aforesaid, who are to pay the same to the mayor for the time being, and he to pay it over to the overseers of the poor of both sides equally, to be by them employed in cloths for poor, old and impotent persons, and for a stock to set the younger sort on work. Which sum, if any person hereafter such promise made and licence granted shall refuse, to pay, then the said Justices are forthwith desired to take such his licence from him and to suppress him from selling any more beer. And it is further agreed on and ordered that the brewers of this borough (to which also they being present do assent) shall not sell any beer to any such alehouse keepers by gallons or other measure save only by the hogshead or barrel, to the end the poor may not be defrauded of the same sum; and further monthly to give in a note to such persons as shall be chosen collectors of the said sum yearly, how many hogsheads or barrels they have in that time sold on to each party to prevent the abuse of the alehouse keeper in not giving in a just account of what beer he has sold within that month. And lastly it is agreed on that Christopher Hall shall be collector of the said sum in Weymouth side and Leonard Hillard in Melcombe side for the next year.

Upon the same day by a like general consent it is agreed on that Mr Fabian Hodder and John Allin the elder of Waymouth shall look to all defects of the quays and to take care for amendment of the same; And also to order the placing and displacing of ships within this harbour according to former constitutions heretofore made concerning the same. And further to take notice of .all forfeitures committed by a person or persons for the breach of any constitution made for the keeping of the harbour, and to levy all such forfeitures according to the said constitutions to the use of this Incorporation, and to render an account of the same when ever they shall be thereto required. All which they are to be perform for this year to come; And it is further agreed on that yearly hereafter two able men shall be appointed, one of Weymouth the other of Melcombe, in their steads; who shall always have a *Warrant Dormant* [a warrant that lasts for an indefinite length of time] under the town seal to authorize them to execute the premises.

Upon the same day by a like general consent it is agreed on that whereas many abuses have been committed by the pilots of this borough in bringing in strangers that come into this harbour to inns and private houses without making Mr Mayor or any officer of this town acquainted therewith, by means whereof many abuses have been and are daily committed which escape unpunished, and many a dangerous and suspicious person departs unexamined. It be ordered: that for the future no pilot allowed by the town shall bring any person on shore out of any ship that shall come into this harbour or road (of what quality soever) but he shall first bring such parties to the mayor for the time being, or in his absence to the then bailiffs, that notice may be taken: what he is, whence he came, whither bound, and such other questions demanded of him as shall the be thought fit and the quality of the person shall require, upon pain that each pilot offending herein shall upon the offence proved or confessed before Mr Mayor be turned-out of his office and another chosen in his stead.

[page 167] Where as notice has been taken that many boats called Bridport Boats and other ships and vessels have been by their owners and by the pilots of this town by their appointment moored in the hold and other places within this harbour below the bridge, and suffered to lie all the winter time, which has been and is to the great prejudice of the harbour. It is thereupon by the like general consent ordered that no Bridport boat or other ship or vessel shall hereafter be suffered to lie or harbour in the winter time below the bridge, but shall be compelled to be moored above the bridge, where there are places enough sufficient for that purpose. And that if any be the pilots shall warn the owners of such vessels forthwith to remove them, which if they shall not perform then the said pilots are to do it at the charge of the owners of such vessels. And if any of the said pilots shall be negligent herein, then upon complaint and proof of such his neglect before Mr, Mayor of this borough for the time being he shall be turned out of his office forthwith.

25 October 1639

Upon this present day at a general meeting of the mayor, aldermen, bailiffs and burgesses in the Guildhall of this borough it is concluded and agreed on that Mr John Pitt, collector of the petty customs shall make seizure of Mr Hill's iron brought from Wales for the petty customs due to this Incorporation for the same with all the arrears thereof.

Upon the same day, by a like general consent, thirty shillings is given to Mr John Pitt, collector of the petty customs, over and above the allowance formerly given him for his pains in collecting the said petty customs.

Upon this present day at a general assembly of the mayor, aldermen, bailiffs and principal or capital burgesses of this borough in the Guildhall there it was and is agreed that every inhabitant of the same borough shall pave and pitch with stone before their doors, lands and dwelling houses all such places as are yet unpaved and unpitched, and such as have been formerly paved and now decayed each person is to amend the defects thereof, home to the gutters in every street, at his own costs and charges, and the gutters to be made and amended at the town charge as formerly they have been. And this is to be done by every inhabitant by Midsummer next upon pain for each person neglecting or refusing so to do to forfeit the sum of [blank] for every yard of ground that shall be unpaved and unpitched to the use of this Incorporation, to be levied as other forfeitures have been formerly ordered to believed.

29 November 1639

Memorandum that by a general consent of the mayor, aldermen, bailiffs and burgesses this day in the Guildhall assembled a piece of timber containing 42 feet in all was delivered to Thomas Lovelesse for the use of Mr Giles Grene, the said Thomas Lovelesse having promised to give satisfaction for the same.

[page 168] Upon the same day Mr Cuttance is desired to take to him a workman and to view and consider of the decays of the house in the Marsh, and if it shall be found too far decayed to to be repaired to cause the materials to be taken down and preserved to the town's use.

31 January 1640

Upon this present day Mr Thomas Ledoze, Mr James Giear of Waymouth, Mr John Cade and Mr George Florry of Melcomb are appointed raters for assessing the sum of money imposed on the borough for and towards the setting forth of a ship of war for his Majesty's service which is thirty and seven pounds.

24 April 1640

Upon this present day Mr Matthew Allin, William Charity and John Cotton, are nominated and appointed to be overseers of the poor of Waymouth, and Mr Thomas Wallis, Nathaniel Allin and Thomas Hingstone overseers of the poor of Melcomb Regis; and to join with the churchwardens of each side therein.

14 August 1640

Whereas twenty bars of iron of the goods of Mr John Hill, merchant, were lately seized by order of this court for that he refused to pay petty customs for the same pretending that because it is Welsh iron no petty customs are due whereupon he has threatened to commence an action against the party that seized the said iron. It is by a general consent of the mayor, aldermen, bailiffs and burgesses now agreed on that in case a suit be commenced for the said iron, the said suit shall be defended at the general charge of this borough out of the revenues of this Incorporation, and the party that made the said seizure shall be saved, harmless from any damage that may happen to him by means thereof. And it is further agreed on that in case any action be brought either against Mr Mayor or any of his officers for seizing a bag of hops of a certain man of Hastings as foreign bought and foreign sold, the same shall likewise be defended at the general charge of this Incorporation, and he and they secured from any damages it may happen therefore.

Upon this present day by a general consent of the mayor, aldermen, bailiffs and burgesses of this borough in the Guildhall there assembled it was and is agreed on that Mr Mayor shall provide some fit person (such as he shall think fit of) to be scavenger of this whole town, who shall cleanse the streets by carrying away the dirt and filth forth of all the streets twice in the week (viz.) Saturdays and Wednesdays, and each inhabitant to cause the street before his door to be swept, and the sweeping thereof to be laid up in a heap in readiness against his coming; with whom Mr Mayor is desired to make as easy a composition as he can for wages which shall, be paid out of the town revenues.

Upon this present by a like assembly John Waall of Waymouth, mariner, is admitted and sworn a freeman of this Incorporation upon payment of five pounds, which he paying into court, three pounds thereof was restored him again. And forthwith the said John Waall was elected and sworn one of the capital and principal burgesses of this borough.

[page 169] Upon this present day James Cornish, the son of Gabriel Cornish of this borough, was admitted and sworn a freeman of this Incorporation by patrimony.

18 September 1640

Upon this present day Thomas Loveles paid £1 10s 6d for the piece of timber heretofore delivered to him for Mr Giles Green's use, but if the timber shall be found to be worth more then he is to pay the full value or to bring and deliver a long and as good a piece of timber for it.

Upon the same day Robert Sanders, shoemaker, is allowed to use his trade within this borough upon payment of ten shillings, which forthwith paid.

21 September 1640

Upon this present day Mr James Giear is elected to be mayor of this borough for the year ensuing, Mr Matthew Allin, Mr John Thornton and Mr Edward Cuttance being named in election with him.

Upon the same day Mr Edward Linzey and Mr Thomas Leddoze are elected to be bailiffs of this borough for the year following.

Upon the same day Mr George Churchey the present mayor is elected to be treasurer and receiver of the town's revenues for the year ensuing. He giving security to yield a true account of all such money as shall come to his hands to the use of this Incorporation.

Upon the same day Mr Bailiffs elected Mr John Cade, Mr Edward Cuttance, Mr Harison and Mr Cornish are elected to be auditors to audit the accounts of the treasurer for the year past.

25 September 1640

Upon this present day by a general consent it is ordered that the treasurer of the town's revenues shall pay to Steven Pollard the sum of ten shillings towards his charges in getting a *spell* [substitute] to go a soldier in his stead to serve his Majesty in the wars against the Scots.

Upon the same day it is ordered that Mr Fabian Hodder shall provide a cable for the town lighter, which shall be allowed to him upon his account.

Upon the same day it is ordered that the roof over the walk, the Custom House and the Jury Chamber shall be laid with bricks and covered with plaster of Paris, and that Howsley of Portland be treated with to do the same, and go in hand with it forthwith.

Upon the same day the timber of the old house in the Marsh is sold to William Skinner for the sum of nine and thirty shillings.

[page 170] **29 September 1640**
Richard Rogers of Bryanston, esquire, chosen and sworn a freeman of this Incorporation *ex gratia*.

16 October 1640
Gerard Napper of More Critchell, esquire, elected and sworn a freeman of this Incorporation *ex gratia*.

22 October 1640
Sir Walter Erle, knight, elected and sworn a freeman of this Incorporation *ex gratia*.

28 September 1640
Upon this present day it is agreed on by a general consent that the petty customs and the town duties shall be kept in the town's hands this next year, and that the same shall be collected by Mr. Robert Wise who is to give his account, and to pay such monies as he shall receive to the treasurer at the end of every month, and to give security so to do. And he is to be paid for collecting the same as formerly was paid to Mr Pitt.

Upon the same day the fees and duties for cartage within this borough are let to farm to Mr Henry Cuttance at the rent of three and twenty pounds and ten shillings for the year following to be paid half yearly.

Upon the same day the profits of the market are let to farm to Mr Henry Rose at the rent of twelve pounds and ten shillings, to be paid half yearly.

Upon the same day the profits of the bridge and drawbridge are let to farm to Mr Henry Mitchell for the next year at the rent of six pounds and ten shillings to be paid half yearly.

2 October 1640
Upon this present day five and twenty pounds, part of Mr Middleton's money, is lent to Mr Richard Harison, which is to be secured by Mr, James Giear and Leonard Hellard, and notice to be given for the letting of the rest [at] the next court day.

Upon the same day agreement is made with Howseley of Portland to work about the roof of the walk, etc. at the rate of two shillings and two pence a day.

[page 171] Upon the same day the profits of the ballast, the forfeitures for breach of any constitutions for keeping clean the quays and harbour, for removing of ships, etc. are let to farm to Mr George Churchey at the rent of eleven pounds and ten shillings. And it is ordered that every stranger shall pay him four pence per tonne for ballast, and every townsman, that is free, two pence per tonne, and to fetch the same at the places appointed upon the former constitutions.

9 November 1640

Upon this day it is agreed that Thomas Loveles shall continue to lay his timber in the lane where formerly he laid the same, paying to the town twenty shillings per annum rent for the same. And that Angell Watts shall remove all his timber thence by the first day of December next.

Upon the same [day] five and twenty pounds, part of Mr Midleton's money that was formerly let to Robert Monday is let to James Cornish payable at Michaelmas 1643, which money is secured by Gabriel Cornish and William Skinner.

Upon the same day five and twenty pounds, part of the same money, formerly lent to Owen Holman, is let to Jonathan Ledoze, and secured by Thomas Ledoze and Henry Cuttance.

Upon the same day five and twenty pounds more of the same money, formerly lent to Gregory Babbidge is let to John Hodder, and secured by Edward Hodder and Fabian Hodder.

16 November 1640

It is agreed that the town clerk shall ride to London to prefer a petition on the town's behalf to the court of Parliament, and to solicit Sir John Strangeways, Sir Walter Erle, Mr Gerard Naper and Mr King or burgesses therein, and for his expenses he is to have three shillings four pence a day.

20 November 1640

John Whyte sworn a freeman of this borough by service, and pays three shillings four pence for his admittance according to a former constitution.

[page 172] Upon the present day Gregory Babbidge paid the sum of four pounds for breach of constitution in not enrolling John White, his apprentice, with one year after he was bound, two shillings and six pence for every quarter for eight years together. At which time by a general consent three pounds and ten shillings was given back to him again, part for two *balkins* which he demanded as lent to Thomas Lovelesse for the use of the town about the bridge, and part *ex mia*.

4 January 1641

Upon this day by a general consent it is thought fit and ordered that the town clerk do draw a petition to his Majesty or to the Lords of the Counsel for ammunition to our ordnance, which are 15 demi-culverins and seven sakers of which fourteen are his Majesty's and eight the town's.

Upon the same day it is ordered, being first by a general consent agreed on, that Mr Matthew Allin shall ride to London to solicit the house of Parliament concerning the grievance of the town, and-he is to have three shillings and four pence the day for his expenses there.

15 March 1641
Upon this day it is agreed on that Mr. Henry Michell, Mr Henry Cuttance, Mr Henry Rose and Mr Gabriel Cornish shall ride to Dorchester together with the constables on Thursday next to attend the commissioners of the subsidies, etc.

11 June 1641
Upon this day it is agreed by a general consent that Mr Henry Rose and Mr Fabian Hodder shall collect the town rents of Melcomb Regis together with all the arrears thereof, and for that purpose Mr Cade is desired to deliver to then the rental of that town now remaining in his custody.

20 August 1641
Upon this day by a general consent Mr Rose and Mr Charity are appointed to view the decays of the quays, molehead and jetty, and to get workmen and labourers to repair the same decays, wherein they are to take the advice of Mr Henry Russell, and the treasurer is to pay the charges upon the workmen's note delivered and signed by Mr Rose and Mr Charity.

[page 173] 21 September 1641
Upon this present day Edward Cuttance of Waymouth is elected to be mayor of this borough for the year following and Mr Matthew Allin, Mr John Thornton and Mr Henry Russell being nominated to be in election with him.

Upon the same day Mr William Charity and Mr Fabyan are elected to be bailiffs of this borough for the year ensuing.

Upon the same day Mr James Giear, now mayor, is chosen to be receiver and treasurer of the revenues of the town for the next year, he giving security to yield a true account of all such sums of money as he shall during that time receive to the town's use.

Upon the same day Mr Bailiffs elected [blank] are appointed to be auditors to audit the accounts of the treasurer for the year past.

24 September 1641
Whereas certain iron of Mr Hills of Dorchester has been by order attached for that he refused to pay the duties due to this town for the same, for which he threatens to bring an action against Mr George Churchey, then mayor, and yet professes himself willing to pay those duties if we can make it appear that either the city of Bristol the city of Exeter or the town of Southampton do demand and receive any duties for iron, Viz: for English or Welsh iron. It is thereupon this present day by a general consent of the mayor, aldermen, bailiffs and burgesses now assembled agreed on that Mr Churchey shall ride to Southampton, Mr Fabyan Hodder to Exeter and Mr Haryson to Bristol to search in the customs houses there, and to bring a certificate from thence of what

duties are paid for such iron to those several places; whose expenses shall be paid by the treasurer upon their bills delivered in.

28 September 1641

Upon this present day by a general consent it is agreed on that the petty customs and the town duties shall be kept in the town's hands the next year, and that the same shall be collected by Mr Robert Wise, who is at the end of every month to give in an account, and to pay such money as he shall receive to the treasurer, and to give security so to do; and he is to be paid for his pains as formerly he has been paid.

[page 174]

Upon the same day the fees and duties due for the cartage of in and within this borough are let to farm to Mr Edward Linzie for the year following at the rent of four and twenty pounds to be paid half yearly.

Upon the same day the profits of the market are let to farm to Mr James Giear for the year ensuing at the rent of twelve pounds and five shillings to be paid half yearly.

Upon the same day the profits of the bridge and drawbridge are let to farm to Mr Henry Mitchell for the next year, at the rent of six pounds and ten shillings to be paid half yearly.

Upon the same day it is agreed on that the profits of the ballast, [and] the forfeitures for breach of any constitution within this town shall be kept in the town's hands, and a fit man to be sought to collect the same, who is to be paid two shillings and six pence in the pound for all such money as he shall collect or receive for the same.

8 October 1641

Upon this present day Roger Read and John Bury are elected to be two of the porters of this borough, who forthwith together with John Elborne, Richard Chowne, Richard Smyth, and Daniel Winsor took their oaths for the due executing of their places. And they did then agree to pay to Balcomb, a late porter but now infirm and not able to labour six pence by the week out of their labour so long as he shall live.

15 October. 1641

Upon this present day by a general consent of the mayor, aldermen, bailiffs and capital burgesses it is agreed on that George Gayland of Dorchester, plumber, be sent for, and treated with all about covering the Walke, the Grand Jury Chamber and the Custom House with lead and that an agreement be made with him for doing thereof, and materials speedily provided.

[page 175] 8 November 1642

Upon this present day Richard mayor, gentleman, was by a general consent of the mayor, aldermen and bailiffs then assembled elected and sworn common clerk for the borough in the room and stead of Francis Gape, lately removed, who is to have and receive all fees and duties belonging to the said office in as ample manner as the said

Francis Gape had and enjoyed the same.

[page 176] **17 August 1643**
For as much as Mr, Francis Gape, common clerk, for this borough was heretofore wrongly suspended from the execution of the same office of common clerk and Mr Richard mayor elected and sworn in his stead in the same office, but for that the same election of Richard Maior was illegal. It is therefore by a general consent of the mayor, aldermen and bailiffs now assembled thought fit and ordered that the said Mr Francis Gape be readmitted into the said office, and the election of the said Richard mayor utterly vacated as if the same had never been, and agreed that this be entered in the book of constitutions.

Upon the same day Roger Rose of Waymouth was removed from his office of constable and William Barnes sworn to execute the said office in his stead.

[page 177 is blank]
[page 178] **18 October 1644, 20 Charles**
Upon this present day Philip Bugden was admitted a freeman of this town and borough for the fine of five pounds which was forthwith paid to Mr John Thornton, treasurer, and the said Philip took his oath of freeman, etc.

Upon this day John Minterne one of the sergeants of mace was appointed by the mayor, bailiffs, aldermen and capital burgesses now present to gather the profits of the market for the year now to come and to render an account of the same quarterly.

8 November 1644, 20 Charles
Upon this present day Jonathan Leddoze at a full meeting of the mayor, aldermen and burgesses having served George Florie, grocer, deceased, as an apprentice by indenture by the space of seven years to that trade was admitted a freeman of this town and borough and took his oath of a freeman.

29 January 1645, 20 Charles
Upon this present day it was ordered at a full meeting of the mayor, aldermen bailiffs and burgesses that all the dirt in the several street and lanes of this town shall be made up into heaps by the inhabitants of the town before their several and respective houses, grounds, lands and dwellings before Saturday morning next, upon pain of every man making default 3s 4d to be forthwith levied on the goods of those which make default. And that from and after the said Saturday the dirt of the said streets and lanes shall be made up in heaps as aforesaid by the said inhabitants twice in every week. That is to say Wednesday and Saturdays upon pain of every one making default for every time 12d to be levied as aforesaid.

Upon the same day it was agreed upon between the mayor, aldermen, bailiffs and burgesses now present, and Robert Hawkins and William Winter concerning the streets and lanes of Waymouth and Melcomb Regis: that the said Robert and William shall twice in every week, viz. Wednesdays and Saturdays carry away with their horses and pots all the dirt which shall be made up in heaps and lay the same, in such places, as shall not annoy the town or harbour; for which labour of theirs they are to have eight pounds by the year, to be paid quarterly by the treasurer of the town, And further ordered, that the town lighter be forthwith trimmed up and made fit for service.

3 March 1645

Roger Rose was this day elected and sworn a sergeant in the place of Thomas Alexander. Upon the same day William Pitt and Samuel Tackle were elected and sworn constables for Waymouth side; And Mr Philip Bugden was nominated constable in Melcomb side in stead of Philip Kind, deceased.

Upon the same day Mr William Pitt was elected one of the capital burgesses and sworn accordingly.

Upon the same day Mr Thomas Snowdon and Mr William Gillet alias Skinner were elected capital burgesses, and the said William Gillet was sworn accordingly.

[page 179] 14 March 1645

It is agreed upon that the sergeants at mace shall collect the arrears of the town rents in Melcomb until Christmas last past, and form thenceforth after every Michaelmas yearly. And shall pay in the same to the town treasurer as often as they shall be required for their pains herein, the town treasurer is to pay them 12d for every 20s which they shall so collect.

Upon the same day Mr Thomas Waltham, Mr Bailiff Allin, Arthur Holeman and Mr John Wall are appointed to audit Mr Matthew Allin's account, and to make their report to the mayor, aldermen, bailiffs and burgesses on Friday next.

21 March 1645

Upon the same day it was ordered, that such lighters as there shall be occasion of shall be impressed for the use of the town by warrant from the vice-admiral for the carrying away of the soil which now lies in the streets and lanes and that Mr George Churchey and Mr Henry Rose for Melcomb, and Mr James Giear and Mr Gabriel Cornish for Waymouth side do take care that this be performed, and such charges as they shall be herein for labourers, shall be paid them by the town treasurer by a rate to be made upon the town.

Upon the same day Justinian Hingston and Thomas Winter were elected and sworn constables for Melcomb side.

Upon the same day Robert Wall, Theophilus Byat and Richard White were elected capital burgesses of this town, and the said Theophilus Byat and Richard White were sworne accordingly.

Upon the same day Thomas Snowden and John Senior are elected capital burgesses in Melcomb side and the said John Senior was sworn accordingly, and Mr Fabian Hodder and Mr Robert Major, capital burgesses, are put out for discontinuing the meetings at hall.

Upon the. same day John Scoville was at a full hall elected a freeman to the trade of a barber surgeon for the fine of 10s which he is to pay to the town steward.

28 March 1645
Upon this present day at a full Hall the election of Thomas Snowdon a capital burgess is made void by a full vote and captain John Arthur is elected a principal burgess in his room.

[page 180] 4 April 1645
Upon the same day it was ordered, that Mr John Wall and Mr Richard White do take care that the town lighter be forth with prepared and fitted for the town service and that the town steward do pay the charge of the same, and that Mr Wall and Mr White do certify their proceedings here in the next Hall day.

18 April 1645
Upon the same day it was ordered that Mr Thomas Waltham, Mr Arthur Holeman, Mr William Williams and Mr John Wall do audit Mr Matthew Allins account against the next Hall and make their report of what satisfaction they conceive it fit for Mr Allin to have.
    Upon the same day it was ordered, that the same 4 persons with the assistance of the constables and sergeants do make a rate in pursuance of the committee's order, for the cleansing of the town to which purpose the constables and sergeants are to bring a list of all strangers to the same four persons before Monday next.

21 April 1645
Upon the same day Henry Rose, Philip Bugden and John Dudley were nominated overseers for the Melcomb, Leonard Hillard, churchwarden, and Nathaniel Allin, sidesman, Richard White, Theophilus Byet and Robert Wall were elected and nominated overseers of the poor for Waymouth.

18 July 1645
Upon the same day it was ordered, that Mr Henry Rose and the sergeants at mace shall collect the arrears of the rents due for the lands of Melcomb Regis, for which end they have a schedule of the same delivered to them, and a warrant under Mr Mayor's hand and seal, And it is further ordered and agreed that the said Mr Rose and the said sergeants at mace are to have one shilling of the pound of every 20s which they shall collect and pay in to the town treasurer.

1 August 1645
Upon the same day John Bury one of the porters of this town paid to the town steward four and thirty shillings and one penny for cartage lately by him collected.

1 August 1645
Upon the same day Mr Wise paid to Mr John Thorneton, treasurer of this town, five pounds and two shillings for petty customs.

[page 181] 20 September 1645

Upon the same day there was paid in by a tobacco merchant to John Thorneton, the town steward, 20s as a fine for licence to sell his tobacco here.

2 October 1645

Upon this present day Mr Robert Wise paid in to the town steward four pounds for petty customs.

Upon this present day the petty customs were let to Mr James Giear for the year ensuing at four score and one pounds to be paid quarterly, security Mr Thomas Waltham and Mr Henry Rose.

Upon this same day the cartage was let to Mr Thomas Waltham for one year at eleven pounds and five shillings to be paid quarterly. Security Mr James Giear and Mr Henry Rose.

Upon the same day the market was let to Mr Henry Rose for, one year, at nine pounds and five shillings to be paid quarterly. Security Mr James Giear and Mr Thomas Waltham.

Upon the same day it was ordered that the bridge duties shall be kept in the town's hand for the year now to come.

Upon the same day the ballast and forfeitures were let to Mr John Senior at five pounds and five shillings to be paid quarterly, security John Minterne.

Upon the same day John Bury, porter, paid to Mr Thomas Wallis, mayor, for the bridge duties nineteen shillings and seven pence, of which was given to the Porter 19d for the remainder was 18s.

Upon the same day Thomas Hingston did agree to the town to pay 30s each year for his shop, to be paid quarterly to the town steward.

6 October 1645

Upon this present day Mr Thomas Waltham was elected mayor of this borough for the year next ensuing.

[page 182] Upon the same day Mr Thomas Leddoze and Mr Henry Rose were elected bailiffs of this borough for this year next ensuing.

Upon the same day Mr Philip Bugden was sworn one of the principal and capital burgesses.

Thomas Wallis late Maior is elected and nominated treasurer for the year to

Upon the same day Mr James Giear, Mr John Allin senior, Mr Robert Wall, Mr George Churchey, Mr John Arthur and Mr John Swetnam were appointed to be auditors to audit the account of the treasurer for the year past.

10 October 1645

Upon this same day Mr Robert Wall was sworn a principal burgess of this town.

Upon the same day Mr Robert Wall was sworn a freeman generally for the fine five pounds of which sum by the consent of the mayor, aldermen and burgesses then present, there was returned four pounds to the said Mr Wall, for the remainder being twenty shillings was paid to the town steward.

17 October 1645

Upon the present day one Mr Haine, a merchant of Exeter, having this week bought a parcel of hops of one Mr Bennet, a merchant of Hastings, one of the Cinque Ports, paid twenty shillings for a fine, whereof by Mr Mayor's orders 5s was repaid him and the 15s was paid over to Mr Wallis the town steward.

Upon the same day the said Mr Bennet, having also bought of captain Andrew Eburne, being no freeman, a quantity of salt and a parcel of raisins of the said Mr Haines, paid for a fine 20s, of which was given back again 10s, and the other 10s was paid over to the town steward.

Upon the same day Mr Theophilus Byat was admitted and sworn a freeman for the fine of five pounds, but in regard he married an alderman's daughter of this town, viz: the daughter of Mr Henry Cuttance, the mayor and company gave him back four pounds of the same, and the other 20s was paid over to Mr Wallis the town steward.

[page 183] 18 October 1645

At a Hall called the same day for the election of a recorder, whereat was present Mr Thomas Waltham, mayor, Mr Thomas Giear, Mr Matthew Allin, Mr John Thornton, Mr Thomas Wallis, Mr John Lockier, Mr George Churchey and Mr James Giear. The gentlemen's names in this election are William Savage, esquire, and Mr John Bond. The voices for Mr Savage are Mr Matthew Allin, Mr George Churchey; and the voices for Mr Bond are Mr James Giear, Mr John Lockier, Mr Thomas Wallis, Mr John Thornton, Mr Thomas Giear and Mr Thomas Waltham. So that the said Mr Bond was elected recorder of this borough and town in the place of Richard King, esquire, late recorder, deceased, and sworn accordingly.

24 October 1645

Upon the same day John Minterne, sergeant at mace, paid in for the arrears of the market rent since the last account the sum of £3 9s 7d to Mr Thomas Wallis the town steward.

Upon the same day Robert Row the younger, merchant , paid in for a fine for merchandise already sold to foreigners, and for a licence to sell such merchandise and goods as he has yet left here, the sum of ten shillings which was presently delivered over to Mr Wallis, town steward.

1 November 1645

Upon this present day Mr Thomas Waltham, mayor of this town, received warrants from John FitzJames, esquire, sheriff of this county for the election of three burgesses of Parliament for this town as follows:

[Latin] John FitzJames Esquire of Leweston, sheriff of the aforesaid county, to the mayor of the borough or town of Weymouth and Melcombe Regis in the aforesaid county, greeting.

Whereas I recently received a writ from the Lord King, directed to me, which read as follows:

Whereas Gerard Napper and Richard King, esquire, have recently been elected as burgesses of the borough of Melcombe Regis in my County, for the Parliament of the same Lord King begun at the city of Westminster on the third day of November in the sixteenth year of the reign of the said Lord King, and whereas they, thus elected and in due manner returned (in accordance with the form of the statute issued and provided for in such cases) in the lower house, for the Commons of the kingdom of the same King of England, as is fully set out in the Parliamentary records located in the Chancery; And whereas afterwards the same Gerard and Richard, by the judgement of the House of Commons, were rendered incapable of sitting there as members of the same during this Parliament; for which reason the subjects of the Lord King of the aforesaid borough of Melcombe Regis have been deprived of anyone to act on behalf of the said borough in the said Parliament, and the said Lord King, however, not wishing that the Commons of his Kingdom in his said Parliament, assembled to address his affairs and the condition of his Kingdom and that of the Church of England, should for this reason be diminished or weakened, so that those due affairs cannot put into effect, has ordered me, through the aforesaid writ, that I should cause to be elected, in place of the said Gerard and Richard, two other suitable and prudent burgesses of the aforesaid borough (in accordance with the form of the statute issued and provided for in such cases).

Therefore I command you, on behalf of the Lord King, that you should cause to be elected without delay in place of the said Gerard and Richard, two other suitable and prudent burgesses of the aforesaid borough (in accordance with the form of the statute issued and provided for in such cases), and that you should cause the names of the same burgesses to be inserted in certain indentures which are to be drawn up between me and you and those who participated in this election so that I may send, without delay, the names of the same burgesses to the said Lord King in the Chancery, together with the other part of the aforesaid indentures.

Issued under the seal of my office on the last day of October in the twenty first year of the reign of the Lord King of England etc.

[English] Another warrant from the said Sheriff was sent for the chosing of one burgess for the borough of Waymouth in the place of Sir John Strangwaies, knight.

3 November 1645

Mr Mayor having received the warrants as before specified an election of burgesses was made by the mayor, aldermen, burgesses and freeholders of the said borough in the town hall of Melcomb Regis between the hours of 8 and 11 in the forenoon of the same day, viz: of Colonel William Sydenham, governor of this garrison, for the said Sir Jerrard napper, of Mr John Bond, the recorder clerk, for the said King, and Mr Matthew Allin, one of the aldermen of the borough for the said Sir John Strangwaies, which election was published in the said town hall. And on the Saturday before the same election public proclamations were made of the time and place for that election, upon Mr Mayor's command, by the sergeants at mace, in all the public and eminent places in both sides, viz: in Weymouth and Melcomb Regis and fixed on the bridge. And upon this same day these Parliament men being present at the same election in the town hall before the choice was made, viz: Mr Thomas Erle, Mr [blank] Ash and

Mr Richard Rose, the said Colonel Sydenham promised to serve the town freely as a burgess in Parliament without any wages or reward, Captain John Arthur undertook the like for Mr Bond, the recorder clerk, and the said Matthew Allin did promise the like for himself and Captain John Frey, Lieutenant Colonel Robert Coker, Mr John Hill and Mr John Sadler being nominated to stand in the same election, and the said Mr Fry and Mr Coker being present did promise to serve freely. Mr James Giear and Mr John Whiteway undertook the like for Mr Hill, and Colonel Sydenham like for Mr Sadler, at which election Colonel Sydenham had 87 voices, Mr John Bond 76, Captain John Fry 29, Mr Matthew Allin 51, Lieutenant Colonel Coker 35, Mr John Hill 32 and Mr John Sadler 14.

[page 185] **21 November 1645**
Upon a conference about paving the market place before the butchers' shops and the widow Babbidge's house, it is agreed upon that it shall be forthwith paved at the town charge for the present. And that the occupiers of the same lands shall for their neglect here in be proceeded against according to a constitution formerly made. And that Mr Bailiff Rose and Mr Constable Bugden do take care to see this performed accordingly.

19 December 1645
Upon the present day at a hall by the mayor and company John Dudley, clerk of the parish of Melcomb Regis is promised 40s for ringing of the bell from Michaelmas last until Lady Day next at 4 in the morning and 8 at night, and for keeping the clock according to the former custom.

Upon the same day Richard Strong, butcher, having served in the town by the space of about 4 years, and having (as he says) served his apprenticeship seven years with Stephen Barrat of Wimborne, and for that he married the daughter of Thomas Barnes of this town, butcher, is now specially admitted a freeman of the trade of butcher only for the fine of ten shillings, which he paid over to the town steward.

Upon the same day Mr George Churchey paid in to the town steward for ballast money, due in 1640, £7 5s, more he promised to pay the next hall day in balance of that account 10s 6d.

9 January 1646
Upon this present day it was agreed on that Mr Theophilus Byet shall employ someone to carry away the soil before Mr Greene's house with the town lighter and that the town steward shall pay for it.

Upon the same day it was ordered by a general consent that Anthony Webstar of Poole should be admitted to this Corporation to use the trade of block maker and joiner, he paying 50s. Fine to the town and to give security to the town that his family or himself be no charge to the town, as also to be liable to all taxes according to his ability as other townsmen are.

[page 186] **13 February 1646**
Upon this present day it was agreed on that the butchers' shops against Morfield's

premises end in Weymouth which is the town land, and now in the town's lands and not in lease, shall be demised to Thomas Hingston the elder, butcher, for [blank] years, if the said Thomas shall so long live, under the yearly rent of 30s payable quarterly, the first payment at Christmas 1645 [sic.] which 30s shall be disposed in this manner; 20s whereof to the town stock, 5s to the town rent of Weymouth and 5s to the poor of Weymouth, to be paid over to the overseers of the poor, by the town steward, at Michaelmas quarterly. The tenant to repair it.

Upon the same day, whereas Joan Babbidge, widow, by licence of this town, has erected a small shop on the town land adjoining to her dwelling house, now it is agreed between her and the town that she shall pay for the same 4s annually to the town, to be paid quarterly, the first payment to be at Midsummer next. And that the same erected shop shall continue no longer than the town shall think fit, but small at any time by their order be taken down and lie open as formerly. And that the said Joan Babbidge shall have power to take down and lay open the same shop as formerly when she shall think fit and from thenceforth the same rent to the town shall cease and determine.

Whereas Mr George Churchey, one of the aldermen and freemen of this town is charged by captain John Arthur that he, contrary to the oath of a freeman, has coloured foreigner's good, whereby to deprive the town of the petty customs to them due. And that he wrought letters to his correspondents in France to make all their invoices, bills of loading and letters in his, the said Mr Churchey's, name, and not in his brother Mr James Churchey's name. Which said James Churchey had ⅔ parts of the trade between the said brothers, as the said Captain Arthur affirms. And that it appears that the said George Churchey heretofore confessed that he had deceived the town of petty customs and desired to be favourably dealt with in his fine and censure by the town which is affirmed by the testimony of the said Captain Arthur and also by the testimony of Mr Mayor, Mr John Thornton and Mr Thomas Wallis. It is therefore by a full and general consent of all the company now present ordered that the sergeants at mace shall summon the said Mr George Churchey to appear at the hall the next Friday to answer this charge.

Thomas Waltham, mayor,	William Williams
Thomas Leddoze, bailiff	William Holmes
Henry Rose, bailiff	Gabriel Cornish
John Thornton, alderman	Nathaniel Allin
Thomas Wallis, alderman	Richard Bolt
Arthur Holman	John Senior
John Arthur	William Pitt
Theophilus Byet	Robert Wall
Philip Bugden	

[page 187] **20 February 1646**

The said Mr George Churchey appearing this day at the hall before the said mayor, aldermen and burgesses and being charged with the premises gave this answer to the said charge: that the town made him pay £30 for his freedom when he was first admitted freeman of this town, where upon the said Mr Churchey, about 12 years since, did enter in his name some of his brother James Churchey's goods in the custom house within the town, to help make up his money, conceiving as he says that he might have justified the doing thereof in regard of the many great taxes which have been laid upon him by the town. However, [he] submits himself to the censure of the mayor, aldermen and burgesses. And in particular he says that he entered a parcel of *reddings* in his own name , which were his brother's, which goods afterwards were taken up and employed for the use of the garrison soldiers for which he is *Exte* , or his brother never as yet received any satisfaction.

Upon the same day Mr Mayor paid over to Mr Wall, one of the overseers of the poor of Waymouth, 5s for the use of the poor there, which 5s was paid in by Mr Finch in full for his fine for selling of beer without licence.

13 March 1646
Upon the present day Mr George Churchey paid in £8 5s to Mr Thomas Wallis, the town steward, which was the remainder of a former account which has been audited by auditors for ballast money.

20 March 1646
Upon this present day it is ordered and agreed upon that all the inhabitants of this town on Saturday in the afternoon in every week forthwith upon the tolling of the hall bell shall clean the gutters before their several house, lands and grounds by raking them with colerakes and washing them with water and conveying away the same, and shall sweep and cleanse the streets and lanes before their several houses, lands and grounds at the same time and carry away all such dirt and soil to several waste places, viz: those of Waymouth in places void and convenient in Waymouth, and the inhabitants of Melcomb upon the sands without the works, 24 feet from the walls and by Salthouse, upon pain of every making default for, every time breaking this order or any part thereof, for every time 12d. To be levied on their goods by the constables and sergeants at mace, or some of them to the use of this Incorporation. And the said constables and sergeants at mace in either side respectively are to make their presentments to the mayor and bailiffs in writing of the persons which shall break this constitution or any article of it upon every Friday in the forenoon at the town hall in Melcomb Regis.

[page 188] 3 April 1646, 22 King Charles
Upon this present day it was ordered that Mr Edward Hodder shall sufficiently pitch and pave the house that he now dwells in, viz: that part of the street which lies over against the town hall, within one month upon pain of ten shillings to be levied to the use of this Incorporation , and also ten shillings a month for every month after until the same shall be pitched and paved as aforesaid.

30 April 1646
Upon the present day Mr George Churchey, Thomas Winter and John Curtice are

appointed overseers for Melcombe, and Gabriel Cornish, John White and Richard Keate for Waymouth side.

29 May 1646

Memorandum that Colonel William Sydenham, the Governor of this garrison, and one of the Parliament burgesses of this town, on a journey that he lately took to the Parliament gave to the poor of Waymouth and Melcomb Regis to be distributed among them five pounds, of which fifty shillings was this day delivered over to Mr Gabriel Cornish , one of the overseers of the poor of Waymouth, and the other fifty shillings Mr Mayor will take care of, that it shall be distributed amongst the poor people of Melcomb Regis in regards the Governor desired Mr Mayor to take care of the disposing of the whole five pounds.

19 June 1646

For as much as Lieutenant Peter Peeke, cloth worker, came this day to the town hall and desired to be admitted a freeman of that trade, and this company conceiving that he may prove useful and beneficial to the town and not prejudicial to any of the tradesmen of this town. And the said Peter Peeke is admitted a freeman only to the trade of cloth worker, and to make cloth as a clothier for the fine of five shillings which was paid to Mr Thomas Wallis the town's steward.

Upon the same day Alexander Clatworthy of this town, mariner, being an ancient town's man, and born in the town is generally admitted a freeman for the fine of five pounds, which monies he laid down. But in regard that the said Alexander Clatworthy and his ancestors have been ancient townsmen, the said fine was mitigated to the sum of twenty shillings , which twenty shillings was paid over to Mr Thomas Wallis , the town steward, and the other four pounds was paid back to Mr Clatworthy.

[page 189] For as much as the town is generally decayed in paving and pitching, it is ordered that the streets of the town shall be generally pitched and paved, the kennels and gutters of the town charge as formerly. And in case the owner or occupier of houses, lands or grounds shall make default in paying for his or their parts and proportions of paving and pitching before his or their houses, lands or grounds then it shall be lawful to take to goods of the persons so refusing by distress by a warrant to be signed by Mr Mayor to such persons as he direct for the payment for such pitching and paving, returning to the parties the over plus

22 June 1646

Upon this present day it is agreed on, between Mr Mayor and the town on one part and William Baily, mason, and Richard his son on the other part, that the said William Baily and his son shall on this day's night, set themselves, and 3 or 4 others to work out the repairing of the pier which upon view is about 50 feet and shall continue upon that work until it be finished. And shall do the work sufficiently to be approved of by able workmen. And the town is to provide materials and necessaries, viz, a ginn rope and a broad plank, or 2 balkins, 2 hand barrows and iron bars for the work. And to pay to the said William Bayly and his son for the finishing and completing of the work the sum of ten pounds, to be paid twenty shillings weekly until the work shall be finished. And the workmen are to lay the foundation two feet deep in the clay.

26 June 1646

For as much as by daily experience many inconveniences and uncertainties are found by measuring of coals by heaps, in buckets and less measures, both the buyer and seller, viz: sometimes more and sometimes less, according to the care and regard of the measures, and of the buyers and sellers. It is therefore this day by a general consent ordered, that from and after the tenth day of July next, all sea coals to be sold within the harbour and town shall not be any more sold by such measures. And that a measure be forthwith prepared at the town's charge, which shall hold by strength as much and the ancient town bushel, held by heap or exactly filled and measured. And so in like manner for half bushels and pecks. And that every seller of coals sell by such measures upon pain of 10s for the first default herein , and for every default afterwards the value of the coals to be so sold, to be levied by distress and sale of the party's goods breaking any part of this constitution to the use of the Incorporation. And in case no such distress shall be openly found and levied, then the person so offending shall be by the mayor and bailiffs of this town, or any one of them committed to the prison, there to remain until he or they so offending shall have a sufficient surety at the least enter into reconnaissance to our sovereign lord the King's Majesty the principal in £20, and the surety in £10, to answer the breach of the said constitution at the next sessions of the peace, which shall be held for this town after the said offence committed.

Upon the same day it was also by a general consent ordered that all persons, as well strangers as townsmen, which shall hereafter load any stones within the pier, or harbour belonging to the town, shall pay a duty to this Incorporation, viz: every townsman 2d per tonne and every stranger 4d per tonne for every tonne which shall be so loaded.

Upon the same day it is agreed upon between Mr Cornish and the town that Mr Cornish shall oversee the work to be finished at the pier for which he is to be paid 6s 8d per week by the town steward.

10 July 1646

Upon this present day Stephen Edwards, shoemaker, by a general consent of the mayor, aldermen, bailiffs and burgesses was admitted a freeman to the trade of shoemaker for the fine of 10s which was paid over to the town steward.

17 July 1646

Upon this present day John Penny of this town, bodice maker, was admitted a freeman to the trade of a bodice maker and hosier for the fine of ten shillings, which sum he paid over to Mr Wallis the town steward.

[page 191] 2 September 1646

Upon this present day at a full hall of the mayor, aldermen, bailiffs and burgesses assembled at the town hall, the whole business touching Mr George Churchey, one of the aldermen of this town, about his deceiving of the town of petty customs and colouring of his brother James Churchey's goods in his, the said George Churchey's, own name, contrary to his oath. And for that it is very probable it has been a practice of the said Mr Churchey during the space of ten years past. Therefore the said Mr Churchey confesses in his answer that he did so about twelve years past, therefore the said Mr Churchey by the said mayor, aldermen, bailiffs and burgesses assembled in the town hall as aforesaid, by a general consent of them all, is fined and amerced the sum of fifty pounds, to be levied for the use of this Incorporation immediately after the four and twentieth day of this present month of September, in case Mr Churchey shall refuse to pay the same fine of fifty pounds, before on demand made by the sergeants at mace on either of them.

Upon the same day Mr John Allin the elder, being a burgess of this town, and having borne the office of bailiff, was this day admitted a freeman of this Incorporation for the fine of five pounds, but for the reasons aforesaid four pounds of the said five pounds was remitted and the other 20s was paid over to Mr Wallis the treasurer.

21 September 1646
Upon this present day Mr James Giear was chosen mayor of this borough for the year next ensuing.

Upon the same day Mr John Lockier and Mr John Arthur are elected bailiffs for the year ensuing

Upon the same day Dr John Bond took his Oath of recorder of this town, and his oath of Supremacy.

[page 192] 28 September 1646
Upon this present day it was agreed that the petty customs should be kept in the town hands for the year to come.

Upon the same day the cartage was let to Mr John Allin senior for the year next ensuing at fifteen pounds and ten shillings.

Upon the same day the market was let to Mr Henry Rose for one whole [blank] next at ten pounds and ten shillings.

Upon the same day the bridge duties were let to Mr John Allin senior for the year next ensuing at fifty shillings.

Upon the same day the ballast and forfeiture were let to Mr Henry Rose for one year at six pounds.

20 October 1646
Memorandum, there was seized on by John Minterne, sergeant at mace, 10 rolls of tobacco which Jasper Samways of Dorchester, grocer, bought of one Robert Burton, a foreigner, worth as Mr Samwayes says £18. And upon Mr Samwayes real acknowledgement of the truth and his submission to the company his fine is assessed to twenty shillings, which he forthwith paid to Mr Thomas Waltham the town steward.

Memorandum, there was seized on as foreign bought and foreign sold of the goods of Mr John Maddocks as follows, viz, a pack of wares sealed up for one Benjamin

King of Stalbridge and brought in to the cellar of Mr George Churchey by a carrier, one Butler of Upway. The said Mr Maddocks came in to the hall and said that the pack of goods in question is worth near about £20 and says that he can not say it was sold to Mr King or any other, and desires that he may not accuse himself , but says that she should be willing to do or suffer any reasonable thing that the town should put him to or require of him. And further says that there is fifteen pounds worth of goods and wares sold of the wares contained in the said pack of wares. And he, putting himself upon the censure of the bench, is fined five pounds.

[page 193] **4 December 1646**
It is this day agreed upon that the business toughing Mr Hill's iron shall be reserved to the determination of the recorder of this town, in the behalf of the town, and to the recorder of Dorchester in the behalf of Mr Hill, or to other such person as Mr Hill shall nominate. And that the present mayor shall be saved harmless in the premises.

11 December 1646
Whereas there is a rate of twelve shillings weekly imposed by the Committee upon this town for the payment of the payment of the county troop. It is ordered that the town clerk of this town shall draw an answer to the said order for the taking of the said rate showing to them the charges they are at in quartering the soldiers here.

29 December 1646
Upon this present day Mr John Knight of Yetminster came before Mr Mayor and the company and desired to be admitted to set up a Grammar school in this town upon certain terms by himself proposed. But, the town did not admit of his terms, yet were content to admit him as the only teacher of the Latin tongue, upon which he desired one month's respite to give his answer to the town, which was granted to him accordingly.

15 January 1647
Memorandum, there was heretofore collected in the church in Melcomb four pounds, four shillings and six pence for the redeeming of two captives out of Algier, which money was delivered over to Mr George Churchey, one of the overseers of the poor, for the use aforesaid, that is for John Vallance and William Bussell.

29 January 1647
Upon this present day Mr Alexander Clatworthy was by a general consent elected and chosen one of the capital burgesses of this town, in the place and stead of Mr William Williams late deceased, and took his oath accordingly.
    [page 194] Upon the same day Mr Henry Waltham, son of Mr Henry Waltham late of this town, merchant, was this day admitted a freeman ex gratia in regard of his father and ancestors were freemen of this town, and the said Henry Waltham was sworn accordingly.
    Upon the same day it was agreed on that Mr Bailiff Lockier and the town clerk

shall solicit the burgesses of Parliament for this town and the Committee of the navy for some allowance towards the repairing several defects and decays in the harbour belonging to this town.

Upon the same day it was generally agreed on, constituted and ordained that whatsoever person or persons shall from and after the last day of this instant January use any trade, mystery or manual occupation within this town, being no freeman or specially admitted thereto, shall forfeit and lose for every month that he or they shall use or exercise such trade, mystery or manual occupation, being no freeman, the sum of forty shillings per month to the use of this Incorporation to be levied by the constables and sergeants at mace.

Upon the same day it was also agreed on that the £10 14s due to Mr John Hill for iron, for which he has recovered a judgement against Mr James Giear, mayor, shall be paid to Mr Hill by the town steward, when he has the money in cash to pay the same, together with the charges formerly expended in this suit against Mr Churchey and the town sergeants.

Upon the same day it was also agreed on that in regard to Mr Edward Buckler has taken great pains in his Ministry in Melcomb for which he has not had any reward, a dwelling house with appurtenances forthwith be provided for the said Mr Buckler, fit for his quality and condition, at the town's charge.

Upon the same day it was agreed on that four pounds shall be allowed to the schoolmaster, Mr Knight lately proposed to this town towards the rent of a house for him to teach school in.

[page 195] Upon the same day it was also ordered that in regard Mr Ellis Hascall, lately married the widow Kind, who was wife to Philip Kind, deceased, late one of the freemen of this town (and the said Mr Hascall being desirous to be made a freeman) shall be admitted a freeman generally to the trade of merchant for the fine of ten pounds.

5 February 1647
Upon the same day the said Mr Hascall was sworn a freeman for the fine of ten pounds.

26 February 1647
Upon the same day Mr Roger Cuttance of this town, merchant, is this day admitted a freeman for the fine of five pounds, but in regard his father was a freeman and bore office in this town, there was delivered back to him the sum of three pounds, so the other forty shillings was paid over to Mr Thomas Waltham the town treasurer. And the said Mr Cuttance was sworn a freeman accordingly.

26 March 1647
Richard Biles of this town, having served as an apprentice to Mr Thomas Waltham, a freeman of this town, was this day admitted a freeman and sworn accordingly.

21 May 1647
Upon this present day Mr Philip Bugden was appointed churchwarden for this year

to come.

Upon the same day John Dudley was appointed sidesman.

[page 196] Upon the same day Mr Thomas Waltham, Mr Henry Rose and Mr Henry Waltham were chosen and appointed overseers of Melcomb, and Captain John Allin, Roger Rose and William Wintor for Waymouth.

Upon the same day Mr Richard Scovile, town clerk, was generally admitted a freeman for the fine of twenty shillings which was paid over to Mr Thomas Waltham, the town steward, four pounds of which £5 he then laid down, being restored to him, and took his oath of a freeman accordingly.

Upon the same day licence was granted to Captain John Arthur to erect a porch before the door of the dwelling house lately Mr Major's, and to set up a pale before the window in the street, provided that the pale or porch be not set forth to straighten the passage of the street.

29 May 1647

Whereas there was brought into the hall several ware of Mr John Maddocks (he appearing there and confessing the same to be foreign bought and sold to one Benjamin King) being seized on by the officers of this Incorporation, viz: one piece of branched holland, one piece of tuffed holland, 10 pieces of coloured incle, 2 gross of beech hooks, 3 pieces of white Manchester, 14 yards of coloured callicon, 18 ells and ¾ of holland, 1 piece of ferret, 6d ribbon, 2lbs 9½oz of coloured silk and one coarse cloth. It was ordered that the said goods should be forthwith sold for the use of the town, whereupon Mr Philip Bugden bought the same wares, for the sum of ten pounds, amounting by Mr Maddocks' note to £11 2s 7½d.

25 June 1647

Upon the present day Mr Edward Hodder, one of the capital burgesses of this town came into the hall and desired the mayor and the rest of the company there present that he by reason of his age being unable to perform the place of a capital burgess may be exempted from it, which was granted to him and Mr Henry Waltham was chosen a capital burgess in his place.

[page 197] 22 July 1647

Upon this present day there was read an order which is as follows:

16 July 1647

The house being informed that by reason of late storms the several piers and harbour of the port of Waymouth in the county of Dorset are in such decay as not only the trade, and consequently the customs, will be much diminished and prejudiced, besides the danger of shipping resorting to the said port. It is thereupon ordered that it be referred to the committee of the navy to give order for the payment of the sum of one thousand pounds , out of the customs arising from the port of Waymouth, to such person or persons as the said committee shall appoint to receive the sum. The said one thousand pounds to be employed for the repair of the piers and harbour there.

Upon reading the former order Mr Mayor, at the request of the company, promised forthwith to procure Christopher Gibb of Portland and some other able workmen to view the decays of the harbour and to treat with them about the repairing of the same. And it was by a general consent agreed upon that Mr John Lockier shall be overseer of the same works until further order who is to sign all the workmen's bills before they be presented to the mayor, aldermen and bailiffs. And the mayor, aldermen and bailiffs , and in the absence of the mayor the mayor's deputy, or any two of them, whereof the mayor or in his absence the deputy shall be particular of his receipts and disbursements touching the premises. And to pass his account therein before such auditors as the mayor, aldermen, bailiffs and burgesses, or the greater number of them shall appoint at the end of every three months, or sooner if they think fit. And it is further ordered that the said Mr Lockier shall be paid for his pains to be taken in the premises the sum of six shillings and eight pence by the week, the same monies to be paid to Mr Lockier by the town steward.

Upon the same day it was ordered that Captain Lockier shall get the town lighter to be fitted up and shall appoint a sufficient man to manage the same boat for the fetching of materials for the repairing of the premises.

[page 198] Whereas there is now due from Mr Richard Harrison to the town the sum of seven and twenty pounds for the rent of a shop under the town hall. Know for that the said Mr Harrison has not made any use of the same shop for three years last past, and is much decayed on his estate, and unable to pay the same rent. Upon his motion this day to have an abatement of the same rent his case was taken into consideration. And it was this day ordered that the said Mr Harrison shall pay in full of the said rent at Michaelmas next the sum of twelve pounds, otherwise this order to be void, and then he is to take a new lease of the town, at the letting out of the town's revenues, and to give security for the payment of the rent in case he intends to keep it any longer and can agree with the town for the yearly rent.

9 August 1647

Upon this present day it was agreed upon that William Gillet of this town, carpenter, shall be employed forthwith to go to Botleigh for the buying of 40 or 50 tonnes of timber to be used about the repairing of the harbour. And that the treasurer for the town shall pay to him ten pounds to pay as earnest towards the same bargain, and the remainder of the monies which shall grow due for the said timber shall be paid by the town.

Upon the same day there was read letters, the one from the Commissioners of the customs to Captain Arthur and the other from Mr John Randall to the mayor, aldermen and bailiffs, which are as follows:

Captain Arthur

Having received special direction from the honourable Committee for the navy and customs for advancing the sum of £500 to the mayor and bailiffs of the town of Weymouth and Melcomb Regis for the repair of the pier and harbour there now in decay. We desire you out of the monies remaining in your hands, and otherwise as the same shall arise out of the receipts of customs, in the said town of Waymouth under your charge, to pay to the said mayor and bailiffs of the said town of Waymouth the said sum of five hundred pounds, and upon payment thereof to take their acquittance testifying the receipt thereof accordingly, which with these letters shall be your sufficient warrant for the allowance thereof upon your account. And not having else at present we rest, Customs House, London, 27 July 1647

To their loving friend Captain John
Arthur, collector of the customs
in the port of Waymouth

Your loving friends
Richard Bateman
Charles Lloyd
Walter Boothby

[page 199] Gentlemen:
Yours of the 23rd present I have received, and do return you all humble thanks for your kind acceptance of any poor service I am able to do for that my poor native town, which shall be continued by me. I have according to your desires sent the letters enclosed both to Mr Green and Dr Bond being at present out of the town, and shall take care to satisfy any such fees and charges as either of them have been at, and thereof I give you a faithful account . You shall have enclosed receive a warrant to Mr Arthur for the payment of £500, part of the £1000, the other £500 is ordered and remains in Mr Greene's hand, and is to be deposited until such time as an account shall be sent up [of] how the former £500 has been expended for the repairing of the piers, the end for which it was granted, the like is for the town of Lime [Lyme Regis].
I have not else but to assure you that I am your most willing and faithful servant,
John Randall
London, 27 July 1647

7 September 1647
Memorandum, there was seized thirty rolls of tobacco sold by Thomas Squibb, a foreigner, to Robert Hardy, a foreigner, but in appearing that Jonathan Leddoze, a freeman of the town, bought the moiety of the same tobacco. And the said Robert Hardy appearing to the charge laid against him concerning the other moiety of the said parcel of tobacco, and he submitting himself to the censure of the mayor and company. The said company upon his submission, and taking the same into consideration, do fine the said Robert Hardey 40s which the said Mr Hardey paid to Mr Thomas Waltham, the town treasurer, and returned thanks to Mr Mayor and the company for their favour to him.
Upon this present day Mr Richard Scovile, the town clerk, is elected and sworn one of the capital burgesses of this town.
Upon the same day it was ordered that a warrant shall be made against Mr George Churchey to levy the £50 formerly assessed on his goods for a fine for entering colouring his brothers goods being a foreigner in his, the said Mr Churchey's own name, and the same business to be presented and defended at the town's charge.

[page 200] 16 September 1647
Upon this present day at a full hall Mr Barnard Ozler and Mr Edmund Frampton, executors of the last will of Mr Bernard Michell, late one of the aldermen of this town, made a lease to the town, as a pledge of their affection, of a void piece of ground near

the jetty for 2000 years, under the yearly rent of 6d. In consideration whereof the town admitted them both freemen *ex gratia* and they were sworn accordingly.

21 September 1647

Upon this present day Mr Thomas Leddoze was elected mayor of this borough for the year next ensuing.

Upon the same day Mr John Allin senior and Mr Richard Scovile were chosen bailiffs of this town for the next year ensuing.

Upon the same day Mr James Giear was chosen treasurer for the year next ensuing.

Upon the same day Mr John Allen, Mr Richard Scovile, Mr John Thornton, Mr George Churchey, Mr Henry Rose and Mr Thomas Chapple were appointed auditors.

28 September 1647

Upon this present day the petty customs were let to Mr Thomas Chapple set seventy seven pounds for the year next to come.

Upon this present day the cartage was let to Mr John Allen senior at fourteen pounds and ten shillings for the year next to come.

Upon this present day the market of the said town was let to Mr John Senior for eleven pounds and fifteen shillings for the year next ensuing.

[page 201] Upon this present day the bridge duties of this town were let to Mr John Allin senior for five and fifty shillings for the year next ensuing.

Upon this present day the ballast and forfeitures of this town were let to Mr Henry Rose for nine pounds and five shillings for the year next ensuing.

22 October 1647

Upon this present day Mr George Pley, Customer of the port, who married the daughter of Mr Robert Wise, an ancient townsman, is generally admitted a freeman of this town for the fine of five pounds, which he paid Mr Thomas Waltham , the town steward, and took his oath of a freeman accordingly.

Upon the same day it was ordered that Mr John Lockier shall from thence forth be paid ten shillings a week for his care and pains as overseer of the materials and workmen about the harbour.

29 October 1647

Upon the same day that there shall be a quay made from the ballast wharf to the pier near Mr Pitt's land , it being very necessary for the securing of ships in time of stormy weather.

19 November 1647

Upon the same day it was ordered that Mr James Giear do speedily write to Hampton for the procuring of 30 tonnes of timber for piles for the harbour.

22 November 1647

Upon this present day Thomas Snow appearing before the mayor and Company of the full hall and desiring leave to use his trade of a cooper in the town whereto he served apprentice in the city of Exeter by the space of seven years, and alleging that he married the daughter of Mr Cade, one of the late aldermen of this town, is admitted a freeman only to the trade of cooper, for the fine of 10s which he paid to Mr James Giear the town treasurer.

[page 202] **17 December 1647**
Upon this present day Mr Adam Lee, late of this town, mariner, now coming from the West Indies, delivered over to Mr Thomas Leddoze, mayor, five pounds, which he gave to the poor of this town, viz: to the poor of Waymouth forty shillings, and to the poor of Melcombe three pounds.

31 December 1647
Upon this present day Mr Robert Wise paid in for the petty customs due since Michaelmas last five and twenty pounds to the hands of the town treasurer and Mr Mayor gave a receipt to Mr Wise for it.

Upon the same day it was agreed that Mr John Randall shall be paid the monies which he laid out of purse to procure the orders about the thousand pounds allotted by the Parliament for the repair of the harbour which is about one and twenty shillings and four pence, and five pounds more as a gratuity for his pains. And it is desired that Mr James Giear write to Mr Sweete, his correspondent, to pay the money to Mr Randoll.

Upon the same day it was agreed on between the town and Christopher Gibbs and Richard Bayly, masons, that the said Gibbs and Bayly shall make up a quay from Leonard Hillard's Corner to the end of the jetty. The town is to *ridd* the foundation, and to make a back against the work. The workmen to have the stones already *scaffled* in to the bargain and to have 4d per perch for so many perches as are from Hillard's Corner to the jetty head, and to make two pair of stairs in such manner as Mr Mayor and company shall direct. The work be as substantial as that which is already done before the houses of Mr Thornton and Mr Lockier in Waymouth side. The breadth of the work be four foot and half, the lower half and three foot and half the upper half of the work.

[page 203] **7 January 1648**
Upon this present day it was ordered and agreed on that a house be provided for a minister, at the town's charge, for one year from such time as he shall come to dwell in the town. And shall be paid for his pains in preaching for one year twenty marks out of the town stock, in part satisfaction for his pains. And that the said minister for his pains shall likewise receive the voluntary contribution of both towns, beside what he shall receive out of the parsonage of Radipoll and by virtue of any order of Parliament or the committee of plundered ministers. And further the town clerk is appointed to treat with Mr George Thorne to exercise his ministry here for the said year in case he be not settled elsewhere.

Upon the same day Robert Stone, glazier, son of an ancient townswoman had leave to exercise his trade of a glazier in the town . And for his fine shall glaze the Hall windows, as much as come to ten shillings.

Upon the same day William Reape was chosen clerk of the parish in the place of John Dudley, clerk. And he is to receive the usual wages for ringing 4 and 8, 6d for every knell. And he is to teach; according to his own offer, the poor children to write and cipher without any reward for his pains of those whose parents are not able to pay.

20 January 1648

Memorandum there was seized on nine bags of hops sold to Jasper Sanwaies of Dorchester by one Richard Barker of Hastings as foreign bought and foreign sold (as the said Richard acknowledges).

21 January 1648

Upon the same day Jasper Samwaies appearing before the mayor and Company, being charged with the foreign buying of the same hops, and submitting himself to the censure of the company is fines five pounds, which was presently paid by him . But in regard of his submission there was delivered him back twenty shillings, and the other four pounds was paid over to Mr Thomas Waltham.

[page 204] Upon the same day Robert Coker, esquire, late sheriff of this county and late governor of this town, is admitted a freeman *ex gratis* and he was sworn accordingly.

Upon the same day Colonel James Heane, governor of this garrison, is admitted a freeman *ex gratia* and he was sworn accordingly.

4 February 1648

Upon the same day it was agreed that Mr Harrison shall have a new lease of the shop that now he has for one and twenty years at the old rent. To have commencement from Christmas last past.

Upon the same day it was ordered that whereas Mr James Giear in the time of his mayoralty paid to Mr Matthew Allen five pounds, part of the sum of money demanded by the said Mr Allin, and due from the town, at the time of the mayoralty of Mr Allin. The said Mr James Giear being town treasurer for this year shall reimburse himself.

Upon the same day Mr Abraham Dry (upon the request of the Company) had leave to use the trade of a clothier in the town provided he does not cuff or sell cloth by retail.

Upon the same day Mr Richard Bolt (upon the disaster befallen Captain John Lockier) is nominated overseer of the labourers about the harbour in the place and stead of the said Mr Lockier, for which he and the said Mr Bolt are to be paid 7d per week for his labour therein by the treasurer.

[page 205] Upon the same day it is ordered that in regard Mr Lockier, late overseer of the work, broke his leg going home to his house. And he being a great charge about surgeons, etc, in his cure, and thereby in decay, the said Mr Lockier shall be paid by the treasurer so much money as will make up the town rent that he has in his hands ten pounds. And that Mr Lockier shall make up his account about the said town rent.

24 March 1648

Whereas there is due to this town by Mr Benjamin Pitt twenty pounds which is in arrears for the rent of a certain mill and lands in Causeway, now this Company does assign over the same twenty pounds to Mr Henry Rose and does agree with him to bear the charge of any suit that shall be commenced or prosecuted touching the same rent. And the said Henry Rose does agree with this Company to pay to the town steward at Michaelmas next to the use of this Incorporation fifteen pounds, and on the next hall day to seal a bond for the repayment of the same accordingly.

Upon the same day it was agreed upon that all those that from the first day of April next sell or spend in any victualling house, or house of entertainment any beer brewed out of this town shall pay for every tun 4s per tun and so after the same proportion for every lesser quantity. And every one that shall give information of beer of this kind shall have one third of the same forfeiture. And the former constitution of 4d per hogshead for town beer to continue.

31 March 1648

Upon the same day Mr Richard White, farmer of the petty customs, paid in to Mr James Giear the town treasurer towards the rent of the petty customs from Michaelmas last until Michaelmas next the sum of one and twenty pounds.

[page 206] 28 April 1648

Upon this present day Mr John Swetnam, Stephen Edwards and Onesiphorus Penny were appointed overseers of the poor for Melcombe; and Mr John Thornton, Peter wall and John Parminter were made overseers for Waymouth.

5 May 1648

Upon this present day Thomas Bennet, a merchant and baron of Hastings, one of the Cinque Ports, producing the certificate under written, it was ordered that he should be repaid that ten shillings which was paid to Mr Thomas Wallis the town steward the 17 October 1645.

To all Christian people to whom these letters shall come, we the mayor, jurors and commonality of the town and port of Hasting in the county of Sussex, one of the Cinque Ports of our sovereign lord the King, to honour and due reverence as appertains , send greeting, whereas our sovereign lord the King's Majesty that now is, and his most noble predecessors late Kings and Queens of England by their charters and confirmations, and by the authority of diverse parliaments have granted ratified and confirmed to the barons of the said Cinque Ports, and their members , that they shall be free of all toll, and of all customs, (that is to say) of all lastage, passage, carriage, rivage, pontage, poundage, murrage, stallage, peysage, peicage, groundage, terrage and of scott and of geld, hidage, scutage and of all wrecks of the sea. And that they shall be free of all their buying, selling and re-buying through all his Majesty's realms and dominions with socke, sacke, tholl and thern. And that they shall be wreck free, suit free, stallage and lanecop free, and that they shall be quiet from all shires and hundreds, and that they shall have their findall, both by sea and land. And that they be quiet of all their goods and merchandise as his Majesty's freemen. And that they shall have their honours in courts and their liberties throughout his Majesty's dominions wheresoever they come. And that they shall not be impleaded, but where they ought and were want, (that is to say) at Shepeway. And further his Majesty and his predecessors by their said charters do forbid that no person do wrongfully disturb them, or their merchandise on pain of forfeiture of ten pounds. And that they shall not be put in assize juries or reconnaissances, (by reason of any foreign tenure) against their wills. [page 207] And that they shall be free of passage of such wines of their own adventure. Viz: one tun of wine before the mast and another tun after the mast. And that they shall be free of all tallages and of all aid to be given to his Majesty by their ships, except the service reserved by his Majesty's said charters. And further that no man shall be part over with them, against their wills or any goods or merchandise which they shall happen to buy in the realm of Ireland. And finally they shall have and enjoy all their liberties and free customs as apply and as honourably as their predecessors at any time had and enjoyed them in the times of Edward the Confessor, William the first and second, Henry, John, Richard, Henry the second, Edward the first, second and third, sometimes Kings of England, and other Kings and Queens of England, the King's most noble predecessors that now is, as the said charters and confirmations more amply do testify and declare. Know ye now therefore that the bearer hereof, Thomas Bennet, jurate, is one of the barons and freeman of the town and port of Hasting, who ought to have and enjoy all the liberties, privileges, franchises and customs aforesaid, granted to the said barons of the Cinque Port and their members, by the charters and confirmations aforesaid. Wherefore we pray and require you and every of you whom it may concern t at what time or said brother and combination Thomas Bennet, or his goods, cattels, chattels, wares of merchandise shall happen to come amongst you, that you vouchsafe continually and gently to entreat as one of us, not offering to him or to his said goods or merchandise any damage, injury, hurt or violence contrary to the charters and confirmations aforesaid. And as we may do for you in like cases, at any of your requests. In witness whereof the common seal of the said town and port of Hasting to these present we have caused to be fixed. Dated at Hasting aforesaid the two and twentieth day of October in the eighteenth year of the reign of our sovereign lord Charles by the grace of God King of England, Scotland, France and Ireland, defender of the faith, etc, 1642.

[page 208] **24 May 1648**
Whereas on the 29th day of May *anno domini* 1647 there were several goods seized as foreign bought and sold (which goods were sold by John Maddocks to one Benjamin King, both foreigners, and the same were sold for ten pounds paid over to the then treasurer. Now it appearing to the mayor, aldermen and burgesses that the said King

has paid for the same goods to the aforesaid John Maddocks and that the said King is but a poor man and not able to bear the same fine. It is therefore by the consent of the mayor, aldermen and burgesses now present upon a full meeting and debate of the promises that the present town steward shall repay to the said Benjamin King six pounds of the said ten pounds.

Upon the same day it was ordered that the rubble, dung and dirt in the lane leading from the widow Knight's brewhouse towards the sea shall be carried away at the town's charge , that the water may have a free passage (that lane at present being very annoying to the town). And that Thomas Snowdon, tailor, be desired to take care to see the same done and to agree with workmen to that purpose which rubble, dirt and soil is to be carried away to the void plot of ground lately taken in by the jetty.

Upon the same day it was agreed on between the town and John Locke and Thomas Russell that the said Locke and Russell shall pitch the quays at Melcomb side for which they shall have two pence fathering the yard. The town is to find materials only, and the paviers are to break and rid the ground and to provide labourers to attend the work at their own charge. The paviours are to do the work substantially.

Upon the same day it was agreed upon that Mr Arthur Holeman and Mr John Senior shall have the benefit of the constitution touching 12d per hogshead for foreign beer and 4d per hogshead for town's beer made the 13 March last past until Michaelmas next at three pounds. For which the said Mr Holman and Mr Senior are to give their bond to the town, to be paid at Michaelmas next, for the benefit of the poor of the town. This is to begin the 24th day of May instant.

[page 209]

Upon the same day it was agreed on and assented between the town and Mr Richard Bolt, overseer of the works, that from henceforth his wages shall be but five shillings per week.

16 June 1648

Upon the same day Mr Peter Wall of this town, merchant, being an ancient town's man, and son of Mr John Wall, a freeman, was admitted a freeman for the fine of five pounds, but in regard of the promises three pounds of the same was delivered back to him and the other forty shillings paid in o Mr James Giear the town treasurer, and he took his oath accordingly.

Upon the same day Mr Peter Wall was chosen one of the capital burgesses of this town in the place of Mr Richard White, lately deceased, and he was sworn accordingly.

Upon the same day Gregory Babbidge, son of Gregory Babbidge the elder, merchant, was admitted a freeman by descent, and he was sworn accordingly.

[page 210] capital burgesses chosen since the 1st of October 1644

Mr Richard White	179
Captain John Arthur	179
Mr Philip Bugden	182
Mr Alexander Clatworthy	193
Mr Henry Waltham	196
Mr Richard Scovile	199
Mr Peter Wall	209
Mr George Pitt	222
Mr Jonathan Leddoze	222
Mr Thomas Winter	222
Mr George Pley	224
Mr Roger Cuttance	224
Stephen Abbott	224
Stephen Edwards	225
Matthew Caseway	225
Mr John Eyres	225
Mr John Rowe	226
Mr James Studleigh	231
Mr John Penny	231
Mr Thomas Hide	248
Mr William Bond	258
Mr Andrew Buckler	259
Mr Samuel Cooke	259
Mr Benjamin Gatch	261
Mr Richard Peircy	262
Mr John Allenbridge	262
Mr Richard Yardley	266

[page 211]

Enrolment of apprentices by indenture with freemen and inhabitants of this borough and town and the day and times of their enrolments according to a constitution heretofore made by the mayor, aldermen, bailiffs and capital burgesses of the said borough and town to that end and purpose by the same constitution more at large appear:

10 June 1641: Peter Neale, son of Andrew Neale of this borough, deceased, has placed himself an apprentice to and with William Neale of the same place, mariner, by indenture bearing the date 4 September 1641 to serve from the day and date of that indenture for the term of eight years the next ensuing

9 November 1641: David Heckles, son of George Heckles of Hebborne in the county of Northumberland, has put himself an apprentice to Thomas Damon of this borough, mariner and shipwright, by indenture sated 20 August 1641 to serve for seven years from the date thereof.

21 January 1645: William Pooke, son of William Pooke of Blandford Forum in the county of Dorset, inn holder, bound apprentice yo Philip Bugden senior of this town, merchant, from the feast of the birth of Our Lord God 1645 for seven years.

29 December 1647: Thomas Samwaies, son of James Samwaies of Bincomb in the county of Dorset, clothier, bound apprentice to John Hodder, mercer, by indenture dated 12 June 1647 to serve for 7 years from the first of January 1646.

10 June 1647: Samuel Cooke, son of John Cooke, late of Dorchester, mercer, bound apprentice to Captain John Arthur of this town, merchant, by indenture bearing date the fifteenth day of June, to serve from the 25th of July 1646 for the term of seven years.

2 July 1649: Erasmus Holland, son of John Holland of Tickleton in the county of Dorset, cloth worker, by indenture dated 18 May 1649 bound apprentice to Stephen Edwards of this town, shoemaker, to serve for 7 years from the date of the same indenture.

23 December 1649; Thomas Tunstall, son of Margaret Tunstall of Waymouth and Melcomb Regis in the county of Dorset, widow, by indenture dated 25 December 1648 bound apprentice to Gregory Babbidge of this town, merchant, to serve for 8 years from the date of the same indenture.

[page 212] 30 May 1651: Nicholas Starr, son of Dorothy Starr of Beere within the parish of Seaton in the county of Devon, widow, by indentures dated 24 September 1650 bound apprentice to Gregory Babbidge of this town, merchant, to serve for 7 years from Michaelmas 1650.

18 June 1652: Jonathan Edwards, son of Mr Stephen Edwards one of the burgesses and freemen of this town, by an indenture bearing the date the four and twentieth day of June 1651, bound apprentice to his father to serve him in the trade of merchant from the day of the date of the indenture.

11 February 1653: John Swetnam, son of William Swetnam of Shaston in the county of Dorset, yeoman, by an indenture bearing the date the 29th day of September in the year of Our Lord 1647 bound apprentice to John Swetnam of Waymouth and Melcomb Regis, woollen draper, to serve him in the trade of woollen draper from the date of the indenture for the term of seven years.

25 July 1653: Thomas Samwayes, son of James Samwayes of Bincombe in the county of Dorset, clothier, by indenture bearing the date 12th day of June in the year of Our Lord 1647 bound apprentice to John Hodder of this town, mercer, to serve him in the trade of mercer from the first of January last past before the date of the indenture for the term of seven years.

25 July 1653 Peter Bagwell, son of Edward Bagwell of Watchcomb in the parish of Culleton in the county of Devon, husbandman, by indenture bearing the date the 25th of January in the year of Our Lord 1649 bound apprentice to John Hodder of this town, mercer, and Elizabeth his wife, to serve them in the trade of mercer from the second day of February next ensuing the date of the indenture for the term of seven years.

18 October 1653: James Wallis, son of Thomas Wallis of Withell in the county of Somerset, yeoman, by indenture bearing date the 29th day of September 1653 bound apprentice to John Hodder a freeman of this town, grocer, and Elizabeth his wife to serve them in the trade of grocer and merchant from the day of the date of the indenture for the term of seven years.

24 March 1653: Bartholomew Attwoll, son of Alexander Attwoll, of the island of Portland, by indenture bearing the date the 20th day of March 1651 bound apprentice to John White the elder, of this town, mariner, to serve the seven years from the date of the same indenture.

6 May 1654: Thomas Dashwood, son of John Dashwood of Lulworth in the county of Dorset, gentleman,, by indenture bearing date the 18th day of March 1653 bound apprentice to John Swetnam, a freeman of this town, woollen draper, and Agnes his wife, to serve them in the trade of woollen draper and mixed draper from the five and twentieth day of March next ensuing the date of the indenture for the term of seven years or eight years as in the said indenture.

1 March 1652: William Bryar, son of John Bryar of Sutton Points in the county of Dorset, yeoman, by indenture bearing date the 24th day of February 1653, bound apprentice to James Giear of this town, merchant, to serve him for seven years from the date of the same indenture.

[page 213] The names of the freemen of this borough and town made since October 1644 by patrimony, service and fine, see previous pages 14, 15, 16, 17 [The names of freemen to 1639 appear on pages 14-17].

Mr Philip Bugden by fine.	178
Jonathan Leddoze by service	178
John Scovile by fine	179, 222
Mr Robert Wall by fine	182
Mr Theophilus Byet by fine	182
Richard Strong by fine for his trade only	185
Lieutenant Peter Peeke by fine for his trade only	188
Mr Alexander Clatworthy by fine	188
Stephen Edwards by fine	190, 225
John Penny by fine	190, 226
Mr John Allin senior by fine	191
Mr Henry Waltham by descent	194
Ellis Hasall by fine	195
Mr Roger Cuttance by fine	195
Richard Biles by service	195
Mr Richard Scovile by fine	196
Mr Barnard Ozler gratis	200
Mr Edmund Frampton gratis	200
Mr George Pley by fine	201
Thomas Snow by fine for his trade only	201
Robert Coker esquire gratis	204
Colonel James Haine gratis	204
Mr Peter Wall by fine	209

John Senior by patrimony   274
Humphrey Weld esquire ex gratia   274
Henry Rose junior by patrimony   275
Mr George Pinsow by fine   276
Mr Christopher Collier by fine   278
Mr Richard Wallis   282

[page 214, this page is blank]

[page 215] **25 September 1648**
At a full hall it appearing that a Dutch skipper named Falke Anderson, master of the Falke of the port of Horne, did much damage lately to the bridge by not safely mooring of his ship, is by a full consent awarded to pay £15 towards the same damage which Mr Mayor Leddoze has promised to pay in.

18 August 1648
It is by a general consent ordered and constituted that all persons that have made any *mixons* or laid any soil or dung in any of the streets or lands of the town shall carry the same away to void ground enclosed at the jetty, before the first day of September next coming, upon pain of every one making default herein five shillings, and so 5s per week until the same be done. And whosoever shall from henceforth lay any dirt, soil, or dung or make any mixon in any of the streets or lanes of this town shall for every time for offending forfeit and pay the like sum of 5s weekly until the same be removed. And it is also ordered that the sergeants at mace shall levy the said pains and forfeitures and pay in the monies to the town steward, giving in an account of their proceedings herein, when they shall be thereto required, for which pains be taken by the said sergeants they shall be allowed out of every twenty shillings so levied two shillings. And for every default weekly, which the sergeants shall make in their care and diligence in levying the said pains and forfeitures or in returning of their accounts as aforesaid, they shall forfeit for every time 12d a piece.

25 August 1648
Upon this day it is agreed that Mr Richard Harrison, Mr John Swetnam, Mr John Senior and Mr Philip Bugden shall against the next Friday give in a particular of all the martial officers and soldiers in the town, and others that are not freemen that use any trade or manual occupation, art or mystery or that keep any shops or are employed as factors to the great prejudice and damage of the townsmen.

Upon the same day it is also agreed on between this company and Thomas Newman that Thomas Newman shall be the general scavenger of these towns Waymouth and Melcomb Regis for the carrying away of all the dirt, rubble and dust from the lands, grounds and gutters into the void ground newly enclosed at the jetty. And that Waymouth above the bridge westwards to the void place near the house of Thomas Barnes and below the bridge against the wall of Mr Denny's brewhouse. And the said scavenger is to carry away the same dirt, rubble and dust as aforesaid twice in every week, weekly, from henceforth until Michaelmas next twelve month, on every Wednesday and Saturday if the weather will permit. And that all the inhabitants of the town shall on every day before those days rake and cleanse the gutters and grounds before their several houses, walls and lands and make the same up into heaps, that it may be stiff and put into the scavenger's pot, upon pain for every one making default herein, for every time, twelve pence to be levied on their goods by the sergeants at mace. For which the said sergeants at mace shall be allowed two shillings of the pound of money so levied. For which pains to be taken, the said scavenger is to have the sole benefit of the common belonging to the town and ten shillings for his pains until Michaelmas next, and five pounds more for the other year, to be paid quarterly by the town treasurer upon a note from Mr Mayor.

21 September 1648, [St] Matthew's Day

Upon this present day Mr Henry Rose was elected and sworn one of the aldermen of this borough.

Upon the same time there was presented to the company a protestation under the hands of diverse inhabitants of the said town which is as follows:

We whose names are here under subscribed do protest against four of those who gave their voices for Mr Henry Rose to be alderman, viz: Mr George Churchey, Mr James Giear, Mr Philip Bugden, and Mr John Hodder, they being men exempted by an ordnance of Parliament from having any voice in the election of any officers in any incorporated towns.

Upon the same day Mr William Holmes was elected mayor of this borough for the year to come.

Upon the same day Mr Thomas Leddoze and Mr John Arthur were chosen bailiffs for the year to come.

Upon the same day Mr Thomas Leddoze, Mr John Arthur, Mr John Senior, Mr Robert Wall, Mr Theophilus Byat and Mr Henry Waltham were appointed auditors for the year to come.

Upon the same time another protestation was presented from diverse other inhabitants of this town as follows:

Whereas by an ordnance of the Parliament of England sitting at Westminster bearing the date the fourth day of October 1647, (which we are by a late order of the 5th of September required to take special notice of) it is provided that no person shall be elected to the office of mayor or bailiffs in any borough within the kingdom of England who has been in arms against the Parliament, aiding or assisting to the enemy, or is duly sequestered or sequestrable.

[page 217] Not withstanding which ordnance the aldermen of this borough of Waymouth and Melcomb Regis have put into the election of the office of mayor Henry Rose who has been in arms against the Parliament; being a sergeant under Captain John Cade; Gabriel Cornish who has been in arms against the Parliament; being the master of ordnance when this town was a garrison against the Parliament; George Churchey who has aided and assisted the enemy and is daily sequestrable. All which persons being provided against the said ordnance we, whose names are hereunto subscribed, do openly protest against the proceedings of the said aldermen in the particulars about expressed and they the said Henry Rose, Gabriel Cornish and George Churchey as persons not capable of being chosen to the said office of mayor and do expect that our protestation be entered among the public records of this court. And whereas by the aforementioned ordnance all that have been in arms against the Parliament, or have aided or assisted the forces of the enemy, not being compelled thereto are denied their voice in the election of any mayor, etc, we do further protest against all such as have any voices in such election.

Dated 21 September 1648.

25 September 1648

At a full hall Nicholas Mynor, William Shattick and William Gillet, carpenters, being examined by the mayor and company about damage done to the town bridge by Richard Wilson, in suffering his ship for want of mooring to gage the said bridge, at four pounds, which this company does approve of and award the said Richard Wilson to pay, and as touching damage done to the piles they refer themselves to the constitution.

28 September 1648

The petty customs of this town are to be kept in the town's hands for this year to come.

The cartage is to be kept in the town's hands for the year ensuing

The market is this day let to Mr Henry Rose for the year to come for eleven pounds and seven shillings.

The ballast and forfeitures are this day let to Mr Henry Rose for nine pounds and fifteen shillings for the year to come.

The bridge duties were this day ordered to be kept in the town's hands for the year to come.

29 September 1648

Upon this present day Mr Churchey brought to the hall and delivered over to the town an ancient book of records of this town which was lately in the hands of his brother Mr Francis Gape.

[page 218] 27 October 1648

Upon this present day Roger Reade, one of the proters [protectors?] of this town paid in to Mr Mayor 18s 3d for the cartage and bridge duties.

3 November 1648

Upon this present day Mr Gabriel Cornish, one of the capital burgesses of this town came in to the hall and did voluntarily resign up his office of common council man and did desire that another might be chosen in his room, which resignation was accepted of.

7 November 1648

Upon this present day Benjamin Hanham, gentleman, came before William Holmes, mayor, and John Arthur, esquire, one of the bailiffs of this borough, and did voluntarily depose that his late mother, the Lady Mary Hastings (whose inheritance of the farm of Rodipoll with appurtenances was during her life) did in her life time lay her commands on this deponent that in regard there had been some suit and controversy in law between the occupiers of the said farm, viz: from about Timeswell to the gate northwards commonly called the Bulwarks, which lands are known by the name of the common belonging to the said town. That he this deponent should not contend with the said townsmen any further about the same lands , for that she the said Lady Mary Hastings then said that she did verily believe that the same lands did belong to the town aforesaid . And that if the same should be detained from them the poor of the said town would curse the detainers, or use words to the like effect. And further this deponent says that his said mother did deliver to his, this deponent, the possession of the said farm and lands with appurtenances with this condition, that he this deponent should permit and suffer the townsmen of Weymouth and Melcomb Regis aforesaid quietly and peaceably to hold and enjoy the same lands called the Common aforesaid.

10 November 1648
Upon the same day was issued out an order from the mayor as follows:

The borough of Waymouth and Melcomb Regis; William Holmes, mayor of the said borough and town and one of the King's Majesty's justices of the peace and quay there, and John Arthur, esquire, one of the bailiffs and justices of the same borough and town, to the sergeants at mace of Waymouth and Melcomb Regis aforesaid, and to every of them greeting. Whereas John Wall, merchant, one of the capital and principal burgesses of this borough and town has lately taken into his house in Waymouth aforesaid one Henry Tizer, a foreigner, with his wife and children, likely to be chargeable to the said borough contrary to a constitution heretofore made by the mayor, aldermen, bailiffs and burgesses of the said borough and town. And although the said John Wall has had public notice given him of the breach of the said constitution, and has been required to remove his said tenant and his family, yet he the said John Wall does refuse to remove them in contempt of the authority of the said town, whereby he the said John Wall has forfeited twenty pounds to the use of the said Corporation according to the tenor and purport of the before written constitution . These are therefore to will and require you to levy by way of distress and sale on the goods of the said John Wall the aforesaid twenty pounds, rendering to him the over plus that shall remain upon the sale of his said goods and that you pay in the same sum so by you levied to the treasurer of the borough and town aforesaid. Hereof fail you not, as you will answer the contrary at your peril. And this shall be your sufficient warrant, given under our hands and seals, etc.

15 December 1648
Upon this present day Henry Edwards of this town, mariner, being examined on his voluntary oath says that yesterday he saw an excise bill for 13 fardells of *dowlas* [coarse cloth] granted to Mr John Prescot. And he further says that he heard a Frenchman and Mr John Prescott, 2 foreigners, treating and discoursing about the buying and

selling of the said 13 fardells of *dowlas* in this deponent's own house in Melcombe Regis where the said dowlas lay.

Edmund Speare on his voluntary oath deposed that yesterday the said Mr John Prescott came to this examinant and desired of him an excise bill for 13 fardells of dowlas containing 44 pieces of dowlas which, as he said, he had then bought of a Frenchman. And this deponent desired the said Mr Prescot to spare him two pieces of the said 13 fardells, to which the said Mr Prescot answered that he could not open the fardells because he was to send them all whole to Bristol.

Upon this present day Henry Tizer has liberty until the day fortnight peremptory to give bond with sufficient security in £100 to save the town harmless from this charge.

15 December 1648

Henry Edwards being again examined on his voluntary oath deposes, concerning the seizure aforesaid of foreign goods bought by Mr Prescott, that he, this examinant, has received from the hands of Mr John Prescott the sum of one hundred and twenty nine pounds, fourteen shillings and six pence, the which said sum he received of the said Mr Prescot to pay it to a French merchant of Rasco, in the province of Brittant in the Kingdom of France, as soon as the said merchant had delivered for the said John Prescot's use, in a cart, eleven packets of dowlas, which did contain 43 pieces and [a] half. [page 220] And this deponent further says that in pursuit of the same bargain the said French merchant did deliver to the aforesaid Mr Prescott the said eleven packets which did contain forty three pieces and [a] half aforesaid. And this deponent did by Mr Prescot's order cause the porters of the town to load it on a cart, and being so loaded (before the cart could be driven out of the town) it was seized on for the use of the Incorporation. And this deponent does acknowledge that he did before the delivery of the said goods give Mr Prescott a receipt for the said one hundred [and] twenty nine pounds, fourteen shillings and six pence to be delivered by this deponent to the said French merchant as soon as the packets of cloth should be delivered to the use of the said John Prescot.

20 December 1648

Upon this present day James Lemen of Rasco [Roscoff] in Brittany, merchant, being examined did voluntarily depose that the said Mr Prescot came to this deponent 2 or 3 several times at the house of Henry Edwards in this town and treated with the deponent concerning certain ballads of cloth which he, this deponent, had to sell and on or about the twelfth day of this instant month of December he bought of this deponent eleven ballets of cloth containing 43 pieces and [a] half for the sum of £261 3s according to a note hereunder written; and further says that he this deponent did [on] the fourteenth of this instant December deliver over to the said Mr Prescot the said 11 ballads of cloth. And that the said Mr Prescot did carry away with him out of the same pieces of cloth, and this deponent further says that the day (before the same ballads were delivered) Henry Edwards told this deponent that he, the said Henry Edwards, had received of Mr John Prescot £129 14s 6d in part of payment for the same goods. And that the same day the goods were delivered in the morning, before delivery thereof, Mr George Cole's servant and Mr Prescot came to Henry Edwards in [the] presence of this deponent and delivered certain bags of money then untold to Henry Edwards containing (as Mr Prescot then said) £131 8s 6d being the residue of the said £261 3s to and for the use of this deponent for the cloth aforesaid; which said sum of £131 8s 6d he the said Mr Prescot then said he had not time to tell over before he had dispatched away the said cloth in a cart, and further says that he was presently to receive the money without any further condition.

17 pieces of dowlas at £6 a piece	£102 00 00
13 pieces of dowlas at £5 a piece	£169 11 00
13 pieces and ½ in three ballads according to a note sold him for	£086 02 00
more 10s which I am to have over and above	£000 10 00
more omitted	£003 00 00
[Total]	£261 03 00

[page 221] At a hall held **4 January 1649**
The mayor and company taking the said seizure and the circumstances thereof into their consideration, and being unwilling to retard the Frenchman and his company, do assess the fine for breaking the privileges of the Incorporation of eleven pounds, out of which the charge of the same seizure, viz. about 5 nobles, is to be deducted, and twenty shillings repaid to the Frenchman, and the rest to be paid to Mr Mayor Holmes.

At a hall **19 January 1649**
Upon this present day diverse of the aldermen and capital burgesses did surrender their several offices as by the ensuing writing appears:
    We of the aldermen and common council men of the town and borough of Waymouth and Melcomb Regis in the county of Dorset, whose names are subscribed do for diverse causes us moving freely and voluntarily resign, and yield up to the mayor, bailiffs, aldermen and commonality of the said borough our several places and offices of aldermen and common council men of the same borough so that the same mayor, bailiffs, aldermen and commonality of the said borough or any others to whom the right does belong may be at liberty to make such election as if we were really dead or otherwise outed of our said offices and places, provided that this, our resignations, may not or shall not be any way construed to the prejudice of any of our persons, credits, reputations or estates in any other thing save in relation to the said offices and places. In testimony whereof we have hereto subscribed our names and set our seals the 18 day of January anno domini 1648 [1649].
    This was signed and sealed in the presence of :
William Sydenham
George Churchey
Joseph Derby
James Giear
Thomas Hughes

Henry Rose
James Heane
Richard Harrison
John Maddockes
John Hodder
George Pley
John Allenbridge
Peter Pecke
Alexander Clatworthy
Richard George

[page 222] At a hall held on Friday **26 January 1649**
Upon this present day Mr John Browne, Mr John Arthur, Mr Richard Scovile and Mr Henry Waltham are elected aldermen for this town.

Upon the same day Mr Andrew Buckler, Mr Roger Cuttance, Mr Jonathan Leddoze, Andrew Patrick, Thomas Winter and George Pitt are elected capital and principal burgesses for this town.

At a hall the **9 February 1649**
Upon this present day Mr John Arthur and Mr Henry Waltham were sworn aldermen.

Upon the same day George Pitt, Jonathan Leddoze and Thomas Winter were sworn capital burgesses.

At a full hall on Friday **16 February 1649**
John Scovile was this day admitted a freeman generally of this Incorporation and sworn for the common fine of five pounds, of which the company remitted 50s and the other 50s was paid to Mr Mayor.

At a full hall **23 February 1649**
Upon this present day Edward Duggles (who heretofore served Mr William Holmes, merchant, the present mayor, to the trade of a merchant within this town by indenture for the space of seven years) was this day admitted a freeman generally to the trade of a merchant for no fine, but paying the ordinary fees for his said admission, and took his oath of freeman accordingly.

Upon the same day it was ordered that the town pump shall be repaired, for which the town is to be at one half the charge, and Mr Bugden and the rest of the neighbours are to be at the other half.

16 March 1649
Upon this present day John Bury, one of the porters, paid in to Mr Mayor for the cartage and bridge duties 47s 6d. Also Richard Scovile, town clerk, was sworn by one the aldermen.

[page 223] Bonds belonging to the public use of the town, and in the town chest 24 March 1649:

Mr Middleton's gift:

Mr John Hodder, Fabian Hodder and John Swetnam, by a bond dated 29 September 1643 for £25, 29 September 1648 principal, £25.

Mr Nathaniel Allen, Mr John Hodder and Mr John Swetnam, by bond dated 30 September 1647 payable 30 September 1650 principal, £25.

The same day was paid in by Mr Gabriel Cornish of Mr Middleton's gift money £25, and 12s 6d for interest money, which 12s and 6d was delivered Mr Mayor for the overseers of Waymouth poor, and the other £25 was put into the chest. £25.

Memorandum: 25 March 1649 this £25 was lent to Mr Philip Bugden according to the ancient order upon security of John Hodder and Leonard Hillard.

Andrew Eburne and Leonard Hillard by bond dated 26 March 1647 in £20 condition to pay £10 for the use of the poor, viz: £5 for Waymouth side and £5 for Melcombe side 25 March 1648; and the interest proportionable £10 between both sides, which £10 was the gift of John Gould of Upway, esquire, deceased.

William Pitt, Robert Wall and Francis Edwards for £5 8s, 6 September 1646, £5 money due to the poor of Melcombe by bond dated 5 September 1645, principal.

Mr Matthew Allin and his son John Allin for £54, the poor money 30 September 1635, dated 30 September 1634, belonging to Melcomb poor. £54.

Thomas Allin, Mr Matthew Allin and John Allin, by bond dated 24 September 1638 for £20 12s, 29 September 1639, the poor's money of Waymouth. £20 12s.

Philip Kind and William Charity by bond dated 27 March 1639 for £20 12s, the poor's money of Waymouth payable 28 March 1640. £20 12s.

Joseph Underwood and Mr George Churchey by bill dated 8 April 1640 for £400 16s, 8 July 1640, the poor's money of Melcomb. £40 16s.

[page 224] Mr Thomas Waltham and Mr Thomas Giear by bond dated 16 December 1630 for £50 principal, £3 per annum interest, whereof 20s per annum for the maintenance of Melcomb Regis Church and £10 per annum to Melcomb poor, Lady Browne's gift.

Mr George Churchey, Matthew Caseway and Leonard Hillard by bill dated 15 January 1638 for £43 4s to the poor of Melcomb Regis, 16 January 1639.

James Osborne, yeoman, to Mr David Gyar for fifty shillings 24 June 1630. This 50s is not mentioned for what use it is. £2 10s.

At a hall Friday **6 April 1649**

Upon this present day it is ordered that the town lighter shall be hauled up and trimmed and Mr Richard Bolt and Mr Robert Wall are desired to take care thereof.

Upon the same day Mr George Play was elected one of the capital burgesses of this town.

At a hall held **11 April 1649**

Upon this present day Mr George Pley was sworn a capital burgess.

At a hall **23 April 1649**

Upon a letter received from Dr John Bond, the recorder, of his desire of resignation of his recordership, for the reasons conveyed in the same letter, Samuel Bond, esquire, barrister at law, is by a unanimous consent chosen recorder of the town in the place and stead of his brother the late recorder.

Upon the same day Mr Roger Cuttance was sworn one of the capital burgesses of this town.

At a hall held **27 April 1649**
Upon this present day John Elborne paid in to the mayor for cartage and bridge duties £2 18s.

Upon the same day there was paid over to Mr Mayor Holmes forty shillings of the monies belonging to the poor of Waymouth to be by him delivered over to the overseers there for the use of the poor.

[page 225] At a hall held **1 June 1649**
Upon this present day Mr John Eyres was admitted a freeman of this town for the fine of five pounds and also chosen one of the capital burgesses of this town.

Upon the same day Steven Abbot, mariner, was admitted a freeman generally for the fine of five pounds which he laid down, but fifty shillings thereof was given him back, and the other fifty shillings was paid over to Mr Mayor and he was sworn accordingly.

Upon the same day the said Steven Abbot was chosen one of the common council of this borough and took his oath accordingly.

Upon the same day Mr Stephen Edwards and Matthew Caseway were elected capital burgesses of this town and sworn accordingly.

Upon the same day the said Stephen Edwards was admitted a freeman generally for the fine of five pounds, of which three pounds was remitted, and the other forty shillings paid over, and he took his oath accordingly.

Upon the same day the said Matthew Caseway was admitted a freeman generally for the fine of five pounds, but £3 10s was given him back, and the other thirty shillings was paid over to Mr Mayor, and he was sworn accordingly.

At a Hall **15 June 1649**
Upon this present day Mr John Eyres, according to a former election, was sworn a freeman generally and a capital burgess of this borough.

6 July 1649
Upon this present day John Elborne, one of the porters of this town, paid in to Mr Leddoze, the town treasurer, for the cartage and bridge duties 21s 8d.

At a hall held **3 August 1649**
Upon this present day it was ordered that whereas the bridge and harbour are at several places in much decay Mr Robert Wall, Mr Peter Wall, Mr Roger Cuttance, Mr George Pley, Mr John Eyres with some of the town carpenters and masons, whom they are to call to their assistance, are to take a view of the same and what the charge

may amount to for the repair thereof, and to make their report of the same the next Friday.

[page 226] Upon the same day William Bond was admitted a freeman generally for the fine of five pounds, which he laid down, but in regard he married Mr Mayor's daughter, twenty shillings thereof was redelivered him, and the other four pounds was paid to Mr Thomas Leddoze, treasurer, and he was sworn accordingly.

At a hall **27 August 1647**

Upon the same day it was agreed on that the petty customs shall always hereafter be called by the name of wharfage, bomage, cranage, anchorage and boyage, and shall be so let out in the future.

Upon the same day it is also agreed that the ballast and forfeitures and bridge duties shall be from henceforth employed only for the repairs of the quays, bridge and harbour.

Upon the same day it was also ordered and agreed upon that whereas diverse goods of Mr George Churchey's were lately seized by this Incorporation for the satisfaction of a fine of fifty pounds, imposed on him by the mayor, aldermen, bailiffs and burgesses of this town, for colouring of the goods of his brother Churchey, a foreigner. Now the said Mr Churchey shall have the same goods redelivered him for the fine of twenty pounds; and also paying thirty shillings for charge about the same seizure; which he accordingly did and the said twenty pounds was delivered over to Mr Thomas Leddoze, treasurer.

Upon the same day Mr John Row was admitted a freeman, generally, for the fine of five pounds and was sworn accordingly.

Upon the same day the said Mr Row was sworn a capital burgess of this borough.

Upon the same day Mr John Penny was admitted a freeman, generally, for the fine of five pounds which he paid down and was sworn accordingly.

31 August 1649

Upon this present day Robert Clarke, roper, was admitted a freeman, generally, for the fine of five pounds, which he paid down, and took his oath accordingly.

Upon the same day diverse of the town were appointed to view the ground overflowed by the sea between Melcomb and Rodipoll, whether the taking of it will not be a damage to the harbour.

Upon the same day Mr Thomas Winter [rest of entry blank]

[page 227] At a meeting of the merchants and principal mariners of this town at a hall held **3 September 1649**.

Reasons given why the water coming towards Rodipoll is not to be stopped of its cause without prejudicing the harbour;

If the in draught be stopped the tide will have but little recourse in the harbour by reason that the tide does cross the bay coming from the bill of Portland to the White North, so that the harbour has only the benefit of the last half ebb in the offering to fill it up within, the east and west moons making a full sea, in the harbour and it being not full sea at Portland before the moon is south east.

The tide coming out of the bay from the northward crossing the harbour brings in so much trash and sand, out of the sea into the harbour's mouth, that it will not be cleared without the tide has a free course as now it has.

But it was conceived, that if any of the ground be taken in, there must be the whole channel left in the middle and bank of both sides, so that the tide must have its full recourse as far up as Radipoll as now it has, otherwise it will be the destruction of the harbour.

11 September 1649
Upon this present day Samuel Bond, esquire, was sworn recorder of this borough in the room of his brother John Bond, esquire.

14 September 1649
Upon the same day it was agreed upon that Mistress Cade shall be forthwith paid by the treasurer forty shillings to cloth her children and forty shillings more yearly for three years to be paid quarterly to commence from Michaelmas next.

28 September 1649
Upon this present day the wharfage, bomage, cranage, anchorage and boyage, formerly called by the name of the petty customs, was kept in the town's hands for the year ensuing

Upon the same day the cartage of this town was let to Mr Henry Waltham at £11 15s for the year ensuing, security Mr Thomas Waltham and Mr Henry Rose.

[page 228] Upon the same day the markets of this town was let to Mr Henry Waltham for ten pounds fifteen shillings for the year following.

Upon the same day the bridge duties were kept in the town's hands for the year ensuing

Upon the same day the ballast and forfeitures were let to Mr Henry Waltham at ten pounds for the year ensuing

Upon the same day there was paid in by the porters for cartage and bridge duties to the town treasurer 5s.

Matthew's day 21 September 1649
Upon the same day John Browne, esquire, was elected mayor for the ensuing year.

Upon the same day Mr Henry Waltham and Mr Robert Wall are elected bailiffs for the year to come.

Upon the same day Mr William Holmes is chosen treasurer for the ensuing year.

Upon the same day Mr Henry Waltham, Mr Robert Wall, Mr Thomas Waltham, Mr Thomas Leddoze, Mr Roger Cuttance and Mr John Swetnam were appointed auditors to audit the account of the last treasurer.

Upon the same day it was ordered that Mr John Browne shall take his oath of the mayor of the town according to the election before the eighth day of October next under the pain of one hundred pounds.

30 September 1649
The petty customs being kept in the town's hands for the ensuing year are to be collected by Mr Robert Wise.

[page 229] 8 October 1649
Upon the same day John Browne esquire was fined £100 for not coming in to be sworn mayor of this borough according to a former order.

19 October 1649
Upon the same day it was by a full consent ordered and agreed on that the mayor for this year to come, and so for the future, yearly, forever, shall be paid ten pounds per annum towards his expenses out of the public revenue of the town by the town treasurer.

29 October 1649
Upon this day Captain John Arthur and Mr Stephen Edwards certified the company that on the town's petition to the committee of the county of Dorset about the common, the committee made this answer: that they could not determine the right petitioned in point of law, but were contented that the town should make their entry upon it, and they would not oppose it, but would discharge Mr Adams, the present tenant, of so much rent that so he might become tenant to the town of the same, or used words to like effect.

2 November 1649
Upon this present day the sergeants at mace certified the company that on Wednesday last they, together with Henry Cox, Richard George, Onesiphorus Penny and John Beere, constables, with the scholars and many others went on to the common belonging to the town and did there sow half a bushel and half a peck of wheat in the same common over the grounds. And they went to the boundaries of the town.

   Upon the same day it was agreed on that the governor of this garrison shall be paid by the town treasurer ten pounds to fill up the new work so far as the second post behind the work westward directly over as far as the jetty on a straight line from the said second post.

   Upon the same day it was also agreed on that the fines imposed on John Browne esquire for not coming in to take his oath of mayor shall be discharged.

   [page 230] Upon the same day it is agreed upon that Briant Wood's business as a scavenger shall be fully consummated at the next hall. The propositions whereof are that he shall have four shillings by the week as the common scavenger to be paid weekly by the treasurer. And that he should also be the common beadle for the same wages, and to keep clean the market place, and not to undertake at any time any labour but about these works for the town and so to employ himself as a day labourer daily unless in the extremity of weather when he is not able to labour.

16 November 1649
Upon the same day it was ordered and agreed on that whereas Mr William White of Dorchester does owe to the town for the town duties, heretofore called petty customs, £4 1s 9d and does refuse to pay it, alleging that he ought not because he is a freeman of London. Now there shall be a seizure made of his goods for the same monies.

14 December 1649
Upon this day Richard Peircey, son of Hugh Peircey, deceased, was this day admitted a free man generally of this Incorporation by descent, and he was sworn accordingly.

29 March 1650
Upon this day it is by a general and full consent ordered that no goods or merchandise that arrive at this port by *port cockquet* or *let pass* shall be landed and carried away before the town duties shall be fully satisfied to the collector of the same duties upon pain for every owner of such goods to forfeit for every offence contrary to this constitution the sum of twenty shillings.

Upon this same day the sergeants at mace of this borough did seize on one butt of Zant. currants, one hogshead of Smerna raisins of Mr William White for the arrears of the town duties.

Upon this day it is ordered that the bonds shall be put in suit against Mr John Allen senior for the town use.

19 April 1650
Upon this day it is agreed that in case Mr William White shall not pay the town duties by Friday next, for which seizure was made of his goods, then the same goods shall be put to sale for the same duties and the over plus be restored to the owner.

Upon this day it is agreed that sergeant Thomas Alexander shall take care for the sowing of one peck of barley in the common to be scattered abroad upon the barley grounds.

Upon this day it is agreed that a writ be written to Mr Dennis Bond about the common, to be sent to Captain Arthur next week.

[page 231] Upon the same day it is agreed that Captain John Arthur shall have liberty to set out an oven in the Backelane over against his new house, four foot wide and ten foot along by the house and to set out a gate in the same land, four foot on the town waste, for all which by way of fine he is to pay five shillings to the town, which he paid to the town treasurer forthwith.

17 May 1650
Memorandum: that on Monday last was fortnight Mr Mayor Holmes and Mr Bailiffs nominated according to the form of the statute Mr John Allen senior, Richard Wilson and Christopher Hall overseers of the poor for Waymouth, and Mr John Arthur, Mr George Pley and Robert White for Melcomb Regis.

At a hall held **31 May 1650**

Mr White's goods formerly seized on, being one vessel of Smerna raisins and one bag of *gawles* for duties of the town, time having been given to the said Mr White to come in to redeem them, and pre-emptory day being given him to that purpose which is now expired. It is agreed on that the same vessel of Smerna raisins shall be sold this afternoon by a candle in the town hall, and if any over plus remain on such sale the same is to be returned to the said Mr White.

Upon the same day it is agreed that a seizure shall be speedily made of Mr Samuel Mico goods for £3 18s 11d which is due from Mr Mico for the town duties.

Upon the same day it is ordered that the town timber now lying over the channel by Mr Fry's house shall be removed over under the wall of Mr Babbidge's house.

Upon the same day it is agreed on that Mr James Studleigh, Mr Thomas Waltham's son in law, shall be admitted a freeman for the fine of five pounds, which he paid down upon the table and, in regard the said Mr Studleigh married an alderman's daughter, forty shillings of the five pounds was restored to him. And the said Mr Studleigh was then elected also a burgess of the said town.

Upon the same day it is agreed on and so ordered that a rate shall be made for the paving of the streets in Melcomb Regis for the raising of sixteen pounds for the purpose aforesaid wherein Mr George Pley, Mr John Senior and Mr Jonathan Leddoze are nominated raters to be made against Friday next and returned in and approved of by the mayor, etc, and the pitcher be treated with by all. The town clerk to come down to work on Monday night, against which time materials shall be provided.

[page 232] To all whom these presents shall come I George Pley, mayor of the town of Waymouth and Melcomb Regis aforesaid and one of the justices of the peace there send greeting. Whereas I am informed by some of the parishioners of West Lulworth in the said county that there has been lately a claim made by the parishioners of Winfrith Newborough in the county aforesaid to certain lands commonly called west Lulworth Down, within the said parish of West Lulworth, pretending thereby that the said parishioners of West Lulworth have only a slight within the said lands for their cattle to feed and departure there only until eleven of the clock in the forenoon every day, and that the soil and the rest of the herbage and pasturage of the said lands doe belong to them in the said parish of Winfrith Newborough. Now know you that the day of the date hereof John Hamwell of the town aforesaid, mariner, aged four score and four years or there abouts, and Thomas Vey of the said town, leather dresser, aged fifty years or there abouts, came before me and did severally and voluntarily swear and depose upon the Holy Evangelist as follows: that is to say the said John Hamwell did depose that in the year of Our Lord one thousand five hundred eighty eight he, this deponent did dwell and inhabit in West Lulworth aforesaid as a servant to one John Say of the same place, yeoman, and did keep sheep for his said master on the said lands called West Lulworth Down for many days and nights together, sand so did the other parishioners of the said parish f West Lulworth as of their own right without any let or contradiction. And this deponent further deposed that there was a certain break or ridge of furzes on the north-east part of the said Down which was accounted part of the boundaries between the lands of the said parishioners of West Lulworth and Winfrith Newborough to the utmost bounds eastwards and northwards, of which said break or ridge of furzes the parishioners of West Lulworth did use to feed and depasture their said sheep. And the said parishioners of Winfrith Newborough did feed and depasture their said sheep on the Down called Winfrith Down lying on the north part of the said break or ridge of furzes. And the said Thomas Vey deposed that he was born in the said parish of West Lulworth and there lived until he was of the age of nineteen years or thereabouts and for many years before he left his dwelling in the same parish this deponent kept sheep for his uncle Jonas Vey on the said West Lulworth Down where also the other parishioners of West Lulworth aforesaid kept their sheep all the year long for many years together for as long in the year as they pleased, both day and night, as far eastwards and northwards as leads to the utmost bounds of the said break and ridge of furze without any let or contradiction. And that the said parishioners of Winfrith Newborough aforesaid did feed and depasture their said sheep on Winfrith Down lying on the north part of the said break or ridge of furze. And the said Thomas Vey further deposed that for many years together after he was of remembrance he went on procession, as the custom then was, with the minister and parishioners of West Lulworth aforesaid, whereby to view the boundaries of the said parish which was performed in this manner: first the said minister and parishioners went to a place called Blacklands Yeate or Gate and from thence to a white thorn at a place called Hemerhill Foot and from thence to a place called Mildowns or Mildons Barrow and from thence straight along the ridge eastwards to a pit called Furzymire where they had small beer and cake-bread. And the said Thomas Vey further deposed that the parishioners of West Lulworth aforesaid did usually, during the time of the deponant's dwelling and residence there, cut and carry away the furzes growing on the said West Lulworth Down to the utmost boundaries of the said Down. [page 233] Which voluntary depositions the said parishioners of West Lulworth aforesaid desired me to take and that the same might be registered among the public records of the town. In testimony of all which I have here to subscribed my name and affixed the seal of mayoralty of the said town the last day of August in the year of |Our Lord one thousand six hundred and fifty two, 1652.

George Pley, mayor

[Latin] Know all those present that I Joshua Bennett of Plymouth in the county of Devon, merchant, am held firmly bound to William Hide junior of Yarmouth in the Isle of Wight, in the county of Hampshire, merchant, for one hundred and twenty pounds of legal money of England to be paid by the same William Hide or his attorney, executors, administrators or assigns. To making which payment well and faithfully I firmly bind my heirs, executors and administrators by my seal and signature, dated 20 October in the 22 year of the reign of King Charles [1646].

[English] The condition of this obligation is such that if the above bound Joshua Bennett, his heirs, executors, administrators or assigns, or any one of them do well and truly content, satisfy and pay, or be cause to be well and truly contented, satisfied and paid to the above named William Hide his executors, administrators or assigns the full and whole sum of sixty and one pounds sixteen shillings of good and lawful money of England in, at, or upon the first day of December next ensuing the date of the presents without any fraud, deceit or further delay, that then this obligation to be frustrate, void and of none effect, or else the same obligation to be in full force and effect.

Sealed and dated in the presence of: Andrew Hall, scrivener, Joshua Bennett, John Pooly.

[page 234] At a full hall **21 June 1650**
Whereas there was an order made the thirtieth day of October 1635 concerning brewers' and other carts coming into this town reciting whereas the Corporation has lately been at great charges about pitching the streets; and the carters and their carts did much damage thereto, every brewer and others bringing or driving any cart into this town should pay four pence for every offence. It is now agreed on by a general consent that the same constitution be of force, and that for every carter or brewer bringing or driving any wagon or cart into this town with wheels bound with iron bands, studs or dowles shall for every wheel of such wagon or cart so bound or every offence pay two pence.

Upon the same day it is ordered and agreed on that whereas diverse foreigners do bring into their town beer to be sold by several innkeepers and alehouse keepers to the great prejudice of diverse inhabitants of this town. Now every innkeeper, alehouse keeper or victualler selling in his or her house any such beer or ale shall pay for every hogshead brought into this town from and after the four and twentieth day of this instant June by him or her sold the sum of 12d the same be paid over for the use of the poor of both towns. Viz: the one moiety thereof to the poor of Waymouth and the other moiety for the poor of Melcomb Regis to be collected by the sergeants at mace and such others as from time to time shall be therefore authorised by a warrant under the hand and seal of the mayor for the time being. And in case any further innkeeper, alehouse keeper or victualler shall refuse to pay the 12d per hogshead, then Mr Mayor for the time being shall give a warrant under the seal to take distress of every offender herein.

At a hall held **28 June 1650**
collectors for the minister nominated;
      For Waymouth: Mr Theophilus Biatt, Mr Stephen Abbott
      For Melcomb: Mr Stephen Edwards, Mr Thomas Winter
      Upon this same day Thomas Hall, Mr William White's man, coming to the town hall about the seizure of his master's goods, viz: one vessel of Smerna raisins and one bag of gawles, Mr Mayor and the company offered to deliver to him the said bag of gawls.

[page 235] At a full hall held **18 September 1650**
Upon this day by a general consent agreed upon and so ordered that five pounds shall be paid by the treasurer to Mr Recorder for his charge, pains and attendance in executing the town's interest about the lands called the common of Melcomb.

28 September 1650

Upon this present day the wharfage, boomage, cranage and anchorage and boyage formerly called by the name of the petty customs was kept in the town's hands for the year ensuing

Upon the same day the cartage was kept in the town's hands for the year ensuing

Upon the same day the markets were kept in the town's hands for the year ensuing

Upon the same day the bridge duties were let to Mr Gregory Babbidge at £4 5s for the year ensuing, security Mr Thomas Leddoze and Mr George Pley.

Upon the same day the ballast and for forfeitures were let to Mr Gregory Babbidge at £12 5s for the year ensuing security Mr Thomas Leddoze and Mr George Pley.

Upon the same day the widow Chubb, making it appear that the lands which was a close of Peter Joy's at the north end of town, is now of no profit to her, there being a fort built on it for the use of the state, it is ordered that the town remit the town rent for the same close, being 18d per annum yearly, until she or her heirs receive some benefit thereby.

3 October 1650

The Corporation by indenture dated 26 September 1636 did for the consideration of 40s demise for Nicholas Jervis, since deceased, a tenement and garden with appurtenances in New Street, to hold to the said Nicholas for four score and nineteen years if the said Nicholas, Rachel his wife, now wife of Robert Bindle and Joan Payne or any of them so long live, rent 5s per annum. Now in regard it is certified by Mr Thomas Waltham and others that Thomas Welman, a poor man of the town, at the town's request lived in part of it rent free until the time of his death upon agreement that the twelve shillings per annum should be remitted for that time, and the said Welman dying since Michaelmas last was twelve month, the said Rachel paid in this day to Thomas Alexander, one of the town sergeants to be placed in account of the late bailiff Mr Henry Waltham 5s for one year's rent ended at Michaelmas 1650 and so all arrears of that rent are discharged.

[page 236] At a full hall held the **12 October 1650**

Upon this day it was ordered that all the inhabitants of this town shall every Friday at two o'clock in the afternoon, weekly rake up and sweep the several streets before their doors upon pains of twelve pence on every one for every time offending herein. And that there shall be a horse and pot bought at the town's charge, and that there shall be a rate made throughout the whole town of Waymouth and Melcomb Regis on all inhabitants thereof for the paying of a scavenger (who is in the next court to be chosen) and for the keeping of the said horse and pot. And the same dirt so raked up in Melcomb Regis shall be carried to the void place in the jetty. And that the dirt of Waymouth shall be the scavenger be brought to the quay by Joseph Bryar's house, and so carried over by a boat to the void place at the jetty, the charge to which boat and of men's wages thereabout shall be paid out of the same rate. And it is further ordered that Mr Bailiff Biatt and Mr Bailiff Pley, Mr Thomas Leddoze and Mr Theodore Waltham do consider what the charge will amount to yearly for keeping the same horse, and paying the scavenger's wages, and that they make a rate for the same upon the inhabitants of this town.

Upon the same day it was ordered that Mr Bailiff Pley, Mr Edwards, Mr Leddoze and Mr Thomas Winter shall view what is necessary to be raised on the inhabitants of Melcombe for the repair of the church and other necessaries, and to make a rate accordingly, and also to audit the account of Mr John Senior the present churchwarden.

At a full hall 18 October 1650
Whereas Whereas Mr Robert wall by his obligation dated 5 October 1645 became bound with William Pitt to the Incorporation for payment of five pounds six shillings, it is ordered that upon Mr Walls paying of five pounds, the principal money, he shall have his bond delivered up, and that until such payment Mr Bailiff Pley shall keep the bond in his custody.

[page 237] At a full hall held 1 November 1650
Upon the same day the porters paid to Mr Holmes the treasurer for cartage since Michaelmas last 25s 3d.

Upon the same day the arrears due from William Gillett for the town rent, whereon he lays his timber and all estreats upon him set in the lawdays was taken into consideration the same amounting to twenty pounds and upwards, the said William Gillet referring and submitting himself to the vote of the company and promising to stand to their award in the premises which the company have assessed to £10 in the whole. And he is to pay 20s per annum for the future at Michaelmas yearly and to keep the gutter clean from time to time which he refused to submit to. And therefore a suit is to be forthwith commenced against him.

At a hall held 8 November 1650
William Seagar, miller, being convened before Mr Mayor and the company for selling of meal by a short half peck, viz: half a pint on every half peck which practice by his own confession he has used by space of five years last past, and one week with another does sell twenty bushels of wheat in meal within this town of Waymouth and Melcomb Regis for which offence by way of *Mulet* he refers himself to the censure of the company, that the poor of each town may reap the benefit of it. And the company taking it into consideration do assess his fine to twenty pounds, viz, ten pounds of it at Christmas next and the other ten pounds at Our Lady Day next.

Mr Mayor Arthur upon his motion (relinquishing his liberty to build a gate on the town waste adjoining to his new house in Melcomb Regis which was granted to him by the company the nineteenth day of April in the year of Our Lord one thousand six hundred and fifty upon a fine) is now granted of the same ground in length twenty foot and in breadth four foot eight inches and besides that more of the said waste to set a house of office on in length ten foot and in breadth four foot eight inches for so much the said gate would have contained.

At a hall held **3 January 1651**
William George aforesaid this day paid in ten pounds, which he gave bonds for, payable at Christmas in part of twenty pounds which he was assessed at for selling of meal by short measure, which was delivered over to the overseers of the town, viz: five pounds to the overseers of Waymouth and five pounds to the overseers of Melcomb Regis to apparel such poor people of the said town.

Daniel Windsor, one of the porters of the town, paid into Mr William Holmes, treasurer, for cartage in money forty shillings and seven pence.

[page 238] Upon the same day Mr Gregory Babbidge paid in for his quarter's rent for the bridge and ballast and forfeitures to Mr Treasurer, eight pounds seventeen shillings and six pence.

Also upon the same day he paid in full of seven pounds seventeen shillings and three pence which his grandmother, the old Mrs Babbidge, deceased, did owe to the Incorporation that the town disbursed for paving the streets before her land; the two pounds seventeen shillings and three pence being forgiven him.

At a hall held **21 March 1651**
Upon the same day it was agreed on and so ordered that on Wednesday next Mr Bailiff Pley, Mr John Lockier, Mr Thomas Leddoze, Mr Thomas Waltham, Mr John Senior and Mr Robert Wall shall at nine of the clock in the morning meet at the town hall and the sergeants at mace to attend them and the six, or any four, of them shall make a rate on the inhabitants and house keepers of the two towns for the maintenance of the town scavenger, horse and pot with the appurtenances of the same rate not exceeding twenty pounds per annum to be paid quarterly, by each person rated, to the sergeants at mace who are to collect the same by a rate in writing, which the town clerk does promise to transcribe fairly in parchment out of the paper rate to be subscribed by the said raters, or four of them, and the original rate to remain amongst the records of the town. And the said sergeants are to pay over the money quarterly collected to the town treasurer and to pass their account for the same to the mayor and company at all times upon demand. And the said raters, or any three, four or more of them, are to appoint the said scavenger, the time and manner of the cleansing of the towns and fitting up of the void land taken in at the jetty.

At a hall held the **28 March 1651**
Upon this day it was agreed between Mr Mayor and the company on the one part and Giles Fowler and Edward Courtney, masons, on the other part touching the marsh as follows, viz: that the said masons shall make up the old wall of the marsh four foot high from the highest part of the foundation, and so level all along, and of the same breadth that the wall was before and back it sufficiently with clay. And shall make a bank level with the top of the said wall, six foot in breadth, behind the adjoining wall besides the stone work of which six foot they are to back sufficiently the stone work one foot and half with blue clay. And to use good materials about it and to make it tight so as to keep out the water. All materials to be provided at their charge save only

such tools as are in the town's custody fit for the work, the workmen giving a note of receipt of them to the sergeants and to make good the same tools at the end of the work. They are to complete the work by the last of August next. And the town is to pay them three score pounds for the work in case they shall sufficiently complete it by the time aforesaid, to be paid in manner following, viz: ten pounds in hand and afterwards ten pounds by the month, save only the workmen are sufficiently to finish the work before the last ten pounds of the said three score pounds shall be paid them.

[page 239] At a hall **19 April 1651**
Whereas upon the same day Mr Robert Wall, lately one of the bailiffs of this town, did disburse toward the payment of the town rent of Waymouth, which this Incorporation is to repay him; and whereas the said Robert Wall was by a bond dated the fifth day of September in the year of Our Lord one thousand six hundred forty and five bound with William Pitt and Francis Edwards for the payment of the five pounds and eight shillings on the sixth day of September in the year of Our Lord one thousand six hundred forty and six to the mayor, aldermen, bailiffs, burgesses and communality for the poor of Melcomb Regis; it is ordered that upon Mr Robert Walls paying five pounds (he being only a surety) the bond shall be delivered him, which 20s Mr Wall presently paid in and thereupon the same 20s was paid over to Giles Fowler, one of the workmen about the marsh for the town's use. And it was ordered that the interest for the five pounds shall be paid by the Incorporation to the use of the poor until they are able to repay the same.

At a hall held **21 April 1651**
Upon the same day whereas Colonel James Heane and Lieutenant Colonel Joyce have towards the repair of the bridge between the two towns made a grant to the Incorporation of thirty trees of timber in the late King's forest of Hampshire, being a parcel of the trees allotted them by the Parliament, viz: to the said Colonel Heane twenty and to the said Lieutenant Colonel Joyce ten. Now it is ordered that Stephen Coven, one of the constables of this town do ride along with the said Lieutenant Colonel Joyce (who is now going to Hampshire) to mark up the said trees and to take care for the cutting down and embarking thereof. And that the said Stephen Coven be paid towards his expenses in hand the sum of three pounds, and that the town shall repay him such other money as he shall disburse about the premises, and give him content for his pains.

At a hall held **2 May 1651**
Upon the same day it was agreed upon that an assignment shall be made of the piece of ground to Thomas Wayman by the town for four pounds of which he has paid already to Mr Thomas Leddoze, the late treasurer, fifty shillings and thirty shillings more he is to pay upon sealing the lease,

At a hall held **12 May 1651**
Upon the same day whereas the bridge and the quays of this town are very much in

decay, so that the town stock is not sufficient to repair the same, it is ordered that a rate of thirty pounds towards the repairs thereof be made on the inhabitants of this town, the same to be levied by the constables of the said town. And in case any shall refuse to pay the same it is ordered that their goods be distrained for the payment thereof. And that Mr Thomas Leddoze, Mr Thomas Waltham, Mr John Senior, Stephen Edwards, George Pitt and Stephen Abbott do forthwith make the same rate and bring it on Friday next to the hall.

At a hall held **13 June 1651**
Upon the same day the porters paid in for the cartage seven and fifty shillings and six pence, of which the treasurer allowed the town clerk 6d for double transcribing the town duties in parchment.

[page 240] At a hall held **23 July 1651**
Upon the same day it was agreed and so ordered that the marsh lately again enclosed by the town shall be made tenantable and sufficiently fenced by the town, save to the cleansing of the ditched and levelling of the ground, which is to be done by the tenant of the town, to repair the highways and level it as has been formerly accustomed and the town to be at the change of a gate and stiles. The tenant to repair all sufficiently during the term and so to leave it at the end of the said term. But in case any eminent, inevitable breach shall fall out and not by the neglect of the tenant, the repair whereof costing five pounds or upwards, that charge shall be born and defrayed by the town. To let it out for seven years from Michaelmas next to the best tenant at a certain yearly rent, payable half yearly, and foot path to be allowed as has been anciently accustomed, but not to be ploughed up or tilled. Upon the same day the marsh was let to Mr Bailiff Pley for the term of seven years, to commence and begin at Michaelmas next, of the yearly rent of fourteen pounds and ten shillings payable quarterly, and to have the liberty to plough up the marsh or dig or delve it for the first three years of his term, but is now to sow it with oats.

And there has been in out of public stock for the making up of the said marsh these sums following, for which interest must be paid by the Incorporation until the same sums be repaid to the public stock.

Of monies belonging to the poor of Melcombe Regis for which George Churchey, Matthew Caseway and Leonard Hillard gave their bond formerly, forty pounds, paid in manner following, viz: £20 of it paid by Matthew Caseway to the masons and £20 paid by Mr George Churchey to Thomas Winter which he paid over to the same masons, £40 paid in by Mr Robert Wall to the same masons 10s out of the £5. Paid by Mr Thomas Leddoze to the said masons 40s. Paid to Me Thomas Waltham for Mr Henry Waltham £5.

At a hall held **8 August 1651**
Upon the same day it was agreed on that John Smith shall have a lease of the house now in the possession of Maud Welman and Robert Bindle for four score and nineteen years from the determination of the present estate, so as he yield up to the town the

rooms now in his possession fifteen days before Michaelmas next, now in the Friary to make a school house, reserving the former rent of five shillings per annum to the town and he is to pay of this estate to the town for the fine three pounds.

To all whom these presents shall come, the mayor, aldermen, bailiffs, burgesses and commonality of Weymouth and Melcomb Regis in the county of Dorset send greeting. Whereas through the decay of trade and by means of the late warrants the revenue of the said town has been wholly exhausted, the town duties to the point of customs (being formerly the chief revenue of the Incorporation) for some years past having amounted to no considerable sum. Yet the issuing forth of monies has been far greater than in peaceable times in that the town has been at great charges about the soldiers and in cleaning and paving of the streets since the late siege.. And whereas the ground called Waymouth marsh has been lately built up and fenced at a great charge, which was thrown down in the late wars, for the repair and settling whereof this Incorporation has been necessitated to take up the sum of three score and ten pounds out of monies belonging to the poor stock of Melcomb. Now know ye that the said mayor, aldermen, bailiffs, burgesses and communality do hereby promise and engage that the Incorporation shall yearly and every year pay to the overseers of the poor of Melcomb Regis the interest of the said three score and ten pounds for and towards the relief of the poor there until the same money shall be raised and paid in to the poor stock of Melcomb Regis aforesaid. In testimony whereof the said mayor, aldermen, bailiffs, burgesses and communality have caused the seal of the said Incorporation to be here to affixed. And this act to be registered among the public records of the said Incorporation and the overseers book for the poor of Melcomb Regis aforesaid, the fifteenth day of August in the year of Our Lord one thousand six hundred fifty and one.

[page 241] **Matthew's day 21 September 1651**
Upon the same day Mr George Pley was elected mayor for the ensuing year.

Upon the same day Mr William Holmes and Mr John Swetnam were elected bailiffs for the year to come.

Upon the same day Mr John Arthur was chosen treasurer for the ensuing year.

Upon the same day Mr William Holmes, Mr John Swetnam, Mr Jonathan Leddoze, Mr Thomas Waltham, Mr John Senior and Mr Robert Wall were appointed auditors for the year to come.

Upon the same day Samuel Bond, esquire, recorded of this town, was admitted a freeman of the Incorporation and took the oath of a freeman accordingly.

At a hall held **25 August 1651**
Upon this present day it was ordered by a general consent that Mr Thomas Waltham shall pay in to the town clerk eighteen pounds on Friday next and the treasurer forty shillings more to make the eighteen pounds [up to] twenty pounds for his journey to London about the obtaining of the common for the town's use.

At a hall **1 September 1651**

Upon the same day Richard Keate, being summoned to appear at the town hall on information of encroaching on the town quay adjoining to his house, and having taken in seven feet and three inches to the northward and nineteen feet and half in length on the said quay and he appearing at the hall, refers himself to the company. It was ordered that the said Richard Keate shall pay to this Incorporation the sum of five shillings per annum as a yearly rent for the said ground so taken in by him forever, to commence from Michaelmas next, to be paid quarterly. And that a lease to that purpose be accordingly granted to him by this Incorporation.

Upon the same day Edmond Speare was admitted a freeman generally for the fine of five pounds which was paid over to Mr Mayor and he was sworn accordingly.

Upon the same day Stephen Coven was admitted a freeman in regard he has been two journeys for the town about their timber and is to go once more about it, and is only to have his charges borne by the town and he was sworn accordingly.

At the hall held **5 September 1651**
Upon the same day it was agreed on between the ensuing Incorporation and William Shatticke, carpenter, that the said William Shatticke shall and will rip and take up the town's lighter and employ as much of the same as shall be useful, for and toward the railing, all along the bank of the marsh in the inside thereof, and shall dig the grounds and set in posts all along the same, every post two feet and half into the earth and shall put two planks for the strengthening of the same work when need shall be and shall pin every plank thereof to the same post, and that the said William Shatticke shall have towards the work so many of the old spikes of the same lighter as are necessary to be employed about the same work [page 242] and shall deliver over to this Incorporation the bolts and remainder of the iron work. The same pieces of the same lighter the said William is to bring to the town court for which work the said Incorporation is to pay him three pounds and to allow him the charge of a boat to carry the same to the marsh.

At a hall held **29 September 1651**
Upon the same day Daniel Winsor, one of the porters of this town paid in to the cartage six and forty shillings out of which there was paid twelve shillings for gathering the cartage money the last year, and five shillings for the porters sweeping the quays, and the remainder being nine and thirty shillings was paid over to Mr Mayor Arthur.

Upon the same day the said Daniel Winsor paid in three and twenty shillings for wheel money which was paid in to Mr Treasurer Holmes.

At a hall held **3 October 1651**
Upon the same day Mr John Senior paid over to Mr Mayor Arthur ten pounds in part of the twenty pounds due from him by bill to the poor of Waymouth, out of which Mr Mayor presently paid Giles Fowler and Edward Courtney seven pounds towards the making up of the marsh and to Matthew Shaddicke three and twenty shillings and to John Mansell thirty two shillings and eight pence.

Memoranda, at a hall **23 January 1652**

Upon the same day Mr John Senior paid in the other ten pounds residue of the said twenty pounds which twenty pounds was put in for the use of the marsh in the same manner which Melcomb poor's money was.

Upon the same third day of October 1651 Andrew Eburne did also pay in to Mr Mayor five pounds in part of the money due by bill to the poor of each side.

Upon the same day John Bury, one of the porters of this town, paid in to Mr Mayor Arthur forty four shillings and five pence for the market and has paid in.

The order of John Arthur, mayor of the said town, and George Pley, bailiff, two of the justices of the peace there, made the third day of October 1651 concerning a base child born of the body of Joan Butcher. For as much as the said Joan has upon her oath accused the said William to be the father of the said child upon her examination taken before the said justices which does probably appear by several circumstances of the said examination contained. Now the said justices do by force and virtue of the statute in that case made and provided order that the said William Ward shall pay twenty pence weekly to the said Joan or the overseer of the poor of the town aforesaid, for the time being from the birth of the said child for and towards the maintenance of the said child , until the said child shall attain its age of seven years. And that the said William Ward, and one other person of sufficient surety for the said William, shall enter into an obligation of the penal sum of forty pounds to the overseers of the poor of the borough of Waymouth and Melcomb Regis aforesaid with condition thereto subscribed that the said William shall from time to time and at all times well and sufficiently save and keep harmless the inhabitants of the town aforesaid, and also the parishioners of the parish church of Weeke Regis in the county aforesaid, of and from the maintenance of the said child. And that he the said William Ward shall pay and discharge all such costs and charges [page 243] as the said inhabitants or parishioners or any of them shall at any time be necessarily put to for and towards the maintenance and education of the said child. Given under our hands and seals the day and year above said.

At a hall held 30 October 1651

Upon the same day it was agreed on by a general and full consent that four pounds per annum shall be paid to Mr John Knight, the schoolmaster, in part of a recompense for teaching of scholars in the town as long as he shall please to continue the said school. And in regard Mr Knight is to fit the school in the Friary at his own charge, he is to be paid the first year's annuity of four pounds in hand by Mr Treasurer. And then at Christmas come twelve month he is to be paid twenty shillings more and from thence forth 20s quarterly during the time aforesaid.

At a hall held 12 December 1651

It is agreed upon that Mr John Hodder upon the security of Mr John Swetnam and Mr John Beer, grocer, paying the interest and charges shall continue the five and twenty pounds part of Mr Middleton's money heretofore lent to Mr Nathaniel Allen.

Upon the same day it was agreed on that a rate should be made for the scavenger on both towns to raise sixteen pounds per annum for the maintenance of the scavenger, that he may likewise at leisure times fill up the said grounds at the jetty with sand, a breach being first made in the upper end of it near the widow Day's house, that he may pass in with his horse and pot to begin from Michaelmas last past and to be paid quarterly. This rate is to be made this next week by Mr Bailiff Holmes, Mr Thomas Leddoze, and Mr Robert Wall for Waymouth, Mr Thomas Waltham, Mr John Senior and Mr Jonathan Leddoze for Melcombe or any five, four or three of them.

At a hall held **23 January 1652**
Upon the same day there was paid to Giles Fowler five pounds being the remainder of three score pounds expended for the new fencing and walling of the marsh according to a former agreement with the town.

At a hall held **20 February 1652**
Richard Brownwell, barber surgeon, came this day and again desired to use his said trade in the town which was granted to him for the fine of twenty shillings. And the first apprentice that he takes is to be of the town, and then afterwards every second apprentice to be taken by him shall be of the town, which twenty shillings he paid to Mr Mayor Pley for the treasurer.

13 April 1652
By the trustees for sale of fee farm rents, whereas Mr Josiah Dewye contracted with us on the 16 December 1651:

The fee farm of the town of Melcomb Regis per annum 20s lying and being in the county of Dorset and has paid to the treasury the whole purchase money due on the said contract. It is this day ordered that the several ad respective owners, occupiers and tenants of the premises do pay the aforesaid rents which were due and payable on the 25 March last to the said Josias Dewye, his assignee or assigns; and so from thence forwards to continue the payment thereof to the said Josias Dewye, his assignee or assigns, at such usual days and times as the same from time to time shall grow and due payable and not to the former receiver and collector thereof. [page 244] And a copy of this order left with the said owners, occupiers or tenants of the premises shall be their sufficient warrant and discharge for their paying the said rents to the said Josias Dewye, his assignee or assigns accordingly. And further ordered that Sir Henry Croke, knight clerk of the pipe, discharge the said premises in his rental and records from paying the said rents to the state due on the five and twentieth day of March last, or which shall from hence forward grow due and payable, and that he give notice thereof to the sheriff, receiver, bailiff or collector of the premises that they demand not nor distrain for the said rents which were due and payable on the said five and twentieth day of March last or which shall from thence forward grow due and payable. But that they leave the same to be received by the said Josias Dewye, his assignee or assigns, according to the order.

Richard Salton, *stally*, Edward Cussett, Thomas Ayres, John Hunt, Thomas Hubbert

At a hall held **18 June 1654**
Upon the same day it was agreed on that the porters shall make all carts loaded with fuel, hay or any provisions whatsoever henceforward to pay according to the constitutions and for every such cart as loads no goods the said porters are to be allowed one penny out of four pence for every such cart.

Upon the same day the said porters paid to Mr Treasurer Arthur for bridge duties fifteen shillings and four pence.

Upon the same day they paid Mr Treasurer for cartage money two and thirty shillings and eight pence. Upon the same day Mr John Wetmany of Newcastle, mariner, paid to captain John Arthur, the town treasurer, forty shillings for discharging his guns in the harbour and gave reparation to the parties grieved.

At a hall held **21 June 1652**
Upon the same day it was agreed Nathaniel Abbott, having discharged one gun into the harbour contrary to the constitution, shall pay twenty shillings, of which fine he was repaid back fifteen shillings.

At a hall held **10 September 1652**
Upon the same day liberty is granted to William Gillett to lay timber on convenient places of the new enclosed ground in Melcombe after the rate of forty shillings per annum to be paid quarterly as long as he holds it, to begin at Michaelmas next.

Upon the same day a convenient place was granted to Mr Mayor Pley and Mr Thomas Waltham to dig a well in on the town waste, without the town, for their own use, so as it may not be any annoyance or prejudice to passengers or dangerous for cattle, at four shillings per annum rent to be paid at Michaelmas yearly.

Matthew's Day 21 September 1652
Upon the same day Mr John Swetnam was elected mayor for the ensuing year.

Upon the same day Mr Thomas Waltham and Mr Robert Wall were elected bailiffs for the year to come.

Upon the same day Mr George Pley was chosen treasurer for the ensuing year.

Upon the same day Mr Thomas Waltham, Mr Robert Wall, Mr Thomas Leddoze, Mr George Pley, John Allen and Mr James Studley were appointed auditors for the year to come.

[page 245] At a hall held **1 October 1652**
Upon the same day it was agreed on that Mr Jonathan Leddoze shall have Martha Pitt's house of Caseway in the county of Dorset, spinster, during her life, paying fifty shillings yearly to the overseers of the poor of Melcomb Regis for the said Martha Pitt's use.

Upon the same day it was agreed upon that Mr Humphrey Favell shall have that plot of ground situated, lying and being in Waymouth within the town of Waymouth and Melcomb Regis bounded with the land of Robert Clarke on the west, past the highway going to Sandfoote Castle on the east, past the land of Mr Andrew Buckler on the south, and the highway leading to Weeke church on the north part thereof containing by estimation one hundred and twenty feet in length and four and twenty feet in breadth, paying three pounds for it. To hold to the said Humphrey, his heirs and assigns, forever and yielding and paying one penny yearly to this Incorporation. And that deed of the premises to that purpose he accordingly granted to him by the said Incorporation.

Upon the same day it was agreed upon that Mr Mayor Pley shall have three years longer time in the marsh added to his former lease, he being the last three years of his term to let the marsh lie to meadow.

Upon the same day the cartage was let to Mr Thomas Waltham at £13 12s for the year ensuing, Mr George Pley and Mr James Studley.

Upon the same day the bridge duties were let to Captain John Arthur at £5 15s for the year ensuing, security Mr Thomas Leddoze and Mr Humphrey Favell.

Upon the same day the markets were let to Captain John Arthur at £12 5s for the year ensuing, security Mr Thomas Leddoze and Mr Humphrey Favell.

Upon the same day the ballast and forfeitures were let to Captain John Arthur at £10 5s for the year ensuing, the same security.

At a hall held **29 October 1652**

Upon the same day it was agreed by a general consent ordered and so agreed upon that Briant Wood, the scavenger, shall have the use of the horse and pot now in his possession until Michaelmas next and so from year to year as long as it shall please the mayor and company upon this condition: that the said Briant shall maintain and feed the said horse from this time and shall repair the pot and wheels, and all other things belonging to the same, at his own costs without any salary or reward from the Incorporation. And that the said Briant shall keep clean the market place and churchyard and ground before the main guard and other waste places in the town. And to agree with other persons for carrying away their dirt on such terms as he can and to take the monies of them to his own use; for the maintenance of the said horse and pot. And shall not use or let out the said horse to hackney or carrying any burdens in any place out of the jurisdiction of the town, and shall carry all the earth and rubble and dirt to the new enclosed ground at the jetty, but shall not fetch or carry any water or beer with his said horse, but may carry wood and other fuel from the quay to any person's house in the town.

Upon the same day it is agreed on that the three pounds thirteen shillings and eight pence being the arrears of the money due for gaoled and maimed soldiers at Our Lady Day 1652 shall be paid out of the church rate which was made in the time of Mr James Studley, the late churchwarden, in case that the rate will amount to it, if not then the now churchwarden and overseers of the poor, or the greater number of them, shall make another rate for the raising of the same three pounds thirteen shillings and eight pence, or so much of the same as shall not be raised as aforesaid in Melcomb Regis, and the same monies to be repaid into the poor stock from whence it was taken.

Upon the same day Andrew Eburne paid by way of allowance for his pension five and twenty shillings and for David Doves twenty shillings, which five and forty shillings is allowed to the said Andrew in part of five pounds principal monies he owes to the poor of Melcomb Regis.

17 June 1653 [later annotation]
Upon the same day Andrew Eburne paid to Mr Mayor three pounds.

At a hall held **9 November 1652**
Upon the same day it was agreed on that Mr George Pley, the present tenant to the marsh, shall pay in the interest of such monies as he has of the poor's stock to the overseers of the poor of each town respectively and the same monies so paid shall be allowed him out of the rent reserved by the lease and that Mr Pley shall pay to the said overseers out of the same rent the arrears of the interest money due to the poor and so to continue the payment of the same quarterly to the said overseers.

At a hall held **4 February 1653**
Upon the same day it was agreed on that Thomas Parson, William Flight and John Yeatman of Fawly near Cashwood Castle, seamen, would bring down the town timber, being ninety tonnes, from Ely at six shillings per tonne. They are not to shorten any of the timbers, but to saw the short pieces that can not be stowed conveniently without sawing. The town is to bear the charge of sawing those short pieces and to make the said seamen some allowance towards the charge of loading it.

Upon the same day the widow Amy Gibson paid to Mr Mayor Swetnam forty shillings in full of all arrears of rents for the barber's shop near the quay until Michaelmas one thousand six hundred fifty and two, which money was afterwards paid to Mr Treasurer Pley, he coming in before the company rose, and the company offered her a lease of it for twenty shillings per annum because so much is offered for it by the year as is averred.

8 February 1653
Thomas Newman on his oath says that yesterday one Robert Hutchings of Lymington, servant of one Francis Goodier of that place, did acknowledge to this deponent that he had sold to one Stephen Gardner of Puddletown, another foreigner within this town, four and twenty quarters of white salt at 2s 1od per bushel. And the said Stephen Gardner also acknowledged to this deponent that he bought the same salt of the Hutchens in Waymouth and the said Gardner told this deponent that he should have what part he would of it.

At a hall held **11 February 1653**
The aforesaid Robert Hutchens appearing at the hall this day did acknowledge that he first sold twenty quarters of the said salt to the said Stephen Gardner as aforesaid, and saying that afterwards the bargain between him and the said Gardner before the delivery of the said salt was made void and afterwards the said Robert Hutchens sold

the said salt to John Beere, mercer (who is no freeman yet admitted) and received two shillings and six pence from the said John Beere in earnest for the said bargain.

[page 247] Upon the same day the said John Beere, submitting the said foreign bargain to the judgement of the court, who awarded him to pay forty shillings, and so the same seizure shall be discharged, out of which forty shillings the treasurer is to allow the sergeant five shillings for the said seizure.

Upon the same day the ground on which the widow Amy Gibson's shop stands is this day let to Richard Scovile, town clerk of this town, for one and twenty years to commence from Our Lady Day next at sixteen shillings per annum rent. And the said widow Amy Gibson sold the same shop to the said Richard Scovile for twenty pounds with the furnace, all ceilings and benches belonging to the said shop, and he is to enter into it at Our Lady Day next.

Upon the same day, it appearing that the said John Beere has served seven years apprenticeship to John Hodder of this town, mercer, is admitted a freeman of this Corporation, and paid down for the same the common duties besides three shillings and four pence for his admission.

At a hall held **22 April 1653**

Upon the same day it was agreed on that Mr Samuel Osborne, the town a gentleman, shall have ten pounds for his pains for soliciting the common business over and above all charges and that Dennis Bond, esquire, John Brown, esquire, John Trenchard esquire, and Colonel William Sidenham, members of Parliament, shall be the town trustees and that the lands shall be settled and vested in those four gentlemen and their heirs for the use of the town according to the order of the house.

Upon the same day it was agreed on that Mr Richard Scovile shall have a lease for the ground for the barber's shop with the appurtenances for four score and nineteen years at sixteen shillings per annum rent.

Upon the same day John Rowswell and John Curtice, constables for the time being, paid in to the overseers of the poor of the town of Waymouth and Melcomb Regis the sum of twenty four shillings and eight pence for foreign beer, whereof four shillings was paid to John Russell for intelligence and two shillings to the constables for gathering it, so there remains eighteen shillings and eight pence.

Upon the same day John Hingston and John Cole, viewers of the market for flesh, paid to the overseers of the poor of this town twelve shillings and six pence for thirteen bulls which were killed by several butchers.

At a hall held **27 May 1653**

Upon the same day Lewis Jones had liberty granted him to use his trade of a haberdasher of hats in this town on the security of his father in law John Barber, clothier, of this town, in forty pounds to save the town harmless, and he is to pay the fine of twenty shillings for such his liberty.

At a hall held **5 August 1653**

Upon the same day it was agreed on that the town treasurer shall pay to Thomas

Holland for measuring of Melcomb common forty shillings, he having returned in a plot of the same lands in which plot the other lands of the town formerly let out to Thomas Newman at eight pounds per annum are now included. The number of acres amount to two hundred twenty and seven acres and seventy eight goads, viz: on the east side of Dorchester Way 172 acres 23 goads on the west side 54 acres 55 goads.

[page 248] Upon the same day Mr Thomas Hide was admitted a freeman generally for the fine of five pounds and also chosen one of the capital burgesses of this town.

At a hall held **30 September 1653**
Upon the same day it was agreed upon that the ordinary for the lecture shall be held at a public place of entertainment. The same house to provide for four ordinaries weekly whereof the preacher for the time being to be always one and Mr Thorne another if he pleased and two other lecturers, and when Mr Thorne himself preaches the lecture three other lecturers to be weekly invited by Mr Mayor's order, the charge of it to be paid quarterly by the town treasurer to Mr Mayor in lieu of his ten pounds for his kitchen and Mr Mayor to appoint the house for his ordinaries and to give order for the invitations.

At a hall held **7 October 1653**
Upon the same day the cartage was kept in the town's hands for the year ensuing.

Upon the same day the bridge was let to Mr George Pley for the ensuing year, security Mr Thomas Leddoze, Mr William Holmes at £3 12s.

Upon the same day the market was let to Mr Thomas Hide at £13 12s for the ensuing year, security Mr Robert Wall, Mr Jonathan Leddoze.

Upon the same day the common was let to John Edwards at 50s for the year ensuing, security Thomas Winter, sergeant Mineterne. And Bryant Wood is to have liberty to tie his horse there.

Upon the same day the anchorage, keyage, boomage, wharfage was kept in the town's hands for the year ensuing.

At a hall held **15 October 1653**
Upon the same day Mr George Pley bought of the town materials a parcel of boards and old timbers amounting to 31s 4d which he paid to Mr Mayor Wall in the townhall and Mr Mayor has the bill signed with Mr Pley's hand.

At a hall held **19 October 1653**
Upon the same day Mr Richard Harrison paid in to Mr Treasurer Swetnam three pounds for the rent of his shop due at Michaelmas 1653.

At a hall held **28 October 1653**
Upon the same day all the stones at Cold Harbour Fort except the three lower course of great asher stones and the stones standing westwards as a boundary against the sea. The top coping stones and the stones northward not yet removed are sold to Mr James

Studley for two and twenty pounds and five shillings except before excepted.

Upon the same day the new Fort stones next to Mountjoy (except the coping stones) are sold to Mr John Senior for ten pounds and five shillings.

Upon the same day the stones at Mountjoy Fort were sold to Mr John Senior for six and thirty shillings.

Upon the same day all the stones laid in the Fryery Green lately bought hither were sold to Mr Jonathan Leddoz for one and twenty shillings.

[page 249] At a hall held **28 October 1653**

Upon the same day the wall stones at the North Fort in Waymouth were sold to Mr Stephen Edwards for four pounds and one shilling.

Upon the same day the healing stones at the North Fort were sold to Mr Andrew Buckler for nine and forty shillings.

Upon the same day the stones of the Chappill Fort (except the now building there and the four pillar stones) were sold to Mr Peter Wall for ten pounds and five shillings.

Upon the same day the guardhouse at the widow Day's (the gunner's room excepted) sold to Mr Thomas Snowdon for four pounds.

Upon the same day the gunners' room at the widow Day's Fort sold to Mr John Senior for six and twenty shillings.

At a hall held **11 November 1653**

Upon the same [day] liberty was granted to John Rowsewell and Giles Hownsell, ropers, to set their posts and ropes on convenient places about the town's end, so on the highways and passages leading into the town be not annoyed. The said John having made use of it but a little time last past is to pay 10s and the said Giles Hownsell is to pay 20s for the time past to the town treasurer, both of them are to pay 20s per annum a piece for the future, quarterly, to such person or persons as shall collect the town rents, to commence from Michaelmas last past.

At a hall held **25 November 1653**

Upon the same day Robert Clarke, roper, brought a bill for 43s wherein were one and fifty deal boards delivered to Shattock and Mr Clarke, having compounded with the Corporation for his ropers' field until Michaelmas last for the sum of 43s. This bill is discharged and Mr Clarke is to pay to the town 20s per annum for his ropers' field to be allotted out from Michaelmas last past.

At a hall held **20 January 1654**

Upon the same day Mr Thomas Hide paid into the town treasurer, Mr Swetnam, three pounds six shillings and three pence for his quarter year's rent [*quartridge*] for the market due at Christmas last past.

Upon the same day was paid into Mr Mayor Wall by the town clerk twelve pounds of Mr George Phippens, clerk, his gift money to the poor of the town, viz: four pounds for Waymouth poor and eight pounds for Melcomb poor. To be let at interest for the poor's use.

At a hall held 3 March 1654

Upon the same day Mr John Arthur, one of the aldermen of the town, on the decease of Mr Bailiff Leddoze, is elected bailiff in the room of the said Mr Leddoze and was sworn bailiff.

Upon the same day was paid to Mablyn Staplyn for his pension ten shillings, of which five shillings was paid to Mr John Arthur and five shillings to Mr John Swetnam in part of their church rates in Mr Studley's time of churchwardenship, to be defaulted out of the rates on Mr Studley church account.

Upon the same day Mr John Senior paid to Mr Wall for the stones at Mountjoy Fort three and thirty shillings in full, and the town is to pay the charges of the court.

[page 250] At a hall held 28 April 1654

Upon the same day the *mayne* guard was sold to Gregory Babbidge, merchant, for thirteen pounds to be in hand paid and to be removed at his charge in one month next ensuing

Upon the same day the buildings of the Chappell Fort and pavements (but not the timber and things placed on it) were sold to Mr Robert wall to be removed in two months and the monies to be in hand paid.

Upon the same day the stones and platform at Mr Thomas Waltham's house were sold to Mr Thomas Waltham for five and twenty shillings to be received in a month.

At a hall held 9 June 1654

Upon the same day Edward Tucker, clothier, having for many years past married one of the daughters of Mr Richard White, deceased, late one of the burgesses of this town and having lived in the town with his family for some years past desired to be generally a freeman of this Corporation which was granted to him for the fine of five pounds and the usual fees. Which said five pounds was paid over to Mr Treasurer Swetnam and was sworn a freeman accordingly.

Upon the same day Thomas Samways, mercer, having served seven years apprenticeship to John Hodder, mercer, a general freeman of this town by indenture enrolled, was generally admitted a freeman of the Incorporation for the fine of three shillings and four pence, which was paid to Mr Treasurer Swetnam in court and was sworn a freeman accordingly.

Upon the same day Richard Wilson, mariner, being born in this town and having married the daughter in law of Mr Edward Cuttance, deceased, late alderman of this town, was also this day generally admitted a freeman of this Incorporation for the fine of five pounds, which was paid to Mr Treasurer Swetnam in court and was sworn a freeman accordingly.

Upon the same day Mr Treasurer Swetnam was ordered to pay to the widow Reape five and forty shillings for three quarters of a year for her husband's wages as clerk. And she is to see that the birth, burials and marriages be lawfully recorded before she be paid any more monies.

At a hall 15 July 1654
Upon the same day Leonard Hillard, vintner, was generally admitted a freeman of this Incorporation for the fine of four pounds which was paid to Mr Treasurer Swetnam and was sworn a freeman accordingly.

Upon the same day Richard George paid for keyage since Michaelmas last three pounds fourteen shillings and six pence to Mr Treasurer Swetnam out of which was allowed Richard George 5s.

[page 251] At a hall held 4 August 1654
Upon the same day it was agreed on by a general consent that John Edwards, the present clerk, shall be allowed out of the town stock three pounds yearly, as was formerly paid to Mr Reap for ringing the bell and keeping the clock all the year long.

Upon the same day it was agreed on by a general consent, because the burial place is so little and the burials may prove annoying and dangerous to the town in general if the town be not carefully looked to, that the bedeman [*bedman*] shall not dig any grave but by the appointment of the churchwarden or sidesmen, or one of them, unless such as shall be buried near the widow Gibon's wall. And that the bedeman shall always dig the graves four feet deep in case he can conveniently do it without digging upon the bodies of such as have been newly interred, upon pain of every default herein by the bedeman two shillings and six pence. And that the bedman shall keep the churchyard clean and take care that none do annoy the churchyard by filthing in it. And that he likewise walk up and down every Sabbath day in the church and churchyard for keeping of the boys in order and to give the justices information of those from time to time that do offend.

At a hall 18 August 1654
William Pooke having served Mr Philip Bugden, deceased, to the trade of merchant by indenture enrolled dated the one and twentieth day of January in the year of Our Lord 1645 [1646] by the space of near about six years and then offering to serve out the remainder of his time with his mistress or any other freeman of this town. And he having several times presented himself to the company for his freedom, and now presenting a letter from John Trenchard, esquire, for that purpose was generally admitted a freeman of this Incorporation for the fine of 3s 4d and paying the other common duties and accordingly took his oath a freeman.

Upon the same day it was ordered that Mr Treasurer Swetnam does pay to sergeant Bennett his bill coming to £3 3s and he to repair all the ironwork of the clock for three years next ensuing at his own charge unless in case any imminent disaster touching the said clock shall happen. And the said Mr Bennett is to assist and instruct the clerk in setting and keeping of the said clock for three years as aforesaid.

21 September 1654, Matthew's Day
Upon the same day Mr Robert Giear was elected mayor for the year to come.

Upon the same day Mr John Senior and Mr Stephen Abbott were chosen bailiffs for the year to come.

Upon the same day Mr Robert Wall was chosen treasurer for the year ensuing

Upon the same day Mr John Smith, Mr Stephen Abbott, Mr Thomas Waltham, Mr Robert Wall, Mr William Holmes and Mr John Row were appointed auditors for the year to come.

[page 252] At a hall held **2 October 1654**

Upon the same day Mr Robert Giear (being elected mayor for the year ensuing) was generally admitted a freeman of this Incorporation, and was sworn a freeman accordingly, and also was chosen mayor of this borough and town for the year to come.

Upon a hall held **28 October 1654**

Upon the same day it was agreed that Mr John Allambridge shall collect the town duties formerly called the petty customs and also the ballast and forfeitures and shall have for his pains in collecting the same two shillings of the pounds he [collects]. Accounting every month or upon every entry in the customs house and paying in the monies for which Mr Thomas Waltham has engaged to Mr Mayor and company.

At a hall held **8 December 1654**

Upon the same day Thomas Browne, gentleman, son of John Browne, esquire, was, out of the company's respect to him and his ancestors having been benefactors of the town, freely and generally admitted a freeman to the trade of merchant within this Corporation and took his oath of freeman accordingly.

18 May 1655

Upon the same day the timber boards and planks in the Chappell Fort were sold to Mr Robert Wall for the sum of five pounds, which five pounds Mr Wall was ordered to pay to Mr Bailiff Abbott, which he paid to Mr Dawbney Williams to make up Waymouth rent due at Michaelmas last past.

At a hall held **10 August 1655**

Upon the same day it was ordered that the streets shall be pitched by Goodman Broome, the pitcher, if he may be got. The town is to be at the charge of the stones, pitching the channels and gutters as have been accustomed. And that the inhabitants shall pay the workman's wages for pitching before their several lands, according to the usual rate by the yard, and shall make their work even and level with the town channels and with their next neighbour's work upon the pain in the constitution. And Mr Pley is desired and has promised to take an account of what boats and stones shall be brought in. And that the boats be fully loaded. And Bryant Wood is to be paid 2s by the day for fetching up of the stones and sand for the workmen with the horse and pot for so many whole days as he shall work about the same.

Be it remembered that the first day of September 1654 the widow Comfrey's deed was put in the town chest.

[page 253] Enrolments of apprentices by indenture with freeman and inhabitants of this borough and town and the days and times of their enrolments according to the constitution heretofore made by the mayor, aldermen, bailiffs and capital burgesses of the said borough and town at that end and purpose as by the same constitution more at large appears.

17 November 1655

Jasper, son of Ephraim Westley of Whitecliffe in the parish of Brixton Deverell in the county of Wiltshire, gentleman, by indenture bearing date the 15 November 1655 bound apprentice to John Swetnam a freeman of this town, woollen draper. And Agnes his wife in the trade of woollen draper to serve them from the day of the date of the indenture for a term of seven years.

30 April 1656

Bartholomew Beere, son of Thomas Beere of Halstock in the county of Dorset, yeoman, by indenture bearing the date the 18 October 1650 bound apprentice to John Beere a freeman of this town, mercer, to serve him in the trade of mercer from the day of the date of the indenture for the term of seven years.

7 November 1656

John Wilson son of Richard Wilson, one of the freemen of this town, by indenture bearing date the eight and twentieth day of September 1656 bound apprentice to his father to serve him in the trade of a merchant from the day of the date of the indenture.

Francis son of John Read of Puddlebridge, in county Devon, tanner, by indenture 28 September 1656 bound to John Hodder, merchant, and his wife for 7 years to it.

20 April 1659

Oliver Jacob, son of Edward Jacob of West Lidford in the county of Somerset, clerk, by indenture bearing the date the 15 April 1659 bound apprentice to John Hodder, merchant and freeman of this town, to serve him in that trade from 25 March last for 7 years.

2 August 1659

John Bennett, son of John Bennett of Windsome in the county of Somerset, husbandman, by indenture bearing date the 20 day of July last bound apprentice to John Senior, mercer and freeman of this town to serve him in that trade from the 8 May last for 7 years.

22 November 1659

Paul Waldron, son of Paul Waldron of Allens Loscombe in the parish of Poorestock and county of Dorset, yeomen, by indenture bearing date the first day of April last, bound apprentice to Robert Giear, merchant, a freeman of this town, to serve him from the 29 September 1658 for 8 years.

16 July 1661
Hugh Peircy, son of Richard Peircy of this town, merchant, by indenture bearing date the 24 June 1661 bound apprentice to his said father, a freeman of this town, to serve him from 25 July last for 7 years.

John Russell, the eldest son of John Russell of this town, mariner, by indenture bearing the date the 24 July 1690 bound apprentice to his said father, a freeman of this town, to serve him for seven years from the date.

[page 254] 8 April 1663
Richard Tucker, son of Edward Tucker of this town, merchant by indenture dated 24th March last, bound apprentice to the said Edward being a general freeman of the said town to serve from the day of the date of the said indenture for 7 years.

6 June 1665
John Burnard, son of Robert Burnard of Knowle within the parish of Long Sutton in the county of Somerset, yeoman, by indenture dated 1st May last, bound apprentice to James Bud, a general freeman of this Town, to serve from the 25th March last for 7 years.

19 June 1665
Thomas Adams, son of Thomas Adams of Corshill within the parish of Rodipoll in the county of Dorset, clothier, bound apprentice unto Francis Reade of this town, merchaht (a general freeman of this town) his executors and assigns by indenture dated 24th June 1664. To serve from the day of the date of the same indenture for the term of seven years.

11 July 1665
Crispian Hounsell, son of Giles Hounsell of this town, ropemaker, by indenture dated 1st July last, bound apprentice unto his said father a general freeman of this town to serve from the day of the date of the said indenture for 7 years.

1 May 1666
Stephen Hitchcocke, son of Robert Hitchcocke of Broadwindsor in the county of Dorset, by indenture dated the thirtieth of April last, bound apprentice to Giles Hounsell, ropemaker, for that trade to serve from the day of the date of the said indenture for 7 years.

29 September 1666
John Penny, son of Onesiphorus Penny of Yeovell in the county of Somerset, maltster, by indenture dated 29th September 1665, bound apprentice unto Thomas Tunstall of this town, merchant, to that trade for seven years from the date of the said indenture.

10 January 1667
Edward Cooke, son of Edward Cooke, late of Somerton in the county of Somerset, yeoman, by indenture bearing date 25th day of November last, bound apprentice unto James Budd of this town, mercer, for the term of seven years from the date of the said indenture.

12 February 1667
Ezekiel Russell, son of Ezekiel Russell of Halstock in the county of Dorset, yeoman, by indenture dated yesterday bound apprentice to John Senior a general freeman of this town to serve for 7 years from the day of the date of the said indenture.

Henry Russell, son of the said Ezekiel Russell by indenture dated this present day bound apprentice to the said John Senior, Rebecka his wife and Hannah Senior to serve for 7 years from the day of the date of the said indenture.

[page 255] To all whom these presents shall come, the mayor, aldermen, bailiffs, burgesses and commonality of Waymouth and Melcomb Regis in the county of Dorset send greetings. Whereas through the decay of trade and by means of the late wars the revenue of the said town has been wholly exhausted, the town duties in point of customs (being formerly the choice revenue of the Incorporation)for some years past having amounted to no considerable sum, yet the issuing forth of monies has been far greater than in peaceable times, in that the town has been at great charges about the soldiers and and in cleaning and paving of the streets since the last siege. And whereas lately the grounds called Waymouth marsh have been built up and fenced at a great charge (which was thrown down and ruined in the said late wars) for the repair and settling of this Incorporation have been reconstituted to take up the sum of five and twenty pounds out of monies belonging to the poor stock of Waymouth. Now, know you that the said mayor, aldermen, bailiffs, burgesses and commonality do hereby promise and engage that this Incorporation shall yearly and every year pay and certify to the overseers of the poor of Waymouth the interest of the said five and twenty pounds for and towards the relief of the poor there until the same monies shall be again raised and paid into the poor stock of Waymouth aforesaid. In testimony whereof the said mayor, aldermen, bailiffs, burgesses and commonality have caused the seal of the said Incorporation to be hereto affixed. And this act to be registered among the public records of the said Incorporation and in the overseer's book for the poor of Waymouth aforesaid, the twentieth day of October in the year of Our Lord one thousand six hundred and fifty four.

[page 256] **26 May 1668**
Roger Moores junior, son of Roger Moores of Sherborne in the county of Dorset senior, bound apprentice to Giles Hounsill, ropemaker and Margaret his wife, by indenture dated this day to serve them from this day for eight years.

20 August 1668
Peter Blagden, son of John Blagden of Tiverton in the county of Devon gent by

indenture dated the seventh day of August past, bound apprentice unto Simon Orchard, merchant, a general freeman of this town, to serve for 7 years from the date of the indenture.

1 February 1669, enrolled 17 March 1669
John Rose, son of John Rose of Kingston in Purbeck, by indenture dated 1 February 1668 bound apprentice unto Captain Lambert Cornelius of this town, mariner, to serve him for seven years from the date of the indenture in the art, mystery or occupation of a mariner.

25 March 1669
Samuel, son of Richard Standerwick of Buckland Mary in the county of Somerset, gent, by indenture dated the day and year last abovementioned bound apprentice to John Senior, mercer, to serve him and his assigns to the said trade of a mercer for seven years from the date of the same indenture.

12 July 1669
Philip Tailor, son of Mary Tailor of Alweston, Dorset, widow. [Aged] 14-? bound apprentice to James Budd of this town, merchant, for seven years from the day and year aforesaid by indenture, then bearing date and Enrolled both parts of the same indenture.

[Date omitted]
William, the son of Mrs Joan Smart of Galton in the county of Dorset, widow, by indenture bearing date the two and twentieth day of October 1669 bound apprentice unto Jacob Chubb of this town, a general freeman of this incororation for the term of seven years to commence from the date of the said indenture.

[page 257] 21 September 1655
Upon this present day Mr Thomas Waltham was elected mayor of this town for the ensuing year; there also being in the election Mr Roger Cuttance, Mr John Senior and Mr Theophilus Byatt.

Upon the same day Mr Theophilus Byatt and Mr Thomas Hide were elected bailiffs of this town for the ensuing year.

Upon the same day Mr Robert Giear, present mayor, is elected treasurer of this town for the ensuing year.

Upon the same day Mr Bailiffs elected Mr John Lockier, Mr Henry Waltham, Mr James Studley and Mr Stephen Abbott were elected auditors to audit the account of the treasurer for the year past.

28 September 1655
Upon this present day it is ordered that John Rowsell, roper, shall have a lease of a parcel of ground adjoining to his lands in Melcomb next the line above the blockhouse, containing in length about twelve feet and in breadth about 12 feet for

999 years; rent 4s per annum , commencing at Michaelmas next, Rowsell to fence and repair it towards the sea.

Upon the same day leave was granted to Mr John penny to set out a porch three feet without his wall at the house where Mr Andrew Buckler now dwells at St Mary street late in the tenure of Roger Cooper, pipe maker.

26 October 1655
Upon this present day the market was let to Mr Stephen Edwards for one year from Michaelmas last for £10 5s on the security of himself, Mr Thomas Winter and Mr Daniel Arding.

Upon the same day the anchorage, keyage, wharfage and boomage of this town were let to Mr Thomas Hide and Mr John Alambridge for £41 10s upon their own and Mr James Studlie's security.

Upon the same day the cartage was let to Mr Thomas Hide for £8 5s on the security of himself and Mr John Senior and Mr James Studly.

Upon the same day the bridge duties were let to Mr Thomas Hide for £3 10s on the security of himself and Mr John Senior and Mr James Studley.

Upon the same day the ballast and forfeitures were let to Mr John Alambridge for £8 6s on the security of himself and Mr John Senior and Mr James Studley.

2 November 1655
Upon this present day was read an order from the committee for preservation of the customs as follows:

At the committee for the preservation of the customs, Thursday 3 May 1655.

It is ordered that the committee for the customs do give order to their collector in the port of Waymouth to pay out of the monies in his hands arising by the collection of the new imposition on coals in that port between 12 October 1654 and the 26 March following to the mayor and aldermen of the town of Waymouth to be by them with the consent of the said collector [page 258] and the checker of the customs then distributed for the use of the poor of Waymouth the sum of four pounds six shillings and five pence. And for so doing this shall be their warrant, the committee names John Stone, George Bennett, William Roberts, George Baynes, John Syres, which £4 6s 5d captain John Arthur, collector for this port, now paid in. Out of which was allowed him 2s 5d in full of 2s 6d which he paid the clerk for the order. The remainder £3 4s was by the consent of the company divided thus: 24s to Waymouth and 42s to Melcomb poor's stock, and to that end the £4 4s was left in Mr Robert Wall's hands to be put in the town chest.

16 November 1655
Upon this present day there was lent to Matthew Spencer of this town, parchment maker, of the poor's stock of Waymouth in the name of the Corporation, on the security of himself and Henry Gawdon, mariner, to be paid in a year next, which £5 rises thus: 40s of the 42s paid above by captain Arthur and the other £3 was taken out of the town chest.

31 December 1655
Upon the same day Mr Theophilus Byatt, Mr Robert Wall, Mr Stephen Abbott and Mr Robert Saunders having viewed a piece of ground adjoining to Mr Thomas Hide's house next to the harbour, which he desires to enclose, ranging even with the town quay, and reporting that it will be no way prejudicial to the harbour provided it be be built sloping even with every foot of the old stairs against Mr Morris his wall. It is agreed on that the said Mr Hide shall extend his backside towards the harbour the breadth of twelve feet and the length to be even with the whole range of the house, and the west end next to Mr Morris his stairs to be build sloping. For which he is to pay five shillings per annum, to build a sufficient pair of stairs for boats to land at the east end of his house, to maintain the same stairs, and to make a sufficient gutter for the water pass.

15 February 1656
Upon this present day John Edwards , the parish clerk, demanding for his salary for ringing the bell at 4 and 8 for one year and 3 quarters past, and his rent due for the common for one year and half being taken into consideration, as also he alleging that he was disturbed in the possession of the common by the tenants in possession of Radipoll Farm, it was ordered that the town steward should pay to him 40s for his said service until Christmas last, and that he be discharged the rent of the said common.

22 February 1656
Upon this present day Mr William Bond was sworn a capital burgess of this town, he being formerly chosen at a full hall.

Upon the same day a lease of a 1000 years was agreed on to be granted to Nicholas Minol, carpenter, of a plot of ground between his and Andrew Eburne's houses, as far downwards to the sea on the east part thereof as the wall of the town stands, and as far westward on to range even with the dwelling house of the said Andrew northwards and southwards, he leaving a passage and way there down to the sea out of the street in breadth from north to south 4 feet and in height 6 feet and half under the timber work on the plain ground or pitching. Nicholas Minol to repair the same at his own costs and to keep the gutter for the street water and dirt clean and free so as the said water and dirt may have a free passage onto the street, through the said plot of ground, in to the sea, and to pay 5s per annum at Michaelmas and Lady Day.

[page 259] 30 April 1656
Upon this present day it is agreed on that the Corporation shall pay to Mr George Thorne, the minister of this town, for so long time as he shall continue his ministry here, eight pounds per annum payable quarterly. The first payment to begin at midsummer next. Which eight pound s to be paid yearly shall be secured to him by some instrument in writing under the seals of the Corporation. And that the said Mr Thorne shall also have and receive yearly, during his ministry here, the rent of the

parsonage house now in the tenure of Thomas Growt, felt maker.

16 May 1656

Upon this present day the common was let to John Prince at 24s per annum rent for one year from Lady Day last. That is to say as far as the sluice leading to Sutton, as far westwards as the town's right, and as far northward as the ditch by the highway side. And Briant Wood, the scavenger's horse, is to go there without paying anything during the said time. And in case the farmers of Radipoll shall impound his horse for feeding in the town common as before expressed the town will save him harmless for any suit in law that shall be commenced touching the same.

Upon the same day it is agreed on that the eight pounds per annum formerly ordered Mr George Thorne, minister here, for his house rent shall issue out of the marsh grounds and lands in Waymouth for which he shall have an annuity under the town seal for 60 years, in case he shall so long live and exercise his ministry here, to be paid quarterly. The first payment to begin in midsummer next. And Mr George Pley who rents the marsh is to pay him this annuity and to be allowed the same out of his rent for the remainder of his term.

26 September 1656

Upon this present day Samuel Cooke having served an apprenticeship to John Arthur, merchant, by the space of seven years to the trade of merchant, as by the enrolment of his indenture of his apprenticeship appears, is generally admitted a freeman of this Incorporation for the common fine of 3s 4d paid to Mr Mayor in court.

Upon the same day Arthur Buckler, gentleman, and Samuel Cooke, merchant, were both admitted and sworn capital burgesses of this borough and town.

21 September 1656

Upon this present day Mr James Giear was chosen mayor of this town for the ensuing year, there being in the election Mr Roger Cuttance, Mr John Senior and Mr Theophilus Byatt.

Upon the same day Mr Richard Scovile and Mr Robert Wall were elected bailiffs of this town for the ensuing year.

Upon the same day Mr Bailiffs elected Mr Lockier, Mr Pley, Mr Stephen Abbott and Mr James Studley were elected auditors to audit the account of the old treasurer.

9 October 1656

Upon this day the market was let to Mr James Giear for £9 5s for the ensuing year on the security of himself, Mr Thomas Hide and Mr John Allambridge.

Upon the same day the cartage was let to John Minterne, sergeant, at £8 15s on the security of himself, Mr John Hodder and Mr Stephen Edwards.

Upon the same day the bridge duties were let to William Skinner on the security of himself, Henry Angell and Henry Taunton the younger for £3 10s.

[page 260] Upon the same day the ballast and forfeitures were let to Mr John Allambridge for £7 5s upon the security of himself and Mr James Giear and Mr

Thomas Hide.

Upon the same day the anchorage, boomage, keyage, wharfage and other petty town duties were let to Mr John Allambridge for £40 5s on the security of himself and Mr James Giear and Mr Thomas Hide.

21 October 1656

Upon this present day Mr Robert wall and Mr Alexander Clatworthy are desired to take care for the placing and fastening of posts for the mooring of ships, and they are desired also to speak with Mr John Allambridge about setting up of the boom, the doing whereof the treasurer is to pay for.

23 January 1657

Upon this present day it is agreed that Briant wood, the scavenger, shall have a new horse bought and he to have the old horse and £6 per annum to be paid quarterly. That is to say 40s out of the town stock and £4 to be raised on the inhabitants of Melcomb by rate. And that the treasurer Waltham shall pay him 20s that was due to him at Christmas last that he may make some present provision for his horse.

Upon the same day it is agreed upon and ordered by a full consent that the duty to this Incorporation for all Portland stone loaded here shall be two pence per tonne and no more to be paid by strangers.

4 June 1657

Upon this present day it is agreed upon that James Moaner shall be scavenger for the time to come for the market and the bridge, and shall have 40s per annum payable quarterly for his pains. And that all inhabitants that hold any houses, cellars, walls, grounds or lands before any of the market places shall rake and sweep up into heaps the dirt and filth in the gutters and streets before their houses, cellars, walls, lands and grounds every Friday at three of the clock in the afternoon that the same may be fit for the scavenger to carry away in his barrow to the void ground by the Jetty Fort upon pain of every one making default for every time 12d. And every inhabitant or housekeeper that shall lay any ashes, rubbish, soil or dirt in any of the streets of the town (unless it be in time of their necessary building or repairs) shall forfeit for every time for offending the like sum of twelve pence. And it is also ordered that all the inhabitants of this town not living in the market place shall rake, sweep and cleanse the streets and gutters before their houses and cellars, shops, walls, lands and grounds and carry away the dirt and filth there every Friday or Saturday weekly to the void ground by the Jetty Fort, or else to some other lands of their own or other convenient place where it may not annoy the town people or passengers, on pain of 12d for every such default for every time. All the said forfeitures to be levied by the sergeants at mace and the said scavenger on the goods of the persons offending, without any further or other warrant for the doing of the same, and the same sums to be accounted for to the town treasurer once a month, out of which the said treasurer o allow to the said sergeants and scavenger one third part of of the said fines for their pains. And it is further ordered that the said scavenger shall cleanse the market place from the higher part of the church northward down as far as as the post on the town quay in the middle or chief street by the custom house, as far westward as the town pump, and as far eastward as the passage and entry into the town hall [page 261], for doing of which the Corporation shall provide a wheel barrow and shovel now at first, which the said scavenger is afterwards to provide and repair at his own charge. And the said scavenger is once a week to cleanse and make clean the said bridge and market place and to carry away the filth and dirt to the said void ground near the Jetty Fort on pain for every time that he shall make default 12d.

Upon the same day Mr Benjamin Gatch, of this town, mariner, is admitted a freeman generally of this Incorporation for the fine of five pounds, which he laid down, but forty shillings of it was given him back again, and the other £3 paid to Mr Robert Wall in part of the monies due to him from the town. Also the said Benjamin Gatch was this day chosen one of the capital burgesses of this town and sworn accordingly.

4 September 1657
Upon this present day it is agreed upon that the quay at Richard Peircy's corner in Waymouth side shall be viewed by Mr Bailiff Wall, Mr Pley, Mr Biatt and Mr Bond who are to make their report of it to Mr Mayor and the company at the next hall day. And it is also ordered that the stairs of the quay against the middle street in Melcombe are to be forthwith repaired at the town charge.

Upon the same day it was ordered that a collection should be made in the churches of Weeke and Melcomb Regis for one Hannibal Jennings, a poor, sick, infirm man taken at sea by pirates and landed in these parts and for his attendance, *physicke* and *medicaments*.

21 September 1657
Upon this present day Mr Henry Waltham was chosen mayor for this town for the ensuing year, there being in the election Mr Roger Cuttance, Mr John Senior and Mr Theophilus Byatt.

Upon the same day Captain Alexander Clatworthy and Mr Steven Edwards are elected bailiffs of the town for the ensuing year.

Upon the same day Mr James Giear is elected treasurer for the ensuing year.

Upon the same day the elected bailiffs Mr George Pley, Mr Robert Wall, Mr Stephen Abbott and Mr Samuel Cooke are elected auditors to audit the account of the old treasurer.

28 September 1657
Upon this present day the market was let to Mr Thomas Hide from a month after Michaelmas until Michaelmas following for £11 on security of himself, Mr Thomas Waltham and Mr John Allambridge.

Upon the same day the cartage was let to Mr Henry Rose for £10 on the security of himself, Mr James Giear and Mr Thomas Hide.

Upon the same day the bridge duties were let to Mr Theophilus Byatt for £5 10s on the security of himself, Mr Robert Wall and Mr Thomas Hide.

Upon the same day the ballast and forfeitures were let to Mr Thomas Hide at £6 15s on the security of himself, Mr Thomas Waltham and Mr John Allambridge.

Upon the same day the anchorage, keyage, boomage, wharfage, etc. were let to Mr Henry Waltham for £44 on the security of himself, Mr Thomas Waltham and Mr Henry Rose.

[page 262] 23 October 1657

Upon this present day Peter Bagwell, having served an apprenticeship by indenture with with Mr John Hodder of this town, mercer, by the space of seven years to that trade is generally admitted a freeman of this Incorporation for the usual fine of 3s 4d, which he paid to Mr James Giear, treasurer, and the said Peter was sworn accordingly.

Upon the same day Mr Jonathan Pelham is admitted a freeman of this Incorporation for the fine of five pounds paid down to Mr James Giear, treasurer, and he took his oath accordingly.

Upon the same day John Allambridge having married the daughter of Mr Thomas Giear, late one of the aldermen of this town, who served several times as a burgess in Parliament, is admitted a freeman of this Incorporation for £5 but for the considerations above £4 10s thereof was returned to him and the other 10s paid over to Mr James Giear, treasurer, and the said John sworn accordingly.

Upon the same day Mr Richard Peircy and Mr John Allambridge were admitted and sworn capital burgesses of this town.

24 December 1657

Upon this present day Thomas Tunstall, having served as an apprentice by indenture enrolled with Gregory Babbidge, merchant, by space of eight years, is now admitted a freeman of this town for the common fine of three shillings and four pence paid to Mr James Giear, and he was sworn accordingly.

25 February 1658

Upon this present day the room now used for the excise office is let to Mr Henry Waltham, mayor, for 20s per annum for so long as he and the Corporation shall agree, to commence at Michaelmas last. And Mr Samuel Cooke is to have the customs house at 40s per annum as long as the Corporation and he shall agree.

Upon the same day it is agreed and ordered that all the inhabitants of Melcomb shall once every week, or more often if need require, to make clean the channels and grounds before their several houses and lands (except in the places hereafter mentioned) and carry the dirt and soil into places of their own where it may be no annoyance or otherwise to the void ground at the jetty on pain of everyone making default for every time 12d to be levied by Mr John Swetnam and Mr Samuel Cooke (according to their own offer) on the goods of the offender by warrant from Mr Mayor under his hand and seal. The exception is as follows; that is to say from the lower part of Mr Pley's dwelling down to the posts on the quay, from the corner of the customs house down to the same posts, and from the common pump to the same posts where the several inhabitants or owners are to rake up the dirt and sweep before their doors, houses and lands. And Briant Wood, the town scavenger, is to carry the same away, for which the said Briant shall have 20s quarterly paid him out of the town's stock. The first payment to begin at Lady Day next. And in consideration whereof the said Briant is to execute the office of beadle for the town and to have 12d for each time that he does execution by whipping of any person and to be paid out of the town stock.

[page 263] **23 July 1658**
Upon the same day licence is granted to Mr Henry Waltham, the present mayor, to erect a porch before the door of his dwelling house over against the White Hart in St Thomas street of four feet and half breadth from the wall of the said dwelling house.

Upon the same day the like licence is granted to Mr John Row, one of the capital burgesses of this Incorporation to erect the like porch before the street door of his dwelling house in the street leading from the town pump to the bridge.

Upon the same day the like licence is granted to Mr Bailiff Edwards to erect the like porch before the door of his dwelling house now in the possession of Mr Samuel Cooke.

17 September 1658
Upon this present day Mr Nathaniel Abbott coming to the hall and desiring to be made a freeman is admitted a freeman generally for the fine of £5, which he paid down, but in regard he is an ancient townsman born here £3 of the money was given him back again, and the other 40s was paid over to Mr James Giear, treasurer, and he took the oath accordingly.

Upon the same day Henry Flower is admitted a freeman generally of this town for the fine of £5, but because he was Mr Mayor's servant, on Mr Mayor's desire three pounds of the money was given him back, and the other 40s was delivered to Mr James Giear the treasurer, and the said Harry Flower took the oath accordingly.

Upon the same day it is agreed on and ordered that whereas several persons are in arrears for several rents due and owing to this Incorporation, diverse of whom are very poor and not able to pay, and diverse pretend that they do not owe so much as is in the rental. That it shall be in the power of Mr Mayor and Mr Robert Wall to order the same rent as they shall think fit, and to abate the same to such parties as they shall see cause for.

Upon the same day Jacob Chub is admitted a freeman generally for the fine of £5 which he paid. And in regard he was born in town £3 thereof was given him back and the other 40s was paid to the treasurer, and he was sworn accordingly.

Upon the same day leave is granted to Mr Henry Waltham, the present mayor, to continue his cistern which he has set out in the back street called St Nicholas Street, and for which he was presented and amerced the last law day, he the said Henry paying the said amercement.

Upon the same day liberty is given to Pascho Corbin to continue the porch now before his door near The Globe in St Mary Street.

[page 264] **21 September 1658**

Upon this present day Captain Roger Cuttance was chosen mayor of this town for the ensuing year.

Upon the same day Mr James Giear and Mr James Studley were chosen bailiffs of this town for the ensuing year.

Upon the same day the elected bailiffs, Mr Clatworthy, Mr Robert Wall, Mr Robert Giear, Mr Thomas Hide and Mr Stephen Abbott were chosen auditors.

1 October 1658
Upon this present day it is ordered and agreed that the cartage and all other duties of this town shall be kept in the town's hands for the ensuing year. And that the duties called the petty customs shall be collected by Mr John Allambridge, who shall account for it monthly, and the market, bridge and cartage by the porters, who shall likewise account for it monthly with the treasurer.

6 January 1659
Upon the same day the mayor of this town having received a warrant from the sheriff of this county for the electing of burgesses for this town for the ensuing Parliament which follows in these words:

Dorset PP John Strode esquire, sheriff of the county aforesaid, to the mayor of the borough of Waymouth and Melcomb Regis, greetings. By virtue of a writ of his highness Richard, Lord Protector of the Commonwealth of England, etc, to me directed reciting that by the advice and consent of his Highness' council for certain great and weighty affairs concerning his Highness and the state of defence of the said Commonwealth. His Highness has ordained his Parliament to be held in his Highness' city of Westminster the 27th day of January next coming and there to confer and treat with the great men and nobles of the said Commonwealth. These are therefore to will and require you that on receipt hereof you cause to be freely and indifferently chosen by them who shall be present at such election of the most discrete and sufficient of your borough's four burgesses according to the form of the statute thereupon made and provided. And the names of the said burgesses so to be chosen whether they be present or absent you insert in certain indentures there upon to be made between me and you. So that the said burgesses may have full and sufficient power to do and consent to those things which then and there by common council of the said Commonwealth by God's assistance shall happen to be ordained on the affairs aforesaid, so that for defect of such like power or by reason of improvident choice of burgesses aforesaid the said affairs may not remain undone in any ways. [page 265] And that the said choice so by you made you make known to me in form aforesaid without delay, so that I may distinctly and openly certify to his said Highness in the court of Chancery such choice at the day and place aforesaid. And hereof fail you not. Given under the seal of my office the third day of January 1659

The Incorporation proceeded to the election of four burgesses for the town aforesaid, there being nominated for the purpose John Trenchard esquire, Colonel Waldire Lago, Colonel John Clarke, Thomas Sydenham, Mr Peter Middleton, Mr Richard Bury and Mr Henry Waltham and the said John Trenchard, Colonel Lago,

Colonel Clarke and Mr Middleton were chosen the four burgesses for the town.

21 January 1659
Upon the same day it is agreed on and ordered that whereas there is eighteen years chief rent due to this Incorporation from Joan Tompson, widow, or others claiming under her for a certain decayed house in Maiden Street adjoining to the house of John Jourdan at 3d per annum for which rent there has not been found any goods on the said lands to take distress, that the town shall forthwith make a re-entry on the said lands.

11 March 1659
Upon this present day it is ordered and agreed on that no person whatsoever shall from henceforth take any ballast but out of the harbour of this port between the pier head and bridge in the channel at least three feet from the quays on either side of which no duty shall be paid to the Incorporation by any townsman and every stranger is to pay twelve pence by the tonne for every tonne, that is to say four pence to the Incorporation and eight pence to the takers up, and every person taking up the ballast elsewhere shall forfeit the ballast so taken to be seized on by the farmer and formers, or by the water bailiff for the time being, for the use of this Incorporation.

Upon the same day it is ordered that the Chappell Ground shall be viewed and bounded out, and that labourers shall be treated with all about the reading, levelling and planning of it, and Mr Wall, Mr Biatt and Mr Clatworthy and Mr Peircy are desired to take care of the business and to make their report thereof the next hall day.

21 September 1659
Upon this day Mr George Pley was elected mayor for the year now ensuing there standing also upon the election Mr John Senior, Mr Theophilus Byett and Mr Alexander Clatworthy.

Upon the same day were chosen bailiffs of this town for the year ensuing Mr John Swetnam and Mr Andrew Bucker.

Upon the same day was chosen treasurer for the year ensuing Mr Robert Giear.

Upon the same day Mr Bailiffs elect Mr Robert Wall and Mr Alexander Clatworthy, Mr Thomas Hide and Mr Samuel Cooke were chosen auditors of accounts.

Upon the same day Edmund Burrow, Christopher Colier of Waymouth and John Comfry and Henry Angell of Melcomb Regis were chosen constables for the year ensuing.

[page 266] 30 September 1659
Petty customs and ballast, forfeitures and anchorage being offered to be let out this day for want of takers were kept in the town's hands.

The market for the same cause was kept in the town's hands

Cartage was this day let to Mr James Giear for the ensuing year at £8 15s to be paid quarterly by even portions upon his own and the security of Mr Robert Wall and Mr Alexander Clatworthy.

Bridge duties let to the town clerk for the year ensuing on the security of himself, Mr James Giear and Mr Robert Wall for £4 5s to be paid quarterly in even portions.

At an assembly of the mayor, aldermen, bailiffs and burgesses of the Incorporation aforesaid the second day of December 1659 Francis Bennet, merchant, who married the daughter of Mr John Swetnam, one of the aldermen of this town, was this present day upon his humble motion upon laying down five pounds was generally admitted a freeman of this town. But for the cause aforesaid 40s of the same monies was remitted and the other three pounds was paid over to Mr Robert Giear, treasurer, and the same Francis was then sworn a freeman.

Henry Cuttance, the son of Captain Roger Cuttance, was this day admitted generally a freeman of this town by birth for the common fine of three shillings and four pence paid to Mr Robert Giear the town treasurer, and the said Henry took his oath of freeman accordingly.

9 March 1660
At a hall held this day Lieutenant Colonel Richard Yardley was *ex gratia* admitted a freeman of this town, and then chosen a capital burgess of this Incorporation, and was accordingly sworn a freeman and capital burgess.

By virtue of a precept under the hand and seal of John Strode, esquire, sheriff of the county of Dorset, in these words following, viz: Dorset PP John Strode, esquire, sheriff of the county of Dorset to the mayor of the boroughs of Waymouth and Melcombe Regis greeting. By virtue of a writ of the keepers of the liberty of England, etc, to me directed I command you that on receipt of this my precept you cause to be freely and indifferently chosen four burgesses of the most discrete and sufficient to serve for your said boroughs in Parliament to be held at Westminster of the five and twentieth day of this instant April according to the form of the statute thereupon made and provided. And the names of such burgesses so to be chosen, whether they be present or absent, you cause to be inserted in certain indentures thereupon to be made between me and them that shall be present at such election so that I may cause them to come at the day and place aforesaid. And that you shall do in the promises you make manifest to me, at or before the eighteenth day of this instant April, so that I may certify the same to the said keepers in the high court of Chancery at the day and time first aforesaid distinctly and openly under the seal of them that shall be present at such election according to the said writ as in itself requires. And hereof fail you not, given under the seal of my office the second day of April 1660. John Strode, esquire, sheriff.

By virtue of which precept the ninth day of the aforesaid month of April the Incorporation proceeded to the election of four burgesses for the boroughs aforesaid, there standing in the election General Edward Montague, Sir William pen, knight, Samuel Bond, esquire, recorder of the said town, [page 267] John Browne, esquire, Mr Peter Middleton, Mr Samuel Mico, merchants, and Mr Henry Waltham, one of the aldermen of the said town. And the said General Montague and Sir William Penwere chosen and published Parliament burgesses for Waymouth and the said

Peter Middleton and Henry Waltham, Parliament burgesses for Melcomb Regis.

Shortly after which election, the said General Montague being removed into the house of the peers, the aforesaid mayor received another precept from the said sheriff to elect one other burgess to serve in Parliament in the room and place of the said General Montague. And thereupon the Incorporation proceeded to an election on the two and twentieth day of June in the aforesaid year of Our Lord 1660. And they standing on that election Colonel Bullen Reymes and the aforesaid Mr Samuel Mico, the said Colonel Bullen Reymes was elected and chosen at Parliament, burgess in the room and place of the said General Montague and published accordingly.

24 August 1660

It being this day certified to the mayor, aldermen, bailiffs and capital burgesses of the borough and town aforesaid by the sergeants at mace that they had taken on the estreats of the law day of the goods of Mr Thomas Hide four pieces of ordnance, the fines amercements and penalties on the same estreats amounting to seven pounds two shillings and six pence. Upon the submission of the said Mr Hide the moiety of the said £7 2s 6d was remitted to him and his goods to be restored on payment of the said moiety.

There being also taken by virtue of the said estreats sixty five yards of canvas cloth of the goods of James Budd, valued at thirty shillings, the same was sold by a piece of candle. And after the said James Budd coming to the town hall and promising that he and his family would leave the town at midsummer next. It is ordered by a full and general consent of the mayor, aldermen, bailiffs and capital burgesses that the sergeants shall redeliver the said cloth on payment of twenty shillings. But afterwards upon the humble request of the said James Budd, he having married a freeman's widow, for the fine of eight pounds paid to Mr Robert Giear, treasurer, he was (as much as in the company lay, he not taking the oath of a freeman) generally admitted a freeman. And for the same monies his amercement was discharged.

[page 268] 28 September 1660

At a meeting this day by the mayor, aldermen, bailiffs and burgesses in the Guildhall in Melcomb Regis.

This day George Pley the younger son of Mr George Pley, the present mayor, was admitted a freeman generally of this Incorporation for the fine of 3s 4d paid to Mr Robert Giear, treasurer, and took his oath of a freeman.

This day George Churchey the younger son of Mr George Churchey, one of the aldermen of this town, was by patrimony generally admitted a freeman of this Incorporation for the common fine of 3s 4d paid to Mr Robert Giear, treasurer, who took his oath of a freeman.

This day the petty customs was let to Mr Henry Waltham for eighty seven pounds and one shilling upon his own security and on the security of Mr James Studley and Mr John Allambridge.

Cartage let to sergeant Rose at eight pounds ten shillings upon the security of himself, Mr John Senior and Mr John Penny.

Market let to the town clerk for ten pounds fifteen shillings, security Mr Robert Wall and Mr John Swetnam.

Bridge let to Henry Gaudoon for three pounds two shillings upon this Mr Rowe's and Mr Allambridge security.

Ballast and forfeitures let to Mr Henry Rose for nine pounds fifteen shillings, security himself, Mr Henry Waltham and Mr Robert Giear.

5 October 1660

At a meeting this day of the mayor, aldermen, bailiffs and burgesses at the townhall of Melcomb Regis.

Mr James Giear the younger son of Mr James Giear the elder was this present day by patrimony generally admitted a freeman of this Incorporation for the common fine of three shillings and four pence paid to Mr Treasurer Pley, and took the oath of freeman.

[page 269] The same day it is by a general consent agreed that Mr Thomas Cooke of Tinden in the county of Somerset shall have the like lease with Mr Thomas Hyde to range even with Mr Hide's building against the harbour at the rent of five shillings per annum. And to commence from Michaelmas 1660.

At the same time Mr Robert Giear and Mr Alexander Clatworth of Waymouth and Mr Robert Giear and Mr Richard Yardley of Melcomb Regis all desired by Mr Mayor and the company to view the general defects in the harbour and to make the report of the same.

11 October 1660

At a meeting of the mayor, aldermen, bailiffs and burgesses held in the Guildhall of Melcomb Regis.

It is generally agreed on that Mr Henry Waltham, who rents the petty customs, remits twenty pounds of that rent to Colonel Bullen Reymes, one of the Parliament burgesses of these boroughs, touching the procuring of monies for the repair of the harbour by himself and the rest of the Parliament burgesses for the said boroughs.

23 December 1660

It was this day agreed on by the mayor, aldermen, bailiffs and principal burgesses that both the sergeants at mace shall from henceforth collect the town rents in Melcomb Regis for which they are to have the same allowance as Mr Osborne had.

This day William Bell, having for some years past lived in this town and in Portland, came this day and petitioned for his freedom which was granted him by a general consent of the mayor, aldermen, bailiffs and burgesses for the fine of five pounds which [was] paid down to Mr Treasurer Pley and took his oath of a freeman accordingly.

GENERAL INDEX

Cannons, Customs and Duties, Goods and Commodities, Livestock, Occupations, Officers, Ships, and Weymouth and Melcombe Regis places will be found grouped under these headings.

Abbot (Abbott), Cardyn, 140; Hugh, 47; Nathaniel, 181, 207, 226; Stephen (Steven), 178, 181, 190, 197, 202, 215, 219, 221-2, 224, 227
Abram, Richard, 46
Adams, Thomas, 61, 74, 217
Alexander (Allexsander), Philip, 16, 46-7, 49; Thomas, 156, 194, 198
Algiers, 85, 92, 167
Aliens, 13, 101, 110
Allambridge (Allenbridge), John, 178, 181, 188, 215, 220, 222-5, 227, 230
Allens Loscombe in Powerstock parish, 216
Allin (Allinn, Allyn, Allynn), Bartholomew, 50, 74; Edward, 29, 46, 47, 49, 66; John, 58, 145, 147, 158, 166, 169, 172, 180, 189, 194, 207; Matthew, 1-2, 10, 12, 14-15, 18-19, 22, 25, 33, 41-2, 46-7, 49, 53, 64-5, 69, 71-4, 78, 86, 90, 93-4, 96-8, 100, 103-6, 111, 113, 115-16, 130, 133, 136, 138, 141, 144, 146, 149-50, 152-3, 156-7, 159-61, 174, 189; Nathaniel, 50, 53, 128, 149, 157, 162, 189, 205; Richard, 10, 12, 15, 18, 21, 24-5, 33, 35-8, 41-2, 49-51, 53, 56, 58, 60-5, 72, 74, 81, 83-5, 88, 90, 93-4, 98; Samuel, 62, 65, 74; Thomas, 189
Alweston in Folke parish, 219
Ammunition, 152
Anderson, Falke, 182
Andney, Widow, 47
Andrewes, Joseph, 107; Thomas, 65
Angell, Henry, 222, 228
Applebee, Peter, 46
Arthur, John, 17, 135, 157-8, 161-2, 166, 169, 178-9, 183, 185, 188, 193-4, 203, 205, 207-8, 213, 220, 222
Ashe (Ash), Richard, 47; William, 110
Ashley, Francis, 115
Assizes, 34, 66, 67, 132
Attwoll, Alexander, 180; Bartholomew, 180
Avery, William, 47

Ayres, see Eyres

Babbidge (Babbag, Babbidg, Bubbage, Bubbidge), Christopher, 118; Gregory, 16, 87, 104, 121, 143, 152, 177, 179, 181, 198, 200, 213, 225; Jeremiah, 111; Jeremy, 16, 36, 38, 49, 53, 67, 71, 75-8, 81, 87, 89, 101, 106, 113, 123, 130-1; Joan, 162; Mrs, 200; widow, 161
Bacaban, Alice, 35
Backway (Backwaye), Henry, 58, 65, 75
Backwell, Henry, 49, 56
Bagg, John, 12, 34, 66; Justinian, 114; Thomas, 15, 46-9
Bagwell, Edward, 179; Peter, 179, 181, 225
Baily (Baiyly, Bayly), Clement, 110; Edward, 99; Richard, 173; William, 12, 56-8, 75, 81, 82, 89, 164-5
Balcomb, a porter, 154
Baldwin, Thomas, 108-9
Ball, John, 25
Baltic Sea, 85
Banfild, William, 34, 45
Barber, John, 210
Barfoote, John, 53, 75
Barger, Peter, 49
Barker, Richard, 174
Barnes, Roger, 60-1, 75; Thomas, 47, 51, 66, 75, 161, 182; William, 155
Barrat, Stephen, 161
Bartlett, John, 48
Barton, James, 51, 52, 75
Bascombe (Bascomb), John, 117; Thomas, 106, 117, 126
Bassett, Arnold, 101
Bateman, Richard, 171
Batter, 46, Christopher, 46
Battlements, 3, 23
Baunton in Dorset (unidentified), 29
Baynes, George, 220
Beer (Beere), Bartholomew, 216; John, 181,

...Oil, 31, 35
...Pearl, 31
...Pilchards, 31, 35
...Pillow, 22
...Pitch, 31, 35
...Plaster of Paris, 31, 39, 151
...Playing cards, 31
...Raisins, 31, 35, 95, 117, 159, 194-5, 197
...Ribbon, 169
...Rice, 31
...Salsa perilla (sarsaparilla roo), 32
...Salt, 22-4, 32-3, 45, 96, 101, 133, 159, 209-10
...Saucers, 22
...Shovel, 144, 224
...Shumacke, 35, 36
...Silver bullion, 31
...Soap, 30, 32
...Stools, 22
...Sugar, 31, 35, 90, 107
...Tar, 31, 35
...Timber, 35-6, 106-8, 113-14, 120, 124, 138, 141, 149-52, 170, 172, 195, 199, 201, 204, 207, 209, 213, 215, 221
...Tin, 32
...Tobacco, 158, 166, 171
...Vinegar, 32, 35, 36
...Walnuts, 31
...Wheat, 193, 199
...Wheel barrow, 144, 224
...Wine (bastard), 31
...Wine (Malmsey), 31
...Wine (Muscatel), 31
...Wine (sack, sacke), 31, 83, 104, 118, 120-1
...Wine, fortified, 104
...Wine, French, 30
...Wine, Gascoigne, 98, 101
...Wine, 30, 35, 98, 101, 103-4, 115, 176
...Woad (towlas oade), 32
...Wool, 30, 32, 35, 36, 88
...Woolcard, 32
Gorge, Ferdinando, 73
Gould, John, 18, 189; Thomas, 50, 59, 62, 65, 75; the widow, 46-7, 49
Greene (Green, Grene), Giles, 15, 33, 42, 62, 65, 68, 72, 74-5, 77, 83, 93, 99, 100, 149-50
Gregory, Daniel, 58-9, 75; Henry, 66; John, 50-1, 55
Grindum's heirs, 48
Growte (Grout), Brandinn, 46; John, 77; Lancelot, 77; Roger, 66; Thomas, 222
Gyer (Giair, Geare, Giar, Giare, Giear, Guyer,

Gyar), David, 5, 16, 28, 39, 47, 50, 68, 72, 75, 79-80, 82-94, 98-101, 103-5, 107, 109, 111, 113, 116, 120, 129, 189; James, 16, 116, 130, 132, 134-5, 137-9, 142, 144, 146, 149-51, 153-4, 156, 158-9, 161, 166, 168, 172-5, 177, 180-1, 183, 187, 222-9, 231; Mary, 145; Robert, 16, 181, 215, 217, 219, 227, 228, 229, 230, 231; Thomas, 1-2, 4, 8, 12, 15, 19, 22, 24-5, 33-8, 41-2, 45, 48, 55-6, 58-9, 75, 80, 83-4, 86, 90, 92-4, 96, 98, 100, 105-6, 110, 113, 116, 127, 129-30, 159, 189, 225
Haine (Haines), James, 180
Hall, Andrew, 197; Christopher, 105, 147, 194; Thomas, 197
Halstock parish (Dorset), 216, 218
Hamell, Martin, 140
Hamon, John, 46, 64, 75, 103
Hamwell, John, 195
Hanam, James, 96
Hanham, Benjamin, 184
Hansford, Richard, 93
Hanson, Richard, 139
Hardy (Hardey), Jeffrey, 47, 49; John, 26, 35; Robert, 171
Harrison (Harison, Harrisone, Harryson, Haryson), Mary, 56; Richard, 16, 28, 43, 56, 58, 75, 78, 80, 82-3, 86, 90, 98, 100, 101, 104-6, 123, 128, 133, 137-8, 140-1, 151, 170, 182, 188, 211
Harvest, Richard, 65
Harvy, Edward, 66
Hascall (Hasall), Ellis, 168, 180
Hastings, Mary, 185
Hastings (Sussex), 149, 159, 174-6, 185
Haught (Haughte, Hought), Henry, 13, 46, 48, 56-7, 75
Hawkins, Henry, 48; Robert, 155
Hayse, John, 26; Robert, 26
Hayward, Robert, 49
Heane, Colonel, 201; James, 174, 188, 201
Heath, Robert, 114
Hebberd, William, 48
Hebbert, Henry, 47
Hebburn (Northumberland)
Heckles, David, 178; George, 178
Hedgcocke, Robert, 47
Hedmore, Henry, 66
Hibbard, Robert, 121
Hicke (Hickes, Hicks), John, 108; Richard, 66
Hickman, Simon, 64, 75
Hide, Thomas, 221; William, 196

www.ingramcontent.com/pod-product-compliance
Lightning Source LLC
Chambersburg PA
CBHW080543110426
42813CB00006B/1196